Designing Hexagonal Architecture with Java

Build maintainable and long-lasting applications with
Java and Quarkus

Davi Vieira

BIRMINGHAM—MUMBAI

Designing Hexagonal Architecture with Java

Group Product Manager: Kunal Sawant

Publishing Product Manager: Akash Sharma

Senior Editor: Nisha Cleetus

Technical Editor: Shruti Thingalaya

Copy Editor: Safis Editing

Proofreader: Safis Editing

Project Manager: Deeksha Thakkar

Indexer: Rekha Nair

Production Designer: Nilesh Mohite

Business Development Executive: Kriti Sharma

Developer Relations Marketing Executives: Rayyan Khan and Sonia Chauhan

First published: January 2022
Second edition: September 2023

Production reference: 1220923
Published by Packt Publishing Ltd.
Grosvenor House
11 St Paul's Square
Birmingham
B3 1RB, UK

ISBN 978-1-83763-511-5

www.packtpub.com

To the memory of my mother, Rosimar Pinheiro, who instilled in me the desire to learn. To my father, Davi, for teaching me the value of persistence. To my brother, Bruno Pinheiro, for his influence on my character and career. To my wife, Eloise, for being my loving partner throughout our joint life journey. To my son, Davi, who brings immense joy and happiness to my life.

– Davi Vieira

Contributors

About the author

Davi Vieira is a software craftsman with a vested interest in the challenges faced by large enterprises in software design, development, and architecture. He has more than 10 years of experience in constructing and maintaining complex, long-lasting, and mission-critical systems using object-oriented languages. He values the good lessons and the software development tradition left by others who came before him. Inspired by this software tradition, he develops and evolves his ideas.

I want to especially thank my wife, Eloise, and my son, Davi, for the motivation to keep moving forward. I also wish to thank Fagner Silva, a person I admire and who is responsible for introducing me to hexagonal architecture. This book would not have been possible if I had not met him. I want to thank Pooja Yadav for coming to me with the idea to write this second edition. And thanks to the fantastic Packt team, with special mention to Deeksha Thakkar and Nisha Cleetus, for being my partners and supporting me throughout this long journey.

About the reviewers

Vikranth Etikyala is a senior staff software engineer at Fintech SoFi and a speaker who talks about cloud and storage technologies. He is currently leading a team of engineers building SoFi Bank's infrastructure using modern cloud technologies. Previously, he was an early member of Amazon **Simple Storage Service** (**S3**), a planet-scale storage system, where he was involved in building foundational storage infrastructure and leading efforts to scale S3 during its exponential growth. He spearheaded features such as List v2 , Transfer Acceleration, and Intelligent Archival, which now handle millions of transactions per second, moving petabytes of data. He also holds a master's degree in computer science from Northeastern University.

Muhammad Edwin is a senior consultant at Red Hat's APAC Global Professional Services specializing in cloud-native application and integration architectures. He loves technology and getting his hands dirty exploring new tech, frameworks, and patterns. He lives in the suburbs of Jakarta, Indonesia, and, when not involved in tech stuff, spends most of his time playing classic Japanese RPGs on his gaming rig.

Table of Contents

3

Handling Behavior with Ports and Use Cases   55

4

Creating Adapters to Interact with the Outside World   73

5

Exploring the Nature of Driving and Driven Operations   107

Part 2: Using Hexagons to Create a Solid Foundation

6

Building the Domain Hexagon   139

7

Building the Application Hexagon   175

8

Building the Framework Hexagon   201

9

Applying Dependency Inversion with Java Modules   223

Part 3: Becoming Cloud-Native

10

11

12

Part 4: Hexagonal Architecture and Beyond

15

Comparing Hexagonal Architecture with Layered Architecture 345

16

Using SOLID Principles with Hexagonal Architecture 363

17

Good Design Practices for Your Hexagonal Application 379

Index 397

Other Books You May Enjoy 408

Preface

Sometimes, solving problems and expressing our ideas through code is challenging. What looks like an obvious solution in our minds may look unnecessarily complex in the minds of others. But that's alright if we are open to new ideas and perspectives because we set our minds to learning unexpected things when we have a persistent attitude and a willingness to embrace everything that comes.

I was not expecting it when I was first introduced to hexagonal architecture.

I remember working in a company where most of the software was developed by consultants. Those folks would come, deliver their code, and leave. Although my team and I tried to establish specific standards to ensure consistency in the applications we were responsible for, the harsh reality was that we needed more knowledge to maintain our applications properly. Given the number of systems and the different approaches and architectures employed to build them, it took a lot of work to maintain and add new features to such systems. That's when a teammate told me about the hexagonal architecture and how it could help us tackle hard-to-maintain software problems.

At that time, there weren't many books covering the hexagonal architecture. Most of the resources were scattered on the internet through video courses and articles explaining how someone implemented hexagonal architecture. The lack of resources was a considerable obstacle, but using an architecture that could improve software maintainability was very attractive to me. So, I kept researching and experimenting in my own job with the ideas, which would ultimately lead to me writing the first edition of this book.

I am fortunate to have had the opportunity to write the first, and now the second, edition of a book dealing with such a fascinating topic as hexagonal architecture. The second edition has allowed me to employ hexagonal architecture ideas with more recent versions of Java and Quarkus. This edition preserves the fundamentals from the previous one while exploring modern Java's new and cool features. Also, this edition explores how hexagonal architecture can be used with the acclaimed SOLID principles and how it relates to the widely used layered architecture.

Concepts such as ports, adapters, and use cases are combined with **Domain-Driven Design (DDD)** elements such as entities and value objects to provide an in-depth guide explaining how to assemble those concepts to untangle the exciting puzzle of designing highly change-tolerable applications with hexagonal architecture. Considering the contemporary cloud-native practices that dictate most enterprise development today, we deep dive into Quarkus to learn how to blend hexagonal architecture ideas with cloud-native development, which enables us to create enterprise-grade hexagonal applications ready to be deployed in any major cloud provider.

So, I encourage you to have a persistent attitude and a willingness to embrace everything that comes and embark with me on this fascinating journey to explore hexagonal architecture.

Who this book is for

This book is suited for Java architects and Java developers at senior and intermediate levels. The reader is expected to have previous knowledge of object-oriented language principles and be acquainted with the Java programming language. Previous professional Java experience is also recommended, as this book is concerned with problems that usually happen in enterprise software development projects using Java.

What this book covers

Chapter 1, Why Hexagonal Architecture?, starts by discussing how software that is not well organized and lacks sound architectural principles may work fine but will present a high risk of developing technical debt. As new features are added, the software tends to become more complex to maintain because there is no common ground to guide the addition or change of features. Based on this problem, this chapter explains why hexagonal architecture helps tackle technical debt by establishing an approach where business code is decoupled from technology code, allowing the former to evolve without dependency on the latter.

Chapter 2, Wrapping Business Rules inside the Domain Hexagon, follows a domain-driven approach and describes what domain entities are, what role they play within hexagonal architecture, and how they wrap business rules and data in simple Java POJOs. It explains why domain entities are the most important part of code and why they should not depend on anything other than other domain entities. Finally, it explains how business rules inside a domain entity can be implemented using the Specification design pattern.

Chapter 3, Handling Behavior with Ports and Uses Cases, covers what use cases are, explaining that they are used to define software intent with interfaces describing things the software can do. Then, it explains what input ports are and the classes that implement use case interfaces, and specifies in concrete ways how the software intent should be accomplished. It talks about output ports and their role in abstractly defining the behavior of operations that need to get data from outside the software. Finally, this chapter explains how use cases and ports are grouped in what's called the Application hexagon.

Chapter 4, Creating Adapters to Interact with the Outside World, shows how adapters allow the software to integrate with different technologies. It explains that the same port can have multiple adapters. Input adapters, bound to input ports, enable the application to expose its functionalities through different communication protocols, such as REST, gRPC, or WebSocket. Output adapters, bound to output ports, allow the application to communicate with varying data sources, whether it be databases or even message queues or other applications. Finally, the chapter shows how all adapters are grouped in the Framework hexagon.

Chapter 5, Exploring the Nature of Driving and Driven Operations, explains that driver operations drive the software behavior by starting one of its exposed functions. It details the driver operations life cycle, showing how a request is captured on the Framework hexagon through an input adapter and then handed down to an input port on the Application hexagon until it reaches the entities from the Domain hexagon. It shows that a use case starts driven operations from the Application hexagon when the software needs to get data from outside, going from an output port to an output adapter to fulfill the use case needs.

Chapter 6, Building the Domain Hexagon, shows how to start developing a telco's network and topology inventory application by first creating the Domain hexagon as a Java module. Then, this chapter shows how business rules and data are mapped to domain entities' classes and methods. The business rules are arranged in different algorithms with the aim of the Specification design pattern. Finally, it shows how to unit test the Domain hexagon.

Chapter 7, Building the Application Hexagon, starts by adding the Application hexagon as the second Java module on the application. It then explains how to create the use case interface that describes the software's operations to manage the network and topology inventory. It shows how to implement the use case with an input port, giving a detailed description of how the code should be arranged. It details the creation of an output port interface and its role in obtaining data from external sources. Finally, it explains how to test the Application hexagon.

Chapter 8, Building the Framework Hexagon, starts by adding the Framework hexagon as the third Java module on the application. Then, it teaches you how to create an input adapter and how it will carry out its operations through an input port. After that, an output adapter is created through the implementation of an output port. The output adapter will show how data can be fetched from external sources and converted to be dealt with in Domain hexagon terms. Finally, the chapter explains how to test the Framework hexagon.

Chapter 9, Applying Dependency Inversion with Java Modules, talks a little bit about Java modules, explaining why they are important to enforce the hexagonal architecture principles related to dependency inversion. It explains that Java modules don't allow cyclic dependencies and because of that, there is no way to make two modules depend on each other at the same time. You will learn how to configure the module descriptor in the hexagonal application.

Chapter 10, Adding Quarkus to a Modularized Hexagonal Application, briefly explains the Quarkus framework and its main features. Then, it advances to show how to add Quarkus to the hexagonal application that was developed in the previous chapters. It introduces the creation of a fourth module, called Bootstrap, which serves to get the application started and is used to group the Domain, Application, and Framework modules.

Chapter 11, Leveraging CDI Beans to Manage Ports and Use Cases, explains how to transform the already developed ports and use cases into CDI beans, leveraging enterprise Java's power in the hexagonal architecture. It starts by explaining what CDI beans are, then it shows how to implement them on input and output ports. Finally, the chapter describes how to adjust the application framework tests to use Quarkus CDI bean test features.

Chapter 12, Using RESTEasy Reactive to Implement Input Adapters, starts by comparing reactive and imperative approaches for REST endpoints, detailing why the reactive approach performs better. It explains how to implement input adapters with Quarkus RESTEasy Reactive capabilities by explaining how to add the correct annotations and inject the proper dependencies to call input ports. In order to expose the hexagonal application APIs, this chapter explains how to add OpenAPI and Swagger UI. Finally, it shows how to test the reactive input port with Quarkus test tools.

Chapter 13, Persisting Data with Output Adapters and Hibernate Reactive, talks about Hibernate Reactive and how it helps Quarkus to provide reactive capabilities for data persistence. It explains how to create a reactive output adapter to persist data to a MySQL database. Finally, it shows how to test the reactive output adapter with Quarkus test tools.

Chapter 14, Setting Up Dockerfile and Kubernetes Objects for Cloud Deployment, explains how to create a Dockerfile for the hexagonal application based on Quarkus. It explains in detail how to package all the modules and dependencies in one single Docker image. It then shows how to create Kubernetes objects such as Deployment and Service for the hexagonal application and test them in a minikube local Kubernetes cluster.

Chapter 15, Comparing Hexagonal Architecture with Layered Architecture, describes layered architecture and explores how layers handle specific system responsibilities, such as persistence and presentation. We then develop an application using layered architecture principles. Finally, to highlight the differences between layered and hexagonal architecture, we refactor the previously layer-based application into a hexagonal one.

Chapter 16, Using SOLID Principles with Hexagonal Architecture, starts by reviewing SOLID principles and observing how each principle helps to build applications with improved maintainability. Then, it explores how SOLID principles can be applied to a system developed with hexagonal architecture. Finally, it presents some common design patterns that can be used while building a hexagonal system.

Chapter 17, Good Design Practices for Your Hexagonal Application, talks about some good practices you can adopt while creating each hexagon for your application. Starting with the Domain hexagon, we focus on DDD aspects to clarify the business problems the application is supposed to solve. Then, we move on to a discussion about the alternative ways to set up use cases and ports in the Application hexagon. Finally, we discuss the consequences of having to maintain multiple adapters.

To get the most out of this book

The examples provided are based on Java 17, but you should be able to run them with more recent Java versions. Maven 3.8 is required to build the example projects. Docker is also needed for the examples of running the application inside a container.

Software/hardware covered in the book	Operating system requirements
Maven 3.8	Windows, macOS, or Linux
Java 17 SE Development Kit	Windows, macOS, or Linux
Docker	Windows, macOS, or Linux
Postman	Windows, macOS, or Linux
Newman	Windows, macOS, or Linux
Kafka	macOS or Linux

You will need Postman, Newman, and Kafka to run the examples in *Chapter 5*.

If you are using the digital version of this book, we advise you to type the code yourself or access the code from the book's GitHub repository (a link is available in the next section). Doing so will help you avoid any potential errors related to the copying and pasting of code.

Download the example code files

You can download the example code files for this book from GitHub at `https://github.com/PacktPublishing/-Designing-Hexagonal-Architecture-with-Java---Second-Edition`. If there's an update to the code, it will be updated in the GitHub repository.

We also have other code bundles from our rich catalog of books and videos available at `https://github.com/PacktPublishing/`. Check them out!

Conventions used

There are a number of text conventions used throughout this book.

`Code in text`: Indicates code words in text, database table names, folder names, filenames, file extensions, pathnames, dummy URLs, user input, and Twitter handles. Here is an example: "Mount the downloaded `WebStorm-10*.dmg` disk image file as another disk in your system."

A block of code is set as follows:

```
public interface RouterNetworkUseCase {

    Router addNetworkToRouter(RouterId,
    Network network);

    Router getRouter(RouterId routerId);
}
```

When we wish to draw your attention to a particular part of a code block, the relevant lines or items are set in bold:

```
function getRouter() {
    const routerId = document.
    getElementById("routerId").value;
    var xhttp = new XMLHttpRequest();
    xhttp.onreadystatechange = function() {
        console.log(this.responseText);
        if (this.readyState == 4 && this.status == 200) {
            const json = JSON.parse(this.responseText)
            createTree(json)
        }
```

Any command-line input or output is written as follows:

```
java -jar target/topology-inventory-1.0-SNAPSHOT-jar-with-
dependencies.jar rest
REST endpoint listening on port 8080...
Topology & Inventory WebSocket started on port 8887...
```

Bold: Indicates a new term, an important word, or words that you see onscreen. For instance, words in menus or dialog boxes appear in **bold**. Here is an example: "Select **System info** from the **Administration** panel."

> **Tips or important notes**
> Appear like this.

Get in touch

Feedback from our readers is always welcome.

General feedback: If you have questions about any aspect of this book, email us at customercare@ packtpub.com and mention the book title in the subject of your message.

Errata: Although we have taken every care to ensure the accuracy of our content, mistakes do happen. If you have found a mistake in this book, we would be grateful if you would report this to us. Please visit www.packtpub.com/support/errata and fill in the form.

Piracy: If you come across any illegal copies of our works in any form on the internet, we would be grateful if you would provide us with the location address or website name. Please contact us at copyright@packt.com with a link to the material.

If you are interested in becoming an author: If there is a topic that you have expertise in and you are interested in either writing or contributing to a book, please visit authors.packtpub.com.

Share Your Thoughts

Once you've read *Designing Hexagonal Architecture with Java, Second Edition*, we'd love to hear your thoughts! Scan the QR code below to go straight to the Amazon review page for this book and share your feedback.

https://packt.link/r/1837635110

Your review is important to us and the tech community and will help us make sure we're delivering excellent quality content.

Download a free PDF copy of this book

Thanks for purchasing this book!

Do you like to read on the go but are unable to carry your print books everywhere?

Is your eBook purchase not compatible with the device of your choice?

Don't worry, now with every Packt book you get a DRM-free PDF version of that book at no cost.

Read anywhere, any place, on any device. Search, copy, and paste code from your favorite technical books directly into your application.

The perks don't stop there, you can get exclusive access to discounts, newsletters, and great free content in your inbox daily

Follow these simple steps to get the benefits:

1. Scan the QR code or visit the link below

https://packt.link/free-ebook/9781837635115

2. Submit your proof of purchase
3. That's it! We'll send your free PDF and other benefits to your email directly

Part 1:
Architecture Fundamentals

In this part, you will gain a solid understanding of hexagonal architecture elements: domain entities, use cases, ports, and adapters. Starting with a discussion about why we would apply hexagonal architecture principles to our project, we progressively advance our exploration by learning how to organize problem domain code with domain-driven design techniques.

Then, we examine the important role use cases and ports play in expressing system behaviors. Moving ahead, we explore how adapters allow the hexagonal system to be compatible with different protocols and technologies. Finally, we close this part by discussing how driving and driven operations influence the behaviors of a hexagonal system.

This part has the following chapters:

1

Why Hexagonal Architecture?

Software that's not well organized and lacks sound software architecture principles may work just fine but develop technical debt over time. As new features are added, the software may become more complex to maintain because there is no common ground to guide code changes. Based on that problem, this chapter explains how hexagonal architecture helps to build software prepared to accommodate changes from unexpected requirements and, by doing so, allows us to increase software maintainability and keep technical debt under control.

We tackle the technical debt problem that arises when shortcuts are taken to overcome the difficulty of introducing changes caused by an inflexible software architecture. We will see how hexagonal architecture helps us improve maintainability by providing the principles to decouple the business logic (code that should purely represent a business problem) from the technology code (code that integrates the system with different technologies such as databases, messaging queues, and external APIs to support the business logic).

I have seen systems developed with business logic closely related to the technology code. Some of those systems would rarely change, so the coupling between business logic and technology code would never be a problem. However, significant refactorings would be necessary for other systems where the requirements would change often and substantially. That was because the business logic was so tightly coupled with the technology code that rewriting the business logic was the only plausible solution.

Using hexagonal architecture may help you to save time and effort due to the software rewrites caused by such scenarios where requirements change often and significantly.

In this chapter, we will cover the following topics:

- Reviewing software architecture
- Understanding hexagonal architecture

By the end of this chapter, you will have learned about the main concepts of hexagonal architecture: entities, use cases, ports, and adapters. Also, you'll know the basic techniques to start applying hexagonal principles in your projects.

Technical requirements

To compile and run the code examples presented in this chapter, you need the latest Java SE Development Kit and Maven 3.8 installed on your computer. They are both available for Linux, macOS, and Windows operating systems.

You can find the code files for this chapter on GitHub at `https://github.com/PacktPublishing/-Designing-Hexagonal-Architecture-with-Java---Second-Edition/tree/main/Chapter01`.

Reviewing software architecture

The word architecture is old. Its origin traces back to times when people used to build things with rudimentary tools, often with their own hands. Yet, each generation repeatedly overcame the limitations of its era and constructed magnificent buildings that stand to this day. Take a look at the Florence Cathedral and its dome designed by Filippo Brunelleschi – what an excellent example of architecture!

Architects are more than just ordinary builders who build things without much thinking. Quite the opposite; they are the ones who care the most about aesthetics, underlying structures, and design principles. Sometimes, they play a fundamental role by pushing the limits of what is possible to do with the resources at hand. The Florence Cathedral, as has already been mentioned, proves that point.

I'll not take this analogy too far because software is not like a physical building. And although there are some similarities between building and software architects, the latter differs considerably because of the living and evolving nature of their software craft. But we can agree that both share the same goal: to build things right.

This goal helps us understand what software architecture is. If we're aiming to build not just working but also easily maintainable and well-structured software, it can even be considered to a certain degree as a piece of art because of the care and attention to detail we employ to build it. So, we can take this activity of building easily maintainable and well-structured software as a noble definition of software architecture.

It's also important to state that a software architect's role should not only be constrained to deciding how things should be made. As in the Florence Cathedral example, where Filippo Brunelleschi himself helped to afix bricks to the building to prove his ideas were sound, a software architect, in the same vein, should soil their hands to prove their architecture is good.

Software architecture should not be the fruit of one person's mind. Although there are a few who urge others to pursue a path of technical excellence by providing guidance and establishing the foundations, for an architecture to evolve and mature, it's necessary to utilize the collaboration and experience of everyone involved in the effort to improve the software quality.

What follows is a discussion around the technical and organizational challenges we may encounter in our journey to create and evolve a software architecture to help us tackle the threat of chaos and indomitable complexity.

Making decisions

All this discussion around software architecture concerns is relevant because we may undermine our capability to maintain and evolve software in the long run if we ignore those concerns. Of course, there are situations where we're not so ambitious about how sophisticated, maintainable, and feature-rich our software will be. It may not be worth all the time and effort to build things in the right way for such situations because what's needed is working software delivered as fast as possible. In the end, it's a matter of priorities. But we should be cautious not to fall into the trap that we can fix things later. Sometimes we may have the money to do so but sometimes we may not. Bad decisions at the beginning of a project can cost us a high price in the future.

The decisions we take regarding code structure and software architecture lead us to what is called internal quality. The degree to which software code is well organized and maintainable corresponds to the internal quality. On the other hand, the value perception about how valuable and good software can be from a user's perspective corresponds to the external quality. Internal and external quality are not directly connected. It's not difficult to find useful software with a messy code base.

The effort spent on internal quality should be seen as an investment where the return is not immediate and visible to the user. The investment return comes as the software evolves. The value is perceived by constantly adding changes to the software without increasing the time and money required to add such changes, as the following pseudo-graph depicts:

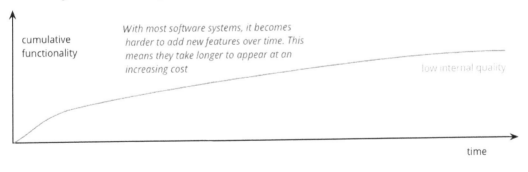

Figure 1.1 – Pseudo-graph showing the impact of changes

But how can we make the right decisions? That's a trick question because we often don't have enough information to assist in a decision-making process that will lead to software architecture that best meets the business needs. Sometimes, even the users don't know completely what they want, leading to new or changed requirements as the project evolves. We tackle such unpredictability by using a software architecture that helps us add changes in a sustainable way to ensure the code base grows without increased complexity and decreased maintainability.

The ability to quickly introduce changes is a major concern in software design, but we should be cautious about how much time we spend thinking about it. If we spend too much time designing, we may end up with an overengineered and possibly overpriced solution. On the other hand, if we ignore or do not reflect enough on design concerns, we may end up with a complex and hard-to-maintain solution. As pointed out by *Extreme Programming Explained: Embrace Change*, the resources spent on design efforts should match a system's need to handle changes at an acceptable pace and cost.

In the end, we want the flexibility of adding new stuff while keeping complexity under control. With that in mind, this book is concerned with software architecture ideas that allow us to handle software design decisions to meet changing business needs. The hexagonal architecture helps us to build change-tolerant systems to support those needs.

The invisible things

Software development is not a trivial activity. It demands considerable effort to become competent in any programming language, and even greater effort to use that skill to build software that generates profit. Surprisingly, sometimes it may not be enough to just make profitable software.

When we talk about profitable software, we're talking about software that solves real-world problems. Or, in the context of large enterprises, to speak more precisely, we mean software that meets business needs. Anyone who has worked in a large enterprise will know that the client generally doesn't want to know how the software is built. They are interested in what they can see: working software meeting business expectations. After all, that's what pays the bills at the end of the day.

But the things that clients cannot see also have some importance. Such things are known as non-functional requirements. They are things related to security, maintainability, operability, scalability, reliability and other capabilities. If adequate care is not taken, those things unseen from the client's perspective can compromise the whole purpose of the software. That compromise can occur subtly and gradually, giving origin to several problems, including technical debt.

I've mentioned previously that software architecture is about doing things right. So, it means that among its concerns, we should include both unseen and seen things. For things that are seen by the client, it's essential to deeply understand the problem domain. That's where techniques such as domain-driven design can help us approach the problem in a way that allows us to structure the software in a form that makes sense not only for programmers but also for everyone involved in the problem domain. Domain-driven design also plays a key role in shaping the unseen part by cohesively defining the underlying structures that will allow us to solve client needs and doing that in a well-structured and maintainable manner.

Technical debt

Coined by Ward Cunningham, technical debt is a term used to describe how much unnecessary complexity exists in software code. Such unnecessary complexity may also be referred to as cruft – that is, the difference between the current code and how it would ideally be. We'll see next how technical debt can appear in a software project.

Developing software that just works is one thing. You assemble code in a way you think is adequate to meet business needs, and then package and deploy it to production. In production, your software meets clients' expectations, so everything is fine and life goes on. Sometime later, another developer comes in to add new features to that software you created. Like you, this developer assembles code in a way they think is adequate to meet business needs, but there are things in your code this developer doesn't clearly understand. Hence, they add elements to the software in a slightly different manner than you would. The software makes its way into production, and the customer is satisfied. So, the cycle repeats.

Software working as expected is what we can clearly see in the previous scenario. But what we cannot see so clearly is that the lack of common ground defining how features should be added or modified leaves a gap that every developer will try to fill whenever they do not know how to handle such changes. This very gap leaves space for the growth of things such as technical debt.

Reality very often pushes us to situations where we just cannot avoid technical debt. Tight schedules, poor planning, unskilled people, and, of course, a lack of software architecture are some of the factors that can contribute to the creation of technical debt. Needless to say, we should not believe that the enforcement of software architecture will magically solve all our technical debt problems. Far from that; here, we're just tackling one facet of the problem. All other technical debt factors will remain and can actually undermine our efforts to build maintainable software.

Vicious cycle

Financial debts tend to continue to grow regardless if you don't pay them. Also, the bank and authorities can come after you and your assets if you don't pay those debts in time. Contrary to its financial counterpart, technical debt doesn't necessarily grow if you don't pay it. What determines its growth, though, is the rate and nature of software changes. Based on that, we can assume that frequent and complex changes have a higher potential to increase technical debt.

You always have the prerogative not to pay technical debt – sometimes that's the best choice depending on the circumstance – but you diminish your capacity to change the software as you do so. With higher technical debt rates, the code becomes more and more unmanageable, causing developers to either avoid touching the code at all or find awkward workarounds to solve the issues.

I believe most of us will have had at least once the unpleasant experience of maintaining brittle, insanely complex systems. In such scenarios, instead of spending time working on things that are valuable to the software, we spend more time fighting technical debt to open space to introduce new features.

If we don't keep the technical debt under control, one day, it will not be worth adding new features to the technical debt-overloaded system. That's when people decide to abandon applications, start a new one, and repeat the cycle. So, the effort required to tackle technical debt should be considered worth it to break that cycle.

It's not for everyone

This zest for quality and correctness that emerges from any serious architectural undertaking is not always present, There are scenarios where the most profit-driving software in a company is an absolute big ball of mud. It's software that has grown without any sense of order and is complicated to understand and maintain. Developers who dare to tackle the complexity posed by this kind of system are like warriors fighting a hydra. The refactoring effort required to impose any order in such complexity is sometimes not worth it.

The big ball of mud is not the only problem. There are also cultural and organizational factors that can undermine any software architecture effort. Very often, I've stumbled upon teammates who simply didn't care about architectural principles. The least-effort path to deliver code into production is the norm to be followed in their minds. It's not hard to find this kind of person in projects with a high turnaround of developers. Because there is no sense of ownership in terms of quality and high standards, there is no incentive to produce high-quality code.

Pushing the discipline to follow a software architecture is hard. Both the technical team and management should be aligned on the advantages and implications of following such discipline. It's important to understand that spending more time upfront on dealing with technical aspects that don't add much value in terms of customer features may pay dividends in the long term. All the effort is paid back with more maintainable software, relieving developers who no longer need to fight hydras and managers who are now better positioned to meet business deadlines.

Before trying to promote, let alone enforce, any software architecture principle, it is advisable to assess the circumstances to make sure there are neither cultural nor organizational factors playing against the attitude of a few trying to meet or raise the bar to better-developed systems.

Monolithic or distributed

There is a recurring discussion in the software community about the organization of a system's components and responsibilities. In the past, where expensive computing resources and network bandwidth were the problems that influenced the software architecture, developers tended to group plenty of responsibilities in a single software unit to optimize resource usage and avoid the network overhead that would occur in a distributed environment. But there is a tenuous line separating a maintainable and cohesive monolith from an entangled and hard-to-maintain one.

The crossing of such a line is a red flag showing the system has accumulated so many responsibilities and has become so complex to maintain that any change poses a severe risk of breaking down the entire software. I'm not saying that every monolithic that grows becomes a mess. I'm trying to convey that the accumulation of responsibilities can cause serious problems in a monolithic system when such responsibility aggregation is not handled with care. Apart from this responsibility issue, it's also equally important to make sure the software is easy to develop, test, and deploy. If the software is too large, developers may have difficulty trying to run and test it locally. It can also have a serious impact on continuous integration pipelines, impacting the compiling, testing, and deployment stages of such pipelines, ultimately compromising the feedback loop that is so crucial in a DevOps context.

On the other hand, if we know when a system accumulates sufficient responsibility, we can rethink the overall software architecture and break down the large monolithic into smaller and more manageable, sometimes autonomous, software components that are often isolated in their own runtime environments. This approach got strong adoption with **Service-Oriented Architecture (SOA)** and then with what can be considered its evolution: the **microservice architecture**. Both SOA and microservices can be considered different flavors of distributed systems. Microservice architecture, in particular, is made possible mainly because computing and network resources are not as expensive as they used to be, bringing lots of benefits related to strong decoupling and faster software delivery. However, this comes with costs because earlier we had to deal with complexity in just one place, whereas now the challenge is dealing with complexity scattered around multiple services in the network.

This book proposes hexagonal architecture ideas that you can apply to monolithic and distributed systems. With monolithic, you may have the application being consumed by a frontend and, at the same time, consuming data from a database or other data sources. The hexagonal approach can help us develop a more change-tolerant monolithic system, testable even without the frontend and the database. The following diagram illustrates a common monolithic system:

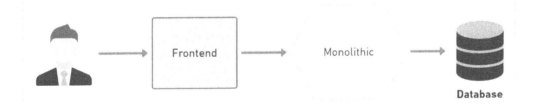

Figure 1.2 – Hexagonal architecture with a monolithic system

In distributed systems, we may be dealing with lots of different technologies. The hexagonal architecture shines in these scenarios because its ports and adapters allow the software to deal with constant technology changes. The following diagram shows a typical microservice architecture where we could apply hexagonal principles:

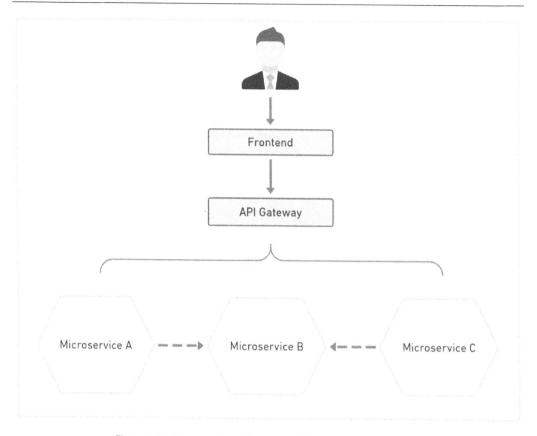

Figure 1.3 – Hexagonal architecture with a microservices system

One of the great advantages of microservice architecture is that we can use different technologies and programming languages to compose the whole system. We can develop a frontend application using JavaScript, some APIs with Java, and a data processing application with Python. Hexagonal architecture can help us in this kind of heterogeneous technological scenario.

Now that we're aware of some of the problems related to software architecture, we're in a better position to explore possible solutions to mitigate those issues. To help us in that effort, let's start by looking into the fundamentals of hexagonal architecture.

Understanding hexagonal architecture

"Create your application to work without either a UI or a database so you can run automated regression-tests against the application, work when the database becomes unavailable, and link applications together without any user involvement."

– Alistair Cockburn.

That quote lays the ground for understanding hexagonal architecture. We can go even further with Cockburn's idea and make our application work without any technology, not just the ones related to the UI or database.

One of the main ideas of hexagonal architecture is to separate business code from technology code. Not just that, we must also make sure the technology side depends on the business one so that the latter can evolve without any concerns regarding which technology is used to fulfill business goals. Having the business logic independent of any technology details gives a system the flexibility to change technologies without disrupting its business logic. In that sense, the business logic represents the foundation through which the application is developed and from which all other system components will derive.

We must be able to change technology code without causing harm to its business counterpart. To achieve this, we must determine a place where the business code will exist, isolated and protected from any technology concerns. It'll give rise to the creation of our first hexagon: the Domain hexagon.

In the Domain hexagon, we assemble the elements responsible for describing the core problems we want our software to solve. Entities and value objects are the main elements utilized in the Domain hexagon. Entities represent things we can assign an identity to, and value objects are immutable components that we can use to compose our entities. The meaning this book uses for entities and value objects comes from domain-driven design principles.

We also need ways to use, process, and orchestrate the business rules coming from the Domain hexagon. That's what the Application hexagon does. It sits between the business and technology sides, serving as a middleman to interact with both parts. The Application hexagon utilizes ports and use cases to perform its functions. We will explore those things in more detail in the next section.

The Framework hexagon provides the outside-world interface. That's the place where we have the opportunity to determine how to expose application features – this is where we define REST or gRPC endpoints, for example. To consume things from external sources, we use the Framework hexagon to specify the mechanisms to fetch data from databases, message brokers, or any other system. In the hexagonal architecture, we materialize technology decisions through adapters. The following diagram provides a high-level view of the architecture:

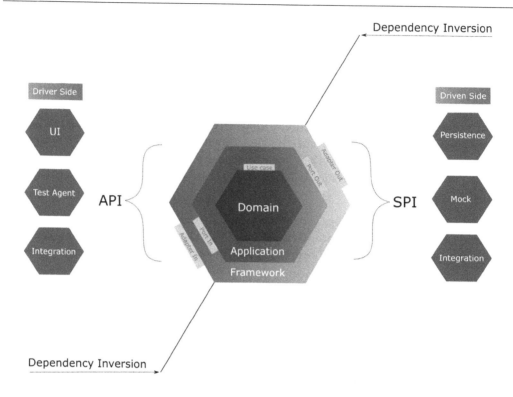

Figure 1.4 – The hexagonal architecture

Next, we'll go deeper into the components, roles, and structures of each hexagon.

Domain hexagon

The Domain hexagon represents an effort to understand and model a real-world problem. Suppose you're working on a project that requires creating a network and topology inventory for a telecom company. This inventory's main purpose is to provide a comprehensive view of all resources that comprise the network. Among those resources, we have routers, switches, racks, shelves, and other equipment types. Our goal here is to use the Domain hexagon to model into code the knowledge required to identify, categorize, and correlate those network and topology elements and provide a lucid and organized view of the desired inventory. That knowledge should be, as much as possible, represented in a technology-agnostic form.

This quest is not a trivial one. Developers involved in such an undertaking may not know much about the telecom business, set aside this inventory thing. As recommended by *Domain-Driven Design: Tackling Complexity in the Heart of Software*, domain experts or other developers who already know the problem domain should be consulted. If none are available, you should try to fill the knowledge gap by searching in books or any other material that teaches about the problem domain.

Inside the Domain hexagon, we have entities corresponding to critical business data and rules. They are critical because they represent a model of the real problem. That model may take some time to evolve and reflect consistently on the problem domain. That's often the case with new software projects where neither developers nor domain experts have a clear vision of the system's purpose in its early stages. In such scenarios, particularly recurrent in start-up environments, it's normal and predictable to have an initial awkward domain model that evolves only as business ideas also evolve and are validated by users and domain experts. It's a curious situation where the domain model is unknown even to the so-called domain experts.

On the other hand, in scenarios where the problem domain exists and is clear in the minds of domain experts, if we fail to grasp that problem domain and how it translates into entities and other domain model elements, such as value objects, we risk building our software based on weak or wrong assumptions.

Weak assumptions can be one of the reasons why software may start simple but, as its code base grows, it accumulates technical debt and becomes harder to maintain. These weak assumptions may lead to fragile and unexpressive code that can initially solve business problems but is not ready to accommodate changes in a cohesive way. Bear in mind that the Domain hexagon is composed of whatever kind of object categories you feel are good for representing the problem domain. Here is a representation based just on entities and value objects:

Figure 1.5 – Domain hexagon

Let's now talk about the components comprising this hexagon.

Entities

Entities help us to build more expressive code. What characterizes an entity is its sense of continuity and identity, as described by *Domain-Driven Design: Tackling Complexity in the Heart of Software*. That continuity is related to the life cycle and mutable characteristics of the object. For example, in our network and topology inventory scenario, we mentioned the existence of routers. For a router, we can define whether its state is enabled or disabled.

Also, we can assign some properties describing the relationship that a router has with different routers and other network equipment. All those properties may change over time, so we can see that the router is not a static thing and its characteristics inside the problem domain can change. Because of that, we can state that the router has a life cycle. Apart from that, every router should be unique in an inventory, so it must have an identity. So, continuity and identity are the elements that determine an entity.

The following code shows a `Router` entity class composed of `RouterType` and `RouterId` value objects:

```
//Router entity class
public class Router {

    private final Type type;
    private final RouterId id;
    public Router(Type type, RouterId id) {
        this.type = type;
        this.id = id;
    }

    public static List<Router> checkRouter(
    Type type, List<Router> routers) {

    var routersList = new ArrayList<Router>();
        routers.forEach(router -> {
        if(router.type == type ){
            routersList.add(router);
        }
    });
    return routersList;
    }
}
```

Value objects

Value objects complement our code's expressiveness when there is no need to identify something uniquely, as well as when we are more concerned about the object's attributes than its identity. We can use value objects to compose an entity object, so we must make them immutable to avoid unforeseen inconsistencies across the domain. In the router example presented previously, we can represent the Type router as a value object attribute from the `Router` entity:

```
public enum Type {
        EDGE,
      CORE;
}
```

Application hexagon

So far, we've been discussing how the Domain hexagon encapsulates business rules with entities and value objects. But there are situations where the software does not need to operate directly at the domain level. *Clean Architecture: A Craftsman's Guide to Software Structure and Design* states that some operations exist solely to allow the automation provided by the software. These operations – although they support business rules – would not exist outside the context of the software. We're talking about application-specific operations.

The Application hexagon is where we abstractly deal with application-specific tasks. I mean abstract because we're not dealing directly with technology concerns yet. This hexagon expresses the software's user intent and features based on the Domain hexagon's business rules.

Based on the same topology and inventory network scenario described previously, suppose you need a way to query routers of the same type. It would require some data handling to produce such results. Your software would need to capture some user input to query for router types. You may want to use a particular business rule to validate user input and another business rule to verify data fetched from external sources. If no constraints are violated, your software then provides the data showing a list of routers of the same type. We can group all those different tasks in a use case. The following diagram depicts the Application hexagon's high-level structure based on use cases, input ports, and output ports:

Figure 1.6 – Application hexagon

The following sections will discuss the components of this hexagon.

Use cases

Use cases represent a system's behavior through application-specific operations that exist within the software realm to support the domain's constraints. Use cases may interact directly with entities and other use cases, making them quite flexible components. In Java, we represent use cases as abstractions defined by interfaces expressing what the software can do. The following example shows a use case that provides an operation to get a filtered list of routers:

```
public interface RouterViewUseCase {
    List<Router> getRouters(Predicate<Router> filter);
}
```

Note the `Predicate` filter. We're going to use it to filter the router list when implementing that use case with an input port.

Input ports

If use cases are just interfaces describing what the software does, we still need to implement the use case interface. That's the role of the input port. By being a component that's directly attached to use cases, at the *Application* level, input ports allow us to implement software intent on domain terms. Here is an input port providing an implementation that fulfills the software intent stated in the use case:

```
public class RouterViewInputPort implements RouterViewUse
  Case {

    private RouterViewOutputPort routerListOutputPort;

    public RouterViewInput
      Port(RouterViewOutputPort  routerViewOutputPort) {
        this.routerListOutputPort = routerViewOutputPort;
    }

    @Override
    public List<Router> getRouters(Predicate<Router> fil
       ter) {
        var routers = routerListOutput
            Port.fetchRouters();
        return Router.retrieveRouter(routers, filter);
    }
}
```

This example shows us how we could use a domain constraint to make sure we're filtering the routers we want to retrieve. From the input port's implementation, we can also get things from outside the application. We can do that using output ports.

Output ports

There are situations in which a use case needs to fetch data from external resources to achieve its goals. That's the role of output ports, which are represented as interfaces describing, in a technology-agnostic way, what kind of data a use case or input port would need to get from outside to perform its operations. I say agnostic because output ports don't care whether the data comes from a particular relational database technology or a filesystem, for example. We assign this responsibility to output adapters, which we'll look at shortly:

```
public interface RouterViewOutputPort {
    List<Router> fetchRouters();
}
```

Now, let's discuss the last type of hexagon.

Framework hexagon

Things seem well organized with our critical business rules constrained to the Domain hexagon, followed by the Application hexagon dealing with some application-specific operations through the means of use cases, input ports, and output ports. Now comes the moment when we need to decide which technologies should be allowed to communicate with our software. That communication can occur in two forms, one known as driving and the other as driven. For the driver side, we use input adapters, and for the driven side, we use output adapters, as shown in the following diagram:

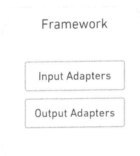

Figure 1.7 – Framework hexagon

Let's look at this in more detail.

Driving operations and input adapters

Driving operations are the ones that request actions from the software. It can be a user with a command-line client or a frontend application on behalf of the user, for example. There may be some testing suites checking the correctness of things exposed by your software. Or it could just be other applications in a large ecosystem needing to interact with some exposed software features. This communication occurs through an **Application Programming Interface (API)** built on top of the input adapters.

This API defines how external entities will interact with your system and then translate their request to your domain's application. The term *driving* is used because those external entities are driving the behavior of the system. Input adapters can define the application's supported communication protocols, as shown here:

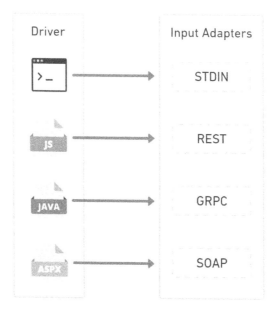

Figure 1.8 – Driver operations and input adapters

Suppose you need to expose some software features to legacy applications that work just with SOAP over HTTP/1.1 and, at the same time, need to make those same features available to new clients who could leverage the advantages of using gRPC over HTTP/2. With the hexagonal architecture, you could create an input adapter for both scenarios, with each adapter attached to the same input port, which would, in turn, translate the request downstream to work in terms of the domain. Here is an input adapter using a use case reference to call one of the input port operations:

```
public class RouterViewCLIAdapter {

    private RouterViewUseCase routerViewUseCase;

    public RouterViewCLIAdapter(){
        setAdapters();
    }

    public List<Router> obtainRelatedRouters(String type) {
        RelatedRoutersCommand relatedRoutersCommand =
            new RelatedRoutersCommand(type);
```

```
        return routerViewUseCase.getRelatedRouters
            (relatedRoutersCommand);
    }

    private void setAdapters(){
        this.routerViewUseCase = new  RouterViewInputPort
            (RouterViewFileAdapter.getInstance());
    }
}
```

This example illustrates the creation of an input adapter that gets data from STDIN. Note the use of the input port through its use case interface. Here, we passed the command that encapsulates input data that's used on the Application hexagon to deal with the Domain hexagon's constraints. If we want to enable other communication forms in our system, such as REST, we just have to create a new REST adapter containing the dependencies to expose a REST communication endpoint. We will do this in the following chapters as we add more features to our hexagonal application.

Driven operations and output adapters

On the other side of the coin, we have driven operations. These operations are triggered from your application and go into the outside world to get data to fulfill the software's needs. A driven operation generally occurs in response to some driving one. As you can guess, the way we define the driven side is through output adapters. These adapters must conform to our output ports by implementing them. Remember, an output port tells the system what kind of data it needs to perform some application-specific task. It's up to the output adapter to describe how it will get the data. Here is a diagram of output adapters and driven operations:

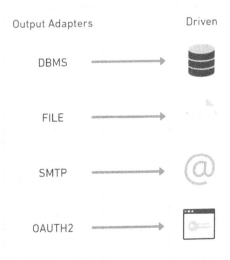

Figure 1.9 – Driven operations and output adapters

Suppose your application started working with Oracle relational databases and, after a while, you decided to change technologies and move on to a NoSQL approach, embracing MongoDB instead as your data source. In the beginning, you'd have just one output adapter to allow persistence with Oracle databases. To enable communication with MongoDB, you'd have to create an output adapter on the Framework hexagon, leaving the Application and, most importantly, Domain hexagons untouched. Because both input and output adapters are pointing inside the hexagon, we're making them depend on both Application and Domain hexagons, hence inverting the dependency.

The term *driven* is used because those operations are driven and controlled by the hexagonal application itself, triggering action in other external systems. Note, in the following example, how the output adapter implements the output port interface to specify how the application is going to obtain external data:

```java
public class RouterViewFileAdapter implements Router
    ViewOutputPort {

    @Override
    public List<Router> fetchRouters() {
        return readFileAsString();
    }

    private static List<Router> readFileAsString() {
        List<Router> routers = new ArrayList<>();
        try (Stream<String> stream = new BufferedReader(
                new InputStreamReader(
                    Objects.requireNonNull(
                    RouterViewFileAdapter.class
                        .getClassLoader().
                    getResourceAsStream
                        ("routers.txt")))).lines()) {
            stream.forEach(line ->{
            String[] routerEntry = line.split(";");
            var id = routerEntry[0];
            var type = routerEntry[1];
            Router router = new Router
                    (RouterType.valueOf(type)
                        ,RouterId.of(id));
                routers.add(router);
            });
        } catch (Exception e){
          e.printStackTrace();
        }
        return routers;
    }
}
```

The output port states what data the application needs from outside. The output adapter in the previous example provides a specific way to get that data through a local file.

Having discussed the various hexagons in this architecture, we will now look at the advantages that this approach brings.

Advantages of the hexagonal approach

If you're looking for a pattern to help you standardize the way software is developed at your company or even in personal projects, hexagonal architecture can be used as the basis to create such standardization by influencing how classes, packages, and the code structure as a whole are organized.

In my experience of working on large projects with multiple vendors and bringing lots of new developers to contribute to the same code base, the hexagonal architecture helps the organization establish the foundational principles on which the software is structured. Whenever a developer switched projects, they had a shallow learning curve to understand how the software was structured because they were already acquainted with hexagonal principles they'd learned about in previous projects. This factor, in particular, is directly related to the long-term benefits of software with a minor degree of technical debt.

Applications with a high degree of maintainability that are easy to change and test are always welcomed. Let's see next how hexagonal architecture helps us to obtain such advantages.

Change-tolerant

Technology changes are happening at a swift pace. New programming languages and a myriad of sophisticated tools are emerging every day. To beat the competition, very often, it's not enough to just stick with well-established and time-tested technologies. The use of cutting-edge technology becomes no longer a choice but a necessity, and if the software is not prepared to accommodate such changes, the company risks losing money and time on big refactoring because the software architecture is not change-tolerant.

So, the port and adapter features of hexagonal architecture give us a strong advantage by providing the architectural principles to create applications that are ready to incorporate technological changes with less friction.

Maintainability

If it's necessary to change some business rule, we know that the only thing that should be changed is the Domain hexagon. On the other hand, if we need to allow an existing feature to be triggered by a client that uses particular technology or protocol that is not yet supported by the application, we just need to create a new adapter, performing this change only on the Framework hexagon.

This separation of concerns seems simple, but when enforced as an architectural principle, it grants a degree of predictability that's enough to decrease the mental overload of grasping the basic software structures before deep diving into its complexities. Time has always been a scarce resource, and if there's a chance to save it through an architectural approach that removes some mental barriers, I think we should at least try it.

Testability

One of the hexagonal architecture's ultimate goals is to allow developers to test the application when its external dependencies are not present, such as its UI and databases, as Alistair Cockburn stated. This does not mean, however, that this architecture ignores integration tests. Far from it – instead, it allows a more loosely coupled approach by giving us the required flexibility to test the most critical part of the code, even in the absence of dependencies such as databases.

By assessing each of the elements comprising the hexagonal architecture and being aware of the advantages such an architecture can bring to our projects, we're now equipped with the fundamentals to develop hexagonal applications.

Summary

In this chapter, we learned how important software architecture is in establishing the foundations to develop robust and high-quality applications. We looked at the pernicious nature of technical debt and how we can tackle it with sound software architecture. Finally, we got an overview of the hexagonal architecture's core components and how they enable us to develop more change-tolerant, maintainable, and testable software.

With that knowledge, we're now able to apply these hexagonal principles to build applications based on the proposed Domain, Application, and Framework hexagons, which will help us establish boundaries between business code and technology code, laying the ground for the development of complete hexagonal systems.

In the next chapter, we're going to explore how to start developing a hexagonal application by looking at its most important part: the Domain hexagon.

Questions

1. What are the three hexagons that comprise the hexagonal architecture?
2. What's the role of the Domain hexagon?
3. When should we utilize use cases?
4. Input and output adapters are present in which hexagon?
5. What's the difference between driving and driven operations?

Further reading

- *Get Your Hands Dirty on Clean Architecture* (Hombergs , 2019)

Answers

1. Domain, Application, and Framework.

2. It provides the business rules and data in the form of entities, value objects, and any other suitable categories of objects that help model the problem domain. It does not depend on any other hexagon above it.

3. When we want to represent a system's behavior through application-specific operations.

4. The Framework hexagon.

5. Driving operations are the ones that request actions from the software. Driven operations are started by the hexagonal application itself. These operations go outside the hexagonal application to fetch data from external sources.

2

Wrapping Business Rules inside Domain Hexagon

In the previous chapter, we learned about the Domain as the first hexagon in hexagonal architecture. By being the innermost hexagon, the Domain does not depend on any code from the Application and Framework hexagons. Also, we make all the other hexagons depend on the Domain to conduct their operations. This kind of arrangement confers the Domain hexagon a degree of responsibility and relevance far higher than other hexagons. We employ such an arrangement because it is in the Domain where we group all the business rules and data that most represent the problem we try to solve.

Among the techniques to model a problem domain, **Domain-Driven Design** (**DDD**) is widely adopted in projects that emphasize software code as a medium to convey knowledge about a business. An ever-present concern to separate what constitutes the core problem domain and what is secondary to it makes DDD a suitable approach to support the hexagonal architecture goal of separating technology code from business code.

The principles and techniques we will see in this chapter will serve as the basis to build the Domain hexagon.

In this chapter, we will cover the following topics:

- Modeling a problem domain with entities
- Enhancing descriptiveness with value objects
- Assuring consistency with aggregates
- Working with domain services
- Using policy and specification patterns to deal with business rules
- Defining business rules as **Plain Old Java Objects** (**POJOs**)

By the end of this chapter, you will have learned the building blocks of DDD and will be able to apply the presented concepts in the development of hexagonal applications.

Technical requirements

To compile and run the code examples presented in this chapter, you need the latest **Java Standard Edition** (**SE**) development kit and **Maven 3.8** installed on your computer. They are all available for the Linux, Mac, and Windows operating systems.

You can find the code files for this chapter on GitHub at `https://github.com/ PacktPublishing/-Designing-Hexagonal-Architecture-with-Java---Second- Edition/tree/main/Chapter02`.

Modeling a problem domain with entities

In DDD, before any code is written, there must be lots of discussions between developers and domain experts—the people who have a deep understanding of their business, which may include other developers as well. Those discussions provide valuable information, acquired through a process called knowledge crunching, which is based on brainstorming between those developers and domain experts. That knowledge is then incorporated into the **ubiquitous language**. This language works as the *lingua franca* among everyone involved in the project and is present in documentation, day-to-day conversations, and – of course – in code.

When we deal with entities, we must always pay attention to how much we can learn about a business by just reading code. Even though just reading code may not be enough. That's when techniques such as knowledge-crunching, where we speak with domain experts to learn more about a business, are instrumental in helping us continuously evolve the ubiquitous language and translate the business knowledge into working code. That's the basis for rich entities that really capture relevant behaviors and are more than mere data objects.

For an entity to be considered an entity, it must have an identity; so, we'll see how to assign identity in a way that is aligned with the hexagonal architecture goal to separate concerns between business and technology code.

The purity of domain entities

When we model a problem domain, the main focus is to capture, as precisely as possible, a real-life scenario in code. That scenario is often composed of several processes working together to support an organization's goals to meet customer expectations. This ability to fulfill customer needs will ultimately determine the organization's capacity to generate profit. So, the problem-domain modeling effort is crucial to determine the overall success of any organization that relies on its software to make money. A failure to understand and translate business requirements into code will obviously result in not satisfied customer expectations.

Central to that problem-domain modeling effort is the creation of entities. Due to the proximity entities have to business requirements, we should strive to shield these entities from technical requirements. We do this to prevent the blurring of business-related code with technology-related code. By technology, I mean those things that exist and make sense only in the context of software.

Those same technology concerns would not make sense if we were only considering the business requirements without the software. We also have to recognize that a problem domain may not always refer to pure business requirements. A problem domain may be purely technological, such as creating a new development framework. I don't think hexagonal architecture is the best approach in those scenarios because its emphasis is on projects trying to solve conventional business problems.

Domain entities should be pure in the sense that they deal only with business concerns. For technology-specific things, we have the option to utilize ports, use cases, and adapters, as we'll see in the following chapters.

Relevant entities

A relevant entity is characterized by the presence of two elements – business rules and business data. It is not unusual to see entity classes modeled almost like database entity objects that express only the data part and forget the business rules represented through the behaviors provided by the entity class methods. These business rules may end up in parts of code other than the Domain hexagon.

This kind of leak, where the business rules end up outside the Domain hexagon, can be harmful because it may make it difficult to understand what the domain entity does. That happens when business rules are defined outside the Domain hexagon and depend, for example, on code that handles database entities, which are not part of the domain model but are a technical detail supporting the domain model. That phenomenon is prevalent in what is called an **anemic domain model**. The entity objects coming from anemic domain models generally have data but lack behavior. By not coupling data with behavior, the anemic domain model goes against the very essence of **Object-Oriented Programming (OOP)**. When behavior is not present in domain objects, we have to go somewhere else to fully grasp what the entity is supposed to do, thus generating a mental overload that can quickly become an onerous burden as a code base grows.

Conversely, we should not overload entity classes with logic that is not intrinsic to the entity we try to model. That's not a trivial thing to do because, at first, we may think an operation is a part of the entity, only to discover later on that it's not.

For things considered not intrinsic to entity behavior, we have the option to use a domain service. With services, we can accommodate those operations that don't fit smoothly into an entity class.

In the previous chapter, we created a `retrieveRouter` method to filter and list routers in the `Router` class, as illustrated in the following code snippet:

```
public static List<Router> retrieveRouter(List<Router>
   routers, Predicate<Router> predicate){
      return routers.stream()
         .filter(predicate)
```

```
        .collect(Collectors.<Router>toList());
}
```

Could we consider this list router's behavior an intrinsic characteristic of routers in the real world? If our problem domain says the opposite, then we should remove this behavior from the entity class. *And what about the constraints that we use to check the router type before we add a router to the list?* If we consider this verification a router-intrinsic behavior, we have the following options:

- Embed this constraint directly in the entity class

- Create a specification to assert the constraint

Specifications are a subject we will cover later in this chapter, but for now, you can see specifications as predicate mechanisms to ensure we work with the correct objects. The following code snippet provides an example of a `Router` entity class with the router type-check constraints embedded directly in it:

```
public class Router {
/** Code omitted **/
    public static Predicate<Router> filterRouterByType
      (RouterType routerType){
        return routerType.equals(RouterType.CORE)
            ? Router.isCore() :
            Router.isEdge();
    }

    private static Predicate<Router> isCore(){
        return p -> p.getRouterType() == RouterType.CORE;
    }

    private static Predicate<Router> isEdge(){
        return p -> p.getRouterType() == RouterType.EDGE;
    }
/** Code omitted **/
}
```

To accommodate the domain service method, we need first to create a domain service class called `RouterSearch` and move to it the `retrieveRouter` method from the `Router` class, as follows:

```
public class RouterSearch {

    public static List<Router> retrieveRouter(List<Router>
      routers, Predicate<Router> predicate){
        return routers.stream()
            .filter(predicate)
            .collect(Collectors.<Router>toList());
```

```
        }
    }
```

The `isCore`, `isEdge`, and `filterRouterByType` constraint methods continue to exist in the `Router` entity class. We only moved the `retrieveRouter` method from `Router` to `RouterSearch`. That `retrieveRouter` method can now be consumed as a service by other objects in the domain and in other hexagons. Later in this chapter, in the *Working with domain services* section, we will take a closer look at domain services.

A question that may arise is how complex the domain model methods should be, especially those that are part of the domain entities. My take is that the complexity will be determined by our knowledge of the problem domain and our ability to translate it into a domain entity that captures, through proper method definitions, only the necessary behaviors required to change the entity state according to the conditions presented by the problem domain. A weak problem domain knowledge may yield unnecessary complexity. So, as our knowledge of the problem domain increases, it also increases our capacity to provide the right level of complexity to the methods we define for the domain entities.

One fundamental characteristic of entities is that they have an identity that uniquely identifies them. Having an identity mechanism is paramount to ensuring that our entities are unique across a system. One way to provide such identity is through the use of UUIDs, a subject we will explore in the section.

Using UUIDs to define identity

You may be familiar with **identifier** (**ID**)-generation techniques that rely on database sequence mechanisms to generate and avoid duplication of IDs. Although it's convenient to delegate this responsibility to a database, by doing so, we couple a crucial aspect of our software to an external system.

Let's suppose we're aiming to develop a hexagonal application that lets us evolve business code with as few technology dependencies as possible. In this case, we need to find a way to turn this identity generation into an independent process.

A common approach to establishing an identity that does not rely on a central authority is with a **universally unique identifier** (**UUID**). This is a 128-bit number widely used to assure universal uniqueness in computer systems. There are four different methods to generate UUIDs – time-based, **Distributed Computer Environment** (**DCE**) security, name-based, and randomly generated. The following code snippet shows how you can create name-based and randomly generated UUIDs:

```
// Name-based UUID
var bytes = new byte[20];
new Random().nextBytes(bytes);
var nameBasedUUID = UUID.nameUUIDFromBytes(bytes);

// Randomly generated UUID
var randomUUID = UUID.randomUUID();
```

Beware of UUIDs, you can have performance issues if your data source is a relational database. Because UUIDs are strings, they consume more memory than the integers created by autogenerated IDs provided by relational databases. The use of UUIDs can cause a considerable impact on the size and index management of databases. There is no free lunch. Computer resources are the price to be paid for such an agnostic ID-generation solution. It's up to you to decide whether the benefits of this approach outweigh the disadvantages.

Once defined, the entity ID should not change, so it becomes an immutable attribute. This immutable characteristic makes the entity ID attribute a suitable candidate to be modeled as a value object. Based on the topology and network inventory example that we dealt with in the previous chapter, the following code snippet shows us a simple approach to creating a value object class to represent the ID of our Router entity:

```
public class RouterId {

    private final UUID id;

    private RouterId(UUID id){
        this.id = id;
    }

    public static RouterId withId(String id){
        return new RouterId(UUID.fromString(id));
    }

    public static RouterId withoutId(){
        return new RouterId(UUID.randomUUID());
    }
}
```

The withId factory method allows the reconstitution of Router entities when we have the ID. The withoutId factory method enables the generation of new IDs if we deal with a new Router entity.

The withId and withoutId methods are both applications of a pattern called the static factory method that allows us to encapsulate object creation. These methods are part of the domain model because they enable identity provisioning, through IDs, on either new or existing router entities.

Entities are first-class citizens in a hexagonal architecture. They are the foundational elements from which other software components will derive. However, they alone aren't enough to create rich domain models because not everything in a domain possesses an identity. We need something to express objects that don't need to be uniquely identified. We fill this need with value objects, a type of object intended to help us increase the descriptiveness of a problem domain.

Enhancing descriptiveness with value objects

In the book *Implementing Domain-Driven Design*, the author Vernon Vaughn points out that we should use value objects to measure, quantify, or describe things from our problem domain. For example, you can describe an ID attribute with a value object instead of a long or integer value. You can wrap a double or big decimal attribute into a specific value object to express quantification more clearly.

We're not fully satisfied with just using the built-in language types to model a problem domain. To make a system more explicit about its nature and purposes, we wrap those built-in language data types – and even our own created types – in well-defined value objects.

This effort to convey meaning is based on the following two fundamental characteristics of value objects:

- They are immutable
- They don't have an identity

Suppose you have painted a picture. Imagine how strange would it be if, for some reason, after you've finished your work, parts of your picture mysteriously change colors. In this analogy, colors are like value objects that we use to create a picture, and each color can be a different value object. So, to ensure that our paint will persist, the colors, once used, must not change and must be immutable once used. I base my argument for value objects on the idea that some characteristics must never change because they are the raw material we use to describe a problem domain.

Raw material alone neither expresses much meaning nor has much value. The real value comes when we combine and work with that raw stuff to form relevant and discernable things. Because value objects alone are like raw material, we don't bother to replace them or throw them away. *And if they are not so important, why should we assign them an identity and take the same care we have with entities?*

The bottom line is that value objects should be discardable and easily replaceable objects that we use to compose an entity or other type of object.

Using value objects to compose entities

When modeling an entity class, for example, we have two options – to use or not use value objects on entity attributes. Here is an example of the second approach:

```java
public class Event implements Comparable<Event> {
    private EventId id;
    private OffsetDateTime timestamp;
    private String protocol;
    private String activity;
    ...
}
```

Consider the following log excerpt as data entries we want to parse into the Event objects:

```
00:44:06.906367 100430035020260940012015 IPV6 casanova.58183 >
menuvivofibra.br.domain: 64865+ PTR? 1.0.0.224.in-addr.arpa. (40)
00:44:06.912775 100430035020260940012016 IPV4 menuvivofibra.br.domain
> casanova.58183: 64865 1/0/0 PTR all-systems.mcast.net. (75)
```

After being properly parsed, we would have Event objects with network traffic activity string fields, as shown here:

`casanova.58183 > menuvivofibra.br.domain`

Before the greater-than sign, we have the source host and, after, the destination host. For the sake of this example, let's see it as an activity representing the source and destination of a packet. By being a string, it leaves a burden for clients that want to retrieve the source or destination host from it, as illustrated here:

```
var srcHost = event.getActivity().split(">")[0]
  //casanova.58183
```

Let's try it with an `Activity` value object, as follows:

```
public class Activity {
    private final String description;
    private final String srcHost;
    private final String dstHost;

    public Activity (String description, String srcHost,
      String dstHost){

        this.description = description;
        this.srcHost = description.split(">")[0];
        this.dstHost = description.split(">")[1];
    }

    public String getSrcHost(){
        return this.srcHost;
    }
}
```

Then, we update the Event entity class, as follows:

```
public class Event implements Comparable<Event> {
    private EventId id;
    private OffsetDateTime timestamp;
    private String protocol;
```

```
    private Activity activity;

    ...

}
```

The client code becomes clearer and more expressive, as we can see in the following snippet. Also, clients don't need to handle the data themselves to retrieve the source and destination hosts:

```
var srcHost = event.getActivity().retrieveSrcHost()
//casanova.58183
```

With value objects, we have more flexibility and control over our data, letting us express the domain model in a more cohesive way.

Assuring consistency with aggregates

So far, we've seen how valuable entities are to represent things in a problem domain. Also, we saw how value objects are essential to enhance the descriptiveness of the model we use. *However, how do we proceed when we have a group of related entities and value objects that express a whole concept when put together?* For such a scenario, we should employ the use of **aggregates**. The idea is that objects inside an aggregate operate in a consistent and isolated manner. To achieve such consistency, we must ensure that any change on any aggregate object is conditioned to the variants imposed by such an aggregate.

An aggregate is like an orchestrator that orchestrates data and behavior on the objects it controls. For this approach to work, we need to define an entry point to interact with the aggregate realm. This entry point is also known as the aggregate root, which keeps references to the entities and value objects that are part of the aggregate. With the boundary provided by aggregates, we're in a better position to assure consistency in the operations conducted by the objects within that boundary. By formally establishing conceptual boundaries to ensure consistency in the activities based on our problem domain, it will be easier for us to incorporate techniques such as optimistic or pessimistic locking, and technologies such as the **Java Transaction API** (**Java JTA**) to support consistent transactional operations. With well-structured aggregates, we have better conditions to apply whatever approach we think is good to enable transactions on our system.

From a performance and scalability perspective, we should always strive to keep our aggregates as small as possible. The reason is simple – large aggregate objects consume more memory. Too many aggregate objects being instantiated at the same time can compromise the overall **Java Virtual Machine** (**JVM**) performance. This rule applies to anything in the OOP world, but we emphasize aggregates because of their ability to integrate objects.

A small aggregate generally contains just one entity that acts as the aggregate root and other value objects. The way to make two different aggregates interact with each other is through their aggregate root, which happens to be an entity root with its unique ID. The aggregate root is used for persistence purposes as well. So, you'll perform changes on aggregate child objects through the aggregate root, and when your changes are done, you'll use the same aggregate root to commit those changes to your persistence system.

Conversely, if you don't see the non-functional requirements of performance and scalability as something critical, I think, with proper care, that aggregates can grow to have more than one entity.

Modeling an aggregate

To illustrate how we can model an aggregate, let's return to our network and topology inventory scenario. One of the business needs is to catalog the equipment and networks connected to a specific **Edge Router**. Below this **Edge Router**, we have a **Level 3 Switch**, responsible for creating **Virtual Local-Area Networks** (**VLANs**) for different networks. The structure would be something like the one shown here:

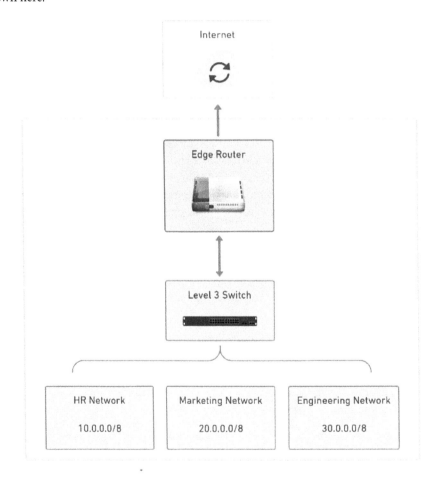

Figure 2.1 – Network components

The catalog of equipment, networks, and relationships is used by the infrastructure department to help them plan and implement changes in the overall network. A router or switch alone doesn't tell us too much about the network. The real value comes when we aggregate all the network components and their interconnections.

This kind of information will allow the infrastructure department to have more visibility and make well-based decisions. The epicenter of our aggregate is the edge router entity, which happens to be our aggregate root. The switch is also an entity. We model its VLAN networks as value objects. The context here is clear – a network composed of HR, marketing, and engineering VLAN networks connected to a switch that, in turn, is connected to the edge router. The internet or other networks can be considered in a different context. Here is a **Unified Modeling Language** (**UML**)-like representation of the aggregate root:

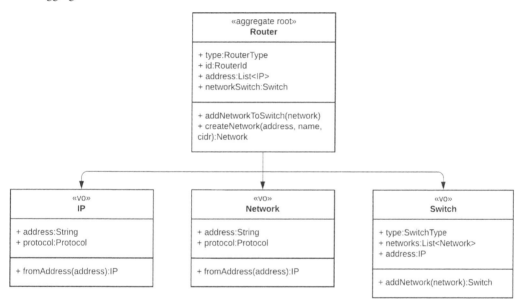

Figure 2.2 – The aggregate grouping together all network components

Starting from the bottom level, we have `Network` as a value object, as illustrated in the following code snippet:

```
public record Network(IP address, String name, int cidr) {

    public Network {
        if (cidr < 1 || cidr > 32) {
            throw new IllegalArgumentException("Invalid
              CIDR
            value");
        }
```

```
        }
    }
```

Note that the **Internet Protocol (IP)** address attribute is a value object as well, as shown in the following code snippet:

```
public class IP {

    private final String address;
    private final Protocol protocol;

    public IP(String address) {
        if(address == null)
        throw new IllegalArgumentException("Null IP
          address");

        if(address.length()<=15) {
            this.protocol = Protocol.IPV4;
        } else {
            this.protocol = Protocol.IPV6;
        }
        this.address = address;
    }

}
```

You may have noted some validation rules in the constructors of the IP and Network value objects' classes. Those validations work as guards to prevent the wrong construction of value objects. Putting those guards in instance creation is one way to free clients from the burden of validating value objects. That's exactly what happens on the Network class, where we just validate the cidr attribute because IP will come already validated.

There's also a Protocol enum value object that we will use to compose the IP value object, as illustrated in the following code snippet:

```
public enum Protocol {
    IPV4,
    IPV6
}
```

After modeling the IP, Network, and Protocol value objects, we have now the necessary objects to model the Switch entity class, as follows:

```
public class Switch {
    private final SwitchType type;
    private final SwitchId switchId;
```

```
    private final List<Network> networkList;
    private final IP address;

  public Switch (SwitchType switchType, SwitchId
    switchId, List<Network> networks, IP address) {
      this.switchType = switchType;
      this.switchId = switchId;
      this.networks = networks;
      this.address = address;
  }

  public Switch addNetwork(Network network, Router rout
    er)
  {
    List<Network> newNetworks =
    new ArrayList<>(router.retrieveNetworks());

  newNetworks.add(network);
  return new Switch(
      this.switchType,
      this.switchId,
      newNetworks,
      this.address);
  }

  public List<Network> getNetworks() {
      return networks;
  }
}
```

Because networks are directly connected to a switch, we create an addNetwork method to support the capability to add more networks to a switch. This method first retrieves the existing networks from the router, adding them to a list. Then, it adds the new network to the list of existing networks. Note that addNetwork does not change the current Switch object but, rather, creates a new Switch instance containing the network we added.

On top of all the value objects we have created so far, and the Switch entity, we need to formalize a boundary with an aggregate root. That's the role of our Router entity class, as illustrated in the following code snippet:

```
public class Router {
    private final RouterType routerType;
    private final RouterId routerid;
```

```java
    private Switch networkSwitch;

    public Router(RouterType, RouterId routerid) {
        this.routerType = routerType;
        this.routerid = routerid;
    }

    public static Predicate<Router>
      filterRouterByType(RouterType routerType) {
        return routerType.equals(RouterType.CORE)
                ? Router.isCore() :
                Router.isEdge();
    }

    public static Predicate<Router> isCore() {
        return p -> p.getRouterType() == RouterType.CORE;
    }

    public static Predicate<Router> isEdge() {
        return p -> p.getRouterType() == RouterType.EDGE;
    }

    public void addNetworkToSwitch(Network network) {
        this.networkSwitch =
          networkSwitch.addNetwork(network, this);
    }

    public Network createNetwork(IP address, String name,
      int cidr) {
        return new Network(address, name, cidr);
    }

    public List<Network> retrieveNetworks() {
        return networkSwitch.getNetworks();
    }

    public RouterType getRouterType() {
        return routerType;
    }
    @Override
    public String toString() {
        return "Router{" +
                "type=" + routerType +
```

```
                ", id=" + routerid +
        '}';
    }
}
```

Along with the `RouterType` and `RouterId` value objects, there is also an entity for the switch. The `networkSwitch` entity represents the switch connected directly to this router. Then, we add two methods, one to create a new network and another to connect an existing network to the switch.

By putting these methods on the aggregate root, we delegate to it the responsibility to handle all the objects under its context, thus enhancing consistency when we deal with such an aggregation of objects. Also, this is an effort to prevent the anemic domain model approach, whereby entities are just data objects without any kind of behavior.

Next, we will see how to use domain services to call those operations contained in the aggregate.

Working with domain services

When modeling a problem domain, we'll certainly face situations where the task at hand does not fit adequately into any of the object categories that we've seen so far in the domain hexagon – entities, value objects, and aggregates. Earlier in this chapter, we encountered a situation where we removed from the `Router` entity a method responsible for retrieving a list of routers. That method seemed to be in the wrong place because, in our topology and network inventory scenario, a router usually doesn't list other routers. To deal with this cumbersome situation, we've refactored the router list method in a separate object. Eric Evans calls such objects **domain services**.

I believe it's important to distinguish domain services from any other type of service. For example, in **Model-View-Controller** (**MVC**) architectures, services are often seen as bridges that connect the different facets of an application, handling data and orchestrating calls within and outside the system. Their usage is often associated with software development frameworks such as Spring that even have a service annotation. However, independent of the context, I believe the main difference between distinguished service types lies not in the meaning but in the scope.

What makes something a service? It's the ability to perform some worthwhile effort. This characteristic is inherent to any service, both in the real world and with computers. However, in the latter case, we should care about the **Separation of Concerns** (**SoC**), modularization, decoupling, and other relevant stuff for good architecture. It's based on those concerns that we put domain services inside the domain hexagon. They perform worthwhile tasks – as with any other services – but within the constrained scope of our problem domain. This means domain services should not call services or other objects that operate in application or framework hexagons. Instead, objects from those hexagons are clients who call domain services.

In the previous section, we created the following two methods in our `Router` entity class, which is also the aggregate root:

```
public void addNetworkToSwitch(Network network) {
    this.networkSwitch = networkSwitch.addNetwork(network,
      this);
}


public Network createNetwork(IP address, String name, long
  cidr) {
    return new Network(address, name, cidr);
}
```

In the following code snippet, we have a service class operating over those two `Router` entity methods:

```
public class NetworkOperation {

    final private int MINIMUM_ALLOWED_CIDR = 8;
    public void createNewNetwork(Router router, IP
      address, String name, int cidr) {

    if(cidr < MINIMUM_ALLOWED_CIDR)
    throw new IllegalArgumentException("CIDR is
      below      "+MINIMUM_ALLOWED_CIDR);

    if(isNetworkAvailable(router, address))
    throw new IllegalArgumentException("Address already
      exist");

    Network =
      router.createNetwork(address,name,cidr);
    router.addNetworkToSwitch(network);
    }

    private boolean isNetworkAvailable(Router router, IP
      address){

        var availability = true;
        for (Network network : router.retrieveNetworks()) {
            if(network.getAddress().equals(address) &&
              network.getCidr() == cidr)
                availability = false;
                break;
```

```
        }
        return availability;
    }
}
```

We have a method called `createNewNetwork` that is responsible for creating a new network object and adding it to the switch linked to our router. We should meet two constraints to be able to create a network. The first, simple one checks whether the minimum **Classless Inter-Domain Routing (CIDR)** has not been violated. The second constraint is somewhat more elaborate. It verifies whether the network address is already used on the whole network.

With this approach, we're delegating to the `NetworkOperation` domain service class the responsibility to deal with tasks that don't fit neatly into entities or value objects. It's also a good way to prevent entity and value object classes from growing too large, with far more features than necessary according to a problem domain.

Until now, we've dealt with invariants directly on entities, value objects, or service classes. Next, we'll see an approach to accommodate those invariants in a more orderly and organized way.

Using policy and specification to deal with business rules

One of the most valuable things a system possesses is its codified business rules. Those rules represent a vital effort to understand a real-world problem and translate that understanding into working software. That's not a trivial task, for sure. In DDD, we learn how crucial it is to work closely with domain experts to model our problem domain correctly. If domain experts are not available, we should seek developers with knowledge of a business. If none of them is available, we have no choice but to embark on a knowledge-seeking journey through books and any other resources that can help us grasp our problem domain's inner workings.

Once the business knowledge is acquired and we have enough relevant information about the problem domain's steps and processes, we can then start the adventure to transform that knowledge into code. At first glance, this process to understand business needs and transform them into software seems simple. Instead, it's been the fruit of very good debates that have given rise to various methodologies and even an important manifesto called the **Agile Manifesto**. It's not my goal here to discuss the best approach to understanding business needs. Instead, the idea here is to present some of the techniques we can use to transform that business knowledge into working software.

We always have the option to do things our way, sometimes ignoring the knowledge resulting from the experience of others who came before us. When dealing with business rules, this is by no means different. In the previous examples, we did this very thing, scattering business rules around code without a second thought. We now have an opportunity to fix that approach and tap into the knowledge of others who came before us.

Policy and specification patterns are two patterns that can help us better organize our code's business rules.

A **policy**, also known as a strategy, is a pattern that encapsulates part of the problem domain in a block of code. For those familiar with the Strategy pattern (*Gang of Four*), the term *algorithm* can be used to describe that encapsulated block of code. The main characteristic of a policy is that it performs some action or processing in the data provided. Policies are intentionally kept separate from entities and value objects to avoid coupling. This decoupling provides the well-known benefit of evolving one part without direct impact or side effects on the other.

Conversely, **specifications** are like conditions or predicates used to ensure the properties of an object. However, what characterizes a specification is its care to encapsulate those predicates in a more expressive way than mere logical operators. Once encapsulated, those specifications can be reused and even combined to express the problem domain better.

When used together, policies and specifications are sound techniques to improve the robustness and consistency of our business rules across code. A specification ensures that only suitable objects are handled by our policies. We have a catalog of different and easily changeable algorithms at our disposal with policies.

To better illustrate how specifications and policies work, we will now explore how to implement them.

Creating specifications

Let's first see how we can refactor our `NetworkOperation` service class to use specifications. We'll start by creating a `Specification` interface, as follows:

```
public interface Specification<T> {
        boolean isSatisfiedBy(T t);
    Specification<T> and(Specification<T> specification);
}
```

It's through the `isSatisfiedBy` implementation that we will define our predicates. Followed by this interface, we need to create an abstract class that implements the `and` method to allow us to combine specifications, as illustrated in the following code snippet:

```
public abstract class AbstractSpecification<T> implements
  Specification<T> {

    public abstract boolean isSatisfiedBy(T t);
    public Specification<T> and(final Specification<T>
      specification) {
        return new AndSpecification<T>(this,
          specification);
    }
}
```

Here, there is only a method for the AND operator because we are not dealing with other operators such as OR and NOT, although it's common to implement methods for those operators. To conclude the creation of our base types, we implement the AndSpecification class, as follows:

```
public class AndSpecification<T> extends AbstractSpecifica
  tion<T> {

    private final Specification<T> spec1;
    private final Specification<T> spec2;

    public AndSpecification(final Specification<T> spec1,
      final Specification<T> spec2) {

        this.spec1 = spec1;
        this.spec2 = spec2;
    }

    public boolean isSatisfiedBy(final T t) {
        return spec1.isSatisfiedBy(t) &&
          spec2.isSatisfiedBy(t);
    }
}
```

We are now ready to create our own specifications. The first one is about the business rule that limits the minimum CIDR allowed for the creation of new networks. The code is illustrated in the following snippet:

```
if(cidr < MINIMUM_ALLOWED_CIDR)
    throw new IllegalArgumentException("CIDR is
      below "+MINIMUM_ALLOWED_CIDR);
```

The corresponding specification will look like this:

```
public class CIDRSpecification extends AbstractSpecifica
  tion<Integer> {

    final static public int MINIMUM_ALLOWED_CIDR = 8;

    @Override
    public boolean isSatisfiedBy(Integer cidr) {
        return cidr > MINIMUM_ALLOWED_CIDR;
    }
}
```

Next, we'll deal with the business rules that check whether the network address is not already used, as follows:

```
if(isNetworkAvailable(router, address))
  throw new IllegalArgumentException("Address already ex
    ist");
private boolean isNetworkAvailable(Router router, IP ad
  dress) {
    var availability = true;
    for (Network network : router.retrieveNetworks()) {
        if(network.getAddress().equals(address) &&
          network.getCidr() == cidr)
                availability = false;
                break;
        }
        return availability;
    }
```

The refactoring of the previous code basically consists of moving the `isNetworkAvailable` method from the entity to the specification class, as shown in the following code snippet:

```
public class NetworkAvailabilitySpecification extends Ab
  stractSpecification<Router> {

    private final IP address;
    private final String name;
    private final int cidr;

    public NetworkAvailabilitySpecification(IP address,
      String name, int cidr) {
        this.address = address;
        this.name = name;
        this.cidr = cidr;
    }

    @Override
    public boolean isSatisfiedBy(Router router) {
        return router!=null &&
          isNetworkAvailable(router);
    }

    private boolean isNetworkAvailable(Router router) {
        return router.retrieveNetworks().stream()
            .noneMatch(
```

```
        network -> network.address().equals(address)
          &&
        network.name().equals(name) &&
        network.cidr() == cidr);
    }
 }
```

To illustrate how to combine two specifications with the and method, we will create two more specifications. The first one is to establish the maximum allowed networks and is shown in the following code snippet:

```
public class NetworkAmountSpecification extends Ab
  stractSpecification<Router> {

    final static public int MAXIMUM_ALLOWED_NETWORKS = 6;
    @Override
    public boolean isSatisfiedBy(Router router) {
        return router.retrieveNetworks().size()
          <=MAXIMUM_ALLOWED_NETWORKS;
    }
}
```

And the second specification is to ensure that we deal only with edge or core routers. This is shown in the following code snippet:

```
public class RouterTypeSpecification extends AbstractSpeci
  fication<Router> {

    @Override
    public boolean isSatisfiedBy(Router router) {
        return
        router.getRouterType().equals(RouterType.EDGE) ||
          router.getRouterType().equals(RouterType.CORE);
    }
}
```

Now that we have defined our specifications, we can use a feature introduced first as a preview in Java 15 and then as definitive in Java 17, allowing us to constrain which classes are permitted to implement an interface or a class. We call it a *sealed class/interface*. As the name implies, this feature seals the class/interface, so it cannot be implemented unless the implementing class/interface name is explicitly declared on the sealed class or interface. Let's check how this feature can work with the specification we just created.

We want to restrict who can implement the `Specification` interface and the `AbstractSpecification` abstract class. In the following code snippet, we can see how we can apply it to the `Specification` interface:

```
public sealed interface Specification<T> permits Ab
  stractSpecification {
/** Code omitted **/
}
```

Note that we restrict which class can implement the interface by using the `permits` clause. Let's seal the `AbstractSpecification` abstract class:

```
public abstract sealed class AbstractSpecification<T> im
  plements Specification<T> permits
        AndSpecification,
        CIDRSpecification,
        NetworkAmountSpecification,
        NetworkAvailabilitySpecification,
        RouterTypeSpecification
{
/** Code omitted **/
}
```

The permit clause now includes all the other classes implementing the `AbstractSpecification`. We still need to ensure the implementing classes are `final`. Therefore, we need to add the `final` clause on every one of those classes, as shown in the following example:

```
public final class NetworkAmountSpecification extends Ab
  stractSpecification<Router> {
/** Code omitted **/
}
```

Once we have finished adjusting the `final` keyword on the implementing specification classes, we have a well-defined set of sealed classes/interfaces, describing which specification classes can be used to define a system's business rules.

We're now ready to refactor our domain service, responsible for creating new networks to use those specifications, as follows:

```
public class NetworkOperation {

    public void createNewNetwork(Router router, IP
      address, String name, int cidr) {
```

```
            var availabilitySpec = new
              NetworkAvailabilitySpecification(address, name,
                cidr);
            var cidrSpec = new CIDRSpecification();
            var routerTypeSpec = new
              RouterTypeSpecification();
            var amountSpec = new
              NetworkAmountSpecification();

            if(cidrSpec.isSatisfiedBy(cidr))
                throw new IllegalArgumentException("CIDR is
                  below
                  "+CIDRSpecification.MINIMUM_ALLOWED_CIDR);

            if(availabilitySpec.isSatisfiedBy(router))
                throw new IllegalArgumentException("Address
                  already exist");

            if(amountSpec.and(routerTypeSpec).isSatisfiedBy
              (router)) {
                Network network =
                  router.createNetwork(address, name, cidr);
                router.addNetworkToSwitch(network);
            }
        }
    }
}
```

Now that we have explored how to implement specifications, let's see how we can create policies.

Creating policies

To understand how policies work, we will create a service class to help us retrieve a list of network events based on a specific algorithm to parse raw event data. This parse algorithm can or cannot be considered part of the problem domain; usually, it's not, but for the sake of this example, let's assume it is.

We will create two policies – the first is to parse string log entries into Event objects using a pure **regular expression (regex)**-based algorithm, where we explicitly inform the regex pattern, while the second one will accomplish the same thing but with a split-based algorithm that uses just a space delimiter. The choice between both policies can be based on performance and the ability to customize the parsing mechanisms, among other factors.

First, we will create an `EventParser` interface, as follows:

```
public interface EventParser {

    DateTimeFormatter formatter =
      DateTimeFormatter.ofPattern("yyyy-MM-dd
        HH:mm:ss.SSS").withZone(ZoneId.of("UTC"));


    Event parseEvent(String event);
}
```

We'll use the `formatter` attribute in both event-parser implementation classes.

Let's start implementing the regex parser policy, as follows:

```
public class RegexEventParser implements EventParser {

    @Override
    public Event parseEvent(String event) {
        final String regex = "(\\\"[^\\\"]+\\\")|\\S+";
        final Pattern pattern = Pattern.compile(regex,
          Pattern.MULTILINE);

        final Matcher matcher = pattern.matcher(event);
        var fields = new ArrayList<>();

        while (matcher.find()) {
            fields.add(matcher.group(0));
        }

        var timestamp =
          LocalDateTime.parse(matcher.group(0),
            formatter).atOffset(ZoneOffset.UTC);
        var id = EventId.of(matcher.group(1));
        var protocol =
          Protocol.valueOf(matcher.group(2));
        var activity = new Activity(matcher.group(3),
          matcher.group(5));
        return new Event(timestamp, id, protocol,
          activity);
    }
}
```

The split parser policy seems simpler, as we can see here:

```
public class SplitEventParser implements EventParser{
        @Override
    public Event parseEvent(String event) {
        var fields = Arrays.asList(event.split(" "));

        var timestamp =
          LocalDateTime.parse(fields.get(0),
            formatter).atOffset(ZoneOffset.UTC);
        var id = EventId.of(fields.get(1));
        var protocol = Protocol.valueOf(fields.get(2));
        var activity = new Activity(fields.get(3),
          fields.get(5));

        return new Event(timestamp,id, protocol,
          activity);
    }
}
```

As we did previously with specifications, the EventParser interface can be turned into a sealed interface:

```
public sealed interface EventParser permits RegexEvent
  Parser, SplitEventParser {
/** Code omitted **/
}
```

Don't forget to include the final keyword on the RegexEventParser and SplitEventParser classes.

Now, returning to the parser policy implementation, note that the Event constructor is called with the parsed attributes. We need to update our Event entity class to enable it to work with our policies. We can do so with the following code:

```
public class Event implements Comparable<Event> {

    private final OffsetDateTime timestamp;
    private final EventId id;
    private final Protocol protocol;
    private final Activity activity;

    public Event(OffsetDateTime timestamp, EventId id,
      Protocol protocol, Activity activity) {

        this.timestamp = timestamp;
        this.id = id;
```

```
        this.protocol = protocol;
        this.activity = activity;
    }

    public static Event parsedEvent(String
      unparsedEvent, ParsePolicyType policy) {

        switch (policy){
          case REGEX -> new
          RegexEventParser().parseEvent(unparsedEvent);
          case SPLIT -> new
          SplitEventParser().parseEvent(unparsedEvent);
        }
    }
  ...
}
```

The switch that allows us to choose between policies relies on the following enum:

```
public enum ParsePolicyType {
    REGEX,
    SPLIT
}
```

We're now ready to create an EventSearch service class with a method to retrieve network events. This domain service will allow us to choose which kind of parse algorithm to use when retrieving events. Here's the code we'll need for this:

```
public class EventSearch {

    public List<Event> retrieveEvents(List<String>
      unparsedEvents, ParsePolicyType policyType){

        var parsedEvents = new ArrayList<Event>();
        unparsedEvents.forEach(event →{
            parsedEvents.add(Event.parsedEvent(event,
        policyType));
        });
        return parsedEvents;
    }
}
```

Now that we are acquainted with policy and specification patterns, let's see the benefits of modeling our business rules on POJOs.

Defining business rules as POJOs

Back in the day, when enterprise development was strongly influenced by Java 2 Platform, **Enterprise Edition (J2EE)** (known today as **Jakarta EE**), there was a technology called **Enterprise JavaBeans (EJBs)**, responsible for lifting from developers all the heavyweight jobs required to manage software development plumbing activities, relating to transaction management, security, and object life cycles. The EJB promise was that developers could focus their energy on developing business features, while the J2EE container would take care of all the infrastructure details. EJBs fulfilled this promise, but not without a price. It was time-consuming and boring to create and maintain EJBs in their first versions. There were lots of things to do, involving various **Extensible Markup Language (XML)** configurations and deployment descriptors, and to make things worse, there was little space to reuse these EJB objects because they had so much boilerplate. They weren't like POJOs – simple and reusable.

This issue with the first EJB versions – version 2 especially – helped to motivate the creation of improved solutions that could leverage the simplicity of POJOs. Among those solutions, we can mention EJB 3 and the technologies derived from frameworks such as Spring and Quarkus. What all those technologies have in common, though, is the incentive and flexibility to work with POJOs.

POJOs are appealing because they are nothing more than regular Java objects. It is simple to understand a POJO because we deal only with Java standard **Application Programming Interfaces (APIs)** instead of custom libraries and frameworks. That's what makes POJOs a category of developer-friendly objects that are easier to understand and reuse across different parts of an application. If we aim for change-tolerant applications, then the use of POJOs is always recommended to diminish coupling with specific technologies, allowing an application to switch between different technologies or frameworks without much friction.

This flexibility offered by POJOs allows them to participate, simultaneously if needed, in different system departments. For example, nothing prevents someone from using the same POJO in transactional, persistence, and user-presentation contexts. We can also use POJOs to represent business rules – the entity, policy, and specification objects presented in this chapter are good examples of how we can embody business rules within POJOs.

By using POJOs to model business rules, we leverage all the benefits related to reusability and simplicity that a POJO can provide. They also go hand in hand with the important goal of keeping domain objects shielded from any technological details, which will ultimately contribute to the essential SoC efforts to support more supple and sober designs.

Summary

The DDD topics we covered in this chapter are paramount in our effort to develop hexagonal applications, as it's through the use of DDD techniques that we'll be able to shape a decoupled, consistent, and business-oriented domain hexagon that will be the foundation for the application and framework hexagons.

It's always essential to understand the basics. By looking closer into the main DDD concepts, we found the basic techniques to aid us in developing the domain hexagon. We covered how to make pure and relevant entities and how to assign an identity to them. With value objects, we understood how important they are in conveying meaning and enhancing the descriptiveness of a problem domain. Aggregates showed us how to group related entities and value objects to describe whole operations in our problem domain. Also, we saw how aggregates are instrumental in assuring consistency with transactions.

Following aggregates, we learned that domain services let us express behaviors that don't fit well into entities or value objects, and to better organize business rules, we learned about policy and specification patterns. Finally, we assessed the benefits of the reusability and simplicity that POJOs provide when defining business rules. With the ideas and techniques explored in this chapter, we can now build a domain hexagon that captures and properly arranges into code the business rules that will influence the behavior of an entire application.

We're now ready to move one step higher in the ladder by entering the realm of the application hexagon, where we'll see how to combine and orchestrate business rules to create software functionality through use cases and ports.

Questions

1. What is the main attribute of entities not found in value objects?
2. Can value objects be mutable?
3. Every aggregate must have an entry-point object to allow communication with other objects controlled by the aggregate. What is the name of this entry-point object?
4. Are domain services allowed to call objects on other hexagons?
5. What is the difference between a policy and a specification?
6. What is the benefit of defining business rules as a POJO?

Further reading

- *Implementing Domain-Driven Design* (Vernon, 2016)
- *Domain-Driven Design: Tackling Complexity in the Heart of Software* (Evans, 2003)
- *Extreme Programming Explained: Embrace Change* (Beck, 1999)

Answers

1. Contrary to value objects, entities have an identity.

2. No. The most important property of a value object is its immutability.

3. The entry-point object for any aggregate is called an aggregate root.

4. No, but objects from other domains and other hexagons can call domain services.

5. A policy is a pattern that encapsulates part of the problem domain knowledge in a block of code or an algorithm. A specification is a pattern that works with predicates to assert the validity of the properties of objects.

6. Because a POJO doesn't depend on external technology details, such as a feature provided by an external library or a framework. Instead, a POJO relies only on a standard Java API, which makes POJOs simple and easy-to-reuse objects. POJOs are helpful for creating business rules objects that aren't blurred by technology details.

3

Handling Behavior with Ports and Use Cases

Once we have defined the business rules in the Domain hexagon, we can start thinking about ways to use those rules to create software features while considering how the system will handle the data coming from users and other applications. Ports and use cases address such concerns in the hexagonal architecture, where we need to orchestrate system data and business rules to provide useful software functionality.

In this chapter, we'll explore how to employ use cases to define the behaviors supported by the software. Through the integration of input and output ports with use cases, we'll understand the role of such ports in establishing the communication flow within the hexagonal system.

We will cover the following topics:

- Expressing software behavior with use cases

- Implementing use cases with input ports

- Using output ports to deal with external data

- Automating behavior with the Application hexagon

"By the end of this chapter, you'll be able to employ ports and use cases to coordinate all the things a hexagonal system must do to fulfill user requirements." Once you have grasped the fundamentals of ports and use cases, it will be possible to utilize them to combine elements from both the Domain and Application hexagons to construct powerful features.

Technical requirements

To compile and run the code examples presented in this chapter, you will need the latest **Java SE Development Kit** and **Maven 3.8** installed on your computer. They are both available for the Linux, Mac, and Windows operating systems.

You can find the code files for this chapter on GitHub at `https://github.com/PacktPublishing/Designing-Hexagonal-Architecture-with-Java/tree/main/Chapter03`.

Expressing software behavior with use cases

A **software system** is nothing more than a set of behaviors working together to achieve the goals defined by users or even other software systems. A software behavior, in turn, is a worthy action that, alone or combined with other software actions, contributes to realizing a worthy software goal. Such goals are intimately connected to the desires expressed by interested users or systems.

We can classify those interested folks as stakeholders or actors from which we will ultimately derive the real-world needs that will be transmuted into goals. These actors' goals will be fulfilled by the **System under Discussion (SuD)**, or simply the software you are developing.

From the hexagonal architecture's standpoint, we can relate these actors to what we saw in *Chapter 1, Why Hexagonal Architecture?*, when discussing driver and driven operations. In the same vein, we can classify the SuD actors: the **driver actor** is a person or system that triggers one of the SuD behaviors, while the **driven actor** is an external system consumed by the SuD.

To express what a system does in both functional and non-functional terms, people such as Ivar Jacobson and Alistair Cockburn and the Agile community, in general, have contributed to developing useful techniques to transform business requirements into meaningful written descriptions of how a system should behave. Among those techniques, one that stands out is that of use cases.

Unlike the UML, which depicts a high-level view of the system through the relationship between diagrams, use cases perform a deeper dive by providing a detailed written description of SuD behaviors. **Use cases** are a valuable technique to set SuD goals, the means or behaviors to fulfill them, the possible failure scenarios, and what to do when they occur. When combined with DDD techniques, use cases are instrumental in bridging the gap of dealing with application-specific activities that mean more to the SuD – and the Application hexagon – than to the problem domain and its business rules in the Domain hexagon. By thinking in terms of use cases, we are making a significant step to improve the separation of concerns in the hexagonal architecture.

We can create use cases by simply writing a description about them, but it's also possible to express them through code. Next, we'll learn how to create use cases both in written and code form.

How to create a use case

There are elaborate approaches to creating written use cases where you may specify detailed and standardized information about the input data, possible behaviors, and use case results. Cockburn classifies those detailed use cases as fully dressed ones. Fully dressed use cases may be helpful in new teams, where people are not used to working together. The standards enforced by the fully dressed approach help provide a clear path about how a use case should be built. It helps prevent situations where a person may consider certain use case aspects that are not present in use cases written by another person. An example of a fully dressed use case is as follows:

- **Actor**: Infrastructure engineer

- **Goal**: To add a new network to an edge router

- **Scope**: Infrastructure department

- **Trigger**: A particular reason to segregate network access through a different network

- **Input data**: Router ID, network name, address, and CIDR

- **Actions**:

    I.   Look up the router ID.

    II.   Validate that the network address doesn't already exist.

    III.   Validate that the CIDR is not below the minimum allowed.

    IV.   If the previous validations are okay, add the network to the informed router.

On the opposite side, we have the less formal and casual types of use cases. The main characteristic of casual use cases is that they don't follow standards about how the information should be recorded. They try to convey as much meaning as possible in one or two paragraphs, as mentioned in the following example.

The infrastructure engineer sends a request to the application containing the router ID, network name, address, and CIDR. The application performs a lookup in the router ID, then validates that the network does not already exist, followed by another validation to confirm that the CIDR value is not below the minimum allowed. If all the validations are okay, then the system proceeds to add the network to the informed router.

Aside from the formal and casual written techniques, it's possible to express user intent directly in the code through automated tests. That approach relies on **behavior-driven design** (**BDD**) principles related to discovery, formulation, and automation. In such an approach, you start talking with business people trying to discover what they need. The output of this discovery process contains examples of situations and behaviors depicting the business need. Then, you move on to the formulation phase, where structured documentation is created based on those examples. Finally, the automation phase is where tests are created and executed to validate those behaviors from examples described and structured in previous phases.

When employing BDD earlier in software development, we have the opportunity to create use cases iteratively based on examples and tests created to validate business ideas.

With the aid of tools such as Cucumber, we can adopt the BDD approach in our hexagonal application. To convert the written use cases we built previously, we need to create a Cucumber feature file:

```
@addNetworkToRouter
Feature: Add network to a router
I want to be able to add a network to an existent router

Scenario: Adding a network to an existent router
Given I provide a router ID and the network details
When I found the router
And The network address is valid and doesn't already exist
And The CIDR is valid
Then Add the network to the router
```

Then, based on the steps provided by the Given, When, And, and Then terms from the feature files, we need to create a test class to automate the validation of our use case steps:

```
public class AddNetworkStepsTest {

  private RouterId routerId;
  private Router router;
  private RouterNetworkFileAdapter routerNetworkFileAdapter
    = RouterNetworkFileAdapter.getInstance();
  Network network = new Network(new IP("20.0.0.0"),
  "Marketing", 8);

  /** Code omitted **/
}
```

First, we have to declare the types and initialize the objects we will use to perform our tests. In the preceding code, we declared the RouterId and Router types. Then, we initialized the RouterNetworkFileAdapter and Network instances.

After preparing the resources we need to test, we can start by implementing the first step of our test:

```
@Given("I provide a router ID and the network details")
public void obtain_routerId() {
  this.routerId = RouterId.withId(
  "ca23800e-9b5a-11eb-a8b3-0242ac130003");
}
```

The @Given annotation describes the retrieval of RouterId. We can use this ID to fetch a router:

```
@When("I found the router")
public void lookup_router() {
```

```
    router =
    routerNetworkFileAdapter.fetchRouterById(routerId);
}
```

By using `RouterNetworkFileAdapter` and `RouterId`, we retrieve a `Router` object. Next, we can check whether the `Network` object meets the desired requirements before adding it to the router:

```
@And(
"The network address is valid and doesn't already exist")
public void check_address_validity_and_existence() {
    var availabilitySpec =
    new NetworkAvailabilitySpecification(
    network.getAddress(), network.getName(),
    network.getCidr());

    if(!availabilitySpec.isSatisfiedBy(router))
    throw new IllegalArgumentException("Address already
    exist");
}
```

To ensure the network is valid, we must apply the rules from `NetworkAvailabilitySpecification`. Next, we must check the network CIDR:

```
@Given("The CIDR is valid")
public void check_cidr() {
    var cidrSpec = new CIDRSpecification();
    if(cidrSpec.isSatisfiedBy(network.getCidr()))
    throw new IllegalArgumentException(
      "CIDR is below"+CIDRSpecification.
        MINIMUM_ALLOWED_CIDR);
}
```

As the last verification step, we must apply the rules from `CIDRSpecification`. If everything is fine, then we can add the network to the router:

```
@Then("Add the network to the router")
public void add_network() {
    router.addNetworkToSwitch(network);
}
```

By calling the `addNetworkToSwitch` method from `Router`, we have added the network to the router.

The following is a visual representation of the formal, casual, and BDD-based types of use cases:

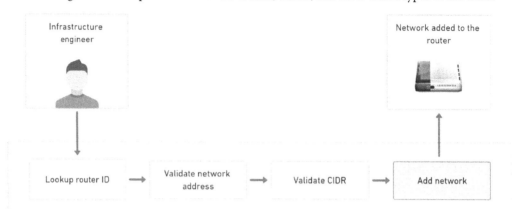

Figure 3.1 – A use case for the topology and inventory network system

Fully dressed, casual, and BDD-based use cases express the same thing. The main difference lies not in the *what* but rather in *how* the three techniques achieve the same objective to describe system behavior. As we may expect, the best choice is conditioned to money, time, and organization constraints.

We could bypass this use case creation/process and go straight on to code the use case. Although I don't consider the formal use case structuring part a required step, I certainly consider it a recommended one. By writing down and structuring the use case's expected behaviors, we're engaging in a valuable additional step to help us clarify and better organize our ideas regarding the use case's arrangement. Once the structuring effort is made, we only need to translate that into its code counterpart.

What I propose in developing hexagonal applications is to design use cases as abstractions rather than implementations. I am using interfaces in these examples, but there is no problem using abstract classes. The following code shows a use case interface based on its written form:

```
public interface RouterNetworkUseCase {

    Router addNetworkToRouter(RouterId routerId, Network
    network);
}
```

We define use cases as interfaces for three reasons:

- To provide different ways of fulfilling the use cases' goals
- To allow dependency on abstraction rather than implementation
- For governance of APIs

The role of use cases in the hexagonal architecture is that they allow us to implement input ports. It's through input ports that we construct the logic that will, for example, call Domain hexagon services, other use cases, and external resources through output ports. The UML representation of the use case and its input port is as follows:

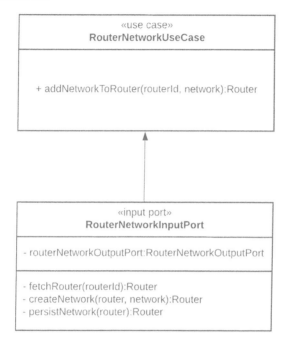

Figure 3.2 – A use case for the topology and inventory network system

Now that we know how to create use cases, both in written and code form, let's explore the ways to implement use cases with input ports.

Implementing use cases with input ports

In the hexagonal architecture, there is this idea about driving and driven operations. We've seen that such classification is also valid to determine which actors interact with the hexagon system. Driving actors are the ones who send requests to the application, while the driven actors represent the external components accessed by the application. We use **input ports** – also known as **primary ports** – to allow the communication flow between driving actors and the driving operations exposed by a hexagonal system. Use cases tell us what behaviors the application will support, while input ports tell us how such behaviors will be performed.

Input ports play an integrating role because they are like pipes that allow the data to flow from driving actors when they hit the hexagonal system through one of its adapters on the Framework hexagon. In the same vein, input ports provide the pipes for communication with business rules from the Domain hexagon. Through input ports, we also orchestrate communication with external systems through output ports and adapters.

Input ports are at the crossroads of a hexagonal system, helping translate what comes from the outside and goes in the direction of the Domain and Application hexagons. Input ports are also essential in orchestrating communication with external systems. In the following diagram, we can see how **Application Hexagon** is the integration point between **Driving Actor** and **Driven Actor** and their respective input and output ports and adapters:

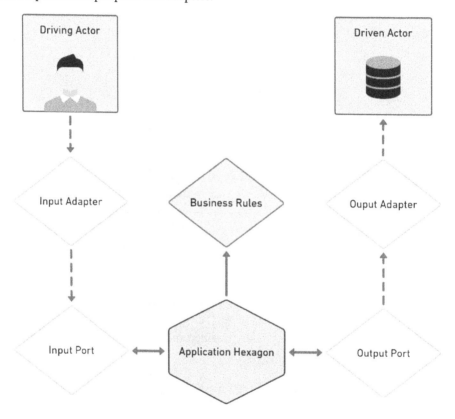

Figure 3.3 – The various ports and the Application hexagon

In the previous section, we defined a use case interface describing an operation that allowed us to add a network to a router. Let's learn how to create an input port by implementing that use case:

```
public class RouterNetworkInputPort implements RouterNet
   workUseCase {
private final RouterNetworkOutputPort
    routerNetworkOutputPort;
public RouterNetworkInputPort(RouterNetworkOutputPort
```

```
        routerNetworkOutputPort) {
        this.routerNetworkOutputPort =
        routerNetworkOutputPort;
    }


    @Override
    public Router addNetworkToRouter(RouterId routerId, Network
        network) {
        var router = fetchRouter(routerId);
        return createNetwork(router, network);
    }

    private Router fetchRouter(RouterId routerId) {
        return
        routerNetworkOutputPort.fetchRouterById(routerId);
    }

    private Router createNetwork(Router router, Network net
      work) {
        var newRouter =
        NetworkOperation.createNewNetwork(router, network);
        return persistNetwork(router) ? newRouter : router;
    }

    private boolean persistNetwork(Router router) {
        return routerNetworkOutputPort.persistRouter(router);
    }


    }
```

With this input port implementation, we have a clear view of what actions the software must perform to fulfill the use case's goal of adding a network to the router. Before we look closer at the input port methods, let's consider the RouterNetworkOutputPort interface's declaration:

```
public interface RouterNetworkOutputPort {

    Router fetchRouterById(RouterId routerId);
    boolean persistRouter(Router router);
}
```

This output port states that the application intends to obtain and persist data from external sources. The hexagon system is not aware of whether the external source is a database, a flat file, or another system. Here, we only state the intention to get data from outside.

The `addNetworkToRouter` method, which returns a `Router` object, is the only public method that's exposed by the input port. We make all other methods private because they are not supposed to be used outside the context of this input port. The input port starts its job by using `RouterId` to retrieve a `Router` object; then, it creates a new `Network` object on that `Router` object. Remember, the `Network` object comprises the address, name, and CIDR attributes, as expressed in the use case's written form. The `fetchRouter` method will try to obtain a `Router` object by passing a `RouterId` ID to the output port's `fetchRouterById` method. That's when the input port will need to coordinate an external call that will be carried out by an output adapter that implements the output port.

If everything goes well, the input port will receive the desired `Router` object and will be able to create a network object and add it to the informed router. At this point, the input port is interacting with a Domain service called `createNewNetwork`. This service works under the constraints imposed by business rules from the Domain hexagon. Finally, the input port coordinates the persistence of the whole operation through the `persistRouter` method from the output port.

This input port does not contain anything specific to the problem domain. Its primary concern is to handle data by orchestrating internal calls with Domain services and external calls with output ports. The input port sets the operation's execution order and provides the Domain hexagon with data in a format it understands.

External calls are interactions that are performed by the hexagonal application to get data from or persist data to external systems. This is the subject of the next section, where we'll learn how to use output ports to deal with things living outside the application.

Using output ports to deal with external data

Output ports, also known as **secondary ports**, represent the application's intent to deal with external data. It's through output ports that we prepare the system to communicate with the outside world. By allowing this communication, we can associate output ports with driven actors and operations. Remember, driven actors are external systems, while driven operations are used to communicate with such systems.

I say that we're preparing the hexagonal application to communicate with the outside world because, at the Application hexagon level, we don't know how that communication will occur yet. This approach is based on Uncle Bob's wise advice to postpone, as much as possible, any decisions concerned about which technologies will be used to fulfill the application's needs. By doing that, we're putting more emphasis on the problem domain than on technological details. I'm not saying that the persistence or messaging mechanisms, for example, are not relevant enough to influence the application's design. Instead, the idea is to not let external technologies dictate how the application is designed.

In the early stages of a software project, it's not uncommon to see people discussing whether to use PostgreSQL or Oracle databases for persistence, Kafka or Redis for pub-sub activities, and so on. Those types of discussions exert a strong influence on how the software solves business problems.

Sometimes, it's hard to imagine such software solving the same business problems but with different technologies. On certain occasions, it's even inconceivable to consider such a thing because the whole application architecture is centered on specific technologies.

As people who work with technology, we're always eager to use the hottest development framework or a modern programming language. That is a good attitude, and I think we should continuously pursue better techniques and sophisticated ways to solve problems. But prudence is advised to properly balance our focus between the technology and problem domain aspects of a system.

It's not only about repositories

You may be used to using terms such as repository or **data access object** (**DAO**) to describe application behaviors related to persistence in a database. In hexagonal applications, we replace repositories with output ports.

Repositories are often associated with database operations, a fact that, by the way, is also enforced by some development frameworks that formalize this association through persistence features offered by the framework. A recurring example of this approach is similar to the following code:

```
public interface PasswordResetTokenRepository extends
   JpaRepository<PasswordResetToken, Long> {

    PasswordResetToken findByToken(String token);
    PasswordResetToken findByUser(User user);
    Stream<PasswordResetToken>
      findAllByExpiryDateLessThan(Date now);
    void deleteByExpiryDateLessThan(Date now);

    @Modifying
    @Query(«delete from PasswordResetToken t where
      t.expiryDate <= ?1")
    void deleteAllExpiredSince(Date now);
}
```

The usage of the `JpaRepository` interface and the `@Query` annotation from the Spring framework reinforces the notion that the password data will come from a relational database. This situation could also be seen as a leaking abstraction condition because our `PasswordResetTokenRepository` interface would also contain all the methods inherited from the `JpaRepository` class that may not be relevant or provide behaviors that don't suit the system's needs.

The underlying idea about output ports is that we're not inferring that persistence or any kind of external communication will occur with a database system. Instead, the output port's scope is broader. Its concern is with communicating with any system, be it a database, a messaging system, or a local or network filesystem, for example.

A more hexagonal approach to the password reset interface shown previously would look something like the following code:

```
public interface PasswordResetTokenOutputPort {

    PasswordResetToken findByToken(String token);
    PasswordResetToken findByUser(User user);
    Stream<PasswordResetToken>
       findAllByExpiryDateLessThan(Date now);
    void deleteByExpiryDateLessThan(Date now);
    void deleteAllExpiredSince(Date now);
}
```

By not extending types from a specific framework and avoiding the usage of annotations such as @ Query, we're turning the output port into a POJO. The usage of annotations per se is not a problem. The issue lies more in the purpose of their usage. If the aim is to use annotations to implement features that only exist in a particular framework, we are then coupling the software to that framework. Instead, if the purpose is to use annotations to implement features based on Java standard specifications, we are making a valuable effort to make the software more tolerant to change.

The data that's obtained from an output port today may come directly from a relational database. Tomorrow, this same data can be obtained from the REST API of some application. Those details are not necessary from the Application hexagon's perspective because the components in this hexagon are not concerned with how the data is obtained.

Their main concern is in expressing what kind of data they need to conduct their activities. The way those Application hexagon components define what data they need is based on the entity and value objects from the Domain hexagon. With this arrangement, where an output port states what type of data it needs, we can plug multiple adapters into the same output port. So, these adapters carry out the necessary tasks to obtain the data, as expressed by the output port. This flow is shown in the following diagram:

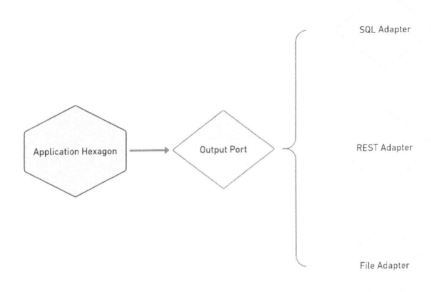

Figure 3.4 – The output port and its adapters

The output port's main goal is to state what kind of data it needs without specifying how it will get that data. That's the reason why we define them as interfaces and not implementations. The implementation part is reserved for output adapters, an essential hexagonal architecture component that we'll look at in the next chapter. To conclude our analysis of output ports, let's explore where they should be used.

Where to use output ports

At the beginning of this chapter, we learned how use cases establish the necessary actions to accomplish something useful in the application. Among these actions, there may be situations that require us to interact with external systems.

So, the reason to create and utilize output ports will be derived from the activities performed by use cases. In code, the reference for an output port will not appear in the use case's interface declaration. The usage of output ports is made explicit when we implement the use case with an input port. That's what we did when we implemented `RouterNetworkUseCase` and declared a `RouterNetworkOutputPort` attribute at the beginning of `RouterNetworkInputPort`:

```
public class RouterNetworkInputPort implements RouterNet
    workUseCase {

        private final RouterNetworkOutputPort
```

```
    routerNetworkOutputPort;

    public RouterNetworkInputPort(RouterNetworkOutputPort
      routerNetworkOutputPort){
        this.routerNetworkOutputPort =
          routerNetworkOutputPort;
    }

    private Router fetchRouter(RouterId routerId) {
        return routerNetworkOutputPort.fetchRouterById
          (routerId);
    }

    private boolean persistNetwork(Router router) {
        return routerNetworkOutputPort.persistRouter
          (router);
    }
  }
}
```

You may be wondering when and how the instance for an output port is created. The previous example shows one approach, where the input port constructor receives a reference for an output port object. This object will be an implementation provided by an output adapter.

Among the operations defined by a use case and implemented by an input port, some operations are responsible for getting data from or persisting data to external sources. That's where output ports come in: to provide the data required to fulfill the use case's goal.

In the same way that a use case goal is used to represent a piece of software's intent, without saying how this intent will be realized, output ports do the same thing by representing what kind of data the application needs, without needing to know how that data will be obtained. Output ports, along with input ports and use cases, are the hexagonal architecture components that support the automation effort that characterizes the Application hexagon. We'll examine this in the next section.

Automating behavior with the Application hexagon

Automation is one of the most valuable things software can do. The advent of computation brought radical changes to how people solve their problems. An interesting scenario is that of the credit card industry in its early years. When banks started to offer credit cards to their customers, most of the back-office activities were done manually. If you wanted to pay for something with a credit card, the person in the store would need to call their bank, who, in turn, would need to contact your card issuer to confirm you had credit. As the technology evolved, computer systems were able to automate this credit verification process.

If we decided to use the hexagonal architecture to build a credit card verification system, those required steps to confirm the cardholder's credit could be expressed using a use case. With an input port, we could handle business rules and all the data necessary to achieve the use case goal, consuming, if necessary, external systems through an output port. When we put all those activities together, the fundamental role of the Application hexagon in automating those activities to fulfill the system's intent becomes more apparent. Here's a code example to illustrate how the credit verification process would look in the Application hexagon:

1. We start by creating a `CreditCard` entity class:

    ```
    public class CreditCard {

        /** Code omitted **/
        double availableCredit;

        public boolean
                isAvailableCreditGreaterOrEqualThan(
                double transactionAmount) {
            return  availableCredit>=transactionAmount;
        }
    }
    ```

    The preceding code only emphasizes the credit availability aspect. So, we have the `availableCredit` attribute and the `isAvailableCreditGreaterOrEqualThan` method to check that there's enough credit for a given transaction.

2. Then, we declare the `CreditCheckUseCase` interface:

    ```
    public interface CreditCheckUseCase {

        boolean hasEnoughCredit(String cardId, double
            transactionAmount);
    }
    ```

    The goal is to check whether the credit card has enough credit for the transaction amount. To do so, we expect the `cardId` and `transactionAmount` attributes. We intend to use `cardId` to get credit card data from somewhere. So, having an output port is required to get data from other places.

3. Here, we declare `CreditCheckOutputPort`:

    ```
    public interface CreditCheckOutputPort {

        CreditCard getCreditCard(String cardId);
    }
    ```

This is a straightforward output port where we pass the `cardId` attribute and expect the `CreditCard` object to contain, among other things, how much credit is available.

4. Suppose credit card data is stored in a MySQL database. We would need an output adapter that implements the previously defined output port:

```
public class CreditCheckMySQLOutputAdapter implements
  CreditCheckOutputPort {
    @Override
    public CreditCard getCreditCard(String cardId) {
        /** Code omitted **/
        return creditCard;
    }
}
```

Inside the `getCreditCard` method, we would probably have some sort of mapping mechanism to convert the data that's retrieved from the database into the domain entity object – that is, `CreditCard`.

5. Finally, we can create the input port by implementing the `CreditCheckUseCase` interface:

```
public class CreditCheckInputPort implements
  CreditCheckUseCase {

    CreditCheckOutputPort creditCheckOutputPort;

    @Override
    public boolean hasEnoughCredit(
    String cardId, double transactionAmount) {
        return
        getCreditCard(cardId)
        .isAvailableCreditGreaterOrEqualThan
        (transactionAmount);
    }

    private CreditCard getCreditCard(String cardId) {
        return creditCheckOutputPort
                .getCreditCard(cardId);
    }
}
```

`CreditCheckInputPort` relies on `CreditCheckOutputPort` to get `CreditCard`, which is used in the `hasEnoughCredit` method, to check whether there is enough credit available.

One advantage of implementing the Application hexagon is that we don't need to be specific about which technologies we should use to fulfill the automation needs of our system. Of course, it's possible to add a fancy development framework to make our lives easier when handling certain activities–such as object life cycle management, which is provided by **Contexts and Dependency Injection (CDI)** mechanisms – but it's that purist approach of not focusing on technological details that makes hexagon systems easier to integrate with different technologies.

As we continue exploring the possibilities offered by the hexagonal architecture, we'll see that using a development framework is not a central point for software development. Instead, in hexagonal systems, frameworks are like ordinary utilitarian libraries that we use to strategically solve a specific problem.

Summary

In this chapter, we learned how to arrange the components that are responsible for organizing and building the features provided by the software. By looking into use cases, we grasped the fundamental principles to translate the behaviors that allow a system to meet users' goals into code. We discovered how input ports play a central role by implementing use cases and acting as middlemen, intermediating the communication flow between internal and external things. With output ports, we can express the need for data from external sources without coupling the hexagonal system with specific technologies. Finally, by using use cases and input and output ports together, we saw how the Application hexagon supports the software's automation effort.

By learning how to arrange things inside the Application hexagon, we can now combine business rules, entities, Domain services, use cases, and other components from both the Application and Domain hexagons to create fully fledged features in the hexagon application, ready to be integrated with different technologies. Such integration can be accomplished with the so-called adapters in the Framework hexagon. That's what we will look at in the next chapter.

Questions

Answer the following questions to test your knowledge of this chapter:

1. What is the purpose of use cases?
2. Input ports implement use cases. Why do we have to do that?
3. Where should output ports be used?
4. What is the advantage of implementing the Application hexagon?

Further reading

To learn more about the topics that were covered in this chapter, take a look at the following resources:

- *Writing Effective Use Cases* (Alistair Cockburn, 2000)
- *Clean Architecture* (Robert Cecil Martin, 2017)

Answers

The following are the answers to this chapter's questions:

1. It's to define software behaviors by establishing who the actors are and what features they expect from a system.

2. Because in the hexagonal architecture, use cases are interfaces that state the supported software capabilities. Input ports, in turn, describe the actions that will enable those capabilities.

3. Output ports appear inside input ports when it is necessary to interact with external systems.

4. By implementing the Application hexagon, we're supporting the overall hexagonal application's effort to automate operations without relying on specific technologies to do so.

4

Creating Adapters to Interact with the Outside World

There is a time in software development at which we need to decide which technologies will be supported by a system. We've discussed in previous chapters how technological choices should not be the primary driver for developing hexagonal applications. In fact, applications based on this architecture present a high degree of changeability, enabling a system to be integrated with different technologies with as little friction as possible. This is because the **hexagonal architecture** establishes a clear frontier between which part of the code is related to business and which is related to technology.

In this chapter, we're going to explore the hexagonal approach to establishing this frontier. We'll learn about the role adapters play when we need to set up technologies or protocols to enable a hexagonal application to communicate with the outside world.

We'll learn about the following topics in this chapter:

- Understanding adapters
- Using input adapters to allow driving operations
- Using output adapters to speak with different data sources

By the end of this chapter, you'll know how input adapters, in conjunction with input ports, can be used to expose the same software features to work with different technologies. In the same vein, you will learn how output adapters are powerful in making your application more versatile when it needs to talk to different data source technologies.

Technical requirements

To compile and run the code examples presented in this chapter, you need the latest **Java SE Development Kit** and **Maven 3.8** installed on your computer. To interact with the adapters, we also recommend installing `curl` and `jq`. All those tools are available for **Linux**, **Mac**, and **Windows** operating systems.

You can find the code files for this chapter on GitHub at `https://github.com/PacktPublishing/-Designing-Hexagonal-Architecture-with-Java---Second-Edition/tree/main/Chapter04`.

Understanding adapters

In hexagonal architecture, adapters have a different role from those employed as a design pattern in object-oriented languages. As a design pattern, we use adapters to make the interfaces of two diverging classes compatible. In the hexagonal architecture, we use adapters to allow a system to be compatible with different technologies or protocols. Although the adapter's role as a hexagonal architecture concept or as a design pattern may differ, it would be correct to state that both approaches share the same purpose: to adapt something to fit correctly into another thing.

A practical analogy to understand the role adapters play in hexagonal architecture is about remote connections to a computer. Every modern operating system is compatible with remote connection protocols. In the past (and even today in certain situations), it was common to use **Telnet** to open a remote connection to a computer. Over time, other protocols emerged, such as **SSH** for console connections, **RDP**, and **Virtual Network Computing (VNC)** for a graphical alternative.

Those protocols only define how you're going to access the operating system, and once you're there, you can execute commands and have access to the features that an operating system provides. It's not uncommon for an operating system to offer more than one protocol to allow remote connection. That's good because it widens the communication possibilities. There may be situations in which it's necessary to support both Telnet and SSH connections simultaneously, maybe because there is an unusual client that works only with Telnet.

By using the preceding analogy, we can replace the operating system with an application developed using **Java**, or any other programming language, and we can replace remote connection protocols such as SSH and Telnet with HTTP-based communication protocols, such as **REST** and **gRPC**. Assuming our Java application is a hexagonal one, the features offered by such applications are organized into use cases, ports, and business rules from the **Application** and **Domain** hexagons. If you want to make those features available for both REST and gRPC clients, you need to create REST and gRPC adapters. Adapters used to expose application features are called **input adapters**. To connect those input adapters to the rest of our system, we associate input ports with input adapters, as illustrated in the following figure:

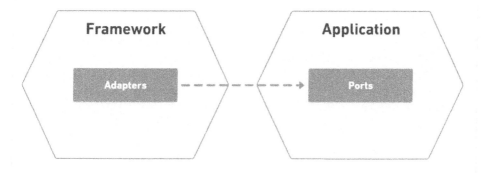

Figure 4.1 – The relationship between adapters and ports

We can define input adapters to allow users and other systems to interact with the application. In the same way, we can also define output adapters to translate data generated by the hexagonal application and communicate with external systems. Here we can see that both input and output adapters live in the extremities of the **Framework** hexagon:

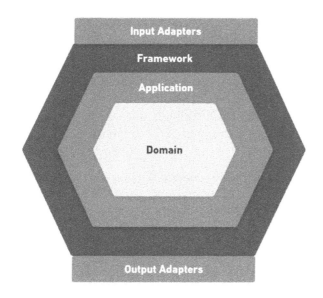

Figure 4.2 – The location of input and output adapters

Let's explore in the next section how we can work with input adapters.

Using input adapters to allow driving operations

You may have heard before that if there's something we can always count on, it's that things will always change. And when we talk about technological changes, that statement is even stronger. We live in an era where computers are not as expensive as they used to be in the past. No matter whether we're dealing with desktops, mobile, or cloud computing, year by year, computer resources, in general, become cheaper and more accessible to everyone. This accessibility means that more people tend to be involved and can collaborate with software development initiatives.

That growing collaboration results in newer programming languages, tools, and development frameworks to support the creative effort to solve people's problems with better and modern solutions. In this innovative and technological heterogeneous context, a good amount of current software development is made. One of the concerns that arises when developing software in this context is how a system will stay relevant and profitable in the face of constant technological changes. If a system is designed to intertwine business rules with technological details, it won't be easy to incorporate new technology without significant refactoring. In hexagonal architecture, input adapters are the elements that help us to make the software compatible with different technologies.

Input adapters are like the remote communication protocols mentioned in the example presented in the previous section. That comparison is valid because input adapters work like protocols, defining which technologies are supported as a means to access the features provided by a hexagonal system. Input adapters mark a clear frontier between what is inside the hexagon and what is outside, and perform what we call driving operations.

From outside the hexagon, there may be users or other systems interacting with the hexagonal application. We have learned that these users and systems are also known as primary actors, playing a pivotal role in shaping application use cases. The interaction between primary actors and the hexagonal application occurs through input adapters. Such interaction is defined by driving operations. We call them driving because primary actors drive, in the sense that they initiate and influence the state and behavior of hexagonal systems.

Input adapters, when put together, form the hexagonal application's API. Because input adapters are in this boundary that exposes the hexagonal system to the outside world, they naturally become the interface for anyone interested in interacting with the system. As we progress in the book, we'll see how to leverage the input adapters' arrangement to structure and expose the application APIs, using tools such as **Swagger**.

We have emphasized the adapters' characteristics to make a system compatible with different technologies or protocols. A more **Domain-Driven Design** (**DDD**) approach suggests other purposes for using an adapter.

A prevalent concern in DDD-based architectures is about integrating the elements of a legacy system into a new one. This occurs in scenarios where a legacy system with relevant knowledge crunched into its domain model solves some important problems but also shows inconsistencies in its design. You don't want to give up the legacy system, but you also don't want the new system design to be influenced by the legacy system's design. To tackle this situation, you can employ what *Implementing Domain-Driven Design* by Vaughn Vernon and *Domain-Driven Design: Tackling Complexity in the Heart of Software* by Eric Evans call an **anti-corruption layer**. This layer is based on the adapters used to integrate bounded contexts from both the legacy and the new systems. In such a scenario, the adapters are responsible for preventing the new system's design from being contaminated by the legacy system's design.

Although we're not applying this kind of usage of adapters in the hexagonal architecture, it's important to be aware that we can use this DDD-based adapter approach for a hexagonal system.

We learned that the connection between primary actors and the hexagonal application occurs through input adapters. Let's see now how to make input adapters connect to other hexagons in the system.

Creating input adapters

Input ports are the means through which we implement use cases, specifying how an input port performs the operations to achieve use case goals. The input port object needs to receive what Jacobson (1992) called a *stimulus* to perform its operations. This stimulus is nothing more than an object calling another. The input port object receives all the necessary data to conduct its operations through the stimulus sent by an input adapter. However, it's at this stage that eventual transformations may take place to convert input data into a format that's compatible with the Domain hexagon.

In the previous chapter, we created a use case to add networks to a router. To achieve the use case goals, we'll create two input adapters: an adapter for communication through HTTP REST and another for command-line execution. In the following UML diagram, we have **RouterNetworkAdapter** as an abstract parent class extended by the **RouterNetworkRestAdapter** and **RouterNetworkCLIAdapter** classes:

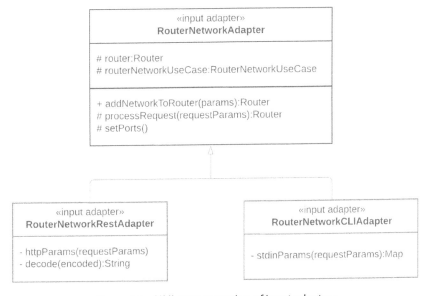

Figure 4.3 – UML representation of input adapters

We will define an adapter abstract base class, followed by two implementations, one for an adapter to receive data from HTTP REST connections and another for the console STDIN connection. To simulate access to these two adapters, we'll create a client class to bootstrap the application.

The base adapter

Let's start by defining the RouterNetworkAdapter abstract base class:

```
public abstract class RouterNetworkAdapter {

    protected Router router;
    protected RouterNetworkUseCase;

    public Router addNetworkToRouter(
    Map<String, String> params){
        var routerId = RouterId.
                withId(params.get("routerId"));
        var network = new Network(IP.fromAddress(
                params.get("address")),
                params.get("name"),
                Integer.valueOf(params.get("cidr")));
        return routerNetworkUseCase.
                addNetworkToRouter(routerId, network);
    }

    public abstract Router processRequest(
                        Object requestParams);
}
```

The idea of this base adapter is to provide standard operations for communicating with the adapter's correspondent input port. In that case, we use the addNetworkToRouter adapter method to receive the parameters required to build the RouterID and Network objects, which are utilized to start the use case operation to add the network to a router. These parameters may come from different sources, either via an HTTP request or via the shell/console with STDIN, but they are treated the same way once they arrive at the addNetworkToRouter method.

We don't refer to input ports directly. Instead, we utilize a use case interface reference. This use case reference is passed and initialized by the input adapter's constructor.

The REST input adapter

Now that we have defined the base `RouterNetworkAdapter` abstract class, we can proceed to create the REST adapter. We start by defining the `RouterNetworkRestAdapter` constructor:

```
public RouterNetworkRestAdapter(RouterNetworkUseCase rout
  erNetworkUseCase){
    this.routerNetworkUseCase = routerNetworkUseCase;
}
```

We use the `RouterNetworkRestAdapter` constructor to receive and initialize the `RouterNetworkUseCase` use case reference.

The following code shows us how a client could call-initialize this `RouterNetworkRestAdapter` input adapter:

```
RouterNetworkOutputPort outputPort = RouterNet
  workH2Adapter.getInstance();
RouterNetworkUseCase usecase = new RouterNetworkInput
  Port(outputPort);
RouterManageNetworkAdapter inputAdapter = new RouterNet
  workRestAdapter(usecase);
```

The intent here is to express that the REST input adapter requires an H2 in-memory database output adapter. Here, we're explicitly stating which output adapter object the input adapter needs to perform its activities. That can be considered a vanilla approach, where we don't use framework-based dependency injection techniques such as **CDI beans**. Later on, all those adapter constructors can be removed to use dependency injection annotations from frameworks such as **Quarkus** or **Spring**.

After defining the `RouterNetworkAdapter` constructor, we then implement the `processRequest` method:

```
/**
 * When implementing a REST adapter, the processRequest
   method receives an Object type parameter
 * that is always cast to an HttpServer type.
 */
@Override
public Router (Object requestParams){
/** code omitted **/
    httpserver.createContext("/network/add", (exchange -> {
      if ("GET".equals(exchange.getRequestMethod())) {
        var query = exchange.getRequestURI().getRawQuery();
        httpParams(query, params);
        router = this.addNetworkToRouter(params);
```

```
        ObjectMapper mapper = new ObjectMapper();
        var routerJson = mapper.writeValueAsString(
        RouterJsonFileMapper.toJson(router));
        exchange.getResponseHeaders().
        set("Content-Type","application/json");
        exchange.sendResponseHeaders(
        200,routerJson.getBytes().length);
        OutputStream output = exchange.getResponseBody();
        output.write(routerJson.getBytes());
        output.flush();
        } else {
          exchange.sendResponseHeaders(405, -1);
        }
  /** code omitted **/
  }
```

This method receives an `httpServer` object, which is used to create the HTTP endpoint to receive GET requests at `/network/add`. The client code that calls `processRequest` is similar to the following excerpt:

```
  var httpserver = HttpServer.create(new InetSocket
    Address(8080), 0);
  routerNetworkAdapter.processRequest(httpserver);
```

The REST adapter receives user data via an HTTP request, parses request parameters, and uses them to call `addNetworkToRouter` defined in the `RouterNetworkAdapter` parent class:

```
  router = this.addNetworkToRouter(params);
```

Remember that the input adapter is responsible for converting user data into suitable parameters used to trigger an input port by using its use case reference:

```
  routerNetworkUseCase.addNetworkToRouter(routerId, network);
```

At this moment, the data leaves the Framework hexagon and goes to the **Application hexagon**. Now, let's see how to connect another adapter to the same input port. The difference, though, is that this adapter is used for command-line execution. This time, the system will not receive data from an HTTP request but rather through a user typing via the keyboard (`STDIN`).

The CLI input adapter

To create the second input adapter, we again extend the base adapter class:

```
  public class RouterNetworkCLIAdapter extends RouterNetwork
    Adapter {
```

```
    public RouterNetworkCLIAdapter(
    RouterNetworkUseCase routerNetworkUseCase){
        this.routerNetworkUseCase = routerNetworkUseCase;
    }
/** code omitted **/
}
```

We define the `RouterNetworkCLIAdapter` constructor to receive and initialize the `RouterNetworkUseCase` use case that this input adapter needs.

For the CLI input adapter, we use a different output adapter. Instead of persisting an in-memory database, this output adapter uses the filesystem.

The following code shows us how a client could initialize the `RouterNetworkCLIAdapter` input adapter:

```
RouterNetworkOutputPort outputPort = RouterNetworkFileA
   dapter.getInstance();
RouterNetworkUseCase usecase = new RouterNetworkInput
   Port(outputPort);
RouterManageNetworkAdapter inputAdapter = new RouterNet
   workCLIAdapter(routerNetworkUseCase);
```

First, we get a `RouterNetworkOutputPort` output port reference. Then, with that reference, we retrieve a `RouterNetworkUseCase` use case. Finally, we get `RouterNetworkAdapter` using the use case defined previously.

The following is how we implement the `processRequest` method for the CLI adapter:

```
@Override
public Router processRequest(Object requestParams){
    var params = stdinParams(requestParams);
    router = this.addNetworkToRouter(params);
    ObjectMapper mapper = new ObjectMapper();
    try {
        var routerJson = mapper.writeValueAsString
                    (RouterJsonFileMapper.toJson(router));
        System.out.println(routerJson);
    } catch (JsonProcessingException e) {
        e.printStackTrace();
    }
    return router;
}
```

In the REST adapter, we have the `httpParams` method to retrieve data from an HTTP request. Now, in `processRequest` from the CLI adapter, we have a `stdinParams` method to retrieve data from the console.

The `processRequest` methods from the REST and CLI adapters have differences in how they handle input data, but both have one thing in common. Once they capture input data into the `params` variable, they both call the `addNetworkToRouter` method inherited from the adapter base class:

```
router = this.addNetworkToRouter(params);
```

From this point on, the data follows the same flow as the one described in the REST adapter scenario, where the input adapter calls the input port through a use case interface reference.

Now that we've finished creating the REST and CLI input adapters, let's see how to call these adapters.

Calling the input adapters

Here is the client code to control which adapter to choose:

```
public class App {
/** code omitted **/
    void setAdapter(String adapter) {
        switch (adapter){
            case "rest" -> {
                outputPort =
                RouterNetworkH2Adapter.getInstance();
                usecase =
                new RouterNetworkInputPort(outputPort);
                inputAdapter =
                new RouterNetworkRestAdapter(usecase);
                rest();
            }
            default -> {
                outputPort =
                RouterNetworkFileAdapter.getInstance();
                usecase =
                new RouterNetworkInputPort(outputPort);
                inputAdapter =
                new RouterNetworkCLIAdapter(usecase);
                cli();
            }
        }
    }
}
```

If we pass `rest` as a parameter when executing the program, the `switch-case` condition will create a REST adapter instance and call the `rest` method:

```
private void rest() {
    try {
        System.out.println("REST endpoint listening on
                            port 8080...");
        var httpserver = HttpServer.create(
        new netSocketAddress(8080), 0);
        routerNetworkAdapter.processRequest(httpserver);
    } catch (IOException e){
        e.printStackTrace();
    }
}
```

The `rest` method, in turn, calls the `processRequest` method from the REST input adapter.

Otherwise, if we pass the `cli` parameter when executing the program, `switch-case` will, by default, create a CLI adapter and call the `cli` method:

```
private void cli() {
    Scanner = new Scanner(System.in);
    routerNetworkAdapter.processRequest(scanner);
}
```

The `cli` method then calls the `processRequest` method from the CLI input adapter.

Here are the steps for calling the input adapters:

1. With the code sample from GitHub within the `chapter4` directory, you can compile the application by running the following command:

   mvn clean package

2. To call the REST adapter, you run the `.jar` file with the `rest` parameter:

   **$ java -jar target/chapter04-1.0-SNAPSHOT-jar-with-dependencies.
   jar rest
   REST endpoint listening on port 8080...**

3. Once the application is up, you can fire up an HTTP GET request to create and add a network:

   **curl -vv "http://localhost:8080/network/add?routerId=ca23800e-
   9b5a-11eb-a8b3-0242ac130003&address=40.0.0.0&name=Finance&c
   idr=8"**

4.   To call the CLI adapter, you run the `.jar` file with no parameters:

```
$ java -jar target/chapter04-1.0-SNAPSHOT-jar-with-dependencies.
jar cli
Please inform the Router ID:
ca23800e-9b5a-11eb-a8b3-0242ac130003
Please inform the IP address:
40.0.0.0
Please inform the Network Name:
Finance
Please inform the CIDR:
8
```

The application will ask you to specify the router ID and other network additional details for calling the CLI adapter. Here, we gave the same data as used to call the REST adapter.

In this section, we learned how to use input adapters to expose hexagonal application features. By defining first a base input adapter, we extended it to create a REST adapter for HTTP requests and a CLI adapter for console/STDIN requests. This arrangement helped us grasp the fundamental role input adapters play in exploring different ways to access the same functionality in the hexagonal system.

Input adapters are the front doors through which we access all the features a hexagonal application can provide. With input adapters, we can easily make the system accessible through different technologies without disturbing business logic. By the same token, we can make the hexagonal application speak to varying data sources. We accomplish that with output adapters, which we'll see in the next section.

Using output adapters to speak with different data sources

What characterizes an object-oriented system is its ability to treat data and behavior as closely related things. This proximity happens to mimic the way things are in the real world. Both animate and inanimate beings have attributes and can perform or be the target of some action. For people starting to learn object-oriented programming, we present examples such as a car, which has four wheels and can drive – wheels being the data and driving the behavior. Examples such as this express the fundamental principle that data and behavior should not be treated as separate things but should be united inside what we call objects.

This object idea has laid the ground for the development of vast and complex systems over the last decades. A good part of those systems is business applications running on enterprise environments. The object paradigm has conquered enterprise development because its high-level approach has allowed people to be more productive and precise when creating software to solve business problems. The procedural paradigm was cumbersome and too low-level for the demands of enterprises.

In addition to object-oriented languages, enterprise software also relies on ways to obtain and persist data. It's hard to imagine a system that is not integrated with data sources such as databases, message queues, or file servers, for example. The need to store things has always been present in computation. The problem, though, has been how this need has influenced and dictated the whole software structure. With the advent of **RDBMSs**, there comes the requirement to formalize data through **schemas** as well. These schemas, then, serve as a reference for establishing data relationships and how the application deals with such relationships. After some time, people started to look for alternatives to avoid the formalism and strict normalization principles imposed by RDBMSs. The problem is not in the formalism per se but in using RDBMSs where there's no need for that.

As an alternative to RDBMSs, there came **NoSQL** databases, proposing a way to store data that didn't rely on tables, columns, and schemas as a means of data organization. The NoSQL approach offers different data storage techniques, based on documents, key-value stores, wide-column stores, and graphs. Not constrained solely by the RDBMS approach, software developers then started using these NoSQL techniques to meet business requirements in a better way and avoid cumbersome solutions that relied on RDBMSs because there were no alternatives.

Aside from databases, other data sources have been used to fulfill software needs to handle data. Filesystems, message brokers, directory-based storage (**LDAP**), and mainframe storage, to name a few, are some of the ways software can handle data. In the world of cloud computing, it's becoming more natural to integrate a system with different technologies to send or receive data. This integration presents some challenges in software development because the system now needs to understand and make itself understandable in a heterogeneous technological context. That situation is even more exacerbated by architectures such as microservices that promote this heterogeneity. To tackle this challenge, we need techniques to overcome the challenges of technologically heterogeneous environments.

We saw in the previous section that we can plug multiple input adapters into the same input port. This also applies to output adapters and ports. Next, we'll see how to create output adapters and plug them into the hexagon system output ports.

Creating output adapters

Together with input adapters, output adapters are the second component that comprises the Framework hexagon. The output adapter's role in a hexagonal architecture is to deal with driven operations. Remember, driven operations are those initiated by the hexagonal application itself to interact with external systems to send or receive some data. These driven operations are described through use cases and are triggered by operations present in the use case's input port implementations. Whenever a use case states the need to deal with data that lives in external systems, this means the hexagonal application will require at least one output adapter and port to meet such requirements.

We learned that output ports present in the Application hexagon express interactions with external systems in abstract ways. Output adapters, in turn, have the responsibility to describe, in concrete terms, how these interactions will occur. With output adapters, we make up our minds about which technologies the system will use to allow data persistence and other types of external integration.

Until now, we have talked about data based solely on the requirements expressed by the domain model we created in the Domain hexagon. After all, it's the domain model from the Domain hexagon that drives the shape of the whole hexagonal system. Technological concerns are just mere details that must adhere to the domain model and not the other way around.

By using the output port as an interface in the Application hexagon and the output adapter as the implementation of that interface in the Framework hexagon, we are structuring the hexagonal system to support different technologies. In this structure, the output adapter in the Framework hexagon must conform to the output port interface in the Application hexagon, which, in turn, must rely on the domain model from the Domain hexagon.

In the previous section, you may have noticed the usage of two different output adapters – the `RouterNetworkH2Adapter` adapter to deal with data from in-memory databases and the `RouterNetworkFileAdapter` adapter to read and persist files from a local filesystem. These two output adapters are implementations of the output ports we created in the Application hexagon:

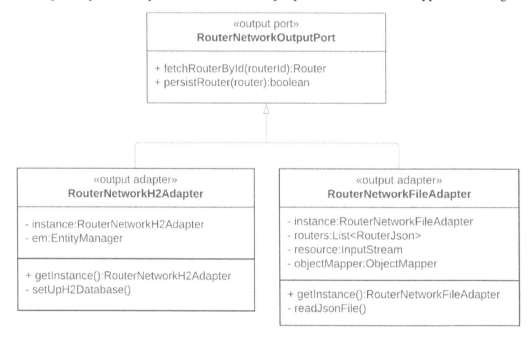

Figure 4.4 – UML representation of output adapters

We'll start by implementing `RouterNetworkH2Adapter`. It uses an H2 in-memory database to set up all the required tables and relationships. This adapter implementation shows us how to adapt the domain model data to a relational database. Then, we proceed to implement `RouterNetworkFileAdapter`, which uses a **JSON** file-backed data structure. Both H2 and JSON file implementations are based on the data provided by the topology and inventory sample system we've been working on. These two adapters will allow two ways to attach an additional network to an existing switch:

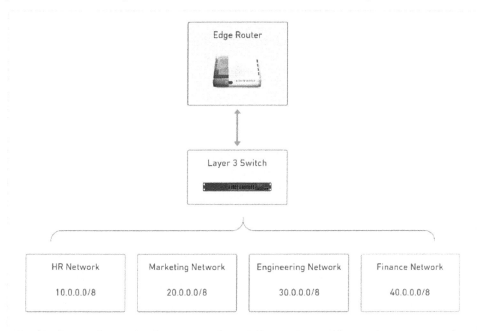

Figure 4.5 – Topology and inventory system with a finance network

Using the same input data from the previous section, we'll attach **Finance Network** to **Layer 3 Switch** from **Edge Router** using one of the available two output adapters.

The H2 output adapter

Before implementing the H2 output adapter, we first need to define the database structure of the topology and inventory system. To determine that structure, we create the `resources/inventory.sql` file with the following SQL statements:

```
CREATE TABLE routers(
    router_id UUID PRIMARY KEY NOT NULL,
    router_type VARCHAR(255)
);
CREATE TABLE switches (
    switch_id UUID PRIMARY KEY NOT NULL,
    router_id UUID,
    switch_type VARCHAR(255),
    switch_ip_protocol VARCHAR(255),
    switch_ip_address VARCHAR(255),
```

```
    PRIMARY KEY (switch_id),
    FOREIGN KEY (router_id) REFERENCES routers(router_id)
);
CREATE TABLE networks (
    network_id int NOT NULL PRIMARY KEY AUTO_INCREMENT,
    switch_id UUID,
    network_protocol VARCHAR(255),
    network_address VARCHAR(255),
    network_name VARCHAR(255),
    network_cidr VARCHAR(255),
    PRIMARY KEY (network_id),
    FOREIGN KEY (switch_id) REFERENCES switches(switch_id)
);
INSERT INTO routers(router_id, router_type) VALUES('ca23800e-9b5a-
11eb-a8b3-0242ac130003', 'EDGE');
INSERT INTO switches(switch_id, router_id, switch_type, switch_ip_
protocol, switch_ip_address)
VALUES('922dbcd5-d071-41bd-920b-00f83eb4bb46', 'ca23800e-9b5a-11eb-
a8b3-0242ac130003', 'LAYER3', 'IPV4', '9.0.0.9');
INSERT INTO networks(switch_id, network_protocol, network_address,
network_name, network_cidr)
VALUES('922dbcd5-d071-41bd-920b-00f83eb4bb46', 'IPV4', '10.0.0.0',
'HR', '8');
INSERT INTO networks(switch_id, network_protocol, network_address,
network_name, network_cidr)
VALUES('922dbcd5-d071-41bd-920b-00f83eb4bb46', 'IPV4', '20.0.0.0',
'Marketing', '8');
INSERT INTO networks(switch_id, network_protocol, network_address,
network_name, network_cidr)
VALUES('922dbcd5-d071-41bd-920b-00f83eb4bb46', 'IPV4', '30.0.0.0',
'Engineering', '8');
```

Although `switches` and `networks` have primary keys, we treat switches as entities and `networks` as value objects that are part of the `Router` entity in the domain model. We are imposing our model on the technological arrangement and not the other way around.

We don't use these primary keys from the `switches` and `networks` tables as references in the domain model. Instead, we use the `router_id` value to correlate the `Router` entity with its `Switch` and `Network` value objects and their respective database tables. This correlation enables the formation of an aggregate where `Router` is the aggregate root, and `Switch` and `Network` are the objects used to compose the aggregate.

Now, we can proceed to implement `RouterNetworkOutputPort` to create the RouterNetworkH2Adapter class:

```
public class RouterNetworkH2Adapter implements RouterNet
   workOutputPort {
      private static RouterNetworkH2Adapter instance;

      @PersistenceContext
      private EntityManager em;
      private RouterNetworkH2Adapter(){
          setUpH2Database();
      }
      @Override
      public Router fetchRouterById(RouterId routerId) {
          var routerData = em.
             getReference(RouterData.class,
             routerId.getUUID());
          return RouterH2Mapper.toDomain(routerData);
      }
      @Override
      public boolean persistRouter(Router router) {
          var routerData = RouterH2Mapper.toH2(router);
          em.persist(routerData);
          return true;
      }
      private void setUpH2Database() {
          var entityManagerFactory = Persistence.
          createEntityManagerFactory("inventory");
          var em = entityManagerFactory.
          createEntityManager();
          this.em = em;
      }
 /** code omitted **/
 }
```

The first method we override is `fetchRouterById`, where we receive `routerId` to fetch a router from the H2 database using our entity manager reference. We cannot use the `Router` domain entity class to map directly to the database. Also, we cannot use the database entity as a domain entity. That's why we use the `toDomain` method on `fetchRouterById` to map data from the H2 database to the domain.

We do the same mapping procedure, using the `toH2` method on `persistRouter` to convert it from a domain model entity into an H2 database entity. The `setUpH2Database` method initiates the database when the application starts. To create only one instance of the H2 adapter, we define a singleton using the getInstance method:

```
public static RouterNetworkH2Adapter getInstance() {
    if (instance == null) {
        instance = new RouterNetworkH2Adapter();
    }
    return instance;
}
```

The instance field is used to provide a singleton object of the H2 output adapter. Note that the constructor calls the setUpH2Database method to create a database connection using EntityManagerFactory. To properly configure the entity manager, we create the resources/META-INF/persistence.xml file with a property to set up the H2 database:

```
<?xml version="1.0" encoding="UTF-8" ?>
<!-- code omitted -->
<property
    name="jakarta.persistence.jdbc.url"
        value="jdbc:h2:mem:inventory;
        MODE=MYSQL;
        DB_CLOSE_DELAY=-1;
        DB_CLOSE_ON_EXIT=FALSE;
        IGNORECASE=TRUE;
        INIT=CREATE SCHEMA IF NOT EXISTS inventory\;
        RUNSCRIPT FROM 'classpath:inventory.sql'" />
<!-- code omitted -->
```

Remember, our domain model comes first, so we don't want to couple the system with database technology. That's why we need to create a RouterData **ORM** class to map directly to the database types. Here, we are using **EclipseLink**, but you can use any **JPA-compliant** implementation:

```
@Getter
@AllArgsConstructor
@NoArgsConstructor
@Entity
@Table(name = "routers")
@SecondaryTable(name = "switches")
@MappedSuperclass
@Converter(name="uuidConverter", converterClass=
  UUIDTypeConverter.class)
public class RouterData implements Serializable {

    @Id
```

```
@Column(name="router_id",
        columnDefinition = "uuid",
        updatable = false )
@Convert("uuidConverter")
private UUID routerId;

@Embedded
@Enumerated(EnumType.STRING)
@Column(name="router_type")
private RouterTypeData routerType;


@OneToOne(cascade = CascadeType.ALL)
@JoinColumn(table = "switches",
        name = "router_id",
        referencedColumnName = "router_id")
private SwitchData networkSwitch;
}
```

We use **Lombok** @Getter, @NoArgsConstructor, and @AllArgsConstructor annotations to diminish the verbosity of the class. We will use the getters and constructor later to convert the data class into a domain model class.

The usage of the @Table and @SecondaryTable annotations serves to represent the relationship between the routers and switches tables. This relationship is mapped using the @OntToOne and @JoinColumn annotations, specifying that both tables must be linked through the router_id attribute.

To use UUID as an ID in EclipseLink, we need to create the following converter class:

```
public class UUIDTypeConverter implements Converter {
    @Override
    public UUID convertObjectValueToDataValue(Object
                    objectValue, Session session) {
        return (UUID) objectValue;
    }
    @Override
    public UUID convertDataValueToObjectValue(Object
                    dataValue, Session session) {
        return (UUID) dataValue;
    }
    @Override
    public boolean isMutable() {
        return true;
```

```
        }
        @Override
        public void initialize(
        DatabaseMapping mapping, Session session){
            DatabaseField field = mapping.getField();
            field.setSqlType(Types.OTHER);
            field.setTypeName("java.util.UUID");
            field.setColumnDefinition("UUID");
        }
    }
}
```

This is the class we use inside the @Converter annotation at the top of the RouterData class. Without this converter, there will be an exception stating a problem in mapping the routerId attribute. Following the declaration of routerId, there is a RouterTypeData attribute called routerType. For every ORM attribute, we add the Data suffix to the class name. Aside from RouterData, we do that with RouterTypeData and SwitchData. Remember that in the domain model, the equivalent types are Router, RouterType, and Switch.

RouterTypeData is the enum in which we store the router type:

```
@Embeddable
public enum RouterTypeData {
      EDGE,
      CORE;
}
```

The @Embeddable annotation allows the enum data to be mapped to the router_type field in the database using the @Embedded annotation:

```
@Embedded
@Enumerated(EnumType.STRING)
@Column(name="router_type")
private RouterTypeData routerType;
```

As the last RouterData field, we refer to SwitchData in the networkSwitch variable, which we use to create the relationship between a router and switch. Let's see how the SwitchData class is implemented:

```
@Getter
@AllArgsConstructor
@NoArgsConstructor
@Entity
@Table(name = "switches")
@SecondaryTable(name = "networks")
@MappedSuperclass
```

```
@Converter(name="uuidConverter", converterClass=
  UUIDTypeConverter.class)
public class SwitchData implements Serializable {

    @Id
    @Column(name="switch_id",
            columnDefinition = "uuid",
            updatable = false )
    @Convert("uuidConverter")
    private UUID switchId;

    @Column(name="router_id")
    @Convert("uuidConverter")
    private UUID routerId;

    @Enumerated(EnumType.STRING)
    @Embedded
    @Column(name = "switch_type")
    private SwitchTypeData switchType;

    @OneToMany
    @JoinColumn(table = "networks",
            name = "switch_id",
            referencedColumnName = "switch_id")
    private List<NetworkData> networks;

    @Embedded
    @AttributeOverrides({
            @AttributeOverride(
                    name = "address",
                    column = @Column(
                            name = "switch_ip_address")),
            @AttributeOverride(
                    name = "protocol",
                    column = @Column(
                            name = "switch_ip_protocol")),
    })
    private IPData ip;
}
```

We apply the same techniques to SwitchData that we applied to RouterData. There is a subtle difference though, which is the relationship established between the switches and networks tables. To create this relationship, we use the @OneToMany and @JoinColumn annotations to create a link between the `SwitchData` and `NetworkData` types using the `switch_id` attribute. A reference to a list of `NetworkData` objects is required because of the `@OneToMany` annotation.

Similar to `RouterDataType`, we have `SwitchDataType`, which is an enum equivalent of `SwitchType` from the domain model:

```
@Embeddable
public enum SwitchTypeData {
    LAYER2,
    LAYER3;
}
```

In the topology and inventory system, we attach networks directly to a switch. To map the domain value object to the H2 database entity, we implement the `NetworkData` class:

```
@Getter
@AllArgsConstructor
@NoArgsConstructor
@Entity
@Table(name = "networks")
@MappedSuperclass
@Converter(name="uuidConverter", converterClass=
  UUIDTypeConverter.class)
public class NetworkData implements Serializable {

    @Id
    @Column(name="network_id")
    private int id;

    @Column(name="switch_id")
    @Convert("uuidConverter")
    private UUID switchId;

    @Embedded
    @AttributeOverrides({
            @AttributeOverride(
                    name = "address",
                    column = @Column(
                            name = "network_address")),
            @AttributeOverride(
                    name = "protocol",
                    column = @Column(
                            name = "network_protocol")),
        })
```

```
    IPData ip;

    @Column(name="network_name")
    String name;

    @Column(name="network_cidr")
    Integer cidr;
/** code omitted **/
}
```

All attributes we have in `NetworkData` are the same ones present in its domain value object counterpart. The only difference is the annotations we add to turn it into a database entity.

Both the `SwitchData` and `NetworkData` classes declare the `IPData` field. We encounter a similar behavior in the domain model, where `Switch` and `Network` classes have an `IP` attribute. Here is how we should implement the `IPData` class:

```
@Embeddable
@Getter
public class IPData {

    private String address;

    @Enumerated(EnumType.STRING)
    @Embedded
    private ProtocolData protocol;

    private IPData(String address){
        if(address == null)
            throw new IllegalArgumentException("Null IP
                        address");
        this.address = address;
        if(address.length()<=15) {
            this.protocol = ProtocolData.IPV4;
        } else {
            this.protocol = ProtocolData.IPV6;
        }
    }

    public IPData() {}

    public static IPData fromAddress(String address){
        return new IPData(address);
    }
}
```

`ProtocolData` follows the same pattern used by other enum-based types:

```
@Embeddable
public enum ProtocolData {
    IPV4,
    IPV6;
}
```

We could argue that there is some repetition in creating all those classes to integrate the system with a database. That's true. It's a trade-off where we give up reusability in favor of changeability, making the application capable of better integration with RDBMSes and other data sources.

Now that we have created all the ORM classes to allow integration with the H2 database, we need to translate database objects into domain model objects and vice versa. We accomplish this by creating a mapper class with mapper methods. Let's start with the methods we use to convert database entities into domain entities:

```
public static Router toDomain(RouterData routerData){
/** code omitted **/
    return new Router(routerType, routerId, networkSwitch);
}
```

The `toDomain` method receives a `RouterData` type representing the database entity and returns a `Router` domain entity.

To convert a list of `NetworkData` database entity objects into a list of `Network` domain value objects, we use the `getNetworksFromData` method:

```
private static List<Network> getNetworksFromData(List<Net
  workData> networkData){
    return networkData
            .stream()
            .map(network -> new Network(
                    IP.fromAddress(
                    network.getIp().getAddress()),
                    network.getName(),
                    network.getCidr()))
            .collect(Collectors.toList());
}
```

It receives a list of `NetworkData` database entity objects and returns a list of `Network` domain entity objects. Then, to convert from a domain model entity into an H2 database entity, we create the `toH2` mapper method:

```
public static RouterData toH2(Router router){
/** code omitted **/
```

```
  return new RouterData(routerId, routerTypeData,
    switchData);
}
```

The `toH2` method receives a `Router` domain entity object as a parameter, to do the proper mapping, and then it returns a `RouterData` object.

Finally, to convert a list of `Network` domain value objects into a list of `NetworkData` database entity objects, we have the `getNetworksFromDomain` method:

```
private static List<NetworkData> getNetworksFromDo
  main(List<Network> networks, UUID switchId){
    return  networks
              .stream()
              .map(network -> new NetworkData(
                    switchId,
                    IPData.fromAddress(
                    network.getAddress().getIPAddress()),
                    network.getName(),
                    network.getCidr()))
              .collect(Collectors.toList());
}
```

The `getNetworksFromDomain` method receives a list of `Network` domain value objects and a UUID-type switch ID as parameters. With that data, this method is able to do the proper mapping, returning a list of `NetworkData` database entity objects.

The `toDomain` static method is used when we need to convert the H2 database object into its domain model counterpart:

```
@Override
public Router fetchRouterById(RouterId routerId) {
    var routerData = em.getReference(
    RouterData.class, routerId.getUUID());
    return RouterH2Mapper.toDomain(routerData);
}
```

When persisting the domain model entity as the H2 database entity, we use the `toH2` static method:

```
@Override
public boolean persistRouter(Router router) {
    var routerData = RouterH2Mapper.toH2(router);
    em.persist(routerData);
    return true;
}
```

The `fetchRouterById` and `persistRouter` methods are called from the `RouterNetworkInputPort` object, using a `RouterNetworkOutputPort` interface reference:

```
private Router fetchRouter(RouterId routerId) {
    return routerNetworkOutputPort.
    fetchRouterById(routerId);
}
/** code omitted **/
private boolean persistNetwork(Router router) {
    return routerNetworkOutputPort.
    persistRouter(router);
}
```

Remember that `RouterNetworkOutputPort` is resolved at runtime based on the parameter we pass to the `RouterNetworkInputPort` constructor. With this technique, we blind the hexagonal system regarding where it needs to go to get data. It can be a relational database or a `.json` file, as we'll see in the next section.

The file adapter

To create the file adapter, we can apply the same ideas used to create the H2 database adapter, with just some minor adjustments to accommodate the file-backed data source. This data source is a `.json` file containing the same data used to create the previous database. So, to start, you can create a `.json` file at `resources/inventory.json` with the following content:

```
[{
    "routerId": "ca23800e-9b5a-11eb-a8b3-0242ac130003",
    "routerType": "EDGE",
    "switch":{
      "switchId": "922dbcd5-d071-41bd-920b-00f83eb4bb46",
      "ip": {
        "protocol": "IPV4", "address": "9.0.0.9"
      },
      "switchType": "LAYER3",
      "networks":[
        {
          "ip": {
            "protocol": "IPV4", "address": "10.0.0.0"
          },
          "networkName": "HR", "networkCidr": "8"
        },
        {
          "ip": {
            "protocol": "IPV4", "address": "20.0.0.0"
```

```
        },
        "networkName": "Marketing", "networkCidr": "8"
      },
      {
        "ip": {
          "protocol": "IPV4", "address": "30.0.0.0"
        },
        "networkName": "Engineering", "networkCidr": "8"
      }
    ]
  }
}]
```

The purpose of adding a network to fulfill our use case goals remains the same, so again we will implement the RouterNetworkOutputPort interface to create RouterNetworkFileAdapter:

```
public class RouterNetworkFileAdapter implements RouterNet
  workOutputPort {
/** code omitted **/
    @Override
    public Router fetchRouterById(RouterId routerId) {
var router = new Router();
        for(RouterJson: routers){
            if(routerJson.getRouterId().
            equals(routerId.getUUID())){
                router =  RouterJsonFileMapper.
                toDomain(routerJson);
            break;
          }
        }
        return router;
    }

    @Override
    public boolean persistRouter(Router router) {
        var routerJson = RouterJsonFileMapper.
                        toJson(router);
        try {
            var localDir = Paths.get("").
                            toAbsolutePath().toString();
            var file = new File(localDir+
                    "/inventory.json");
            file.delete();
            objectMapper.writeValue(file, routerJson);
```

```
        } catch (IOException e) {
            e.printStackTrace();
        }
        return true;
    }
/** code omitted **/
}
```

The `fetchRouterById` method returns a `Router` object by parsing a `.json` file using the `RouterId` parameter. The `persistRouter` method persists changes in the `inventory.json` file.

Instead of using an entity manager and EclipseLink, we use the `Jackson` libraries to serialize and deserialize the JSON data. To load the `inventory.json` file into memory, we use the adapter constructor to call the `readJsonFile` method to load the `inventory.json` file into a list of `RouterJson` objects:

```
private void readJsonFile(){
    try {
        this.routers = objectMapper.readValue(
            resource,
            new TypeReference<List<RouterJson>>(){});
        } catch (Exception e) {
            e.printStackTrace();
        }
}
private RouterNetworkFileAdapter() {
    this.objectMapper = new ObjectMapper();
    this.resource = getClass().getClassLoader().
    getResourceAsStream("inventory.json");
    readJsonFile();
}
```

As in the H2 case, with JSON, we also need to create special classes to map between JSON objects and domain model objects. The classes' structure is similar to the H2 ORM classes, with differences mainly in the annotations used to create adequate mapping. Let's see how to implement the `RouterJson` class:

```
/** Code omitted **/
@JsonInclude(value = JsonInclude.Include.NON_NULL)
public class RouterJson {

    @JsonProperty("routerId")
    private UUID routerId;
    @JsonProperty("routerType")
    private RouterTypeJson routerType;
```

```
    @JsonProperty("switch")
    private SwitchJson networkSwitch;
}
```

We use the `@JsonInclude` and `@JsonProperty` annotations to map class attributes to JSON fields. These JSON mappings are much more straightforward than H2 mappings because we don't need to deal with database relationships. `RouterTypeJson`, `SwitchJson`, and all other JSON map classes are similar in that they use the same annotations to convert JSON and domain model objects.

To convert `RouterJson` into `Router`, we use the `toDomain` method from the `RouterJsonFileMapper` mapper class:

```
RouterJsonFileMapper.toDomain(routerJson);
```

We use the `toJson` method to convert from `Router` into `RouterJson`:

```
RouterJsonFileMapper.toJson(router);
```

`RouterJsonFileMapper` is similar to its H2 counterpart but simpler because we don't need to deal with **one-to-many** or **one-to-one** relationships. Let's start with the methods used to convert JSON objects into domain objects:

```
public static Router toDomain(RouterJson routerJson){
    /** code omitted **/
    return new Router(routerType, routerId, networkSwitch);
}
```

The `toDomain` method here receives a `RouterJson` object as a parameter, performs the proper mapping, and then returns a `Router` object. A similar procedure occurs when we need to convert a list of `NetworkJson` JSON objects into a list of `Network` domain objects:

```
private static List<Network> getNetworksFromJson(List<Net
  workJson> networkJson){
    return networkJson
            .stream()
            .map(json ->  new Network(
                    IP.fromAddress(
                    json.getIp().getAddress()),
                    json.getNetworkName(),
                    Integer.valueOf(json.getCidr()))))
            .collect(Collectors.toList());
}
```

The `getNetworksFromJson` method receives a list of `NetworkJson` objects as parameters and returns an adequately mapped list of `Network` objects.

Let's see the methods used to convert domain objects into JSON objects:

```
public static RouterJson toJson(Router router){
    /** code omitted **/
    return new RouterJson(
                routerId,
                routerTypeJson,
                switchJson);
}
```

The `toJson` method does the opposite of what `toDomain` does. Instead of a JSON object as a parameter, the `toJson` method here receives a `Router` domain object, performs the proper mapping, and returns a `RouterJson` object.

Finally, we have a situation where it's necessary to convert a list of `Network` domain objects into a list of `NetworkJson` JSON objects:

```
private static List<NetworkJson>  getNetworksFromDo
  main(List<Network> networks){
      return networks
                .stream()
                .map(network -> new NetworkJson(
                    IPJson.fromAddress(
                    network.getAddress().getIPAddress()),
                    network.getName(),
                    String.valueOf(network.getCidr())))
                .collect(Collectors.toList());
}
```

By receiving a list of `Network` objects as parameters, the `getNetworksFromDomain` method can proceed to map the needed attributes and return a list of `NetworkJson` objects.

Now that we have completed the file output adapter implementation, let's play around, calling both the file and H2 output adapters.

Calling the output adapters

Before calling the adapter, let's compile the application. Navigate to the `Chapter04` directory and run the following command:

```
mvn clean package
```

To call the H2 output adapter, we need to use the REST input adapter. We can do that by providing the rest parameter when executing the .jar file:

```
$ java -jar target/chapter04-1.0-SNAPSHOT-jar-with-dependencies.jar
rest
$ curl -vv "http://localhost:8080/network/add?routerId=ca23800e-9b5a-
11eb-a8b3-0242ac130003&address=40.0.0.0&name=Finance&cidr=8" | jq
```

The file output adapter is accessible through the CLI input adapter:

```
$ java -jar target/chapter04-1.0-SNAPSHOT-jar-with-dependencies.jar
Please inform the Router ID:
ca23800e-9b5a-11eb-a8b3-0242ac130003
Please inform the IP address:
40.0.0.0
Please inform the Network Name:
Finance
Please inform the CIDR:
8
```

The result of calling both the H2 and file output adapters will be the same:

```
{
    "routerId": "ca23800e-9b5a-11eb-a8b3-0242ac130003",
    "routerType": "EDGE",
    "switch": {
      "switchId": "922dbcd5-d071-41bd-920b-00f83eb4bb46",
      "ip": {
        "address": "9.0.0.9", "protocol": "IPV4"
      },
      "switchType": "LAYER3",
      "networks": [
        {
          "ip": {
            "address": "10.0.0.0", "protocol": "IPV4"
          },
          "networkName": "HR",
          "networkCidr": "8"
        },
        {
          "ip": {
            "address": "20.0.0.0", "protocol": "IPV4"
          },
          "networkName": "Marketing",
          "networkCidr": "8"
```

```
        },
        {
          "ip": {
            "address": "30.0.0.0", "protocol": "IPV4"
          },
          "networkName": "Engineering",
          "networkCidr": "8"
        },
        {
          "ip": {
            "address": "40.0.0.0", "protocol": "IPV4"
          },
          "networkName": "Finance",
          "networkCidr": "8"
        }
      ]
    }
  }
```

Note the `Finance` network block at the end of the output, which confirms that the data was correctly persisted.

By creating these two output adapters, we enabled the hexagonal application to speak with different data sources. The best part was that we didn't need to change anything in the Domain or Application hexagons.

The only requirement for creating an output adapter is implementing an output port interface from the Application hexagon. These output adapter examples showed how a hexagonal approach protects the business logic from technological concerns. Of course, there is a trade-off when we decide to follow this path. However, if we aim to make change-tolerant systems centered in the domain model, the hexagonal architecture provides the necessary techniques needed for that.

Summary

We learned in this chapter that adapters are used to define the technologies that are supported by a hexagonal application. We created two input adapters to allow driving operations, that is, a REST adapter to receive data from HTTP connections and a CLI adapter to receive data from `STDIN`. Both input adapters were attached to the same input port, allowing the hexagonal system to use the same logic to process requests coming in distinct formats.

Then, we created an H2 database output adapter and a JSON file output adapter to allow the hexagonal application to communicate with different data sources. These two output adapters were attached to the same output port, enabling the hexagonal system to persist and obtain data from external sources so that the data source technology did not influence the business logic.

By knowing the purpose of input and output adapters and understanding how to implement them, we can now create systems that can tolerate significant technological changes without substantial refactoring. This benefit is achieved because all the system components, including the adapters, are developed around the domain model.

To fully understand the dynamic between adapters and other hexagonal architecture elements, we're going to look into the life cycle of driving and driven operations in the next chapter.

Questions

1. When should we create an input adapter?

2. What is the benefit of connecting multiple input adapters to the same input port?

3. What interface must we implement to create output adapters?

4. Which hexagon do the input and output adapters belong to?

Answers

1. We create an input adapter when we need to expose software features to be accessed by driving actors. These actors can access the hexagonal application using different technologies or protocols, such as HTTP REST or via the command line.

2. The main benefit is that the same logic, contained in an input port, can be used to treat data that comes from different input adapters.

3. Output adapters must always implement output ports. By doing that, we are sure that the adapters are in line with the requirements expressed by the domain model.

4. They are both from the Framework hexagon.

Further reading

- *Get Your Hands Dirty on Clean Architecture: A hands-on guide to creating clean web applications with code examples in Java*, Tom Hombergs, Packt Publishing Ltd., 2019

- *Object-Oriented Software Engineering: A Use Case Driven Approach*, Ivar Jacobson, Pearson Education, 1992

- *Domain-Driven Design: Tackling Complexity in the Heart of Software*, Eric Evans, Pearson Education, 2003

- *Implementing Domain-Driven Design*, Vaughn Vernon, Pearson Education, 2013

- *Hexagonal architecture* (`https://alistair.cockburn.us/hexagonal-architecture/`), Alistair Cockburn

5

Exploring the Nature of Driving and Driven Operations

We spent the previous chapters analyzing the elements comprising each hexagon in the **hexagonal architecture**. We learned about entities, value objects, and business rules, and how to arrange them in the Domain hexagon to create a meaningful domain model. After that, when dealing with the Application hexagon, we learned how to utilize use cases and ports to create fully fledged software features on top of the domain model. Finally, we learned how to create adapters to integrate the hexagonal application features with different technologies.

To better comprehend a hexagonal system, we also need to be aware of its surroundings. That's why, in this chapter, we explore the nature of driving and driven operations, as they represent the external elements interacting with the hexagonal application. On the driving side, we'll see how frontend applications act as primary actors, driving the behavior of a hexagonal system. On the driven side, we will learn what is necessary to enable a message-based system to be driven by a hexagonal system.

In this chapter, we will cover the following topics:

- Reaching the hexagonal application with driving operations
- Integrating web applications with the hexagonal system
- Running test agents and calling the hexagonal system from other applications
- Handling external resources with driven operations

By the end of this chapter, you will know the most common driving and driven operations. Once you understand these operations and how they influence the inner structure of a hexagonal system, you'll have learned all the building blocks of the hexagonal architecture, enabling you to develop complete hexagonal applications while leveraging all the techniques presented so far.

Technical requirements

To compile and run the code examples presented in this chapter, you need the **Java SE Development Kit (JDK)** (version 17 or higher) and **Maven 3.8** installed on your computer. They are all available for **Linux**, **Mac**, and **Windows** operating systems. You will also need to download these tools: **Postman**, **Newman** (from **npm**), and **Kafka**. We recommend using Linux to run Kafka properly. If you're using a Windows system, you can use **Windows Subsystem for Linux (WSL)** to run Kafka.

You can download the latest version of Kafka from `https://kafka.apache.org/downloads.html`.

You can download the latest version of Postman from `https://www.postman.com/downloads`.

You can download the latest version of Newman from `https://www.npmjs.com/package/newman`.

You can find the code files for this chapter on GitHub:

`https://github.com/PacktPublishing/-Designing-Hexagonal-Architecture-with-Java---Second-Edition/tree/main/Chapter05`

Reaching the hexagonal application with driving operations

We may consider it inconceivable that a system can be self-contained in the sense that no one interacts with it and that this system doesn't interact with other users or systems. Such an arrangement goes against the fundamentals of computer architecture (von Neumann, 1940), which presume the presence of input and output operations in any computer system. Indeed, it's difficult to imagine a useful software program that doesn't receive any data or produce any result.

Through the lens of the hexagonal architecture, the input side of a system is controlled by driving operations. We call them *driving operations* because they actually initiate and drive the behavior of a hexagonal application.

In *Chapter 3, Handling Behavior with Ports and Use Cases*, we related driving operations to primary actors. These actors are in charge of triggering driving operations in the hexagonal system. The driving operations can assume different facets: they can be users interacting directly with the system through a command-line console, a web **User Interface (UI)** application requesting data to present it in a browser, a testing agent wanting to validate a specific test case, or any other system interested in the features exposed by the hexagonal application.

All these different facets are grouped on the **driving side**, as shown in the following diagram:

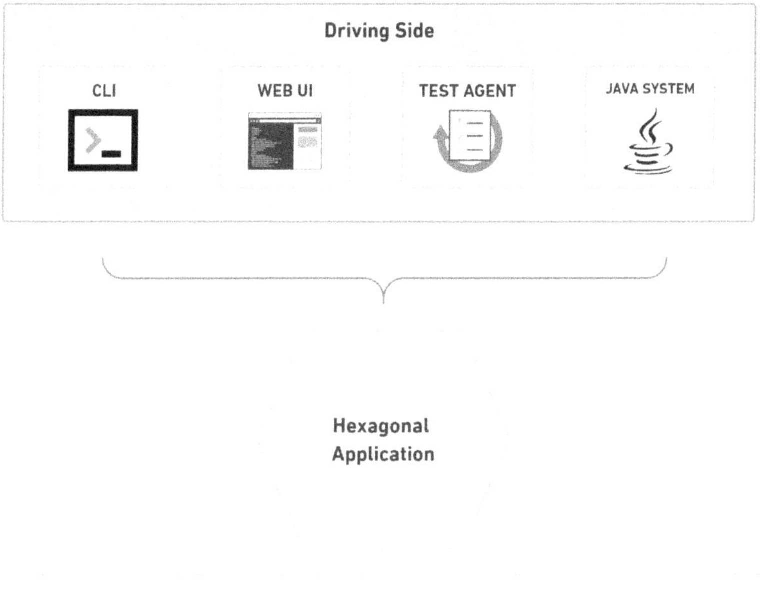

Figure 5.1 – The driving side and the hexagonal application

We saw, in the previous chapter, how to interact with a hexagonal application using a **Command-Line Interface** (**CLI**) and through **HTTP REST**. Now, we'll explore how to integrate other types of driving operations to communicate with the topology and inventory system we've been developing so far.

Once we have these integrations in place, we will analyze the path a request needs to take in order to traverse all the hexagons until it reaches the Domain one. This exercise will help us to understand the role played by each hexagon and its components in processing the request of a driving operation. So, let's start by integrating a web UI with the hexagonal system.

Integrating web applications with the hexagonal system

Nowadays, with the advent of **HTML 5**, modern **JavaScript**, and continuously improving web development techniques, it's possible to build highly sophisticated systems that run directly from the web browser. Faster internet connections, more computational resources, and better and well-established web standards have all contributed to the improvement of web applications. The old and cluttered **Flash** or **Java applet**-based systems, for example, have been replaced by frontend applications based on fancy frameworks such as **Angular**, **React**, or **Vue**.

Not only has the technology evolved and changed, but the practices surrounding web development have evolved too. Encouraged by the **Model-View-Controller** (**MVC**) pattern, developers used to group presentation code with business logic in a single software unit. The MVC's purpose has been to establish clear boundaries between different categories of components – model, view, and controller – in an application. But because the presentation and business code were most often part of the same software project and assembled into the same `.ear` or `.war` package file, it wasn't rare to see that the business logic had leaked into the presentation code.

Java EE (now **Jakarta EE**) and other frameworks, such as **Struts**, utilized technologies such as **Servlets**, **JSP**, and **JSF** to allow full integration between presentation and business code. After some time, people started to realize that this practice of putting frontend and backend code too close to each other could be a source of entropy for their software projects.

As a response to such practices, the industry turned to decoupled architectures where the frontend system is a separate, standalone application that interacts via the network with one or more backend systems.

So, we will create a simple, standalone frontend application that obtains its data from our topology and inventory system. Our application will be based only on HTML 5, CSS, and *vanilla* JavaScript. The application aims to allow users to add networks to a router and retrieve existing routers from the system database. We will also refactor part of the hexagonal application to enable better integration with our frontend application. The result will be a web browser application integrated with the hexagonal system, as shown in the following screenshot:

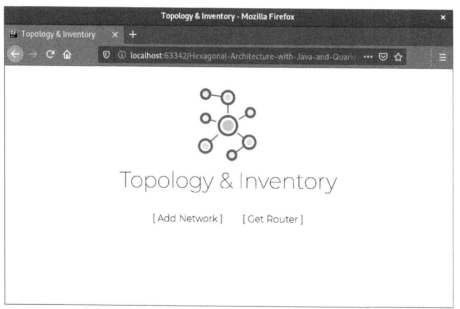

Figure 5.2 – The Topology & Inventory frontend application

The frontend application will allow users to add networks to an existing router and view a graphical representation of the router and its networks.

Let's start enhancing the hexagonal application by adding the getRouter method to the RouterNetworkUseCase interface:

```
public interface RouterNetworkUseCase {

    Router addNetworkToRouter(RouterId,
    Network network);

    Router getRouter(RouterId routerId);
}
```

The getRouter method signature is simple. It receives RouterId and returns a Router object. We need this behavior to allow the frontend application to display a router.

Next, we need to provide an implementation for the getRouter method. We do that by implementing the RouterNetworkUseCase interface with the RouterNetworkInputPort class:

```
public class RouterNetworkInputPort implements RouterNet
  workUseCase {
/** code omitted **/
    @Override
    public Router getRouter(RouterId routerId) {
        return fetchRouter(routerId);
    }

    private Router fetchRouter(RouterId routerId) {
        return routerNetworkOutputPort.
                fetchRouterById(routerId);
    }
/** code omitted **/
}
```

Notice that fetchRouter already existed in the input port implementation, but we didn't have an exposed operation that allowed us to retrieve the router. The fetchRouter method is then used not only by the addNetworkToRouter method but now also by getRouter.

It's necessary to propagate the input port change to the input adapter. We do that by creating a getRouter method on the base input adapter defined in the RouterNetworkAdapter abstract class:

```
public Router getRouter(Map<String, String> params) {
    var routerId = RouterId.
    withId(params.get("routerId"));
    return routerNetworkUseCase.getRouter(routerId);
}
```

Remember that `RouterNetworkAdapter` is the base input adapter for both `RouterNetworkCLIAdapter` and `RouterNetworkRestAdapter`.

To allow the frontend application to communicate with the hexagonal system, we'll use the REST adapter. So, there are some changes we need to make in `RouterNetworkRestAdapter` to allow this communication:

```
@Override
public Router processRequest(Object requestParams){
/** code omitted **/
    if (exchange.
      getRequestURI().getPath().equals("/network/add")) {
        try {
            router = this.addNetworkToRouter(params);
        } catch (Exception e) {
            exchange.sendResponseHeaders(
            400, e.getMessage().getBytes().length);
            OutputStream output = exchange.
            getResponseBody();
            output.write(e.getMessage().getBytes());
            output.flush();
        }
    }
    if (exchange.
      getRequestURI().getPath().contains("/network/get")) {
        router = this.getRouter(params);
    }
/** code omitted **/
}
```

The changes to the `processRequest` method were made so it can properly handle requests coming from the /network/add and /network/get paths.

We can move now to the development of the frontend part of our topology and inventory system. Our focus will be on the HTML and JavaScript elements. We'll create two pages: the first one is to allow users to add networks, and the second one is where users will be able to retrieve a graphical view of a router and its networks.

Creating the Add Network page

Let's start by creating the first HTML page, as shown in the following screenshot:

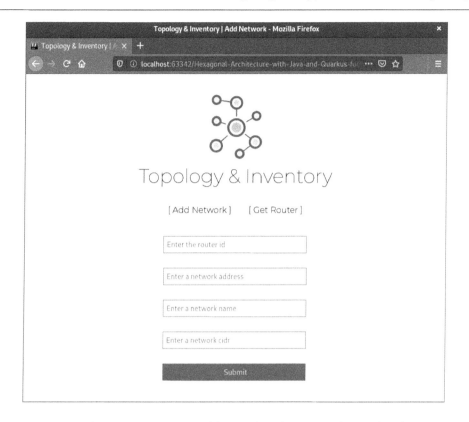

Figure 5.3 – The Add Network page of the Topology & Inventory frontend application

The **Add Network** page contains a form, where users are asked to type the necessary data to add a network to an existing router. Here is the code for the form:

```
<html>
  <head>
    <title>Topology & Inventory | Add Network</title>
    /** code omitted **/
  </head>
  <body>
      /** code omitted **/
      <form name="addNetwork" onsubmit="return
       false;">
      /** code omitted **/
      </form>
    <script src="js/networkTools.js"></script>
  </body>
</html>
```

In order to process the preceding **Add Network** page form, we use a JavaScript function called
addNetworkToRouter, which is present in the networkTools.js file:

```
function addNetworkToRouter() {
    const routerId = document.
    getElementById("routerId").value;
    const address = document.
    getElementById("address").value;
    const name = document.getElementById("name").value;
    const cidr = document.getElementById("cidr").value;
    const xhttp = new XMLHttpRequest();
    xhttp.open("GET",
    "http://localhost:8080/network/add?
        routerId=" + routerId + "&" +
        "address=" + address + "&" +
        "name=" + name + "&" +
        "cidr=" + cidr, true);
    xhttp.onload = function(
        if (xhttp.status === 200) {
            document.
            getElementById("message").
            innerHTML = "Network added with success!"
        } else {
            document.
            getElementById("message").
            innerHTML = "An error occurred while
            trying to add the network."
        }
    };
    xhttp.send();
}
```

We use the XMLHttpRequest object to process GET requests in the /network/add endpoint
exposed by the REST adapter in the hexagonal application. It is a short JavaScript code that captures
the values entered in the HTML form, processes them, and then shows a success message if everything
goes okay or an error message if not, as we can see here:

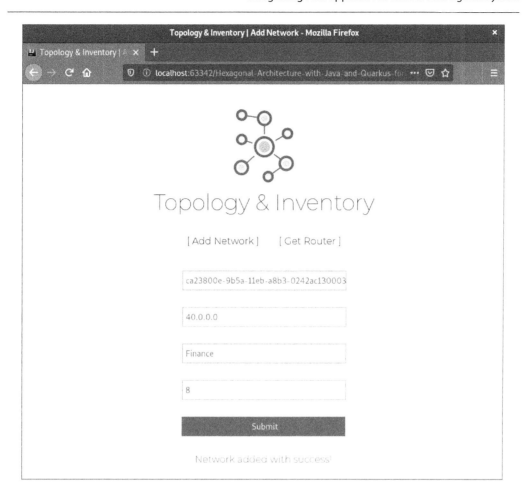

Figure 5.4 – Adding a new network to the topology and inventory application

Now, let's move on to the creation of the **Get Router** page.

Creating the Get Router page

The **Get Router** page contains an HTML form to process the user request, but it also provides a graphical view based on the JSON response obtained from the hexagonal application. Let's start by considering the HTML form:

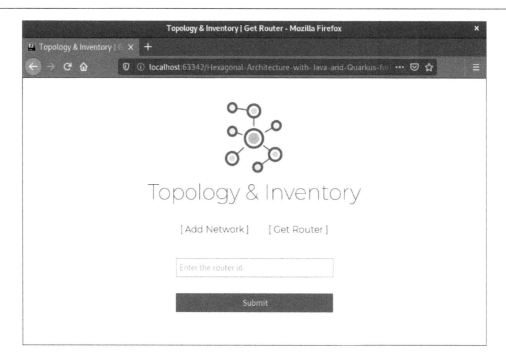

Figure 5.5 – The Get Router page of the topology and inventory frontend application

The **Get Router** HTML page follows the same structure as the one we used on the **Add Network** page, but this form uses only one parameter to query a router from the hexagonal application.

To create a JSON-based graphical view of the router and its networks, we'll use a JavaScript library called D3 that consumes the JSON data and produces the graphical view. The JavaScript code processes the form, and then it uses the JSON response with the D3 libraries:

```
function getRouter() {
    const routerId = document.
    getElementById("routerId").value;
    var xhttp = new XMLHttpRequest();
    xhttp.onreadystatechange = function() {
        console.log(this.responseText);
        if (this.readyState == 4 && this.status == 200) {
            const json = JSON.parse(this.responseText)
            createTree(json)
        }
    };
    xhttp.open(
    "GET",
    "http://localhost:8080/network/get?routerId="+routerId,
```

```
    true);
    xhttp.send();
}

function createTree(json) {
    const container = document.getElementById("container");
    const vt = new VTree(container);
    const reader = new Vtree.reader.Object();

    var data = reader.read(json);
    vt.data(data).update();
}
```

Here, we are passing the `/network/get` endpoint defined previously in the hexagonal application. The `getRouter` function processes the GET requests and uses the JSON response as the parameter for the `createTree` function that will construct the graphical view of the network.

If we fill the form with the router ID, `ca23800e-9b5a-11eb-a8b3-0242ac130003`, to retrieve a router, the result we get is like the one shown in the following screenshot:

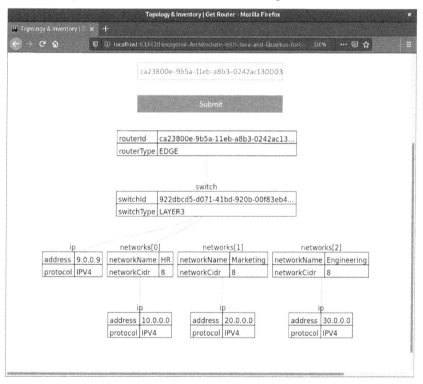

Figure 5.6 – The network graphical view provided by the Get Router page

Remember, the data presented in the preceding screenshot came ultimately from the H2 in-memory database that we attached directly to the REST input adapter used here by the frontend application.

Now, let's see how test agents can be integrated with the topology and inventory system.

Running test agents

Aside from frontend applications, another common type of driven operation comes from test and monitoring agents interacting with the hexagonal system to verify whether its features are working well. With tools such as Postman, we can create comprehensive test cases to validate how the application behaves when faced with certain requests.

In addition, we can periodically issue requests to certain application endpoints to check whether they are healthy. This practice has been popularized with tools such as **Spring Actuator**, which provides a specific endpoint in the application that allows you to check whether it's healthy. Also, some techniques involve the use of probe mechanisms that periodically send a request to the application to see whether it is alive. For example, if the application is not alive or is causing timeouts, then it can be automatically restarted. In cloud-native architectures based on **Kubernetes**, it's common to see systems using probe mechanisms.

This section will explore how to run a simple test case to confirm whether the application behaves according to our expectations. There will be no need to change the topology and inventory system we have been developing so far. Here, we will create a test case using a tool called Postman. In Postman, test cases are known as **testing collections**. Once these testing collections are made, we can execute them using **Newman**, which is a CLI tool used specifically to run Postman collections.

To get started, you have to follow these steps:

1. Download both Postman and Newman. The download links are available in the *Technical requirements* section. The collection used in this chapter is also present in the chapter's GitHub repository (https://github.com/PacktPublishing/-Designing-Hexagonal-Architecture-with-Java---Second-Edition/blob/main/Chapter05/topology-inventory.postman_collection.json).

2. Import the collection to Postman.

3. Once imported, the collection will present two requests. One request is for the getRouter endpoint and the other is for addNetwork. The following screenshot shows how the two requests should appear after importing the collections to Postman:

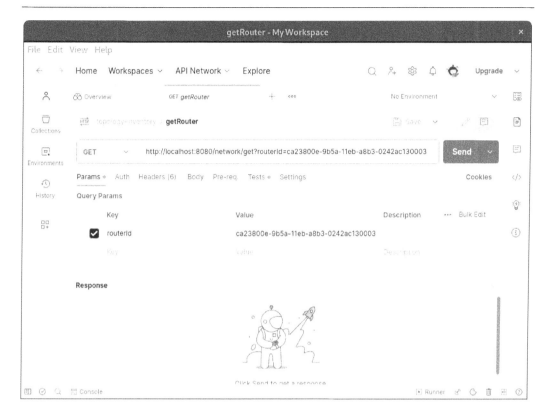

Figure 5.7 – The topology and inventory collection from Postman

4. Before running the test on Postman, be sure to bring up the topology and inventory application by running the following command from the project's `root` directory:

```
java -jar target/topology-inventory-1.0-SNAPSHOT-jar-with-
dependencies.jar rest
```

Our goal in testing the `getRouter` request is to confirm whether the application returns an HTTP `200` response code when we try to retrieve a router by passing a router ID.

5. Then, we want to validate whether the returned value is what we are expecting. In this case, we expect to encounter only three networks in the system: HR, `Marketing`, and `Engineering`. In Postman, we create tests for each request. So, we will create tests for the two requests present in the collection we imported. Let's start by creating a test for the `getRouter` request:

```
pm.test("Status code is 200", () => {
  pm.expect(pm.response.code).to.eql(200);
});

pm.test("The response has all properties", () => {
```

```
const responseJson = pm.response.json();
pm.expect(
    responseJson.switch.networks).
    to.have.lengthOf(3);
pm.expect(
    responseJson.switch.networks[0].networkName).
    to.eql('HR');
pm.expect(
    responseJson.switch.networks[1].networkName).
    to.eql('Marketing');
pm.expect(
    responseJson.switch.networks[2].networkName).
    to.eql('Engineering');
});
```

In the preceding code, we first check whether the HTTP response code is 200. Then, we proceed to parse and peek at the JSON response data to see whether it matches what we expect. In this test, we expect a response containing a router with a switch comprising three networks.

6. The test from the addNetwork request is similar to the getRouter request's test. The difference, though, is that the response expected this time contains the additional Finance network, as we can see in the following test code:

```
pm.test("Status code is 200", () => {
  pm.expect(pm.response.code).to.eql(200);
});

pm.test("The response has all properties", () => {
  const responseJson = pm.response.json();
  pm.expect(
      responseJson.switch.networks).
      to.have.lengthOf(4);
  pm.expect(
      responseJson.switch.networks[3].networkName).
      to.eql('Finance');
});
```

The addNetwork request in that collection adds a network named Finance. That's why we are only checking to see whether the Finance network was correctly added. Also, we expect the length of the list of networks to be 4 after adding the Finance network.

7. If you want to run these tests from outside Postman, you can do that by first exporting the collection to a .json file, then using Newman to execute the tests from that collection:

```
newman run topology-inventory.postman_collection.json
```

The result is something like the one presented in the following screenshot:

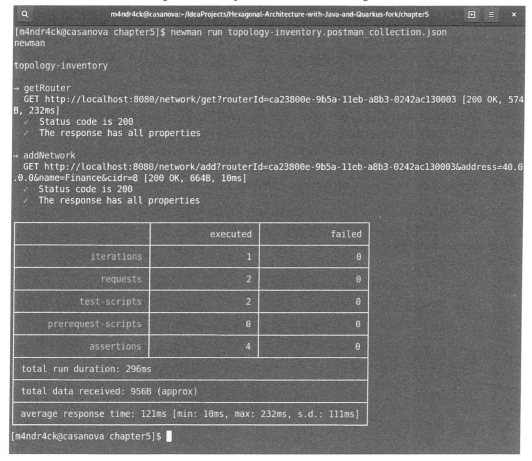

Figure 5.8 – Running topology and inventory application tests with Newman

This kind of test execution using Newman is ideal for integrating the hexagonal application into **Continuous Integration** (**CI**) pipelines. Developers use Postman to create collections and their respective tests, and these same collections are triggered and validated through CI tools (such as **Jenkins**) that can use Newman to execute the tests.

Now that we are acquainted with both frontend applications and test agents as means of driving operations, let's check out one more type of driving operation. Next, we will discuss the driving operation that occurs in distributed or microservices architecture, where different applications from the same system communicate through the network.

Calling the hexagonal system from other applications

There is a recurring debate about whether to develop a monolith or microservices system. In a monolith, we have data flowing directly between objects and method calls. All the software instructions are grouped in the same application, diminishing the communication overhead and centralizing the logs generated by the system.

With both microservices and a distributed system, we have part of the data flowing through the network between standalone, self-contained applications that cooperate in providing the features of the whole system. This approach decouples the development, allowing more modularized components. It also improves compilation times because the packages are smaller, contributing to faster feedback loops in CI tools. Microservices, though, offer some challenges because the logs are not centralized anymore, and the network communication overhead can represent a limiting factor, depending on the system's purpose.

In a distributed approach, two or more hexagonal self-contained systems can comprise the whole hexagonal-based system. In such a scenario, the hexagonal **System A** that initiates the request acts as a primary actor and triggers a driving operation on the hexagonal **System B**, as shown in the following diagram:

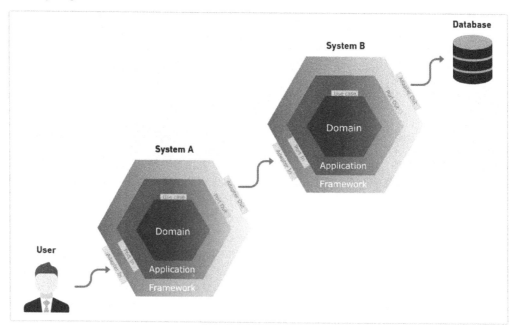

Figure 5.9 – Multiple hexagonal applications

Note that **System A** triggers a request through one of its output adapters. This request goes directly to one of the input adapters from **System B**. An exciting thing about distributed architecture is that you don't need to use the same programming language to develop all the system components.

In a distributed architecture scenario, we could write **System A** in Java and **System B** in Python. As long as they agree on a common medium of communication – JSON and HTTP, for example – they can cooperate in the same system. With the advent of container technologies such as Docker and Kubernetes, it's not a big deal to have a technology-hybrid system.

This section has looked at what driving operations are and how we can use them to interact with the hexagonal system. In the next section, we'll see the other side of the coin: driven operations.

Handling external resources with driven operations

A general characteristic of business applications is their need to send or request data from other systems. We've already seen that output ports and adapters are the hexagonal architecture components we use to allow the hexagonal system to interact with external resources without compromising the business logic. These external resources are also known as *secondary actors* and provide data or capabilities absent in the hexagonal application that requests them.

When the hexagonal application sends a request to a secondary actor – generally, on behalf of a primary actor who first triggered a driving operation from one of the hexagon application's use cases – we call such a request a *driven* operation. It's driven because these operations are controlled and driven by the hexagonal system.

So, *driving* operations come from the primary actor's requests that drive the behavior of a hexagonal system, whereas *driven* operations are the requests initiated by the hexagonal application itself toward secondary actors (such as databases or other systems). The following diagram shows the driven side with some examples of driven operations:

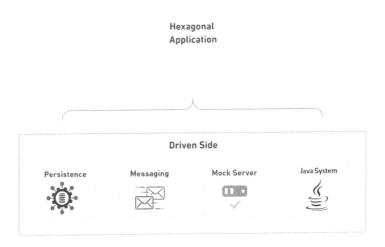

Figure 5.10 – The driven side and the hexagonal application

This section will explore some of the possible driven operations a hexagonal application can perform, as shown in the preceding diagram.

Data persistence

Driven operations based on data persistence are the most common. The H2 output adapter we created in *Chapter 4, Creating Adapters to Interact with the Outside World*, is one example of a driven operation that deals with data persistence by utilizing an in-memory database. This kind of driven operation often leverages **Object-Relational Mapping** (**ORM**) techniques to handle and translate objects between the hexagonal system and a database. In the Java world, **Hibernate** and **EclipseLink** provide robust **Java Persistence API** (**JPA**) implementations with ORM features.

Transaction mechanisms are also a part of persistence-based driven operations. When working with transactions, we can make the hexagonal system directly deal with transactional boundaries or delegate this responsibility to an application server.

Messaging and events

Not every system relies only on synchronous communication. Depending on the situation, you may want to trigger events about your *stuff* without interrupting the runtime flow of your application.

There are types of architecture strongly influenced by techniques where the communication between system components occurs asynchronously. These systems become more loosely coupled by employing such techniques because their components are no longer attached to the interfaces provided by other applications. Instead of relying solely on APIs blocking connections, we let messages and events drive the behavior of applications in a non-blocking way.

By *blocking*, we mean those connections that need to wait for a response to allow the application flow to proceed. The non-blocking approach allows an application to send a request and move forward without the need for an immediate response. There are also situations where an application reacts to messages or events to take some action.

Message-based systems are secondary actors driven by the hexagonal application. Unlike databases, where the communication will start from the hexagonal application, there are scenarios where the message-based system will start the communication with the hexagonal application. But, to receive or send messages, the hexagonal system always needs to first establish a flow of communication with a message system. Such a scenario is widespread when dealing with technologies such as Kafka, where the application can be both a consumer and producer of messages. To be integrated with a message system such as Kafka, the hexagonal application needs to express its intent by joining a **Kafka topic**.

To better understand how a message-based system integrates with a hexagonal application, we'll implement a feature in our topology and inventory system to allow us to see events produced by the application. The backend hexagonal part of the system will send events to Kafka, and the frontend will consume those events in real time and display them in the web browser. We'll implement this feature by executing the following steps:

1. Let's start by bringing up Kafka and creating a topic for our application. The Kafka download URL is available in the *Technical requirements* section. Once you have downloaded the latest Kafka version, extract it:

```
$ curl "https://downloads.apache.org/kafka/3.4.0/kafka_2.12-
3.4.0.tgz" -o ./kafka_2.12-3.4.0.tgz
$ tar -xzf kafka_2.12-3.4.0.tgz
$ cd kafka_2.12-3.4.0
```

2. Before proceeding, be sure to have JDK version 17 or higher installed on your system. Once Java is properly installed and configured, you can start the `zookeeper` service:

```
$ bin/zookeeper-server-start.sh config/zookeeper.properties
```

3. Be sure to open a separate shell session or tab and start the Kafka `broker` service:

```
$ bin/kafka-server-start.sh config/server.properties
```

4. At this point, Kafka is up and running in your environment. Let's now create the topic for our application in a third shell session or tab:

```
bin/kafka-topics.sh --create --topic topoloy-inventory-events
--bootstrap-server localhost:9092
```

5. Now, we need to add proper ports and adapters to enable the hexagonal application to send and consume events from Kafka. Let's do that with the `NotifyEventOutputPort` output port:

```
public interface NotifyEventOutputPort {
    void sendEvent(String Event);
    String getEvent();
}}
```

6. Next, we implement the output port with the `NotifyEventKafkaAdapter` output adapter. We start the `NotifyEventKafkaAdapter` adapter implementation by first defining the Kafka connection properties:

```
public class NotifyEventKafkaAdapter implements Noti
  fyEventOutputPort {
    private static String KAFKA_BROKERS =
      "localhost:9092";
    private static String
      GROUP_ID_CONFIG="consumerGroup1";
    private static String CLIENT_ID="hexagonal-
      client";
```

```
          private static String TOPIC_NAME=
          "topology-inventory-events";
          private static String
            OFFSET_RESET_EARLIER="earliest";
          private static Integer
            MAX_NO_MESSAGE_FOUND_COUNT=100;
          /** code omitted **/
      }
```

Note that the KAFKA_BROKERS variable value, set to localhost:9092, corresponds to the host and port used to bootstrap the Kafka topic. The TOPIC_NAME variable value, set to topology-inventory-events, represents the topic that we use to produce and consume messages.

7. Let's move on now to create the method to send messages to our Kafka topic:

```
    private static Producer<Long, String> getProducer(){
        Properties properties = new Properties();

        properties.put(ProducerConfig.
        BOOTSTRAP_SERVERS_CONFIG, KAFKA_BROKERS);
        properties.put(ProducerConfig.
        CLIENT_ID_CONFIG, CLIENT_ID);
        properties.put(ProducerConfig.
        KEY_SERIALIZER_CLASS_CONFIG,
        LongSerializer.class.getName());
        properties.put(ProducerConfig.
        VALUE_SERIALIZER_CLASS_CONFIG,
        StringSerializer.class.getName());
        return new KafkaProducer<>(properties);
    }
```

The getProducer method configures the Producer properties by setting the required attributes in the ProducerConfig class. Then, it returns a KafkaProducer instance, which we use to produce messages in the Kafka topic.

8. On the other hand, we have the getConsumer method, which consumes the messages generated by the Producer method:

```
    public static Consumer<Long, String> getConsumer(){
        Properties properties = new Properties();

        properties.put(ConsumerConfig.
        BOOTSTRAP_SERVERS_CONFIG,KAFKA_BROKERS);
        properties.put(ConsumerConfig.
        GROUP_ID_CONFIG, GROUP_ID_CONFIG);
```

```
properties.put(ConsumerConfig.
KEY_DESERIALIZER_CLASS_CONFIG,
LongDeserializer.class.getName());
properties.put(ConsumerConfig.
VALUE_DESERIALIZER_CLASS_CONFIG,
StringDeserializer.class.getName());
properties.put
  (ConsumerConfig.MAX_POLL_RECORDS_CONFIG,
          1);
properties.put(ConsumerConfig.
ENABLE_AUTO_COMMIT_CONFIG,"false");
properties.put(ConsumerConfig.
AUTO_OFFSET_RESET_CONFIG, OFFSET_RESET_EARLIER);
Consumer<Long, String> consumer =
new KafkaConsumer<>(properties);
consumer.
subscribe(Collections.singletonList(TOPIC_NAME));
return consumer;
}
```

With the `getConsumer` method, we use the `ConsumerConfig` class to set the required properties. This method returns a `KafkaConsumer` instance that we use to consume and read messages from the Kafka topic.

9. Moving ahead, we override the first method, `sendEvent`, declared in `NotifyEventOutputPort`. It's with this method that we'll be able to send messages to the Kafka Producer instance:

```
@Override
public void sendEvent(String eventMessage){
    var record = new ProducerRecord<Long, String>(
            TOPIC_NAME, eventMessage);
    try {
        var metadata = producer.send(record).get();
        System.out.println("Event message " +
                "sent to the topic "+TOPIC_NAME+": "
                +eventMessage+".");
        getEvent();
    }catch (Exception e){
        e.printStackTrace();
    }
}
```

The first line of the sendEvent method creates a ProducerRecord instance that informs the constructor parameters about the topic name and the message we intend to send as an event. Near the end, we have a call to the getEvent method.

10. As we shall see next in more detail, we call this method to consume messages from Kafka and forward them to a WebSocket server:

```
@Override
public String getEvent(){
    int noMessageToFetch = 0;
    AtomicReference<String> event =
    new AtomicReference<>("");
    while (true) {
    /** code omitted **/
        consumerRecords.forEach(record -> {
            event.set(record.value());
        });
    }
    var eventMessage = event.toString();
    if(sendToWebsocket)
    sendMessage(eventMessage);
    return eventMessage;
}
```

The getEvent method relies on the KafkaConsumer instance assigned to the consumer variable. With that instance, it retrieves messages from the Kafka topic.

11. After retrieving the message, the getEvent method calls the sendMessage method to forward that message to the WebSocket server:

```
public void sendMessage(String message){
    try {
        var client = new WebSocketClientAdapter(
        new URI("ws://localhost:8887"));
        client.connectBlocking();
        client.send(message);
        client.closeBlocking();
    } catch (URISyntaxException |
            InterruptedException e) {
        e.printStackTrace();
    }
}
```

The sendMessage method receives a parameter as a string, containing the consumed Kafka topic message. It then forwards that message to a WebSocket server running on port 8887.

Let's see briefly how that `WebSocket` server is implemented:

```
public class NotifyEventWebSocketAdapter extends WebSock
  etServer {
/** code omitted **/
public static void startServer() throws IOException, Inter
  ruptedException {
    var ws = new NotifyEventWebSocketAdapter(
    new InetSocketAddress("localhost", 8887));
    ws.setReuseAddr(true);
    ws.start();
    System.out.println("Topology & Inventory" +
    " webSocket started on port: " + ws.getPort());
    BufferedReader sysin =
    new BufferedReader(new InputStreamReader(System.in));
    while (true) {
        String in = sysin.readLine();
        ws.broadcast(in);
        if (in.equals("exit")) {
            ws.stop();
            break;
        }
    }
}
/** code omitted **/
}
```

The `startServer` method creates an instance of `NotifyEventWebSocketAdapter`, containing the host and port of the `WebSocket` server. When we are starting the hexagonal application, one of the first things that occurs is the calling of the `startServer` method to bring up the WebSocket server on port `8887`:

```
void setAdapter(String adapter) throws IOException, Inter
  ruptedException {
    switch (adapter) {
        case "rest" -> {
            routerOutputPort =
            RouterNetworkH2Adapter.getInstance();
            notifyOutputPort =
            NotifyEventKafkaAdapter.getInstance();
            usecase =
            new RouterNetworkInputPort(routerOutputPort,
            notifyOutputPort);
            inputAdapter =
```

```
                new RouterNetworkRestAdapter(usecase);
                rest();
                NotifyEventWebSocketAdapter.startServer();
            }
            default -> {
                routerOutputPort =
                RouterNetworkFileAdapter.getInstance();
                usecase =
                new RouterNetworkInputPort(routerOutputPort);
                inputAdapter =
                new RouterNetworkCLIAdapter(usecase);
                cli();
            }
        }
    }
}
```

Along with a WebSocket server class, we also need to implement a WebSocket client class to process the events coming from Kafka:

```java
public class WebSocketClientAdapter extends
    org.java_websocket.client.WebSocketClient {

    public WebSocketClientAdapter(URI serverUri) {
        super(serverUri);
    }

    @Override
    public void onMessage(String message) {
        String channel = message;
    }

    @Override
    public void onOpen(ServerHandshake handshake) {
        System.out.println("Connection has opened");
    }

    @Override
    public void onClose(int code, String reason,
    boolean remote) {
        System.out.println("Connection has closed");
    }

    @Override
    public void onError(Exception e) {
```

```
            System.out.println(
            "An error occurred. Check the exception below:");
            e.printStackTrace();
        }
    }
```

When a message is consumed from the Kafka topic, the hexagonal application uses `WebSocketClientAdapter` to forward the message to the WebSocket server. The `onMessage`, `onOpen`, `onClose`, and `onError` methods represent the WebSocket protocol operations that the `WebSocketClientAdapter` class needs to support.

The last thing we need to do in the hexagonal application is to make the `addNetworkToRouter` and `getRouter` methods send events using the ports and adapters we have just created:

```java
public class RouterNetworkInputPort implements RouterNet
    workUseCase {
    /** Code omitted **/
    @Override
    public Router addNetworkToRouter(
    RouterId routerId,  Network network) {
        var router = fetchRouter(routerId);
        notifyEventOutputPort.
        sendEvent("Adding "+network.getName()
        +" network to router "+router.getId().getUUID());
        return createNetwork(router, network);
    }

    @Override
    public Router getRouter(RouterId routerId) {
        notifyEventOutputPort.
        sendEvent(
        "Retrieving router ID"+routerId.getUUID());
        return fetchRouter(routerId);
    }
    /** Code omitted **/
}
```

Note that now we are calling `sendEvent` on both methods (`addNetworkToRouter` and `getRouter`), so whenever we add a network or retrieve a router, the hexagonal application will send an event informing us what has happened.

We can now add an **Events** page to allow the frontend application to connect with the WebSocket server from the hexagonal application. The following screenshot shows us the **Events** page that we'll create:

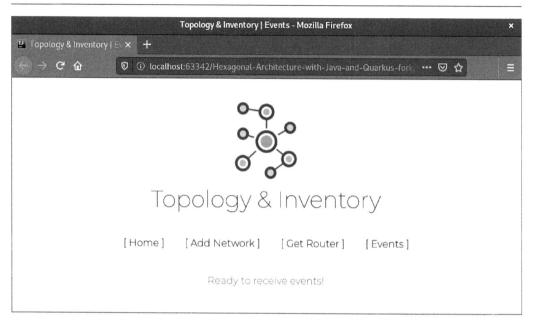

Figure 5.11 – The topology and inventory application Events page

The **Events** page follows the same structure we used in previous pages. The important part of this page is the JavaScript code utilized to connect users to the WebSocket server exposed by our hexagonal application:

```
var wsocket;

function connect() {
    wsocket = new WebSocket("ws://localhost:8887");
    wsocket.onopen = onopen;
    wsocket.onmessage = onmessage;
    wsocket.onclose = onclose;
}

    function onopen() {
    console.log("Connected!");
}

    function onmessage(event) {
    console.log("Data received: " + event.data);
    var tag = document.createElement("div");
    tag.id = "message";
    var text = document.createTextNode(">>"+event.data);
    tag.appendChild(text);
```

```
        var element = document.getElementById("events");
        element.appendChild(tag);
    }


    function onclose(e) {
        console.log("Connection closed.");
    }
    window.addEventListener("load", connect, false);
```

The onmessage method creates and appends a new div HTML element for every new message received from the WebSocket connection. So, every event generated by the hexagonal application will be sent to Kafka and printed in real time in the frontend application. The communication between the frontend, the hexagonal application with WebSocket, and the Kafka message system is represented in the following flow:

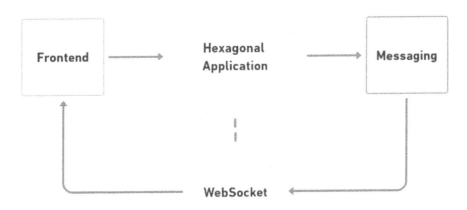

Figure 5.12 – The flow between the frontend, the hexagonal
application with WebSocket, and the message system

To test this flow, make sure to have your local Kafka instance running. Then, start the hexagonal application:

```
java -jar target/topology-inventory-1.0-SNAPSHOT-jar-with-
dependencies.jar rest
REST endpoint listening on port 8080...
Topology & Inventory WebSocket started on port 8887...
```

To create a WebSocket connection between your browser and the application, you need to open the **Events** page from the frontend application. To see the data flowing to the **Events** page, try to add a network or retrieve a router using the `ca23800e-9b5a-11eb-a8b3-0242ac130003` ID. The event entries will appear as follows on the **Events** page:

Figure 5.13 – The frontend application receiving events from Kafka through a WebSocket connection

This integration using Kafka and WebSockets has shown us how a hexagonal application deals with message-driven operations. We didn't need to touch the business logic to add these technologies. All we had to do was create more ports and adapters to augment the system's capabilities.

Now, let's briefly see one more type of driven operation that a hexagonal application can handle.

Mock servers

The typical approach for software development is to have multiple environments, such as development, QA, and production. The first working software releases start going to development environments and then progressively make their way to production. This journey to production is generally conducted by CI pipelines that constantly validate and ensure the software is working well.

Among CI validations, unit and integration tests may happen during the pipeline execution. Integration tests, in particular, depend on external components such as other applications, systems, databases, and services – all of them provided in different environments.

The execution of integration tests in development environments poses a low risk but can cause problems if there is, for example, concurrent usage of resources. This concurrency issue can generate inconsistency in test results. For QA, the situation is slightly more complicated because we must ensure consistency when dealing with test data explicitly tailored to specific scenarios. If that test data changes inadvertently, we may find inconsistencies in test results. We need to be careful because the cost of test failures in QA is even higher than in development environments.

In order to overcome testing obstacles, some tools simulate application endpoints and their responses. Those tools are known as **mock solutions**, and they come in various shapes and forms. You can manually mock the responses and endpoints of a service that your application needs; however, this is not always trivial, and it may take considerable effort. Also, there are sophisticated tools that do the dirty work and let you focus just on the logic. That is the role of mocking servers.

Because mocking servers act as an external entity providing useful resources to the application, we also consider them secondary actors driven by a hexagonal system that wants to leverage mocking server capabilities instead of hitting actual systems.

By no means have we exhausted all the possible driven operations a hexagonal system can have. But, in this section, we peeked into some of the relevant driven operations present in a hexagonal application.

Summary

In this chapter, we had the opportunity to dive deep into the nature of driving and driven operations. Although we had already dealt with them in previous chapters, we examined these operations in more depth.

Starting with *driving operations*, we learned that they drive the hexagonal application behavior by calling its input adapters. To illustrate driving operations, we first created a frontend application to play the role of a primary actor requesting data through the input adapters provided by the topology and inventory hexagonal application. Then, to explore testing tools as driving operations, we created a Postman collection with tests based on API endpoints exposed by the hexagonal application.

On the *driven operations* side, we saw how to enable the hexagonal application to work with message-based systems such as Kafka. To better understand the effects of message-based systems on the hexagonal application, we created ports and adapters that enabled the application to send and consume messages from Kafka. Also, we made a WebSocket server to let the frontend application retrieve the events generated by the hexagonal system in real time.

By handling different kinds of driving and driven operations, we can now better comprehend the inner workings of a hexagonal system, its surroundings, and how the driving and driven operations influence the hexagonal application.

The fundamentals acquired from this chapter and the previous ones provide all the building blocks to start developing robust, change-tolerant systems with the hexagonal architecture instruments.

In the next chapter, we'll apply the things we have learned to initiate the construction of a production-grade hexagonal system that will incorporate features from the Java module system and **Quarkus** framework.

Questions

1. What are driving operations?

2. Give one example of a driving operation.

3. What are driven operations?

4. Give one example of a driven operation.

Answers

1. Driving operations are requests initiated by the primary actors that drive the hexagonal application's behavior.

2. A frontend application calling a hexagonal system through one of its input adapters is an example of a driving operation.

3. Driven operations are requests initiated by the hexagonal application itself, generally on behalf of a use case need, toward secondary actors driven by a hexagonal system.

4. When the hexagonal application accesses a database. In this case, the database is driven by the hexagonal application.

Part 2: Using Hexagons to Create a Solid Foundation

By following a real-world example of a system that manages a telco's network and topology inventory, in this part, you will learn how to implement the building blocks for creating such a system using hexagonal architecture ideas.

This is a hands-on part where we'll have the opportunity to get our hands dirty while applying the hexagonal architecture principles. We start by implementing the Domain hexagon, which contains the domain model of the topology and inventory system. Then, we implement the Application hexagon by using use cases and ports to express system behaviors. To enable and expose the features provided by the hexagonal system, we use adapters to implement the Framework hexagon. Closing this part, we learn how to use Java modules to apply dependency inversion in our hexagonal system.

This part has the following chapters:

Building the Domain Hexagon

In previous chapters, we had the opportunity to employ **Domain-Driven Design** (DDD) techniques, such as entities and value objects, to create a domain model. However, until now, we haven't touched on organizing packages, classes, and modules to fit the hexagonal architecture purpose.

The **Domain hexagon** is the place to start developing a hexagonal application. Based on the domain, we derive all other hexagons. We can say that the Domain hexagon is the brain of hexagonal systems because the core fundamental business logic resides in such a hexagon.

So, in this chapter, we will start to explore how to structure a hexagonal application project from the bottom using a Java module approach. This will help us ensure better encapsulation and unit testing to validate our code as we develop the Domain hexagon components.

We will cover the following topics in this chapter:

- Bootstrapping the Domain hexagon
- Understanding the problem domain
- Defining value objects
- Defining entities and specifications
- Defining domain services
- Testing the Domain hexagon

By the end of this chapter, you will have acquired a hands-on perspective on the development of all the Domain hexagon components. This knowledge will enable you to take care of all the details regarding the structure and arrangement of classes and packages in the Domain hexagon.

Technical requirements

To compile and run the code examples presented in this chapter, you will need the latest **Java SE Development Kit** and **Maven 3.8** installed on your computer. They are all available for Linux, Mac, and Windows operating systems.

You can find the code files for this chapter on GitHub at `https://github.com/PacktPublishing/-Designing-Hexagonal-Architecture-with-Java---Second-Edition/tree/main/Chapter06`.

Bootstrapping the Domain hexagon

The hexagonal application project that we will start in this chapter is actually a continuation of the topology and inventory system that we've developed in the last few chapters. However, the difference here is that we will augment some of the system's capabilities and use the **Java Platform Module System (JPMS)** to encapsulate the Domain hexagon in a Java module.

To get started with bootstrapping the Domain hexagon, let's create a multi-module Maven project, as follows:

1. First, we will create a parent project called `topology-inventory` by executing the following code:

    ```
    mvn archetype:generate \
    -DarchetypeGroupId=org.codehaus.mojo.archetypes \
    -DarchetypeArtifactId=pom-root \
    -DarchetypeVersion=RELEASE \
    -DgroupId=dev.davivieira \
    -DartifactId=topology-inventory \
    -Dversion=1.0-SNAPSHOT \
    -DinteractiveMode=false
    ```

    We use the `archetype:generate` Maven goal to generate a Maven root project for the system. It creates a `pom.xml` file with the coordinates we pass in the command's parameters, such as `groupId` and `artifactId`.

2. Then, we create a module for the Domain hexagon, like this:

    ```
    cd topology-inventory
    mvn archetype:generate \
      -DarchetypeGroupId=de.rieckpil.archetypes  \
      -DarchetypeArtifactId=testing-toolkit \
      -DarchetypeVersion=1.0.0 \
      -DgroupId=dev.davivieira \
      -DartifactId=domain \
      -Dversion=1.0-SNAPSHOT \
      -Dpackage=dev.davivieira.topologyinventory.domain \
      -DinteractiveMode=false
    ```

    We recommend running the preceding command directly on the CMD instead of PowerShell if you use Windows. If you need to use PowerShell, you'll need to wrap each command part in double quotation marks.

As shown in the preceding code snippet, we enter the `topology-inventory` Maven project root directory generated in the first step, and again, we run the `archetype:generate` Maven goal. The result is a Maven module called `domain` that is part of the `topology-inventory` Maven project.

3. After executing the `mvn` commands to create a `topology-inventory` Maven root project and then the `domain` module, you'll have a directory tree similar to the one shown here:

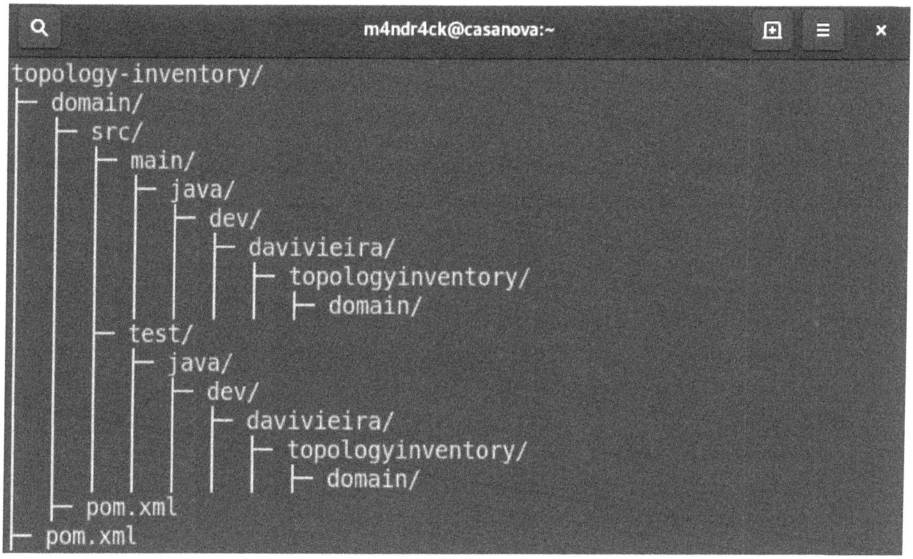

```
topology-inventory/
├─ domain/
│  ├─ src/
│  │  ├─ main/
│  │  │  ├─ java/
│  │  │  │  ├─ dev/
│  │  │  │  │  ├─ davivieira/
│  │  │  │  │  │  ├─ topologyinventory/
│  │  │  │  │  │  │  ├─ domain/
│  │  ├─ test/
│  │  │  ├─ java/
│  │  │  │  ├─ dev/
│  │  │  │  │  ├─ davivieira/
│  │  │  │  │  │  ├─ topologyinventory/
│  │  │  │  │  │  │  ├─ domain/
│  ├─ pom.xml
├─ pom.xml
```

Figure 6.1 – The directory structure of the Domain hexagon

Since the release of **Java 9**, it has been possible to create modules by putting the `module-info.java` module descriptor file into a Java project root directory. When you create a Java module using this file, you close the access to all public packages in that module. To make public packages accessible to other modules, you need to export the desired packages in the module descriptor file. There are other interesting things to say about Java modules, but we have reserved them for *Chapter 9, Applying Dependency Inversion with Java Modules*.

To transform the Domain hexagon in a Java module, you need to create a module descriptor file at `topology-inventory/domain/src/java/module-info.java`, as follows:

```
module domain {
}
```

Because we're not yet allowing access to any public packages, nor depending on other modules, we will leave the `module-info.java` file with no entries.

In order to make not just the Domain but also all other hexagons with less verbose classes, we'll add the `lombok` library to the `pom.xml` project root, as follows:

```
<dependencies>
  <dependency>
      <groupId>org.projectlombok</groupId>
      <artifactId>lombok</artifactId>
      <version>1.18.20</version>
      <scope>compile</scope>
  </dependency>
</dependencies>
```

It's also important to configure the annotation processing paths for `lombok`; otherwise, there will be compilation failures. You can do this by running the following code:

```
<plugins>
  <plugin>
      <groupId>org.apache.maven.plugins</groupId>
      <artifactId>maven-compiler-plugin</artifactId>
      <version>3.8.1</version>
      <configuration>
          <source>17</source>
          <target>17</target>
          <annotationProcessorPaths>
              <path>
                  <groupId>org.projectlombok</groupId>
                  <artifactId>lombok</artifactId>
                  <version>1.18.26</version>
              </path>

          </annotationProcessorPaths>
      </configuration>
  </plugin>
</plugins>
```

It's inside the `maven-compile-plugin` plugin block that we add the configuration for `annotationProcessorPaths`.

Because we add the lombok dependency, we need to update the domain's `module-info.java` file, like this:

```
module domain {
    requires static lombok;
}
```

We are now ready to start developing the Domain hexagon on top of our fully modularized structure. Let's move on to understand the problem domain of our enhanced topology and inventory system.

Understanding the problem domain

We will start modeling the problem domain by considering the fact that a core router can connect to both core and edge routers. Edge routers, in turn, connect to switches and their networks. The following diagram depicts this scenario:

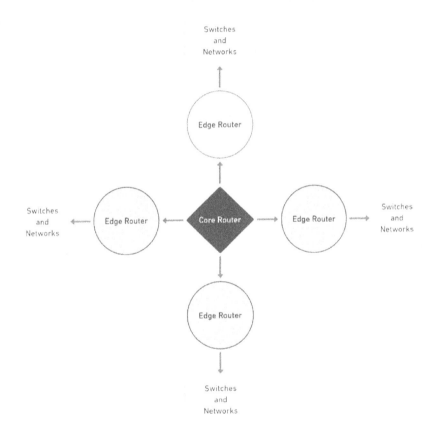

Figure 6.2 – A use case for the topology and inventory network system

Core routers are faster and deal with high traffic loads, and they don't deal directly with the traffic generated from a switch and its networks. Conversely, edge routers deal directly with traffic generated by a switch and its networks. In our scenario, an edge router is not allowed to connect to other edge routers; it can only connect to core routers and switches. A switch can have multiple networks.

Bear in mind that's a particular arrangement established for our scenario. By no means does it represent a strict rule of how to organize network components. Here is a diagram showing the arrangement of our scenario:

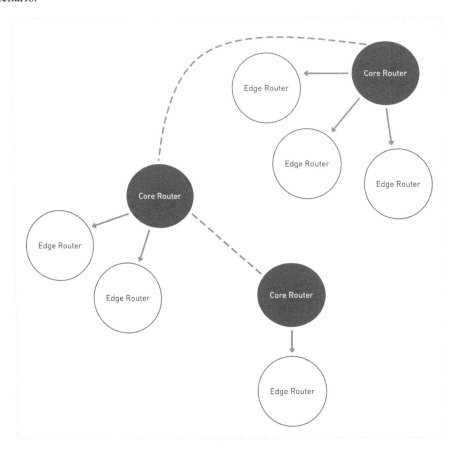

Figure 6.3 – A use case for the topology and inventory network system (continued)

The topology and inventory system's purpose is to allow users to view and manage network assets. By network assets, we mean routers, switches, and networks – routers and switches being physical assets, and networks being logical assets provided by switches. Those assets are spread across different locations, and the system should show the interconnectivity between assets and their sites. A location is composed of the complete address, along with its latitude and longitude.

The management part is based on nothing more than **Create, Read, Update, Delete** (**CRUD**)-like operations, allowing users to exert control over the topology and inventory systems' data.

Our approach to building such a system is to first create a Domain hexagon, using a domain model containing the operations and rules required to fulfill the system's purpose at its highest level. Our intention at the highest level is to validate business ideas straight on the Domain hexagon without the aid of things present on the Application and Framework hexagons. As things move onto these hexagons, they tend to become more technology-specific, operating at a lower level, because technology-specific things are far away from the Domain hexagon. The degree to which we maintain the core system functionalities within the Domain hexagon heavily influences how loosely coupled the hexagonal system will be.

To validate the methods and classes of the Domain hexagon, we'll create unit tests to ensure domain operations work as expected. This will give us a degree of assurance to move forward and use these operations on the Application hexagon.

Next, we will start to build the hexagonal system foundation with value objects, the architecture components that lets us create a domain model to better express the problem domain.

Defining value objects

As we have already seen in *Chapter 2, Wrapping Business Rules inside Domain Hexagon*, entities are the elements we use to classify system components that have an identity. Conversely, the value objects don't have an identity. We use value objects to describe those system parts where there is no need to define an identity. Then, we have aggregates that serve to encapsulate the objects' related entities and values.

I recommend starting by creating value objects first because they are like the building blocks, the raw material we'll use to build more elaborate value objects, and – most importantly – the entities. Now, we'll add all the volume object classes on the Domain hexagon module, which were created in the previous section when we bootstrapped the Domain hexagon. We'll use the following steps to define the value objects:

1. Let's start with the `Id` value object class, as follows:

    ```
    package dev.davivieira.topologyinventory.domain.vo;

    import lombok.EqualsAndHashCode;
    import lombok.Getter;
    import lombok.ToString;

    import java.util.UUID;

    @Getter
    @ToString
    @EqualsAndHashCode
    public class Id {

        private final UUID id;
    ```

```
        private Id(UUID id){
            this.id = id;
        }

        public static Id withId(String id){
            return new Id(UUID.fromString(id));
        }

        public static Id withoutId(){
            return new Id(UUID.randomUUID());
        }
    }
```

The preceding code is very straightforward, with just one UUID attribute that we use to store the id value. We will use the withId static method to create Id instances with a given string. If we want to create something new, we should use the withoutId static method, which randomly generates IDs.

2. The Vendor enum value object class, as we'll see in the *Defining entities and specifications* section, is used on both router and switch entity classes. You can see this class in the following code snippet:

```
package dev.davivieira.topologyinventory.domain.vo;

public enum Vendor {
    CISCO,
    NETGEAR,
    HP,
    TPLINK,
    DLINK,
    JUNIPER
}
```

We will model the Vendor class as enum to let us easily illustrate the system features.

3. We will do the same thing with the Model enum, as follows:

```
package dev.davivieira.topologyinventory.domain.vo;

public enum Model {
    XYZ0001,
    XYZ0002,
    XYZ0003,
    XYZ0004
}
```

4. For `Protocol`, we create an enum value object to represent both the **Internet Protocol version 4 (IPv4)** and **IP version 6 (IPv6)** protocols, as follows:

```
package dev.davivieira.topologyinventory.domain.vo;

public enum Protocol {
    IPV4,
    IPV6;
}
```

5. To help us clearly define which kind of router we're dealing with, we'll create a `RouterType` enum, as follows:

```
package dev.davivieira.topologyinventory.domain.vo;

public enum RouterType {
    EDGE,
    CORE;
}
```

6. The same idea is also applied to available switch types, as we can see here:

```
package dev.davivieira.topologyinventory.domain.vo;

public enum SwitchType {
    LAYER2,
    LAYER3;
}
```

7. As every router and switch has a location, we have to create a `Location` value object class, as follows:

```
package dev.davivieira.topologyinventory.domain.vo;

public record Location (
    String address,
    String city,
    String state,
    int zipCode,
    String country,
    float latitude,
    float longitude
) {}
```

We introduce the `Location` value object with attributes that allow us to identify an address uniquely. That's why we also have `latitude` and `longitude` as class attributes.

The value objects we just created are the most important ones because they are the basic building blocks for the other value objects and entities that comprise the entire system. Next, we can create more elaborate value objects based on those we just created, as follows:

1. Let's start with the IP value object, as illustrated in the following code snippet:

```
/** Code omitted **/
public class IP {
    private final String ipAddress;
    private final Protocol;
    public IP(String ipAddress){
      if(ipAddress == null)
          throw new IllegalArgumentException(
          "Null IP address");
        this.ipAddress = ipAddress;
      if(ipAddress.length()<=15) {
          this.protocol = Protocol.IPV4;
      } else {
        this.protocol = Protocol.IPV6;
      }

    }
/** Code omitted **/
    }
```

With the IP value object class, we can create both IPv4 and IPv6 addresses. The constraint that checks which protocol to use is within the value object constructor. The logic we use to validate the IP address is a simple one, just for the sake of our example. For a more comprehensive validation, we can use the InetAddressValidator class from the commons-validator library.

2. Then, we create a value object to represent networks that will be added to a switch, as follows:

```
package dev.davivieira.topologyinventory.domain.vo;

import lombok.Builder;
import lombok.EqualsAndHashCode;
import lombok.Getter;
import lombok.ToString;

@Builder
@Getter
@ToString
@EqualsAndHashCode
public class Network {
```

```
    private IP networkAddress;
    private String networkName;
    private int networkCidr;

    public Network(IP networkAddress,
    String networkName, int networkCidr){
        if(networkCidr <1 || networkCidr>32){
            throw new IllegalArgumentException(
            "Invalid CIDR value");
        }
        this.networkAddress = networkAddress;
        this.networkName = networkName;
        this.networkCidr = networkCidr;
    }
}
```

We model the Network value object to store the IP address, network name, and **Classless Inter-Domain Routing (CIDR)** attributes. CIDR is a network address notation composed of two numbers. The first number (for example, 10.0.0.0) is the network base IP address. The second number (for example, 24) is used to determine the network subnet mask and how many IP addresses will be available in this network. In the Network class, we refer to the second CIDR number.

Inside the Network constructor, we add the constraint to validate whether the CIDR value is valid.

Finally, you'll have a package and class structure similar to the one shown in the following screenshot:

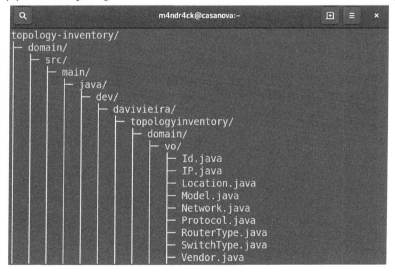

Figure 6.4 – The directory structure of the value objects

Now that we have looked at value objects, which are our Domain hexagon's building blocks, we can move on to creating entities and their specifications.

Defining entities and specifications

Once we have created all the value objects, we can start to think about how to represent the elements in entities that have an identity. Also, we need to develop specifications to define business rules that govern constraints that the entities should obey.

Remember that what characterizes an entity is its identity and the presence of business rules and data. In the topology and inventory system, we have as entities Equipment, Router, and Switch.

Inside the domain Java module we created previously, we'll add the entity classes within a package called entity.

The Equipment and Router abstract entities

Routers and switches are different types of network equipment, so we'll start by creating an Equipment abstract class, as follows:

```
package dev.davivieira.topologyinventory.domain.entity;

import dev.davivieira.topologyinventory.domain.vo.IP;
import dev.davivieira.topologyinventory.domain.vo.Id;
import dev.davivieira.topologyinventory.domain.vo.Location;
import dev.davivieira.topologyinventory.domain.vo.Model;
import dev.davivieira.topologyinventory.domain.vo.Vendor;
import lombok.AllArgsConstructor;
import lombok.Getter;

@Getter
@AllArgsConstructor
public abstract sealed class Equipment
permits Router, Switch {
    protected Id id;
    protected Vendor vendor;
    protected Model model;
    protected IP ip;
    protected Location location;

    public static Predicate<Equipment>
    getVendorPredicate(Vendor vendor){
        return r -> r.getVendor().equals(vendor);
    }
}
```

Most of the value objects created in the previous section are present here in the `Equipment` entity. We use the predicate provided by `getVendorTypePredicate` to apply the filters that only retrieve a specific vendor's equipment.

Deriving from `Equipment`, we create a `Router` abstract class, as follows:

```
package dev.davivieira.topologyinventory.domain.entity;

import dev.davivieira.topologyinventory.domain.vo.IP;
import dev.davivieira.topologyinventory.domain.vo.Id;
import dev.davivieira.topologyinventory.domain.vo.Location;
import dev.davivieira.topologyinventory.domain.vo.Model;
import dev.davivieira.topologyinventory.domain.
   vo.RouterType;
import dev.davivieira.topologyinventory.domain.vo.Vendor;

import lombok.Getter;
import java.util.function.Predicate;

@Getter
public abstract sealed class Router extends Equipment
permits CoreRouter, EdgeRouter {

    protected final RouterType routerType;

    public static Predicate<Router>
    getRouterTypePredicate(RouterType routerType){
        return r -> r.getRouterType().equals(routerType);
    }
    /** Code omitted **/
}
```

The `Router` abstract class defines predicates common to either core or edge routers. We use the predicate provided by `getRouterTypePredicate` to apply filters that retrieve only routers of a specific type.

Here, we have more two predicates from the `Router` abstract class:

```
public static Predicate<Equipment>
  getModelPredicate(Model model){
    return r -> r.getModel().equals(model);
}

public static Predicate<Equipment>
```

```
getCountryPredicate(Location location){
  return p ->
    p.location.country().equals(location.country());
}
```

We use the `getModelPredicate` and `getCountryPredicate` predicates to retrieve routers of a specific model or particular country.

The `Router` abstract class provides the common attributes shared by core and edge routers. It's in the `Router` class that we introduce the predicates to serve as filters when querying lists of routers.

The core router entity and its specifications

Moving ahead, let's implement the `CoreRouter` entity class, as follows:

```
/** Imports omitted **/
public final class CoreRouter extends Router {
    /** Code omitted **/
    public Router addRouter(Router anyRouter){
        var sameCountryRouterSpec =
        new SameCountrySpec(this);
        var sameIpSpec =
        new SameIpSpec(this);

        sameCountryRouterSpec.check(anyRouter);
        sameIpSpec.check(anyRouter);

        return this.routers.put(anyRouter.id, anyRouter);
    }
/** Code omitted **/
}
```

Core routers can be connected to other core and edge routers. To allow such behavior in the `CoreRouter` class, we create an `addRouter` method receiving the `Router` abstract type as a parameter. We also use the `SameCountrySpec` specification to make sure that edge routers are in the same country as the core router. This rule doesn't apply when we try to connect a core router to another core router.

Next, we have the `SameIPSpec` specification to confirm that routers don't have the same IP address. We make the business rules more explicit and the code easier to read and understand by using specifications. You can write this code without any specification and just throw `if-else` conditions with the necessary variables, but the mental load required to understand the code for anyone not acquainted with it would probably be higher.

Here, we have the `removeRouter` method:

```
public Router removeRouter(Router anyRouter){
    var emptyRoutersSpec = new EmptyRouterSpec();
    var emptySwitchSpec = new EmptySwitchSpec();

    switch (anyRouter.routerType) {
        case CORE → {
            var coreRouter = (CoreRouter)anyRouter;
            emptyRoutersSpec.check(coreRouter);
        }
        case EDGE → {
            var edgeRouter = (EdgeRouter)anyRouter;
            emptySwitchSpec.check(edgeRouter);
        }
    }
    return this.routers.remove(anyRouter.id);
}
```

For the `removeRouter` method, we have the `EmptyRouterSpec` specification, which prevents us from removing a router that has any other routers connected to it. The `EmptySwitchSpec` specification checks whether a router has any switch connected to it.

Core routers deal only with other routers. That's why there is no reference to switches in the `CoreRouter` entity class.

Note that the two methods, `addRouter` and `removeRouter`, operate directly on a `Router` type parameter, using domain specifications to check that there are no constraint violations before making any changes. Let's closely examine the specifications used by the `CoreRouter` entity, starting with the `SameCountrySpec` specification. This specification makes sure that edge routers are always from the same country as their core routers.

The `package` specification is where we'll put all the specifications, so that's the package in which we'll put the `SameCountrySpec` specification, as follows:

```
/** Imports omitted **/
public final class SameCountrySpec extends AbstractSpecifi
  cation<Equipment> {

    private final Equipment equipment;

    public SameCountrySpec(Equipment equipment){
        this.equipment = equipment;
    }
/** Code omitted **/
}
```

The `SameCountrySpec` constructor receives an `Equipment` object, which we use to initialize the `equipment` private field.

Continuing with the `SameCountrySpec` implementation, we override the `isSatisfiedBy` method, as follows:

```
@Override
public boolean isSatisfiedBy(Equipment anyEquipment) {
    if(anyEquipment instanceof CoreRouter) {
        return true;
    } else if (
    anyEquipment != null && this.equipment != null) {
        return this
        .equipment
        .getLocation()
        .country()
        .equals(
            anyEquipment.getLocation().country());
    } else{
        return false;
    }
}
```

The `SameCountrySpec` implementation does not apply to core routers. That's why we always return `true` when the object is a `CoreRouter` entity. Otherwise, we proceed with the validation to check that the equipment is not in a different country.

Next, we override the `check` method, as follows:

```
@Override
public void check(Equipment equipment) {
    if(!isSatisfiedBy(equipment))
        throw new GenericSpecificationException(
        "The equipments should be in the same country");
}
```

We use the `check` method to run the specification. Other classes can call this method to verify whether the specification is met or not.

It's possible to connect two core routers from different countries. What's not possible, as stated previously, is to connect edge and core routers that are not present in the same country. Note that this specification is based on the `Equipment` type, allowing us to reuse this specification not just with routers but also on switches.

The following `SameIpSpec` specification ensures that no equipment has the same IP address:

```
/** Imports omitted **/
public final class SameIpSpec extends AbstractSpecification
  <Equipment>{

    private final Equipment equipment;

    public SameIpSpec(Equipment equipment){
        this.equipment = equipment;
    }

    @Override
    public boolean isSatisfiedBy(Equipment anyEquipment) {
        return
        !equipment.getIp().equals(anyEquipment.getIp());
    }
    @Override
    public void check(Equipment equipment) {
        if(!isSatisfiedBy(equipment))
            throw new GenericSpecificationException("It's
              not possible to attach routers with the same
              IP");
    }
}
```

The `SameCountrySpec` and `SameIpSpec` specifications are used by the `addRouter` method to ensure that no constraints are violated before adding any router to a core router.

Moving on, we have the `EmptyRouterSpec` and `EmptySwitchSpec` specifications. Before a router is removed, we must make sure that no other routers or switches are connected to such a router. These are very simple specifications. Let's start by looking at the `EmptyRouterSpec` specification, as follows:

```
/** Imports omitted **/
public final class EmptyRouterSpec extends AbstractSpecification
  <CoreRouter> {

    @Override
    public boolean isSatisfiedBy(CoreRouter coreRouter) {
        return coreRouter.getRouters()==null||
                coreRouter.getRouters().isEmpty();
    }
```

```
    @Override
    public void check(CoreRouter coreRouter) {
        if(!isSatisfiedBy(coreRouter))
            throw new GenericSpecificationException("It
                isn't allowed to remove a core router with
                other routers attached to it");
    }
}
```

This specification is based on the `CoreRouter` type because only core routers can be connected to other core and edge routers.

The `EmptySwitchSpec` class is given as follows:

```
/** Imports omitted **/
public final class EmptySwitchSpec extends AbstractSpecification
  <EdgeRouter> {

    @Override
    public boolean isSatisfiedBy(EdgeRouter edgeRouter) {
        return edgeRouter.getSwitches()==null ||
                edgeRouter.getSwitches().isEmpty();
    }

    @Override
    public void check(EdgeRouter edgeRouter) {
        if(!isSatisfiedBy(edgeRouter))
            throw new GenericSpecificationException("It
                isn't allowed to remove an edge router with a
                switch attached to it");
    }
}
```

The `EmptySwitchSpec` class is very similar to the `EmptyRouterSpec` class. The difference, though, is that only edge routers can have switches. That's why this specification is based on the `EdgeRouter` type.

Edge router entity and its specifications

Now that we're done with the `CoreRouter` entity and its specifications, we can move on to create an `EdgeRouter` entity class, as follows:

```
/** Imports omitted **/
public final class EdgeRouter extends Router {
```

```
    /**Code omitted **/
    private final Map<Id, Switch> switches;

    public void addSwitch(Switch anySwitch){
        var sameCountryRouterSpec =
        new SameCountrySpec(this);
        var sameIpSpec = new SameIpSpec(this);

        sameCountryRouterSpec.check(anySwitch);
        sameIpSpec.check(anySwitch);

        this.switches.put(anySwitch.id,anySwitch);
    }
    /** Code omitted **/
}
```

The addSwitch method's purpose is to connect switches to edge routers. Also, in the EdgeRouter class, we reuse the same SameCountrySpec and SameIpSpec specifications used when implementing the CoreRouter class.

Next, we have the removeSwitch method from the EdgeRouter class, as illustrated in the following code snippet:

```
public Switch removeSwitch(Switch anySwitch){
    var emptyNetworkSpec = new EmptyNetworkSpec();
    emptyNetworkSpec.check(anySwitch);

    return this.switches.remove(anySwitch.id);
}
```

For the removeSwitch method, we have the EmptyNetworkSpec specification to ensure that a switch has no networks connected to it.

As we did in the CoreRouter class, we use the SameCountrySpec and SameIpSpec specifications. However, the context is different because we're adding a switch to a router. The only new specification used in the EdgeRouter class is the EmptyNetworkSpec specification, which is used to ensure all networks are removed from a switch before it can be removed from an edge router.

Switch entity and its specifications

What's left now is the implementation of the `Switch` entity class and its related specifications. The ideas we use here are similar to what we applied in core and edge router entities. Let's start by creating a `Switch` entity class, as follows:

```
/** Imports omitted **/
public final class Switch extends Equipment {

    private final SwitchType switchType;
    private final      List<Network> switchNetworks;
    /** Code omitted **/
    public static Predicate<Switch>getSwitchTypePredicate
      (SwitchType switchType){
        return s -> s.switchType.equals(switchType);
    }
    /** Code omitted **/
}
```

We start the `Switch` class implementation by creating a `getSwitchTypePredicate` method predicate, which we used to filter switch collections by the switch type.

Next, we create an `addNetworkToSwitch` method, as follows:

```
public boolean addNetworkToSwitch(Network network) {
    var availabilitySpec =
    new NetworkAvailabilitySpec(network);
    var cidrSpec = new CIDRSpecification();
    var amountSpec = new NetworkAmountSpec();

    cidrSpec.check(network.getNetworkCidr());
    availabilitySpec.check(this);
    amountSpec.check(this);

    return this.switchNetworks.add(network);
}
```

The `addNetworkToSwitch` method receives a `Network` type parameter, which we use to add a network to a switch. However, before adding the network, we need to check some constraints expressed by the specifications. The first one is the `NetworkAvailabilitySpec` specification, which verifies whether the network already exists on the switch. Then, we use the `CIDRSpecification` specification to check whether the network CIDR is valid. Finally, we use the `NetworkAmountSpec` specification to validate whether we have surpassed the maximum networks allowed on the switch.

Next, we have the `removeNetworkFromSwitch` method, as illustrated in the following code snippet:

```
public boolean removeNetworkFromSwitch(
  Network network){
    return this.switchNetworks.remove(network);
}
```

As there are no constraints to remove networks from a switch, this method does not use any specifications.

To summarize, right at the beginning of the `Switch` class, we declared a predicate to allow us to filter switch collections based on switch types (`LAYER2` and `LAYER3`). The `addNetworktoSwitch` method uses the `NetworkAvailabilitySpec`, `NetworkAmountSpec`, and `CIDRSpecification` specifications that we already defined in *Chapter 2, Wrapping Business Rules inside Domain Hexagon.* If none of these specifications' constraints are violated, a `Network` object will be added to the switch.

Finally, we have the `removeNetworkFromSwitch` method, which doesn't look at any specification to remove networks from a switch.

With the `Switch` entity implementation, we conclude the modeling of the entities and specifications required to fulfill the topology and inventory system's purpose.

For all the entities, you should have a package and class structure similar to this:

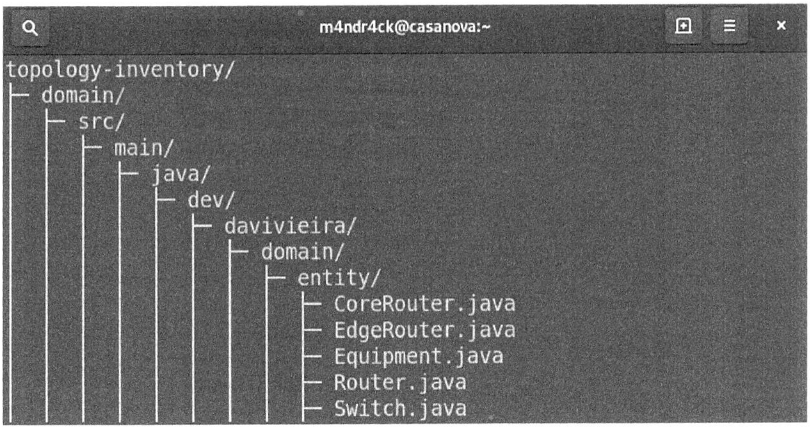

Figure 6.5 – The directory structure of entities

As we can see in the preceding screenshot, we put all the entities inside the `entity` package.

And for all the specifications, the package and class structure should look like this:

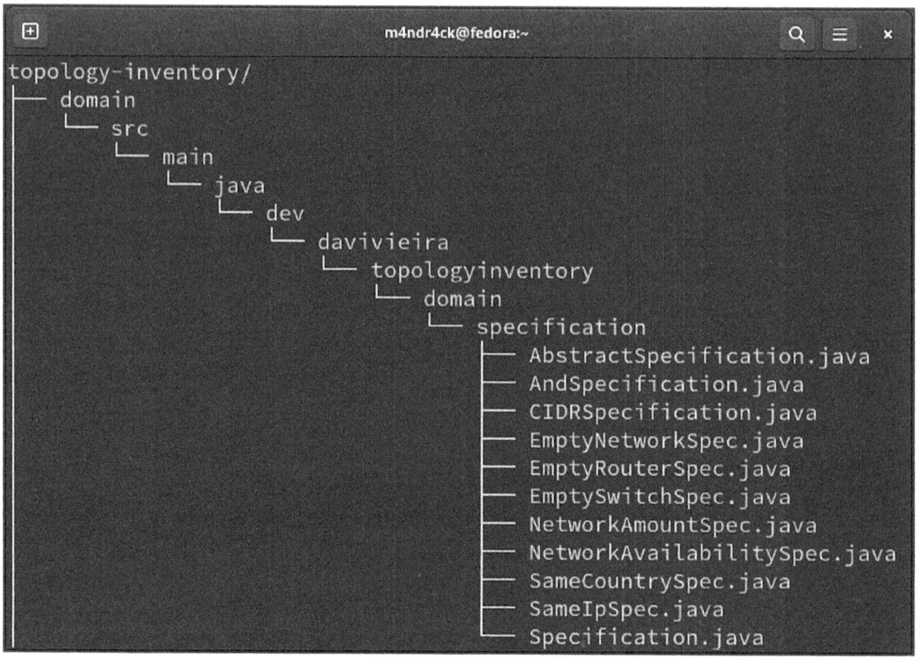

```
topology-inventory/
├── domain
    └── src
        └── main
            └── java
                └── dev
                    └── davivieira
                        └── topologyinventory
                            └── domain
                                └── specification
                                    ├── AbstractSpecification.java
                                    ├── AndSpecification.java
                                    ├── CIDRSpecification.java
                                    ├── EmptyNetworkSpec.java
                                    ├── EmptyRouterSpec.java
                                    ├── EmptySwitchSpec.java
                                    ├── NetworkAmountSpec.java
                                    ├── NetworkAvailabilitySpec.java
                                    ├── SameCountrySpec.java
                                    ├── SameIpSpec.java
                                    └── Specification.java
```

Figure 6.6 – The directory structure of specifications

Some of the specifications used by the topology and inventory system were already created in *Chapter 2, Wrapping Business Rules inside Domain Hexagon*. The remaining specifications are the ones we created in this section.

Based on the entities we have just created, we can now think of tasks that are not directly related to such entities. That is the case of services that work as an alternative to providing capabilities outside domain entities. Let's now see how to implement services that let us find, filter, and retrieve data from the system.

Defining domain services

The topology and inventory system is about the visualization and management of network assets, so we need to enable a user to handle collections of such network assets. One way to do that is through services. With services, we can define behaviors to deal with system entities and value objects.

All the services that we'll create in this section reside in the `service` package.

Let's start by creating a service to deal with collections of routers.

Router service

In the previous section, when implementing the Router, CoreRouter, and EdgeRouter entities, we also created some methods to return predicates to aid us in filtering collections of routers. With a domain service, we can use these predicates to filter such collections, as follows:

```
package dev.davivieira.topologyinventory.domain.service;

import dev.davivieira.topologyinventory.domain.
  entity.Equipment;
import dev.davivieira.topologyinventory.domain.
  entity.Router;
import dev.davivieira.topologyinventory.domain.vo.Id;
import java.util.List;
import java.util.Map;
import java.util.function.Predicate;
import java.util.stream.Collectors;

public class RouterService {

    public static List<Router>
    filterAndRetrieveRouter(List<Router> routers,
    Predicate<Equipment> routerPredicate){
        return routers
                .stream()
                .filter(routerPredicate)
                .collect(Collectors.<Router>toList());
    }

    public static Router findById(
    Map<Id,Router> routers, Id id){
        return routers.get(id);
    }
}
```

For the filterAndRetrieveRouter method, we pass a list of routers and a predicate, to filter the list, as parameters. Then, we define a findById method to retrieve a router, using an Id type parameter.

Now, let's see the service operations we can use to handle switches.

Switch service

This service follows the same idea we applied to the router service. It's primarily based on the predicate provided by the `getSwitchTypePredicate` method to filter collections of switches based on their type. As new predicates arise, we can use them as new criteria to filter switch collections. Also, note that the `findById` method is used again to allow switch retrieval based on the `Id` type parameter. Here is the code:

```
package dev.davivieira.topologyinventory.domain.service;

import dev.davivieira.topologyinventory.domain.
  entity.Switch;
import dev.davivieira.topologyinventory.domain.vo.Id;
import java.util.List;
import java.util.Map;
import java.util.function.Predicate;
import java.util.stream.Collectors;

public class SwitchService {

    public static List<Switch> filterAndRetrieveSwitch
      (List<Switch>    switches, Predicate<Switch>
        switchPredicate){
     return switches
                .stream()
                .filter(switchPredicate)
                .collect(Collectors.<Switch>toList());
    }

    public static Switch findById(Map<Id,Switch> switches,
      Id id){
     return switches.get(id);
    }
}
```

Although we don't model the network as entities in the domain model, there is no issue in creating service classes to handle collections of network value objects.

Let's create a last service class for the topology and inventory system.

Network service

This service is based primarily on a need to filter network collections based on the IP protocol. We can have collections of both IPv4 and IPv6 networks. This service provides the capacity to filter such collections based on the network IP protocol. The following code is used to create a `NetworkService` class:

```
package dev.davivieira.topologyinventory.domain.service;

import dev.davivieira.topologyinventory.domain.vo.Network;
import java.util.List;
import java.util.function.Predicate;
import java.util.stream.Collectors;

public class NetworkService {

    public static List<Network> filterAndRetrieveNetworks
      (List<Network> networks, Predicate<Network>
      networkPredicate){
        return networks
                .stream()
                .filter(networkPredicate)
                .collect(Collectors.<Network>toList());
    }
}
```

The `filterAndRetrieveNetworks` method receives a list of networks and a predicate, to filter the list, as parameters. It returns a filtered list of networks.

With `NetworkService`, we conclude creating domain services.

After creating all these services, you'll have a package and class structure like the one shown here:

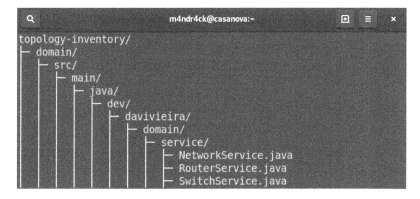

Figure 6.7 – The directory structure of domain services

To drive the development of value objects, entities, specifications, and services, you can adopt a **Test-Driven Development** (**TDD**) approach, where you can start creating broken tests and then implement the correct classes and methods to make those tests pass. We did the contrary here to provide a big picture of the components we needed to create to build the Domain hexagon for the topology and inventory system.

In this section, we created services that operate under the Domain hexagon level. Instead of putting more behaviors directly on entities, we created separate service classes to enable behaviors that we don't consider inherently part of the entities. These services allow us to handle collections of routers, switches, and networks.

Before we move on to the development of the Application hexagon, we need to ensure the operations we created in the Domain hexagon work as expected; otherwise, the upstream hexagons will break when performing these operations. So, in the next section, we'll see how to test the Domain hexagon.

Testing the Domain hexagon

To test the Domain hexagon appropriately, we should rely only on its components, ignoring anything coming from other hexagons. After all, these hexagons should depend on the Domain hexagon and not the other way around. As we have already seen, the Domain hexagon concentrates on the core system logic. It is from that logic that we derive the structure and behavior of the Application and Framework hexagons. By building a robust and well-tested Domain hexagon, we build a solid foundation for the entire system.

Among the operations performed by the topology and inventory system, we can consider adding, removing, and searching network assets as the most important ones. We'll use the following steps to test these operations:

1. Let's start by seeing how we can test the addition of network equipment, as follows:

    ```
    @Test
    public void addNetworkToSwitch(){
        var location = createLocation("US");
        var newNetwork = createTestNetwork("30.0.0.1", 8);
        var networkSwitch =
        createSwitch("30.0.0.0", 8, location);

        assertTrue(
        networkSwitch.addNetworkToSwitch(newNetwork));
    }
    ```

    The `addNetworkToSwitch` method checks the successful path when the system can add a network to a switch. The following test checks the unhappy path for this:

    ```
    @Test
    public void
    ```

```
addNetworkToSwitch_failBecauseSameNetworkAddress(){
    var location = createLocation("US");
    var newNetwork = createTestNetwork("30.0.0.0", 8);
    var networkSwitch = createSwitch(
    "30.0.0.0", 8, location);

    assertThrows(GenericSpecificationException.class,
      () ->
      networkSwitch.addNetworkToSwitch(newNetwork));
}
```

The addNetworkToSwitch_failBecauseSameNetworkAddress method checks the unsuccessful path when we try to add a network that already exists in the switch.

2. Then, we have test scenarios where we want to add a switch to an edge router, as illustrated in the following code snippet:

```
@Test
public void addSwitchToEdgeRouter(){
    edgeRouter.addSwitch(networkSwitch);

    assertEquals(1,edgeRouter.getSwitches().size());
}
```

We added a switch to an edge router with no switches attached; such an edge router should have exactly one switch attached to it. The following code snippet has the unhappy path for the addSwitchToEdgeRouter method:

```
@Test
public void addSwitchToEdgeRouter
  _failBecauseEquipmentOfDifferentCountries(){
    var locationUS = createLocation("US");
    var locationJP = createLocation("JP");
    var networkSwitch =
    createSwitch("30.0.0.0", 8, locationUS);
    var edgeRouter =
    createEdgeRouter(locationJP,"30.0.0.1");

    assertThrows(GenericSpecificationException.class,
    () -> edgeRouter.addSwitch(networkSwitch));
}
```

When we try to add a switch that is for a different country than the edge router, the addSwitchToEdgeRouter method checks the successful path while the addSwitchToEdgeRouter_failBecauseEquipmentOfDifferentCountries method checks the unsuccessful one.

3. Then, we have test scenarios where we want to add an edge router to a core router, as illustrated in the following code snippet:

```
@Test
public void addEdgeToCoreRouter(){
    coreRouter.addRouter(edgeRouter);

    assertEquals(1,coreRouter.getRouters().size());
}
```

The addEdgeToCoreRouter method checks the successful path when we try to add an edge router that is for a different country than the core router. The next code snippet has the unhappy path for the addEdgeToCoreRouter method:

```
@Test
public void addEdgeToCoreRouter
  _failBecauseRoutersOfDifferentCountries(){
    var locationUS = createLocation("US");
    var locationJP = createLocation("JP");
    var edgeRouter =
    createEdgeRouter(locationUS,"30.0.0.1");
    var coreRouter =
    createCoreRouter(locationJP, "40.0.0.1");

    assertThrows(GenericSpecificationException.class,
    () -> coreRouter.addRouter(edgeRouter));
}
```

The addEdgeToCoreRouter_failBecauseRoutersOfDifferentCountries method checks the unsuccessful path when the edge and core routers are in different countries.

4. Then, we have test scenarios where we want to add a core router to another core router, as illustrated in the following code snippet:

```
@Test
public void addCoreToCoreRouter(){
    coreRouter.addRouter(newCoreRouter);
    assertEquals(2,coreRouter.getRouters().size());
}
```

The addCoreToCoreRouter method checks the successful path when we can add a core router to another one. In the following code snippet, we have the unhappy path for this method:

```
@Test
public void addCoreToCoreRouter
  _failBecauseRoutersOfSameIp(){
    var location = createLocation("US");
```

```
var coreRouter = createCoreRouter(
location, "30.0.0.1");
var newCoreRouter = createCoreRouter(
location, "30.0.0.1");

assertThrows(GenericSpecificationException.class,
() -> coreRouter.addRouter(newCoreRouter));
}
```

The addCoreToCoreRouter_failBecauseRoutersOfSameIp method checks the unsuccessful path when we try to add core routers with the same IP address.

With these tests, we can also check whether the specifications work as expected.

5. Then, there are other scenarios where it's necessary to remove any router from a core router, a switch from an edge router, and a network from a switch, as illustrated in the following code snippet:

```
@Test
public void removeRouter(){
    var location = createLocation("US");
    var coreRouter = createCoreRouter(
    location, "30.0.0.1");
    var edgeRouter = createEdgeRouter(
    location, "40.0.0.1");
    var expectedId = edgeRouter.getId();

    coreRouter.addRouter(edgeRouter);
    var actualId =
    coreRouter.removeRouter(edgeRouter).getId();

    assertEquals(expectedId, actualId);
}
```

The removeRouter test method checks whether we can remove an edge router from a core router. In the following code snippet, we test the removal with a switch:

```
@Test
public void removeSwitch(){
    var location = createLocation("US");
    var network = createTestNetwork("30.0.0.0", 8);
    var networkSwitch =
    createSwitch("30.0.0.0", 8, location);
    var edgeRouter = createEdgeRouter(
    location, "40.0.0.1");
```

```
        edgeRouter.addSwitch(networkSwitch);
        networkSwitch.removeNetworkFromSwitch(network);
        var expectedId =
        Id.withId(
        "f8c3de3d-1fea-4d7c-a8b0-29f63c4c3490");
        var actualId=
        edgeRouter.removeSwitch(networkSwitch).getId();

        assertEquals(expectedId, actualId);
    }
```

The removeSwitch test method checks whether we can remove a switch from an edge router. In the following code snippet, we test removal with a network:

```
    @Test
    public void removeNetwork(){
        var location = createLocation("US");
        var network = createTestNetwork("30.0.0.0", 8);
        var networkSwitch =
        createSwitch("30.0.0.0", 8, location);

        assertEquals(
        1, networkSwitch.getSwitchNetworks().size());
        assertTrue(
        networkSwitch.removeNetworkFromSwitch(network));
        assertEquals(
        0, networkSwitch.getSwitchNetworks().size());
    }
```

The removeNetwork test method checks whether we can remove a network from a switch.

After the adding and removing operations, we have to test the filter and retrieve operations.

6. To filter routers by type, we implement the following test:

```
    @Test
    public void filterRouterByType(){
        List<Router> routers = new ArrayList<>();
        var location = createLocation("US");
        var coreRouter = createCoreRouter(
        location, "30.0.0.1");
        var edgeRouter = createEdgeRouter(
        location, "40.0.0.1");

        routers.add(coreRouter);
```

```
        routers.add(edgeRouter);

        var coreRouters =
        RouterService.filterAndRetrieveRouter(routers,
        Router.getRouterTypePredicate(RouterType.CORE));
        var actualCoreType =
        coreRouters.get(0).getRouterType();
        assertEquals(RouterType.CORE, actualCoreType);

        var edgeRouters =
        RouterService.filterAndRetrieveRouter(routers,
        Router.getRouterTypePredicate(RouterType.EDGE));
        var actualEdgeType =
        edgeRouters.get(0).getRouterType();
        assertEquals(RouterType.EDGE, actualEdgeType);
    }
```

The `filterRouterByType` method tests the operations available on the `RouterService` class. In the preceding case, we check whether the `filterAndRetrieveRouter` method can really filter and retrieve CORE or EDGE routers from a list containing different types of routers.

7. To filter routers by vendor, we have the following test:

```
@Test
public void filterRouterByVendor(){
    List<Router> routers = new ArrayList<>();
    var location = createLocation("US");
    var coreRouter = createCoreRouter(
    location, "30.0.0.1");
    var edgeRouter = createEdgeRouter(
    location, "40.0.0.1");

    routers.add(coreRouter);
    routers.add(edgeRouter);

    var actualVendor =
    RouterService.
      filterAndRetrieveRouter(routers,
    Router.getVendorPredicate(
    Vendor.HP)).get(0).getVendor();
    assertEquals(Vendor.HP, actualVendor);

    actualVendor =
    RouterService.filterAndRetrieveRouter(routers,
```

```
Router.getVendorPredicate(
Vendor.CISCO)).get(0).getVendor();
assertEquals(Vendor.CISCO, actualVendor);
}
```

By using a predicate provided by the getVendorPredicate method, we call filterAndRetrieveRouter from the RouterService class. Then, we check whether the retrieved router model is what we are looking for.

8. Next, we test the same filterRouterByLocation method but with a different predicate, as follows:

```
@Test
public void filterRouterByLocation(){
    List<Router> routers = new ArrayList<>();
    var location = createLocation("US");
    var coreRouter = createCoreRouter(
    location, "30.0.0.1");

    routers.add(coreRouter);

    var actualCountry =
    RouterService.filterAndRetrieveRouter(routers,
    Router.getCountryPredicate(
    location)).get(0).getLocation().getCountry();

    assertEquals(
    location.getCountry(), actualCountry);
}
```

By calling the getCountryPredicate method, we receive the predicate to filter routers by country. The result of this method is stored in the actualCountry variable, which we use in the test assertion.

9. Next, we test the filterRouterByModel method, as follows:

```
@Test
public void filterRouterByModel(){
    List<Router> routers = new ArrayList<>();
    var location = createLocation("US");
    var coreRouter = createCoreRouter(
    location, "30.0.0.1");
    var newCoreRouter = createCoreRouter(
    location, "40.0.0.1");

    coreRouter.addRouter(newCoreRouter);
```

```
        routers.add(coreRouter);

        var actualModel=
        RouterService.filterAndRetrieveRouter(routers,
        Router.getModelPredicate(
        Model.XYZ0001)).get(0).getModel();

        assertEquals(Model.XYZ0001, actualModel);
    }
```

The goal here is to confirm whether the `filterAndRetrieveRouter` method works as expected when we need to filter router lists based on the router model.

10. Here, we have a test for the `filterAndRetrieveSwitch` method from the `SwitchService` class:

```
@Test
public void filterSwitchByType(){
    List<Switch> switches = new ArrayList<>();
    var location = createLocation("US");
    var networkSwitch = createSwitch(
    "30.0.0.0", 8, location);

    switches.add(networkSwitch);

    var actualSwitchType =
    SwitchService.filterAndRetrieveSwitch(switches,
    Switch.getSwitchTypePredicate(
    SwitchType.LAYER3)).get(0).getSwitchType();

    assertEquals(
    SwitchType.LAYER3, actualSwitchType);
}
```

The goal here is to check whether it is possible to filter switch lists using the predicate provided by the `getSwitchTypePredicate` method. This is the predicate we use to filter switch lists by type. Finally, the `assertEquals` method checks whether the expected switch type matches what we expect.

11. Then, we test the operations to retrieve routers and switches by using their IDs, as follows:

```
@Test
public void findRouterById() {
    List<Router> routers = new ArrayList<>();
    Map<Id, Router> routersOfCoreRouter =
    new HashMap<>();
```

```
var location = createLocation("US");
var coreRouter = createCoreRouter(
location, "30.0.0.1");
var newCoreRouter = createCoreRouter(
location, "40.0.0.1");

coreRouter.addRouter(newCoreRouter);
routersOfCoreRouter.put(
newCoreRouter.getId(), newCoreRouter);

var expectedId = newCoreRouter.getId();
var actualId =
RouterService.findById(
routersOfCoreRouter, expectedId).getId();

assertEquals(expectedId, actualId);
}
```

With `findRouterById`, we test the `findById` method from `RouterService`.

12. Finally, we implement the `findSwitchById` method, like this:

```
@Test
public void findSwitchById(){
    List<Switch> switches = new ArrayList<>();
    Map<Id, Switch> switchesOfEdgeRouter =
    new HashMap<>();
    var location = createLocation("US");
    var networkSwitch = createSwitch(
    "30.0.0.0", 8, location);

    switchesOfEdgeRouter.put(
    networkSwitch.getId(), networkSwitch);

    var expectedId =
    Id.withId("f8c3de3d-1fea-4d7c-a8b0-29f63c4c3490");
    var actualId =
    SwitchService.findById(
    switchesOfEdgeRouter, expectedId).getId();

    assertEquals(expectedId, actualId);
}
```

With `findSwitchById`, we test the `findById` method from `SwitchService`.

After implementing and executing these tests, you should see the following output, showing that 19 tests were executed successfully:

```
[INFO] ---------------------------------------------------------
[INFO]  T E S T S
[INFO] ---------------------------------------------------------
[INFO] Running dev.davivieira.topologyinventory.domain.DomainTest
[INFO] Tests run: 19, Failures: 0, Errors: 0, Skipped: 0, Time
elapsed: 0.04 s - in dev.davivieira.topologyinventory.domain.
DomainTest
[INFO]
[INFO] Results:
[INFO]
[INFO] Tests run: 19, Failures: 0, Errors: 0, Skipped: 0
```

The successful execution of these tests assures us that the most fundamental operations from the Domain hexagon work as expected.

That's the green light we need to move ahead and start the development of the Application hexagon.

Summary

Based on the topology and inventory system we developed in previous chapters, this chapter provided a hands-on approach to the early steps of developing a hexagonal system. We started by bootstrapping the Domain hexagon as a modularized Maven project and using the JPMS.

We briefly analyzed and understood the problem domain as it relates to the management of network assets. Then, we translated the problem domain into a domain model based on value objects, entities, specifications, and services. Finally, we tested everything we've done to ensure things won't break when we start to develop the Application hexagon on top of the Domain one.

By learning how to develop a robust Domain hexagon, we lay a solid foundation that the Application and Framework hexagons can rely on. In the next chapter, we will learn how to build the Application hexagon by assembling the useful features and everything else we've created on the Domain hexagon.

Questions

1. Which technologies are used to bootstrap the Domain hexagon as a modularized application?

2. Why did we start developing the Domain hexagon by creating value objects first?

3. Once we understand the problem domain, what's the next step?

4. Why is it so important to develop a robust and well-tested Domain hexagon?

Answers

1. Maven and the JPMS.

2. Because value objects are used to compose other value objects and entities.

3. We need to translate that problem domain into a domain model.

4. Because a robust Domain hexagon provides a solid foundation to develop the Application and Framework hexagons.

7

Building the Application Hexagon

Once we have a foundation provided by the Domain hexagon, we can build the remaining part of the system on top of this. It's time to think about how the system will coordinate the handling of different data and behaviors to fulfill the needs of different actors, and we will explore this through a discussion of use case examples. To accomplish this, we need to create the Application hexagon on top of the foundation defined by the Domain hexagon.

To continue building the modular structure initiated in the previous chapter, where we configured the Domain hexagon as a **Java** module, we will continue to use the modular approach by defining the Application hexagon as the second Java module of our hexagonal system.

In order to provide a better view of the system's capabilities, one recommended approach is to use **Cucumber**, which is a well-known behavior-driven development technology that uses concepts such as features and scenarios to describe the system's behavior. So, for the Application hexagon, we'll use Cucumber to help us shape the hexagonal system's use cases.

Cucumber enables us to test the Application hexagon and explain the structure of use cases in a non-technical way.

In this chapter, we'll learn about the following topics:

- Bootstrapping the Application hexagon
- Defining use cases
- Implementing use cases with input ports
- Testing the Application hexagon

By the end of this chapter, you'll know how to utilize use cases as a blueprint to drive the development of the entire Application hexagon. By expressing the user intent through use cases and deriving objects from them to implement ports, you'll be able to develop the code to accomplish use case goals in a structured way.

Technical requirements

To compile and run the code examples presented in this chapter, you need the latest **Java SE Development Kit (JDK)** and **Maven 3.8** installed on your computer. They are all available for the **Linux**, **Mac**, and **Windows** operating systems.

You can find the code files for this chapter on GitHub at `https://github.com/ PacktPublishing/-Designing-Hexagonal-Architecture-with-Java---Second-Edition/tree/main/Chapter07`.

Bootstrapping the Application hexagon

The Application hexagon orchestrates internal requests through the Domain hexagon and external requests through the Framework hexagon. We construct the system's features based on the domain model provided by the Domain hexagon, with ports and use cases. In the Application hexagon, we don't specify any constraint or business rule. Instead, our aim for the Application hexagon is to define and control the data flow in the hexagonal system.

To continue developing the topology and inventory system, we have to bootstrap the Application hexagon as a Maven and Java module. Let's start with the Maven configuration:

```
mvn archetype:generate \
  -DarchetypeGroupId=de.rieckpil.archetypes  \
  -DarchetypeArtifactId=testing-toolkit \
  -DarchetypeVersion=1.0.0 \
  -DgroupId=dev.davivieira \
  -DartifactId=application \
  -Dversion=1.0-SNAPSHOT \
  -Dpackage=dev.davivieira.topologyinventory.application \
  -DinteractiveMode=false
```

The preceding command creates the basic Maven project's structure for the Application hexagon. Here, we set the module's `groupId` coordinate as `dev.davivieira` and `version` as `1.0-SNAPSHOT`, the same ones used for the parent project. We set `artifactId` as `application` to uniquely identify this module in the Maven project.

You need to run the preceding `mvn` command in the Maven project root directory by using the following commands:

```
$ cd topology-inventory
$ mvn archetype:generate ...
```

This creates the skeleton project structure for the Application hexagon. The directory structure will be like the following screenshot:

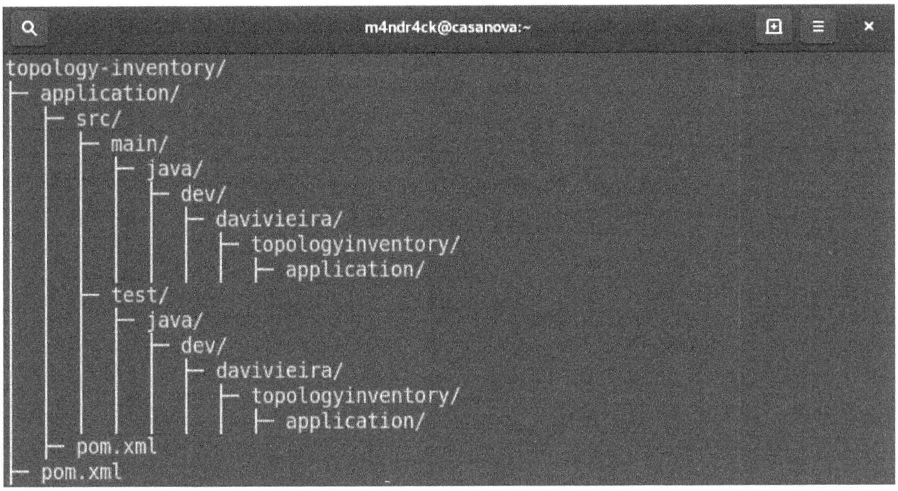

Figure 7.1 – The directory structure of the Application hexagon

The root `pom.xml` file should contain the `application` and `domain` Maven modules:

```
<modules>
    <module>domain</module>
    <module>application</module>
</modules>
```

Following the Maven module project creation, we need to configure the Application hexagon as a Java module by creating the `module` descriptor file in `application/src/java/module-info.java`:

```
module application {
    requires domain;
    requires static lombok;
}
```

Note the first `requires` entry – it states that the `application` module depends on the `domain` module. We need to add the Domain hexagon dependency at `application/pom.xml`:

```
<dependency>
    groupId>dev.davivieira</groupId>
    <artifactId>domain</artifactId>
    <version>1.0-SNAPSHOT</version>
    <scope>compile</scope>
</dependency>
```

The Maven coordinates `groupId`, `artifactId`, and `version` specify the correct parameters to fetch the Domain hexagon's Maven module.

Because we'll utilize Cucumber to provide a written description and also test our use cases, we need to add its dependencies to `application/pom.xml`:

```
<dependency>
    <groupId>io.cucumber</groupId>
    <artifactId>cucumber-java</artifactId>
    <version>6.10.4</version>
    <scope>test</scope>
</dependency>
<dependency>
    <groupId>io.cucumber</groupId>
    <artifactId>cucumber-junit</artifactId>
    <version>6.10.4</version>
    <scope>test</scope>
</dependency>
<dependency>
    <groupId>io.cucumber</groupId>
    <artifactId>cucumber-picocontainer</artifactId>
    <version>6.10.4</version>
    <scope>test</scope>
</dependency>
```

As stated in this chapter's introduction, we'll use Cucumber to structure and test use cases. The Maven dependencies declared in the previous code examples are required to enable Cucumber in the Application hexagon.

Once the Application hexagon's Maven module and Java module are properly configured for the topology and inventory system, we can move on and start defining use cases for the system.

Defining use cases

The topology and inventory system allows users to manage network resources such as routers, switches, and networks. To enable this management, we created a domain model in the previous chapter that represents the relationship between those resources. What we have to do now is construct the system's features in terms of the domain model. These features represent user intent when interacting with the system.

To make it possible to express use cases in both written and code form, we use Cucumber, a valuable tool to enable non-technical people to grasp the use cases that exist in the code.

By relying on Cucumber concepts such as features and scenarios, we can create use case descriptions that are easy to follow. The use case descriptions that are shaped using Cucumber can serve as references to develop use case interfaces.

Before creating the use case interfaces for the topology and inventory system, we first need to structure the use cases in feature files consumed by Cucumber. Feature files are where we'll describe a sequence of written statements that define the use case. This same written description is then used while implementing the classes to test the use case.

Creating written descriptions for router management use cases

To get started, let's create the `RouterAdd.feature` file, which describes the use case related to adding routers to the system:

```
@RouterAdd
Feature: Can I add an edge router to a core router?

  Scenario: Adding an edge router to a core router
    Given I have an edge router
    And I have a core router
    Then I add an edge router to a core router

  Scenario: Adding a core router to another core router
    Given I have a core router
    And I have another core router
    Then I add this core router to the core router
```

This feature file describes two scenarios – the first is when a user wants to add an edge router to a core router; the second is when the user wants to add a core router to another core router.

After that, we have the `RouterCreate.feature` file:

```
@RouterCreate
Feature: Can I create a new router?

  Scenario: Creating a new core router
    Given I provide all required data to create a core
        router
    Then A new core router is created

  Scenario: Creating a new edge router
    Given I provide all required data to create an edge
      router
    Then A new edge router is created
```

Here, we have two scenarios describing the creation of both core and edge routers.

Finally, there is the `RouterRemove.feature` file:

```
@RouterRemove
Feature: Can I remove routers?

  Scenario: Removing an edge router from a core router
    Given The core router has at least one edge
          router connected to it
    And The switch has no networks attached to it
    And The edge router has no switches attached to it
    Then I remove the edge router from the core router

  Scenario: Removing a core router from another core router
    Given The core router has at least one core router
          connected to it
    And The core router has no other routers connected to
        it
    Then I remove the core router from another core router
```

For each of the two scenarios described, we define a specific set of constraints to allow the removal of the router. Once we have Cucumber scenarios describing the supported behaviors regarding router management, we can define the use case interface that will allow the implementation of the operations. These operations will enable such behaviors.

Defining the use case interface for router management

A good use case interface for router management should contain the operations that allow the system to fulfill the scenarios described by the `RouterAdd.feature`, `RouterCreate.feature`, and `RouterRemove.feature` files. The following use case interface is defined in reference to the scenarios we described in the Cucumber feature files:

```
package dev.davivieira.topologyinventory.
  application.usecases;

import dev.davivieira.topologyinventory.domain.
  entity.CoreRouter;
import dev.davivieira.topologyinventory.domain.
  entity.Router;
import dev.davivieira.topologyinventory.domain.vo.IP;
import dev.davivieira.topologyinventory.domain.vo.Id;
import dev.davivieira.topologyinventory.domain.vo.Location;
```

```
import dev.davivieira.topologyinventory.domain.vo.Model;
import dev.davivieira.topologyinventory.domain.
  vo.RouterType;
import dev.davivieira.topologyinventory.domain.vo.Vendor;

public interface RouterManagementUseCase {
    Router createRouter(
            Vendor vendor,
            Model model,
            IP ip,
            Location location,
            RouterType routerType);
    CoreRouter addRouterToCoreRouter(
            Router router, CoreRouter coreRouter);
    Router removeRouterFromCoreRouter(
            Router router, CoreRouter coreRouter);

    Router retrieveRouter(Id id);
    Router persistRouter(Router router);
}
```

The `createRouter` method is based on the `RouterCreate.feature` Cucumber file. The `addRouterToCoreRouter` and `removeRouterFromCoreRouter` methods are for the `RouterAdd.feature` and `RouterRemove.feature` files, respectively. Now, let's move on to creating the written descriptions for the switch management use cases.

Creating written descriptions for switch management use cases

We will start by creating the `SwitchAdd.feature` file:

```
@SwitchAdd
Feature: Can I add a switch to an edge router?

  Scenario: Adding a switch to an edge router
    Given I provide a switch
    Then I add the switch to the edge router
```

This is a very straightforward use case scenario. Given that we provide a valid switch, we can add it to an edge router. There is no mention of the core routers because they are not supposed to receive switch connections.

Then, we create the `SwitchCreate.feature` file:

```
@SwitchCreate
Feature: Can I create new switches?

  Scenario: Creating a new switch
    Given I provide all required data to create a switch
    Then A new switch is created
```

This scenario is similar to the `RouterCreate.feature` file, in the sense that if we provide all the required data, a new `Switch` object is created.

Finally, we create the `SwitchRemove.feature` file:

```
@SwitchRemove
Feature: Can I remove a switch from an edge router?

  Scenario: Removing a switch from an edge router
    Given I know the switch I want to remove
    And The switch has no networks
    Then I remove the switch from the edge router
```

So, to remove a switch from an edge router, we have to make sure the switch has no networks connected to it. This is what the preceding scenario asserts.

Now, let's define the use case interface for switch management, based on the Cucumber scenarios we just created.

Defining the use case interface for switch management

As we did with routers, we will do the same for switches by creating a use case interface to define the switch management operations, based on the written descriptions we made previously in our Cucumber feature files:

```
package dev.davivieira.topologyinventory.
  application.usecases;

import dev.davivieira.topologyinventory.domain.
  entity.EdgeRouter;
import dev.davivieira.topologyinventory.domain.
  entity.Switch;
import dev.davivieira.topologyinventory.domain.vo.IP;
import dev.davivieira.topologyinventory.domain.vo.Location;
import dev.davivieira.topologyinventory.domain.vo.Model;
import dev.davivieira.topologyinventory.domain.
```

```
    vo.SwitchType;
import dev.davivieira.topologyinventory.domain.vo.Vendor;
public interface SwitchManagementUseCase {

    Switch createSwitch(
            Vendor vendor,
            Model model,
            IP ip,
            Location location,
            SwitchType switchType
            );

    EdgeRouter addSwitchToEdgeRouter(Switch networkSwitch,
    EdgeRouter edgeRouter);

    EdgeRouter removeSwitchFromEdgeRouter(Switch
    networkSwitch,
    EdgeRouter edgeRouter);
}
```

The `createSwitch`, `addSwitchToEdgeRouter`, and `removeSwitchFromEdgeRouter` methods correspond to the Cucumber `SwitchCreate.feature`, `SwitchAdd.feature`, and `SwitchRemove.feature` feature files, respectively. The `createSwitch` method receives all the required parameters to construct a `Switch` object. Both the `addSwitchToEdgeRouter` and `removeSwitchFromEdgeRouter` methods receive a switch and an edge router as parameters, and both methods return `EdgeRouter`.

To finish the definition of use cases, we still need to create the Cucumber feature files and interfaces for networks. Let's do that!

Creating written descriptions for network management use cases

For networks, we will continue to follow the same pattern of the add, create, and remove operations previously used on routers and switches. Let's start with the `NetworkAdd.feature` file:

```
@NetworkAdd
Feature: Can I add a network to a switch?

  Scenario: Adding a network to a switch
    Given I have a network
    And I have a switch to add a network
    Then I add the network to the switch
```

This is a simple scenario to ensure that we're able to add networks to a switch.

Following the addition of networks, we have the `NetworkCreate.feature` file:

```
@NetworkCreate
Feature: Can I create new networks?

  Scenario: Creating a new network
    Given I provide all required data to create a network
    Then A new network is created
```

For network creation, as we did with routers and switches, we make sure that all required data is properly provided so that a new network is created.

Finally, we have the `NetworkRemove.feature` file:

```
@NetworkRemove
Feature: Can I remove a network from a switch?

  Scenario: Removing a network from a switch
    Given I know the network I want to remove
    And I have a switch to remove a network
    Then I remove the network from the switch
```

It follows the same structure as the adding scenario but checks the system's capability to remove networks from a switch.

Now that we have Cucumber scenarios for network management, let's define a use case interface to perform such scenarios.

Defining the use case interface for network management

The `NetworkManagementUseCase` interface follows the same structure as previously defined interfaces, where we declared methods for creation, addition, and removal operations:

```
package dev.davivieira.topologyinventory.
  application.usecases;

import dev.davivieira.topologyinventory.domain.
  entity.Switch;
import dev.davivieira.topologyinventory.domain.vo.IP;
import dev.davivieira.topologyinventory.domain.vo.Network;

public interface NetworkManagementUseCase {
```

```
Network createNetwork(
        IP networkAddress,
        String networkName,
        int networkCidr);

Switch addNetworkToSwitch(Network network,
Switch networkSwitch);

Switch removeNetworkFromSwitch(Network network,
Switch networkSwitch);
}
```

Here, again, we declare the `createNetwork`, `addNetworkToSwitch`, and `removeNetworkFromSwitch` methods based on the written descriptions from the Cucumber feature files. These three method declarations in the `NetworkManagementUseCase` interface represent the first step in implementing the capabilities that will allow us to manage networks, as described in the scenarios we created using Cucumber.

In this section, we learned about an approach to start use case development by first describing the behaviors and scenarios expected from the system. Once the scenarios were thoroughly explored, we then utilized them as a reference to define the use case interfaces that will allow the system to perform the behaviors described in the scenarios.

Now that we have all the use case interfaces to manage routers, switches, and networks, we can provide an input port implementation for each of these use case interfaces.

Implementing use cases with input ports

Input ports are a central element of the Application hexagon. They play a crucial integration role because it is through them that we bridge the gap between the Domain and Framework hexagons. We can get external data from an output port and forward that data to the Domain hexagon by using output ports. Once the Domain hexagon's business logic is applied to the data, the Application hexagon moves that data downstream until it reaches one of the output adapters in the Framework hexagon.

When creating the Application hexagon, you're able to define output port interfaces, but because there is no Framework hexagon yet to provide an output adapter as an implementation, you're not able to use these output ports.

You'll see output port declarations in the following code, but they are not being used yet. We're just preparing the Application hexagon to work when we have the Framework hexagon to provide the implementations.

The following steps will help us to implement use cases with input ports:

1. We start by creating a `RouterManagementOutputPort` field in the `RouterManagementInputPort` class:

    ```
    package dev.davivieira.topologyinventory.application.
      ports.input;

    import dev.davivieira.topologyinventory.application.
      ports.output.RouterManagementOutputPort;
    import dev.davivieira.topologyinventory.application.
      usecases.RouterManagementUseCase;
    import dev.davivieira.topologyinventory.domain.entity.
      CoreRouter;
    import dev.davivieira.topologyinventory.domain.
      entity.Router;
    import dev.davivieira.topologyinventory.domain.entity.
      factory.RouterFactory;
    import dev.davivieira.topologyinventory.domain.vo.IP;
    import dev.davivieira.topologyinventory.domain.vo.Id;
    import dev.davivieira.topologyinventory.domain.
      vo.Location;
    import dev.davivieira.topologyinventory.domain.
      vo.Model;
    import dev.davivieira.topologyinventory.domain.
      vo.RouterType;
    import dev.davivieira.topologyinventory.domain.
      vo.Vendor;
    import lombok.NoArgsConstructor;

    @NoArgsConstructor
    public class RouterManagementInputPort implements
      RouterManagementUseCase {

        RouterManagementOutputPort
        routerManagementOutputPort;
        /** Code omitted
    }
    ```

We created this `RouterManagementOutputPort` interface field because we don't want to depend directly on its implementation. Remember, output adapters implement output ports.

2. Next, we implement the `createRouter` method:

```
@Override
public Router createRouter(Vendor vendor,
                           Model model,
                           IP ip,
                           Location location,
                           RouterType routerType) {
    return RouterFactory.getRouter(
            vendor,model,ip,location,routerType);
}
```

With the `createRouter` method, we'll receive all the required parameters to construct a `Router` object. Object creation is delegated to the `getRouter` method from the `RouterFactory` class.

3. Next, we implement the `retrieveRouter` method:

```
@Override
public Router retrieveRouter(Id id) {
    return
        routerManagementOutputPort.retrieveRouter(id);
}
```

It's a very straightforward method that uses `Id` to obtain the `Router` objects, using the `retrieveRouter` method from the `RouterManagementOutputPort` output port.

4. Next, we implement the `persistRouter` method:

```
@Override
public Router persistRouter(Router router) {
    return
        routerManagementOutputPort.persistRouter(router);
}
```

To persist a router, we need to pass the `Router` object we want to persist. This method is generally used after any operation that creates new `Router` objects or causes changes in existing ones.

5. Next, we implement the `addRouterToCoreRouter` method:

```
@Override
public CoreRouter addRouterToCoreRouter(Router router,
  CoreRouter coreRouter) {
    var addedRouter = coreRouter.addRouter(router);
    //persistRouter(addedRouter);
    return addedRouter;
}
```

To add `Router` to `CoreRouter`, we call the `addRouter` method from `CoreRouter`. We're not persisting `Router` because we don't have an adapter to allow us to do that. So, we just return the added `Router` object.

6.   Finally, we implement `removeRouterFromCoreRouter`:

```
@Override
public Router removeRouterFromCoreRouter(Router rout
  er,CoreRouter coreRouter) {
    var removedRouter =
    coreRouter.removeRouter(router);
    //persistRouter(removedRouter);
    return removedRouter;
}
```

Again, we use one of the methods present in the `CoreRoute` class. Here, we call the `removeRouter` method to remove `Router` from `CoreRouter`. Then, we return `removedRouter`, instead of actually removing it from an external data source.

The first method we implemented, `createRouter`, can produce either core or edge routers. To accomplish this, we need to provide a factory method directly in the Domain hexagon, in a class called `RouterFactory`. The following is how we implement this `getRouter` factory method:

```
public static Router getRouter(Vendor vendor,
                               Model model,
                               IP ip,
                               Location location,
                               RouterType routerType){

        switch (routerType){
            case CORE → { return CoreRouter.builder().
                            id(Id.withoutId()).
                            vendor(vendor).
                            model(model).
                            ip(ip).
                            location(location).
                            routerType(routerType).
                            build();
                }
/** Code omitted **/
```

The `RouterType` parameter, which we pass to the `getRouter` method, has only two possible values – CORE and EDGE. The switch looks into one of these two values to determine which `builder` method to use. If `RouterType` is CORE, then the `builder` method from `CoreRouter` is called. Otherwise, the `builder` method from `EdgeRouter` is used, as we can see here:

```
case EDGE → {  return EdgeRouter.builder().
                  id(Id.withoutId()).
                  vendor(vendor).
                  model(model).
                  ip(ip).
                  location(location).
                  routerType(routerType).
                  build();
}
default → throw new UnsupportedOperationException(
    "No valid router type informed");
```

If neither CORE nor EDGE is informed, the default behavior is to throw an exception saying that no valid router type was informed.

Let's implement the `SwitchManagementUseCase` interface with `SwitchManagementInputPort`:

1. We will start by implementing the `createSwitch` method:

    ```
    package dev.davivieira.topologyinventory.application.
      ports.input;

    import dev.davivieira.topologyinventory.application.
      usecases.SwitchManagementUseCase;
    import dev.davivieira.topologyinventory.domain.
      entity.EdgeRouter;
    import dev.davivieira.topologyinventory.domain.
      entity.Switch;
    import dev.davivieira.topologyinventory.domain.vo.IP;
    import dev.davivieira.topologyinventory.domain.vo.Id;
    import dev.davivieira.topologyinventory.domain.
      vo.Location;
    import dev.davivieira.topologyinventory.domain.
      vo.Model;
    import dev.davivieira.topologyinventory.domain.
      vo.SwitchType;
    import dev.davivieira.topologyinventory.domain.
      vo.Vendor;
    ```

```
public class SwitchManagementInputPort implements
  SwitchManagementUseCase {
    @Override
    public Switch createSwitch(
            Vendor vendor,
            Model model,
            IP ip,
            Location location,
            SwitchType switchType) {
        return Switch.builder()
                .id(Id.withoutId())
                .vendor(vendor)
                .model(model)
                .ip(ip)
                .location(location).switchType
                    (switchType).build();
    }
/** Code omitted **/
}
```

For the `createSwitch` method, we don't need a factory method to create objects because there are no `Switch` object variations as compared to routers. Instead, we generate `Switch` objects, using the `builder` method directly from the `Switch` class.

2. Next, we implement the `addSwitchToEdgeRouter` method:

```
@Override
public EdgeRouter addSwitchToEdgeRouter(
  Switch networkSwitch, EdgeRouter edgeRouter) {
    edgeRouter.addSwitch(networkSwitch);
    return edgeRouter;
}
```

Then, we have `addSwitchToEdgeRouter`, which receives `Switch` and `EdgeRouter` as parameters, to add switches to an edge router. There is no way to persist switches without persisting routers as well. That's why we did not put a persistence method here. By doing that, we enforce all switch persistence operations to occur only when we persist routers.

Remember that `Router` is an aggregate (a cluster of domain objects) that controls the life cycle of other entities and value objects, including `Switch`-type objects.

3. Finally, we implement the `removeSwitchFromEdgeRouter` method:

```
@Override
public EdgeRouter removeSwitchFromEdgeRouter(
  Switch networkSwitch, EdgeRouter edgeRouter) {
```

```
        edgeRouter.removeSwitch(networkSwitch);
        return edgeRouter;
    }
```

The last method, removeSwitchFromEdgeRouter, receives the same parameters, Switch and EdgeRouter, and removes switches from edge routers using the removeSwitch method present in an EdgeRouter instance.

Now, let's see how we can implement the NetworkManagementUseCase interface with NetworkManagementInputPort:

1. We start by implementing the createNetwork method:

```
package dev.davivieira.topologyinventory.
    application.ports.input;
import dev.davivieira.topologyinventory.application.
    usecases.NetworkManagementUseCase;
import dev.davivieira.topologyinventory.domain.
    entity.Switch;
import dev.davivieira.topologyinventory.domain.vo.IP;
import dev.davivieira.topologyinventory.domain.
    vo.Network;
import lombok.NoArgsConstructor;
@NoArgsConstructor
public class NetworkManagementInputPort implements
    NetworkManagementUseCase {
        @Override
        public Network createNetwork(
        IP networkAddress, String networkName,
        int networkCidr) {
            return  Network
                    .builder()
                    .networkAddress(networkAddress)
                    .networkName(networkName)
                    .networkCidr(networkCidr).build();
    }
/** Code omitted **/
}
```

To create a new network, we use all the received method parameters in conjunction with the builder method from the Network class.

2. Next, we implement addNetworkToSwitch:

```
@Override
public Switch addNetworkToSwitch(
```

```
Network network, Switch networkSwitch) {
  networkSwitch.addNetworkToSwitch(network);
  return networkSwitch;
}
```

Here, we receive the Network and Switch objects. Then, we call the addNetworkToSwitch method on Switch by passing the Network object as a parameter. Then, we return a Switch object with the added Network object.

3. Finally, we implement the removeNetworkFromSwitch method:

```
@Override
public Switch removeNetworkFromSwitch(
  Network network, Switch networkSwitch) {
    networkSwitch.removeNetworkFromSwitch(network);
    return networkSwitch;
}
```

We receive the Network and Switch objects as parameters, like in the addNetworkToSwitch method. However, to remove the network from a switch, we call removeNetworkFromSwitch from the Switch object.

That completes implementing input ports for router, switch, and network management. To ensure everything works as expected, let's create Cucumber tests based on the written use case descriptions and the input ports we just created.

Testing the Application hexagon

An interesting and useful thing about Cucumber is that we can use the written scenario description provided in the feature file to tailor unit tests. In addition, these written scenarios provide an easy way to understand and implement the hexagonal system's use cases. We're also laying the groundwork for the development of unit tests in the Application hexagon.

So, the tests we're about to build in this section are a continuation of the written scenario descriptions we created for the router, switch, and network management operations. Our goal here is to test input port implementations to ensure these ports work as expected when input adapters call them.

To get started, we need to create the ApplicationTest test class to enable Cucumber:

```
package dev.davivieira.topologyinventory.application;

import io.cucumber.junit.Cucumber;
import io.cucumber.junit.CucumberOptions;
import org.junit.runner.RunWith;

@RunWith(Cucumber.class)
```

```
@CucumberOptions(
        plugin = {"pretty", "html:target/cucumber-result"}
)
public class ApplicationTest {

}
```

The important part is the @RunWith annotation, which triggers the initialization of the Cucumber engine.

Let's start by creating tests to check whether the system is capable of adding routers.

In the same way that we created a RouterAdd.feature file, we'll create its counterpart as a RouterAdd.java test class. The location for both files will resemble the following:

- src/test/java/dev/davivieira/topologyinventory/application/RouterAdd.java

- src/test/resources/dev/davivieira/topologyinventory/application/routers/RouterAdd.feature

The following steps walk you through adding an edge router to a core router:

1. The first step is to get an edge router:

    ```
    @Given("I have an edge router")
    public void assert_edge_router_exists(){
        edgeRouter = (EdgeRouter)
        this.routerManagementUseCase.createRouter(
                Vendor.HP,
                Model.XYZ0004,
                IP.fromAddress("20.0.0.1"),
                locationA,
                EDGE
        );
        assertNotNull(edgeRouter);
    }
    ```

    Here, we use the createRouter method from RouterManagementUseCase to create edge router objects. We need to cast the returned object to an EdgeRouter type because the createRouter method returns Router. Then, to make sure that we received a proper router object, we call assertNotNull on edgeRouter.

2. Now that we have EdgeRouter, we need to create CoreRouter by using the createRouter method again:

    ```
    @And("I have a core router")
    public void assert_core_router_exists(){
    ```

```
coreRouter = (CoreRouter)
this.routerManagementUseCase.createRouter(
        Vendor.CISCO,
        Model.XYZ0001,
        IP.fromAddress("30.0.0.1"),
        locationA,
        CORE
);
assertNotNull(coreRouter);
}
```

This code follows the exact same pattern as the first step. The only difference is that we pass CORE as RouterType to the createRouter method from RouterManagementUseCase.

3. With these two objects, EdgeRouter and CoreRouter, we can now test adding the former to the latter:

```
@Then("I add an edge router to a core router")
public void add_edge_to_core_router(){
    var actualEdgeId = edgeRouter.getId();
    var routerWithEdge =
    (CoreRouter)  this.routerManagementUseCase.
    addRouterToCoreRouter(edgeRouter, coreRouter);
    var expectedEdgeId =
    routerWithEdge.getRouters().get(actualEdgeId).
    getId();
    assertEquals(actualEdgeId, expectedEdgeId);
}
```

The addRouterToCoreRouter method receives EdgeRouter and CoreRouter as parameters. At the end of the method, we compare the actual and expected edge router IDs to confirm whether the edge router has been added correctly to the core router.

To test the execution of the Cucumber scenario steps from RouterAdd.feature, we have to run the following Maven command:

```
mvn test
```

The output will be similar to the one shown here:

```
@RouterAdd
Scenario: Adding an edge router to a core router # dev/davivieira/
topologyinventory/application/routers/RouterAdd.feature:4
Given I have an edge router # dev.davivieira.topologyinventory.
application.RouterAdd.assert_edge_router_exists()
```

```
And I have a core router # dev.davivieira.topologyinventory.
application.RouterAdd.assert_core_router_exists()
Then I add an edge router to a core router # dev.davivieira.
topologyinventory.application.RouterAdd.add_edge_to_core_router()
```

The Cucumber test passes through the testing methods in the RouterAdd.java file in the same order as they were declared in the RouterAdd.feature file.

Now, let's see how we can implement the RouterCreate.java test class for the RouterCreate.feature file. Their file locations will resemble the following:

- RouterCreate.java file: src/test/java/dev/davivieira/topologyinventory/application/RouterCreate.java

- RouterCreate.feature file: src/test/resources/dev/davivieira/topologyinventory/application/routers/RouterCreate.feature

The following scenario steps walk through creating a new core router in the system:

1. The first step is to create a new core router:

```
@Given("I provide all required data to create a core
  router")
public void create_core_router(){
    router =  this.routerManagementUseCase.
            createRouter(
            Vendor.CISCO,
            Model.XYZ0001,
            IP.fromAddress("20.0.0.1"),
            locationA,
            CORE
    );
}
```

We provide all the required data to the createRouter method from RouterManagementUseCase in order to create the new core router.

2. Then, we proceed to confirm whether the router created was indeed a core router:

```
@Then("A new core router is created")
public void a_new_core_router_is_created(){
    assertNotNull(router);
    assertEquals(CORE, router.getRouterType());
}
```

The first assertion checks whether we received a null pointer. The second assertion looks into the router's type to confirm that it's a core router.

The following scenario steps involve checking whether we can simply create an edge router by using the `createRouter` method from `RouterManagementUseCase`:

1. First, we create an edge router:

```
@Given("I provide all required data to create an edge
   router")
public void create_edge_router(){
    router =
      this.routerManagementUseCase.createRouter(
            Vendor.HP,
            Model.XYZ0004,
            IP.fromAddress("30.0.0.1"),
            locationA,
            EDGE
      );
}
```

We follow the same procedure for creating the core router objects, but now, we set the EDGE parameter as `RouterType` for object creation.

2. In the last scenario step, we just execute the assertions:

```
@Then("A new edge router is created")
public void a_new_edge_router_is_created(){
    assertNotNull(router);
    assertEquals(EDGE, router.getRouterType());
}
```

The first assertion checks with the `assertNotNull` method whether the router reference is not `null`. Then, it proceeds by executing `assertEquals` to check whether the router created is `EdgeRouter`.

To run the tests related to the creation of routers, we will execute the following Maven command in the project root directory:

```
mvn test
```

The test result should contain the following output:

```
@RouterCreate
Scenario: Creating a new edge router # dev/davivieira/
topologyinventory/application/routers/RouterCreate.feature:8
Given I provide all required data to create an edge router # dev.
davivieira.topologyinventory.application.RouterCreate.create_edge_
router()
Then A new edge router is created # dev.davivieira.topologyinventory.
application.RouterCreate.a_new_edge_router_is_created()
```

Now that we're done with the scenario to create routers, let's see how to implement the `RouterRemove.java` test class for the `RouterRemove.feature` file. The file locations are as follows:

- `src/test/java/dev/davivieira/topologyinventory/application/RouterRemove.java`

- `src/test/resources/dev/davivieira/topologyinventory/application/routers/RouterRemove.feature`

We have to create the methods to test a scenario where we want to remove an edge router from a core router:

1. To get started, we first need to know whether the core router we are working with has at least an edge router connected to it:

    ```
    @Given("The core router has at least one edge router
      connected to it")
    public void the_core_router_has_at_least_one_edge_
      router_connected_to_it(){
        var predicate =
          Router.getRouterTypePredicate(EDGE);
        edgeRouter = (EdgeRouter)
          this.coreRouter.getRouters().
                entrySet().
                stream().
                map(routerMap -> routerMap.getValue()).
                filter(predicate).
                findFirst().get();
        assertEquals(EDGE, edgeRouter.getRouterType());
    }
    ```

    From a core router, we search for an edge router connected to it. Then, we store the returned edge router in the `edgeRouter` variable. Following that, we assert the type of router to confirm whether we have an edge router.

2. Next, we have to check that there are no networks attached to the switch connected to the edge router. We have to check this; otherwise, we will not be able to remove the switch from the edge router:

    ```
    @And("The switch has no networks attached to it")
    public void the_switch_has_no_networks_
      attached_to_it(){
        var networksSize =
        networkSwitch.getSwitchNetworks().size();
        assertEquals(1, networksSize);
        networkSwitch.removeNetworkFromSwitch(network);
    ```

```
    networksSize =
      networkSwitch.getSwitchNetworks().size();
    assertEquals(0, networksSize);
}
```

To assert a switch has no networks connected to it, we first check the size of the networks on the switch. It should return 1. Then, we remove the network and check the size again. It should return 0.

We must ensure that the switch has no networks attached to it to make that switch eligible for removal.

3. Next, we can proceed to check that there are no switches connected to the edge router:

```
@And("The edge router has no switches attached to it")
public void the_edge_router_has_no_switches_
  attached_to_it(){
    var switchesSize =
      edgeRouter.getSwitches().size();
    assertEquals(1, switchesSize);
    edgeRouter.removeSwitch(networkSwitch);
    switchesSize = edgeRouter.getSwitches().size();
    assertEquals(0, switchesSize);
}
```

Here, we remove the switch using the removeSwitch method, followed by an assertion to confirm that the edge router has no more switches connected.

4. Now, we can test the removal of the edge router from the core router:

```
@Then("I remove the edge router from the core router")
public void edge_router_is_removed_from_core_router(){
    var actualID = edgeRouter.getId();
    var expectedID = this.routerManagementUseCase.
        removeRouterFromCoreRouter(
        edgeRouter, coreRouter).
        getId();
    assertEquals(expectedID, actualID);
}
```

To test the removal of an edge router from the core router, we first get the edge router ID of the router we intend to remove. We store this ID in the actualID variable. Then, we proceed to the actual removal. The removeRouterFromCoreRouter method returns the removed router. So, we can use the removed router ID, stored in the expectedID variable, to check with the assertEquals method whether the router was really removed.

To confirm the tests related to router removal are working, we execute the Maven test goal in the project root directory:

```
mvn test
```

The results you get after executing the tests should be similar to the following output:

```
@RouterRemove
Scenario: Removing an edge router from a core router # dev/davivieira/
topologyinventory/application/routers/RouterRemove.feature:4
Given The core router has at least one edge router connected to it #
dev.davivieira.topologyinventory.application.RouterRemove.the_core_
router_has_at_least_one_edge_router_connected_to_it()
And The switch has no networks attached to it # dev.davivieira.
topologyinventory.application.RouterRemove.the_switch_has_no_networks_
attached_to_it()
And The edge router has no switches attached to it # dev.davivieira.
topologyinventory.application.RouterRemove.the_edge_router_has_no_
switches_attached_to_it()
Then I remove the edge router from the core router # dev.davivieira.
topologyinventory.application.RouterRemove.edge_router_is_removed_
from_core_router()
```

The preceding output provides the execution details of the four testing methods involved in removing the edge router from the core router.

We have completed the testing part of router management. For switch and network management, we follow the same ideas. In the book's GitHub repository, you can access the topology and inventory code with all its tests.

Summary

In this chapter, on top of the Domain hexagon, we built the Application hexagon with use cases and ports. For use cases, we heavily relied on a behavior-driven development tool called Cucumber. With Cucumber, we can express use cases supported by the system not only in code terms but also in written text.

We started by creating Cucumber feature files containing the use case written descriptions, and then we used them as a reference to create use case interfaces. These interfaces were then implemented by input ports that provided a concrete way to achieve the use case goals. Finally, we built use case tests, based again on the written description provided by Cucumber.

By implementing and testing the Application hexagon in this way, we leveraged the special capabilities of Cucumber to express the system's behavior in a declarative and straightforward form, and we used these same capabilities to implement and test the entire Application hexagon.

On top of the Application hexagon and the features it provides, we need to decide how such features will be exposed. Also, some of these require access to external data sources. We'll address all these concerns by developing the Framework hexagon in the next chapter.

Questions

1. What do we call files where we declare Cucumber scenarios?

2. On which other Java module does the Application hexagon depend?

3. Which hexagonal architecture component is used to implement use cases?

Answers

1. They are called feature files.

2. It depends on the Domain hexagon Java module.

3. Input ports are utilized to implement use cases.

8
Building the Framework Hexagon

When building a hexagonal application, the last step consists of exposing the application features by connecting input adapters to input ports. Also, if there is any need to get data from, or persist it inside, external systems, then we need to connect output adapters to output ports. The Framework hexagon is the place where we assemble all the adapters required to make the hexagonal system.

We first created the domain model using things including entities, value objects, and specifications in the Domain hexagon. Then, in the Application hexagon, we expressed the user's intent using use cases and ports. Now, in the Framework hexagon, we have to employ adapters to expose system features and define which technologies will be used to enable such features. After assembling the Domain, Application, and Framework hexagons, we will have an architecture resembling the following figure:

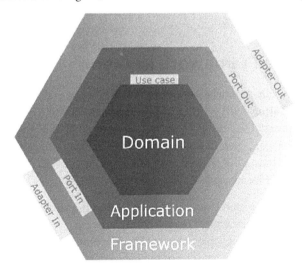

Figure 8.1 – Domain, Application, and Frameworks hexagons assembled

What is so compelling about the hexagonal architecture is that we can add and remove adapters without worrying about changing the core system logic wrapped in the Domain hexagon. Of course, there is a price to be paid in the form of data translation between domain entities and external entities. However, in exchange, we gain a more decoupled system with clear boundaries between its realms of responsibilities.

In this chapter, we will cover the following topics:

- Bootstrapping the Framework hexagon
- Implementing output adapters
- Implementing input adapters
- Testing the Framework hexagon

By the end of this chapter, you'll have learned to create input adapters to make the hexagonal application features accessible to other users and systems. Also, you'll learn how to implement output adapters to enable the hexagonal system to communicate with external data sources.

Technical requirements

To compile and run the code examples presented in this chapter, you'll need the latest **Java SE Development Kit** and **Maven 3.8** installed on your computer. They are all available for the Linux, Mac, and Windows operating systems.

You can find the code files for this chapter on GitHub at `https://github.com/PacktPublishing/-Designing-Hexagonal-Architecture-with-Java---Second-Edition/tree/main/Chapter08`.

Bootstrapping the Framework hexagon

When building a system using hexagonal architecture, you don't need to decide upfront whether the system API will be exposed using REST or gRPC, nor whether the system's primary data source will be a MySQL database or MongoDB. Instead, what you need to do is start modeling your problem domain in the Domain hexagon, then designing and implementing use cases in the Application hexagon. Then, only after creating the previous two hexagons do you need to start thinking about which technologies will enable the hexagonal system's functionalities.

A hexagonal approach centered around **Domain-Driven Design** allows us to postpone the decisions regarding the underlying technologies internal or external to the hexagonal system. Another prerogative of the hexagonal approach is the pluggable nature of the adapters. If you want to expose a certain system feature to be accessible via REST, you create and plug a REST input adapter into an input port. Later on, if you want to expose that same feature to clients using gRPC, you can create and plug a gRPC input adapter into the same input port.

When dealing with external data sources, we have the same pluggable prerogatives using output adapters. You can plug different output adapters into the same output port, changing the underlying data source technology without having to majorly refactor the whole hexagonal system.

To further explore input adapters, we'll have a more in-depth discussion in *Chapter 12, Using RESTEasy Reactive to Implement Input Adapters*. We'll also investigate more possibilities for output adapters in *Chapter 13, Persisting Data with Output Adapters and Hibernate Reactive*.

Let's stick to the basics and create a solid structure for input and output adapters. On top of this structure, later on, we'll be able to add the exciting features provided by the Quarkus framework.

Continuing the development of the topology and inventory system, we need to bootstrap the Framework hexagon as a Maven and Java module.

Inside the topology and inventory Maven root project, we have to run the following command:

```
mvn archetype:generate \
    -DarchetypeGroupId=de.rieckpil.archetypes  \
    -DarchetypeArtifactId=testing-toolkit \
    -DarchetypeVersion=1.0.0 \
    -DgroupId=dev.davivieira \
    -DartifactId=framework \
    -Dversion=1.0-SNAPSHOT \
    -Dpackage=dev.davivieira.topologyinventory.framework \
    -DinteractiveMode=false
```

We recommend running the preceding command directly on CMD instead of PowerShell if you are using Windows. If you need to use PowerShell, you'll need to wrap each part of the command in double quotes.

The mvn `archetype:generate` goal creates a Maven module called `framework` inside `topology-inventory`. This module comes with a skeleton directory structure based on the `groupId` and `artificatId` we passed into the mvn command. Also, it includes a child pom. xml file inside the `framework` directory.

After executing the mvn command to create the `framework` module, the root project's pom.xml file will be updated to contain the new module:

```
<modules>
  <module>domain</module>
  <module>application</module>
  <module>framework</module>
</modules>
```

The `framework` module is inserted at the end as the latest module we have just added.

Because the `framework` module depends on both the `domain` and `application` modules, we need to add them as dependencies to the `framework` module's `pom.xml` file:

```xml
<dependencies>
  <dependency>
    <groupId>dev.davivieira</groupId>
    <artifactId>domain</artifactId>
    <version>1.0-SNAPSHOT</version>
  </dependency>
  <dependency>
    <groupId>dev.davivieira</groupId>
    <artifactId>application</artifactId>
    <version>1.0-SNAPSHOT</version>
  </dependency>
<dependencies>
```

After running the Maven command to create the `framework` module, you should see a directory tree similar to the one shown here:

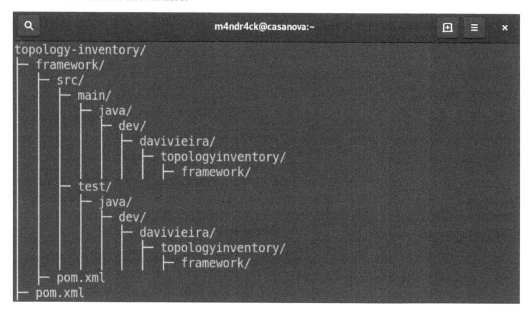

Figure 8.2 – The directory structure of the Framework hexagon

There should be a child `pom.xml` file in the `framework` directory and a parent `pom.xml` file in the `topology-inventory` directory.

Once we have completed the Maven configuration, we can create the descriptor file that turns the `framework` Maven module into a Java module. We do that by creating the following file, `topology-inventory/framework/src/java/module-info.java`:

```
module framework {
    requires domain;
    requires application;
}
```

Because we have added `domain` and `application` as Maven dependencies to the framework's `pom.xml` file, we can also add them as Java module dependencies to the `module-info.java` descriptor file.

With both the Maven and Java modules properly configured for the Framework hexagon, we can move on to creating the output adapters for the topology and inventory system.

Implementing output adapters

We will start by implementing the output adapters to set up the integration between our topology and inventory system and the underlying data source technology, which is an H2 in-memory database. It's also important to implement output adapters first because we refer to them when implementing the input adapters.

The topology and inventory system allows external data retrieval for routers' and switches' entities. So, in this section, we will review the output port interfaces that get external data related to these entities. We'll also provide an output adapter implementation for each output port interface.

The router management output adapter

The router management output adapter we need to create should implement this `RouterManagementOutputPort` interface:

```
package dev.davivieira.topologyinventory.application.
  ports.output;

import
  dev.davivieira.topologyinventory.domain.entity.Router;
import dev.davivieira.topologyinventory.domain.vo.Id;

public interface RouterManagementOutputPort {
    Router retrieveRouter(Id id);

    Router removeRouter(Id id);
```

```
        Router persistRouter(Router router);
    }
```

Both the `retrieveRouter` and `removeRouter` methods' signatures have `Id` as a parameter. We use `Id` to identify the router in the underlying data source. Then, we have the `persistRouter` method signature receiving a `Router` parameter, which can represent both core and edge routers. We use that `Router` parameter to persist the data in the data source.

For the topology and inventory system, for now, we have to implement only one output adapter to allow the system to use an H2 in-memory database.

We start the implementation with the `RouterManagementH2Adapter` class:

```
package dev.davivieira.topologyinventory.framework.
  adapters.output.h2;

import dev.davivieira.topologyinventory.application.ports.
  output.RouterManagementOutputPort;
import dev.davivieira.topologyinventory.domain.
  entity.Router;
import dev.davivieira.topologyinventory.domain.vo.Id;
import dev.davivieira.topologyinventory.framework.adapters.
  output.h2.data.RouterData;
import dev.davivieira.topologyinventory.framework.adapters.
  output.h2.mappers.RouterH2Mapper;
import jakarta.persistence.EntityManager;
import jakarta.persistence.EntityManagerFactory;
import jakarta.persistence.Persistence;
import jakarta.persistence.PersistenceContext;

public class RouterManagementH2Adapter implements
  RouterManagementOutputPort {

    private static RouterManagementH2Adapter instance;

    @PersistenceContext
    private EntityManager em;

    private RouterManagementH2Adapter(){
        setUpH2Database();
    }
    /** Code omitted **/
}
```

The H2 database connection is controlled by `EntityManager`. This connection is configured by the `setUpH2Database` method, which we execute when we call the class's empty constructor. We use the variable called `instance` to provide a singleton so other objects can trigger database operations.

Let's implement each method declared on the output port interface:

1. We start with the `retrieveRouter` method, which receives `Id` as a parameter:

    ```
    @Override
    public Router retrieveRouter(Id id) {
        var routerData = em.getReference(
                        RouterData.class, id.getUuid());
        return RouterH2Mapper.
          routerDataToDomain(routerData);
    }
    ```

    The `getReference` method from `EntityManager` is called with `RouterData.class` and the UUID value is extracted from the `Id` object. `RouterData` is a database entity class that we use to map data coming from the database into the `Router` domain entity class. This mapping is accomplished by the `routerDataToDomain` method from the `RouterH2Mapper` class.

2. Then, we implement the `removeRouter` method, which removes a router from the database:

    ```
    @Override
    public Router removeRouter(Id id) {
        var routerData = em.getReference(
                        RouterData.class, id.getUuid());
        em.remove(routerData);
        return null;
    }
    ```

    To remove a router, we first have to retrieve it by calling the `getReference` method. Once we have a `RouterData` object representing the database entity, we can call the `remove` method from `EntityManager`, which can delete the router from the database.

3. Finally, we implement the `persistRouter` method:

    ```
    @Override
    public Router persistRouter(Router router) {
        var routerData = RouterH2Mapper.
                        routerDomainToData(router);
        em.persist(routerData);
        return router;
    }
    ```

    It receives a `Router` domain entity object that needs to be converted into a `RouterData` database entity object that can be persisted with the `persist` method from `EntityManager`.

By implementing the `retrieveRouter`, `removeRouter`, and `persistRouter` methods, we provide the basic database operations required by the topology and inventory system.

Let's move on to see the switch output adapters' implementation.

The switch management output adapter

The output adapter we implement for the switch is simpler because we don't need to persist switches directly or remove them. The sole purpose of the switch's output adapter is to enable the retrieval of switches from the database. We allow persistence only through the router output adapter.

To get started, let's define the `SwitchManagementOutputPort` interface:

```
package dev.davivieira.topologyinventory.application.
  ports.output;

import dev.davivieira.topologyinventory.domain.
  entity.Switch;
import dev.davivieira.topologyinventory.domain.vo.Id;

public interface SwitchManagementOutputPort {
    Switch retrieveSwitch(Id id);
}
```

We have just one method called `retrieveSwitch`, which receives `Id` and returns `Switch`.

The `SwitchManagementH2Adapter` output adapter implementation is very straightforward and similar to its router counterpart. So, we'll just assess the implementation of the `retrieveSwitch` method:

```
/** Code omitted **/
public class SwitchManagementH2Adapter implements
  SwitchManagementOutputPort {

    /** Code omitted **/
    @Override
    public Switch retrieveSwitch(Id id) {
        var switchData = em.getReference(
                        SwitchData.class, id.getUuid());
        return
        RouterH2Mapper.switchDataToDomain(switchData);
    }
    /** Code omitted **/
}
```

We call the `getReference` method from `EntityManager` with `SwitchData.class` and a UUID value as parameters in order to retrieve a `SwitchData` database entity object. Then, this object is converted into a `Switch` domain entity when we call the `switchDataToDomain` method from the `RouterH2Mapper` class.

Now that we have both `RouterManagementH2Adapter` and `SwitchManagementH2Adapter` properly implemented, we can proceed to implement the input adapters.

Implementing the input adapters

When building the Application hexagon, we need to create use cases and input ports to express system capabilities. To make these capabilities available to users and other systems, we need to build input adapters and connect them to input ports.

For the topology and inventory system, we will implement a set of generic input adapters as Java POJOs. These generic input adapters are the basis for the technologically specific implementation that takes place in *Chapter 12, Using RESTEasy Reactive to Implement Input Adapters*. In that chapter, we will reimplement the generic input adapters as RESTEasy-based input adapters using the Quarkus framework.

The input adapter's central role is to receive requests from outside the hexagonal system and fulfill these requests using an input port.

Continuing to develop the topology and inventory system, let's implement the input adapters that receive requests related to router management.

The router management input adapter

We start by creating the `RouterManagementGenericAdapter` class:

```
public class RouterManagementGenericAdapter {

    private RouterManagementUseCase
      routerManagementUseCase;

    public RouterManagementGenericAdapter(){
        setPorts();
    }
    /** Code omitted **/
}
```

We start the `RouterManagementGenericAdapter` implementation by declaring a class attribute for `RouterManagementUseCase`. Instead of using an input port class reference, we utilize the use case interface reference, `RouterManagementUseCase`, to connect to the input port.

On the constructor of `RouterManagementGenericAdapter`, we call the `setPorts` method, which instantiates `RouterManagementInputPort` with a `RouterManagementH2Adapter` parameter as an output port to connect to the H2 in-memory database that the input port uses.

The following is how we should implement the `setPorts` method:

```
private void setPorts(){
    this.routerManagementUseCase =
            new RouterManagementInputPort(
            RouterManagementH2Adapter.getInstance()
    );
}
/** Code omitted **/
```

The `setPorts` method stores a `RouterManagementInputPort` object in the `RouterManagementUseCase` attribute we defined earlier.

After class initialization, we need to create the methods that expose the operations supported by the hexagonal system. The intent here is to receive the request in the input adapter and forward it to an input port by using its use case interface reference:

1. Here are the operations for retrieving and removing routers from the system:

    ```
    /**
     * GET /router/retrieve/{id}
     * */
    public Router retrieveRouter(Id id){
        return routerManagementUseCase.retrieveRouter(id);
    }

    /**
     * GET /router/remove/{id}
     * */
    public Router removeRouter(Id id){
        return routerManagementUseCase.removeRouter(id);
    }
    ```

    The comments are to remind us that these operations will be transformed into REST endpoints when integrating Quarkus into the hexagonal system. Both `retrieveRouter` and `removeRouter` receive `Id` as a parameter. Then, the request is forwarded to an input port using a use case reference.

2. Then, we have the operation to create a new router:

    ```
    /**
     * POST /router/create
     * */
    ```

```
public Router createRouter(Vendor vendor,
                               Model,
                               IP,
                               Location,
                               RouterType routerType){
    var router = routerManagementUseCase.createRouter(
            null,
            vendor,
            model,
            ip,
            location,
            routerType
    );
    return routerManagementUseCase.
      persistRouter(router);
}
```

From the `RouterManagementUseCase` reference, we first call the `createRouter` method to create a new router, then we persist it using the `persistRouter` method.

3. Remember that in the topology and inventory system, only core routers can receive connections from both core and edge routers. To allow the addition and removal of routers to or from a core router, we first define the following operation to add routers:

```
/**
 * POST /router/add
 * */
public Router addRouterToCoreRouter(
    Id routerId, Id coreRouterId){
    Router = routerManagementUseCase.
    retrieveRouter(routerId);
    CoreRouter =
        (CoreRouter) routerManagementUseCase.
        retrieveRouter(coreRouterId);
    return routerManagementUseCase.
            addRouterToCoreRouter(router, coreRouter);
}
```

For the `addRouterToCoreRouter` method, we pass the routers' `Id` instances as parameters we intend to add along with the target core router's `Id`. With these IDs, we call the `retrieveRouter` method to get the router objects from our data source. Once we have the `Router` and `CoreRouter` objects, we handle the request to the input port using a use case reference, by calling `addRouterToCoreRouter` to add one router to the other.

After that, we define the operation to remove routers from a core router:

```
/**
 * POST /router/remove
 * */
public Router removeRouterFromCoreRouter(
    Id routerId, Id coreRouterId){
    Router =
    routerManagementUseCase.
    retrieveRouter(routerId);
    CoreRouter =
        (CoreRouter) routerManagementUseCase.
        retrieveRouter(coreRouterId);
    return routerManagementUseCase.
        removeRouterFromCoreRouter(router,
            coreRouter);
}
```

For the `removeRouterFromCoreRouter` method, we follow the same steps as those for the `addRouterToCoreRouter` method. The only difference, though, is that at the end, we call `removeRouterFromCoreRouter` from the use case in order to remove one router from the other.

Let's now create the adapter that handles switch-related operations.

The switch management input adapter

Before we define the methods that expose the switch-related operations, we need to configure the proper initialization of the `SwitchManagementGenericAdapter` class:

```
package dev.davivieira.topologyinventory.framework.
    adapters.input.generic;
import dev.davivieira.topologyinventory.application.
    ports.input.*
import dev.davivieira.topologyinventory.application.
    usecases.*;
import dev.davivieira.topologyinventory.domain.entity.*;
import dev.davivieira.topologyinventory.domain.vo.*;
import dev.davivieira.topologyinventory.framework.
    adapters.output.h2.*;

public class SwitchManagementGenericAdapter {

    private SwitchManagementUseCase
        switchManagementUseCase;
```

```
    private RouterManagementUseCase
      routerManagementUseCase;

    public SwitchManagementGenericAdapter(){
        setPorts();
    }
```

SwitchManagementGenericAdapter is connected to two input ports – the first input port is SwitchManagementInputPort from SwitchManagementUseCase, and the second input port is RouterManagementInputPort from RouterManagementUseCase. That's why we start the class implementation by declaring the attributes for SwitchManagementUseCase and RouterManagementUseCase. We are connecting the switch adapter to the router input port because we want to enforce any persistence activity to happen only through a router. The Router entity, as an aggregate, controls the life cycles of the objects that are related to it.

Next, we implement the setPorts method:

```
  private void setPorts(){
      this.switchManagementUseCase =
              new SwitchManagementInputPort(
              SwitchManagementH2Adapter.getInstance()
      );
      this.routerManagementUseCase =
              new RouterManagementInputPort(
              RouterManagementH2Adapter.getInstance()
      );
  }
** Code omitted **
```

With the setPorts method, we initialize both input ports with the SwitchManagementH2Adapter and RouterManagementH2Adapter adapters to allow access to the H2 in-memory database.

Let's see how to implement the methods that expose the switch-related operations:

1. We start with a simple operation that just retrieves a switch:

    ```
      /**
       * GET /switch/retrieve/{id}
       * */
      public Switch retrieveSwitch(Id switchId) {
          return switchManagementUseCase.
            retrieveSwitch(switchId);
      }
    ```

    The retrieveSwitch method receives Id as a parameter. Then, it utilizes a use case reference to forward the request to the input port.

2. Next, we have a method that lets us create and add a switch to an edge router:

```
/**
 * POST /switch/create
 * */
public EdgeRouter createAndAddSwitchToEdgeRouter(
        Vendor,
        Model,
        IP,
        Location,
        SwitchType, Id routerId
) {
    Switch newSwitch = switchManagementUseCase.
    createSwitch(vendor, model, ip, location,
      switchType);

    Router edgeRouter = routerManagementUseCase.
    retrieveRouter(routerId);
    if(!edgeRouter.getRouterType().equals
      (RouterType.EDGE))
        throw new UnsupportedOperationException(
    "Please inform the id of an edge router to add a
      switch");
    Router = switchManagementUseCase.
    addSwitchToEdgeRouter(newSwitch, (EdgeRouter)
      edgeRouter);

    return (EdgeRouter)
    routerManagementUseCase.persistRouter(router);
}
```

We call the switch input port method, `createSwitch`, by passing the parameters received by the `createAndAddSwitchToEdgeRouter` method to create a switch. With `routerId`, we retrieve the edge router by calling the `retrieveRouter` method from the router input port. Once we have the `Switch` and `EdgeRouter` objects, we can call the `addSwitchToEdgeRouter` method to add the switch to the edge router. As the last step, we call the `persistRouter` method to persist the operation in the data source.

3. Finally, we have the `removeSwitchFromEdgeRouter` method, which allows us to remove a switch from an edge router:

```
/**
 * POST /switch/remove
 * */
public EdgeRouter removeSwitchFromEdgeRouter(
```

```
            Id switchId, Id edgeRouterId) {
        EdgeRouter =
                (EdgeRouter) routerManagementUseCase.
                            retrieveRouter(edgeRouterId);
        Switch networkSwitch = edgeRouter.
                                getSwitches().
                                get(switchId);
        Router = switchManagementUseCase.
                        removeSwitchFromEdgeRouter(
                        networkSwitch, edgeRouter);
        return (EdgeRouter) routerManagementUseCase.
        persistRouter(router);
    }
```

removeSwitchFromEdgeRouter receives Id as a parameter for the switch and another Id for the edge router. Then, it retrieves the router by calling the retrieveRouter method. With the switch ID, it retrieves the switch object from the edge router object. Once it gets the Switch and EdgeRouter objects, it calls the removeSwitchFromEdgeRouter method to remove the switch from the edge router.

What's left now is to implement the adapter that deals with the topology and inventory networks.

The network management input adapter

As we did with the router and switch adapters, let's implement the NetworkManagementGenericAdapter class by first defining the ports it needs:

```
package dev.davivieira.topologyinventory.framework.
  adapters.input.generic;
import dev.davivieira.topologyinventory.application.
  ports.input.*;
import dev.davivieira.topologyinventory.application.
  usecases.*;
import dev.davivieira.topologyinventory.domain.
  entity.Switch;
import dev.davivieira.topologyinventory.domain.vo.*;
import dev.davivieira.topologyinventory.framework.
  adapters.output.h2.*;

public class NetworkManagementGenericAdapter {

    private SwitchManagementUseCase
      switchManagementUseCase;
    private NetworkManagementUseCase
```

```
networkManagementUseCase;
public NetworkManagementGenericAdapter(){
    setPorts();
}
```

Besides NetworkManagementUseCase, we also use SwitchManagementUseCase. We need to call the setPorts method from the constructor of NetworkManagementGenericAdapter to properly initialize the input port objects and assign them to their respective use case references. The following is how we implement the setPorts method:

```
private void setPorts(){
    this.switchManagementUseCase =
            new SwitchManagementInputPort(
            SwitchManagementH2Adapter.getInstance());
    this.networkManagementUseCase =
            new NetworkManagementInputPort(
            RouterManagementH2Adapter.getInstance());
}
/** Code omitted **/
```

As we did in previous input adapter implementations, we configure the setPorts method to initialize the input port objects and assign them to the use case references.

Let's implement the network-related methods:

1. First, we implement the addNetworkToSwitch method to add a network to a switch:

    ```
    /**
     * POST /network/add
     * */
    public Switch addNetworkToSwitch(Network network, Id
      switchId) {
        Switch networkSwitch = switchManagementUseCase.
                                retrieveSwitch(switchId);
        return networkManagementUseCase.
                addNetworkToSwitch(
                network, networkSwitch);
    }
    ```

    The addNetworkToSwitch method receives the Network and Id objects as parameters. To proceed, we need to retrieve the Switch object by calling the retrieveSwitch method. Then, we can call the addNetworkToSwitch method to add the network to the switch.

2. Then, we implement the method to remove a network from a switch:

```
/**
 * POST /network/remove
 * */
public Switch removeNetworkFromSwitch(
String networkName, Id switchId) {
    Switch networkSwitch = switchManagementUseCase.
                            retrieveSwitch(switchId);
    return networkManagementUseCase.
            removeNetworkFromSwitch(
            networkName, networkSwitch);
}
```

First, we get a `Switch` object by calling the `retrieveSwitch` method with the `Id` parameter. To remove a network from a switch, we use the network name to find it from a list of networks attached to the switch. We do that by calling the `removeNetworkFromSwitch` method.

The adapter for managing networks is the last input adapter we have to implement. With these three adapters, we can now manage routers, switches, and networks from the Framework hexagon. To make sure these adapters are working well, let's create some tests for them.

Testing the Framework hexagon

By testing the Framework hexagon, we not only have the opportunity to check whether the input and output adapters are working well but we can also test whether the other hexagons, Domain and Application, are doing their part in response to the requests coming from the Framework hexagon.

To test it, we call the input adapters to trigger the execution of everything necessary in the downstream hexagons to fulfill the request. We start by implementing tests for the router management adapters. The tests for switches and networks follow the same pattern and are available in the GitHub repository for this book.

For the routers, we will put our tests into the `RouterTest` class:

```
public class RouterTest extends FrameworkTestData {

    RouterManagementGenericAdapter
    routerManagementGenericAdapter;

    public RouterTest() {
        this.routerManagementGenericAdapter =
        new RouterManagementGenericAdapter();
        loadData();
    }
```

```
    /** Code omitted **/
}
```

In the `RouterTest` constructor, we instantiate the `RouterManagementGenericAdapter` input adapter class that we use to perform the tests. The `loadData` method loads some test data from the `FrameworkTestData` parent class.

Once we have correctly configured the requirements of the tests, we can proceed with the testing:

1. First, we test router retrieval:

    ```
    @Test
    public void retrieveRouter() {
        var id = Id.withId(
        "b832ef4f-f894-4194-8feb-a99c2cd4be0c");
        var actualId = routerManagementGenericAdapter.
                        retrieveRouter(id).getId();
        assertEquals(id, actualId);
    }
    ```

    We call the input adapter, informing it of the router `id` we want to retrieve. With `assertEquals`, we compare the expected ID with the actual ID to see whether they match.

2. To test router creation, we have to implement the `createRouter` test method:

    ```
    @Test
    public void createRouter() {
        var ipAddress = "40.0.0.1";
        var routerId  = this.

        routerManagementGenericAdapter.createRouter(
                Vendor.DLINK,
                Model.XYZ0001,
                IP.fromAddress(ipAddress),
                locationA,
                RouterType.EDGE).getId();
        var router = this.routerManagementGenericAdapter.
        retrieveRouter(routerId);
        assertEquals(routerId, router.getId());
        assertEquals(Vendor.DLINK, router.getVendor());
        assertEquals(Model.XYZ0001, router.getModel());
        assertEquals(ipAddress,
        router.getIp().getIpAddress());
        assertEquals(locationA, router.getLocation());
        assertEquals(RouterType.EDGE,
    ```

```
        router.getRouterType());
    }
```

From the router input adapter, we call the `createRouter` method to create and persist a new router. Then, we call the `retrieveRouter` method with the ID previously generated by the router we have just created. Finally, we run `assertEquals` to confirm whether the router retrieved from the data source is indeed the router we created.

3. To test the addition of a router to a core router, we have the `addRouterToCoreRouter` test method:

```
@Test
public void addRouterToCoreRouter() {
    var routerId = Id.withId(
    "b832ef4f-f894-4194-8feb-a99c2cd4be0b");
    var coreRouterId = Id.withId(
    "b832ef4f-f894-4194-8feb-a99c2cd4be0c");
    var actualRouter =
    (CoreRouter) this.routerManagementGenericAdapter.
    addRouterToCoreRouter(routerId,coreRouterId);
    assertEquals(routerId,
    actualRouter.getRouters().get(routerId).getId());
}
```

We pass the variables, `routerId` and `coreRouterId`, as parameters to the input adapter's `addRouterToCoreRouter` method, which returns a core router. `assertEquals` checks whether the core router has the router we added.

4. To test the removal of a router from a core router, we'll use this code:

```
@Test
public void removeRouterFromCoreRouter(){
    var routerId = Id.withId(
    "b832ef4f-f894-4194-8feb-a99c2cd4be0a");
    var coreRouterId = Id.withId(
    "b832ef4f-f894-4194-8feb-a99c2cd4be0c");
    var removedRouter =
    this.routerManagementGenericAdapter.
    removeRouterFromCoreRouter(routerId,
    coreRouterId);
    var coreRouter =
    (CoreRouter)this.routerManagementGenericAdapter.
    retrieveRouter(coreRouterId);
    assertEquals(routerId, removedRouter.getId());
    assertFalse(
```

```
        coreRouter.getRouters().containsKey(routerId));
    }
```

This test is very similar to the previous one. We again use the `routerId` and `coreRouterId` variables, but now we also use the `removeRouterFromCoreRouter` method, which returns the removed router. `assertEquals` checks whether the removed router's ID matches the ID from the `routerId` variable.

To run these tests, execute the following command in the Maven project root directory:

```
mvn test
```

The output should be similar to the one here:

```
[INFO]  T E S T S
[INFO] -------------------------------------------------------
[INFO] Running dev.davivieira.topologyinventory.framework.NetworkTest
[INFO] Tests run: 2, Failures: 0, Errors: 0, Skipped: 0, Time elapsed:
0.654 s - in dev.davivieira.topologyinventory.framework.NetworkTest
[INFO] Running dev.davivieira.topologyinventory.framework.RouterTest
[INFO] Tests run: 5, Failures: 0, Errors: 0, Skipped: 0, Time elapsed:
0.014 s - in dev.davivieira.topologyinventory.framework.RouterTest
[INFO] Running dev.davivieira.topologyinventory.framework.SwitchTest
[INFO] Tests run: 3, Failures: 0, Errors: 0, Skipped: 0, Time elapsed:
0.006 s - in dev.davivieira.topologyinventory.framework.SwitchTest
```

Along with `RouterTest`, we also have tests from `SwitchTest` and `NetworkTest`, which you can find in the book's GitHub repository, as mentioned before.

By implementing the Framework hexagon tests, we conclude the development of the Framework hexagon and the whole topology and inventory system's backend. Taking what we've learned from this chapter and the previous chapters, we can apply all the techniques covered to create a system following the hexagonal architecture principles.

Summary

We started the Framework hexagon construction by first implementing the output adapters to enable the topology and inventory system to use an H2 in-memory database as its primary data source.

Then, we created three input adapters: one for router operations, another one for switch operations, and the last one for network-related operations. To conclude, we implemented tests to ensure that the adapters and the whole hexagonal system worked as expected. By completing the development of the Framework hexagon, we have finished the development of our overall hexagonal system.

We can improve the hexagonal system we have created by exploring the possibilities offered by the **Java Module Platform System** (**JPMS**). For example, we can leverage the hexagonal modular structure to apply the **Dependency Inversion Principle** (**DIP**). By doing so, we can make the hexagonal system more loosely coupled. We shall examine the DIP and other exciting features in the next chapter.

Questions

1. Which other Java modules does the `Framework hexagon` Java module depend on?

2. Why do we need to create the output adapters?

3. In order to communicate with the input ports, the input adapters instantiate input port objects and assign them to an interface reference. What's that interface?

4. When we test a Framework hexagon's input adapter, we are also testing other hexagons. Why does that happen?

Answers

1. The `Framework hexagon` module depends on the Domain and Application hexagons' Java modules.

2. We create output adapters to enable the hexagonal system to connect to external data sources.

3. It's the use case interface.

4. Because the input adapters depend on the components provided by the Domain and Application hexagons.

9

Applying Dependency Inversion with Java Modules

In the previous chapters, we learned how to develop each hexagon as a Java module. By doing that, we started to enforce the scope and responsibilities of each hexagon in the architecture. However, we did not go too far in exploiting the Java module's features, such as encapsulation and dependency inversion, and how these features can enhance the overall structure of a hexagonal system by making it more robust and loosely coupled.

To understand the role that's played by the **Java Platform Module System** (**JPMS**) in developing a hexagonal system, we need to understand what problems the JPMS aims to solve. Once we know what we can do with the JPMS in terms of encapsulation and dependency inversion, we can apply these techniques in conjunction with the hexagonal architecture.

So, in this chapter, we will learn how to combine the JPMS with the hexagonal architecture to create a well-encapsulated system with clearly defined boundaries that are reinforced by the system's modular structure and dependency inversion techniques. We'll cover the following topics:

- Introducing the JPMS
- Inverting dependencies on a hexagonal application
- Using the Java platform's `ServiceLoader` class to retrieve JPMS provider implementations

By the end of this chapter, you will have learned how to use services, consumers, and providers from the JPMS to apply dependency inversion and encapsulation principles for a hexagonal system.

Technical requirements

To compile and run the code examples presented in this chapter, you will need the latest **Java SE Development Kit** and **Maven 3.8** installed on your computer. They are both available for the Linux, macOS, and Windows operating systems.

You can find the code files for this chapter on GitHub at `https://github.com/PacktPublishing/-Designing-Hexagonal-Architecture-with-Java---Second-Edition/tree/main/Chapter09`.

Introducing the JPMS

Before **Java SE 9**, the only mechanism we had to handle dependencies in Java was the `classpath` parameter. The `classpath` parameter is where we put dependencies in the form of **JAR files**. However, the problem is that there is no way to determine which JAR file a particular dependency came from. If you have two classes with the same name, in the same package, and present in two different JAR files, one of the JAR files would be loaded first, causing one JAR file to be shadowed by the other.

Shadowing is the term we use to refer to a situation where two or more JAR files that contain the same dependency are put into the `classpath` parameter, but only one of the JAR files is loaded, shadowing the rest. This JAR dependency entanglement issue is also known as **JAR hell**. A symptom that indicates that things are not so good with dependencies that have been loaded into the `classpath` parameter is when we see unexpected `ClassNotFoundException` exceptions at system runtime.

The JPMS cannot completely prevent JAR hell issues related to dependency version mismatches and shadowing. Still, the modular approach helps us have a better view of the dependencies that are needed by a system. This broader dependency perspective is helpful to prevent and diagnose such dependency issues.

Before the JPMS, there was no way to control access to public types from different JAR files. The default behavior of a **Java Virtual Machine** (**JVM**) is to always make these public types available between other JAR files, which often leads to collisions involving classes with the same name and package.

The JPMS introduced the `module` path and a strict encapsulation policy that restricts, by default, access to all public types between different modules. No longer can all public types be accessed from other dependencies. With the JPMS, `module` has to state which packages that contain public types are available to other modules. We did that by using the `exports` directive on the `domain` hexagon module:

```
module domain {
    exports dev.davivieira.topologyinventory.domain.entity;
    exports dev.davivieira.topologyinventory.domain.entity
      .factory;
    exports dev.davivieira.topologyinventory.domain
      .service;
    exports dev.davivieira.topologyinventory.domain
      .specification;
    exports dev.davivieira.topologyinventory.domain.vo;
    requires static lombok;
}
```

Then, to access the `domain` hexagon module, we used the `requires` directive in the `application` hexagon module:

```
module application {
    requires domain;
}
```

This modularization mechanism assembles code in a new Java construct called `module`. As we saw previously, `module` may have to determine which package it intends to export and which other modules it requires. In this arrangement, we have more control over the things our application exposes and consumes.

If you're targeting development on cloud-based environments and care for performance and cost, the `module` system's nature allows you to construct a customized Java runtime (known in the past as **JRE**) containing just the modules required to run the application. With a smaller Java runtime, both the application startup time and memory usage will decrease. Let's say we're talking about hundreds – even thousands – of Kubernetes pods running Java in the cloud. With a smaller Java runtime, we can achieve a considerable economy regarding computational resource consumption.

Now that we are more acquainted with the JPMS's motivations and benefits, let's go back to developing our topology and inventory system. We will learn how to use more advanced JPMS features to enhance encapsulation and adherence to dependency inversion principles.

Inverting dependencies on a hexagonal application

The **dependency inversion principle (DIP)**, as introduced by Robert C. Martin, states that high-level components should not depend on low-level components. Instead, both of them should depend on abstractions. At first glance, for some, it may not be so obvious to understand such a concept. *After all, what do the high- and low-level components mean? And what kind of abstractions are we talking about?*

A high-level component has a set of operations orchestrated to enable a major system behavior. A high-level component may rely on low-level components to provide a major system behavior. A low-level component, in turn, utilizes a specialized behavior that supports the goals of a high-level component. We call a piece of client code that acts as the high-level component because it depends on and consumes the functionalities provided by the low-level component.

The high-level component can be either a concrete or abstract element, while the low-level component should be concrete because it always provides implementation details.

Let's consider some client code as a high-level component that calls methods on a serving code. The serving code, in turn, can be regarded as a low-level component. This low-level component contains the implementation details. In procedural programming designs, it's common to see high-level components depending directly on the implementation details provided by low-level components. Martin says that this direct dependency on implementation details is bad because it makes the system rigid. For example, if we change these implementation details on the low-level components, such changes can cause immediate problems for the high-level components that depend directly on them. That's where this rigidity comes from: we cannot change one part of the code without causing side effects in other parts.

To invert the dependency, we need to make the high-level component depend on the same abstraction that the low-level component is derived from. In object-oriented designs, we can achieve this feat by using abstract classes or interfaces. The low-level component implements an abstraction, whereas the high-level component refers to that abstraction instead of the low-level implementation. So, this is what we have to do to invert the dependencies properly.

The JPMS introduced a mechanism to help us avoid this dependency on implementation details. This mechanism is based on consumers, services, and providers. In addition to these three JPMS elements, there is one more, already known in previous Java versions, called `ServiceLoader`, which enables the system to find and retrieve implementations of a given abstraction.

We call a consumer with a module that declares the need to consume a service provided by a provider module through the `uses` directive. This `uses` directive states the name of an interface or abstract class that represents the service we intend to use. The service, in turn, is the object that implements the interface or extends the abstract class that's informed in the `uses` directive. The provider is a module that declares the service interface and its implementations with the providers and directives, respectively.

Let's see how we can use the JPMS to apply this DIP to our hexagonal system, topology, and inventory. We'll also see a representation for inverting dependencies using input adapters, use cases, and input ports.

Providing services with use cases and input ports

When developing the topology and inventory system, we designed use cases as interfaces and input ports as implementations for these interfaces. We can consider use cases and input ports as hexagonal architecture components that match the JPMS definition for a service. The Application hexagon module can be regarded as the module that provides the service. *And what about the consumer?* The Framework hexagon module is the direct consumer of the Application hexagon module.

Based on that reasoning, we'll re-implement both the Application and Framework hexagon modules so that the input adapters from the Framework hexagon will no longer need to depend on the input port implementations from the Application hexagon. Instead, the input adapters will only depend on the use case interface types, rather than the input ports' concrete types. In such a context, we can regard input adapters as high-level components and input ports as low-level components. Input adapters refer to use case interfaces. Input ports implement these use cases. The following diagram illustrates this:

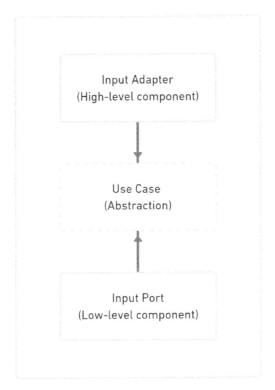

Figure 9.1 – Dependency inversion with an input adapter, use case, and input port

The preceding diagram illustrates how we can approach dependency inversion in the hexagonal architecture. This example considers the dependency inversion between the Framework and Application hexagons, but we can do the same thing with the Domain hexagon as well.

Let's consider how RouterManagementGenericAdapter is currently accessing the implementation details instead of the abstraction:

```
private RouterManagementUseCase;

public RouterManagementGenericAdapter(){
    setPorts();
}

private void setPorts(){
    this.routerManagementUseCase = new
      RouterManagementInputPort(
            RouterManagementH2Adapter.getInstance()
    );
}
```

By calling new `RouterManagementInputPort(RouterManagementH2Adapter.getInstance())`, we are making the input adapter depend on the implementation details of both the `RouterManagementInputPort` input port and the output adapter expressed by `RouterManagementH2Adapter`.

To make an input port class eligible to be used as a provider class in the JPMS, we need to do the following:

1. First, we must add a no-arguments constructor:

    ```
    @NoArgsConstructor
    public class RouterManagementInputPort implements
      RouterManagementUseCase {
    /** Code omitted **/
    }
    ```

2. Then, we must declare the `setOutputPort` method in the use case interface:

    ```
    public interface RouterManagementUseCase {
        void setOutputPort(
        RouterManagementOutputPort
          routerManagementOutputPort);
    }
    ```

3. Lastly, we must implement the `setOutputPort` method in the input port:

    ```
    @Override
    public void setOutputPort(RouterManagementOutputPort
      routerManagementOutputPort) {
        this.routerManagementOutputPort =
        routerManagementOutputPort;
    }
    ```

Now, we can update the Application hexagon's `module` descriptor to define the services that we'll provide by using the use case interfaces and their input port's implementations:

```
module application {
    requires domain;
    requires static lombok;

    exports dev.davivieira.topologyinventory.application
      .ports.
    input;
    exports dev.davivieira.topologyinventory.application
      .ports.
    output;
    exports dev.davivieira.topologyinventory.application
```

```
        .usecases;
/** Code omitted **/
}
```

We start by declaring the dependency that the `application` module has on the Domain hexagon and `lombok` modules. Then, we use `exports` to enable access to the input ports, output ports, and use cases.

Next, we must declare the services we want to provide. We can accomplish this service declaration by providing a use case interface and the input port that implements it. Let's declare the service provider for router management:

```
provides dev.davivieira.topologyinventory.application
    .usecases.
RouterManagementUseCase
with dev.davivieira.topologyinventory.application.ports
    .input.
RouterManagementInputPort;
```

In the preceding code, `RouterManagementUseCase` is being provided by `RouterManagementInputPort`.

Next, we must define the service provider for switch management:

```
provides dev.davivieira.topologyinventory.application
    .usecases.
SwitchManagementUseCase
with dev.davivieira.topologyinventory.application.ports
    .input.
SwitchManagementInputPort;
```

In the preceding code, `SwitchManagementUseCase` is being provided by `SwitchManagementInputPort`.

Finally, we must declare the service provider for network management:

```
provides dev.davivieira.topologyinventory.application
    .usecases.
NetworkManagementUseCase
with dev.davivieira.topologyinventory.application.ports
    .input.
NetworkManagementInputPort;
```

Here, we have `NetworkManagementUseCase` being provided by `NetworkManagementInputPort`.

Before we learn how to access these input ports through JPMS services in input adapters, let's learn how we can invert dependencies when working with output ports and output adapters.

Providing services with output ports and output adapters

In the Framework hexagon, we have output ports as interfaces and output adapters as their implementations. Input ports depend on output ports. In that sense, input ports can be regarded as high-level components because they depend on the abstractions provided by output ports. Output adapters act as low-level components that provide implementations for output port abstractions. The following diagram shows an illustration of this dependency inversion arrangement:

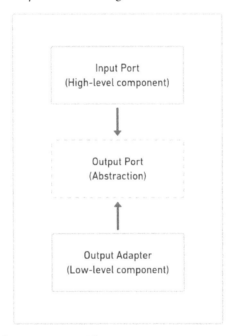

Figure 9.2 – Dependency inversion with an input port, output port, and output adapter

Note that both the input port and the output adapter point to the same output port abstraction. This means that we can use the JPMS to apply the dependency inversion principle with these architecture components.

However, there is one requirement we have to meet to use output adapters as implementation providers. This requirement requires every provider class to have a public constructor with no parameters, which is not the case for the output adapters we implemented in the previous chapters:

```
private RouterManagementH2Adapter(){
    setUpH2Database();
}
```

We implemented the `RouterManagementH2Adapter` constructor as `private` to enforce a singleton pattern. To show how to use this output adapter as a JPMS service provider, we need to disable the singleton pattern by changing the constructor's access modifier from `private` to `public`:

```
public RouterManagementH2Adapter(){
    setUpH2Database();
}
```

Now, we can update the framework hexagon's `module` (the `info.java` file) to define the services:

```
module framework {
    requires domain;
    requires application;

    /** Code omitted **/

    exports dev.davivieira.topologyinventory.framework
      .adapters.
    output.h2.data;
    opens dev.davivieira.topologyinventory.framework
      .adapters.
    output.h2.data;

    provides dev.davivieira.topologyinventory.application
      .ports.
    output.RouterManagementOutputPort
    with dev.davivieira.topologyinventory.framework
      .adapters.output.
    h2.RouterManagementH2Adapter;

    provides dev.davivieira.topologyinventory.application
      .ports.
    output.SwitchManagementOutputPort
    with dev.davivieira.topologyinventory.framework
      .adapters.output.
    h2.SwitchManagementH2Adapter;
}
```

We start by using the `requires` directive to declare the module dependencies on the Domain and Application hexagon modules. Then, we use the `exports` directive to enable access to all public types in the `dev.davivieira.topologyinventory.framework.adapters.output.h2.data` package. We use the `opens` directive to allow runtime reflective access to the output adapters. We need this reflective access because of the database library dependencies that these output adapters have.

Finally, we use the `provides` and `with` directives to inform the output port interfaces, `RouterManagementOutputPort` and `SwitchManagementOutputPort`, along with their respective output adapter implementations, `RouterManagementH2Adapter` and `SwitchManagementH2Adapter`.

Now that we've completed the configuration that's required to enable dependency inversion between the output ports and adapters, let's learn how to configure input adapters to access dependencies through their abstractions.

Making the input adapters dependent on abstractions

The first step in consuming the services we have exposed with the `provides` and `with` directives is to update the `module` descriptor of the consumer's `framework` hexagon module by utilizing the `uses` directive. We'll execute the following steps to do so:

1. Let's start by updating the module descriptor:

    ```
    module framework {
        /** Code omitted **/
        uses dev.davivieira.topologyinventory.application
          .usecases
        .RouterManagementUseCase;
        uses dev.davivieira.topologyinventory.application
          .usecases
        .SwitchManagementUseCase;
        uses dev.davivieira.topologyinventory.application
          .usecases
        .NetworkManagementUseCase;
        uses dev.davivieira.topologyinventory.application
          .ports.output
        .RouterManagementOutputPort;
        uses dev.davivieira.topologyinventory.application
          .ports.output
        .SwitchManagementOutputPort;
    }
    ```

    The first three `uses` directives point to the services provided by the Application hexagon module. The last two `uses` directives refer to the services we exposed in the Framework hexagon module.

    Now that we have the `module` descriptors adequately configured to allow the system to depend on interfaces instead of implementations, we need to refactor the input adapters so that they only rely on use case interfaces from the Application hexagon module and output the port interfaces from the Framework hexagon module.

2. First, we must configure the `RouterManagementGenericAdapter` adapter:

    ```
    public class RouterManagementGenericAdapter {

        private RouterManagementUseCase
          routerManagementUseCase;

        public RouterManagementGenericAdapter(
        RouterManagementUseCase routerManagementUseCase) {
            this.routerManagementUseCase =
              routerManagementUseCase;
        }
        /** Code omitted **/
    }
    ```

    Note that `RouterManagementGenericAdapter` no longer depends on
    `RouterManagementInputPort` and `RouterManagementH2Adapter`, as it did
    previously. There is only one dependency on the `RouterManagementUseCase` interface.

3. For the `SwitchManagementGenericAdapter` input adapter, this is how we should
    configure the dependency:

    ```
    public class SwitchManagementGenericAdapter {

        private SwitchManagementUseCase
          switchManagementUseCase;
        private RouterManagementUseCase
          routerManagementUseCase;

        public SwitchManagementGenericAdapter (
        RouterManagementUseCase,
        SwitchManagementUseCase switchManagementUseCase){
            this.routerManagementUseCase =
              routerManagementUseCase;
            this.switchManagementUseCase =
              switchManagementUseCase;
        }
        /** Code omitted **/
    }
    ```

    The `SwitchManagementGenericAdapter` input adapter depends on both the
    `RouterManagementUseCase` and `SwitchManagementUseCase` use case interfaces
    to perform its activities.

4. To conclude, we have to adjust the `NetworkManagementGenericAdapter` adapter class:

```
public class NetworkManagementGenericAdapter {

    private SwitchManagementUseCase
      switchManagementUseCase;
    private NetworkManagementUseCase
      networkManagementUseCase;

    public NetworkManagementGenericAdapter(
    SwitchManagementUseCase,
    NetworkManagementUseCase networkManagementUseCase) {
        this.switchManagementUseCase =
          switchManagementUseCase;
        this.networkManagementUseCase =
          networkManagementUseCase;
    }
    /** Code omitted **/
}
```

The `NetworkManagementGenericAdapter` input adapter follows the same pattern we used in the previous input adapters and requires use case references in the input adapter's constructor. Here, we're making use of the `SwitchManagementUseCase` and `NetworkManagementUseCase` use case interfaces.

In this section, we touched on a crucial JPMS feature: service providers. By using them, we can bind input port implementations to the use case interfaces. That's how we arrange the code. So, the input adapters can rely on use case abstractions to trigger operations on the Application hexagon.

Now, let's learn how to use `ServiceLoader` to retrieve service implementations based on the JPMS providers we have defined.

Using the Java platform's ServiceLoader class to retrieve JPMS provider implementations

So far, we have configured the `module` descriptor of the Application and Framework hexagon modules. We have refactored the input adapters so that they only depend on the abstractions provided by use case interfaces. *But how can we retrieve the concrete instances that implement those use case interfaces?* That's exactly what the `ServiceLoader` class does.

`ServiceLoader` is not a new class made solely to support JPMS features. Instead, `ServiceLoader` has been present in Java since version **1.6**. From **Java 9** onward, this class was enhanced to work with the Java module's services. It relies on the configuration provided by the `module` descriptor to find implementations for a given service provider interface.

To illustrate how we can use `ServiceLoader`, let's update the `FrameworkTestData` test class by creating a method called `loadPortsAndUseCases`. This method uses `ServiceLoader` to retrieve the objects we need to instantiate the input adapters. We need to create the `loadPortsAndUseCases` method because we'll call it to initialize the input adapters through `ServiceLoader`. Before creating the `loadPortsAndUseCases` method, we need to declare the input adapter variables that we'll use to assign the objects that are instantiated with the aid of `ServiceLoader`:

```
public class FrameworkTestData {
  protected RouterManagementGenericAdapter
  routerManagementGenericAdapter;
  protected SwitchManagementGenericAdapter
  switchManagementGenericAdapter;
  protected NetworkManagementGenericAdapter
  networkManagementGenericAdapter;
  /** Code omitted **/
}
```

The variables we've declared here are used to store references for the input adapters we'll create using the input ports and output adapters objects that we obtained from the `ServiceLoader` class.

Let's start by initializing `RouterManagementGenericAdapter`.

Initializing RouterManagementGenericAdapter

We will start the `loadPortsAndUseCases` method's implementation by using a `ServiceLoader` instance to retrieve the objects that are necessary for instantiating `RouterManagementGenericAdapter`. We'll perform the following steps to do this:

1. The following code shows the `loadPortsAndUseCases` method's initial implementation:

   ```
   protected void loadPortsAndUseCases() {
     // Load router implementations
     ServiceLoader<RouterManagementUseCase>
       loaderUseCaseRouter =
     ServiceLoader.load(RouterManagementUseCase.class);
     RouterManagementUseCase =
     loaderUseCaseRouter.findFirst().get();
     // Code omitted //
   }
   ```

   The `load` method from `ServiceLoader` receives a `RouterManagementUseCase.class` file as a parameter. This method can find all the implementations for the `RouterManagementUseCase` interface. Since `RouterManagementInputPort` is the only implementation that's available for the use case interface, we can call `loaderUseCaseRouter.findFirst().get()` to get that implementation.

Aside from a proper implementation for the `RouterManagementUseCase` interface, we also need to provide an implementation for the `RouterManagementOutputPort` interface.

2. The following code shows how to retrieve a `RouterManagementOutputPort` object:

    ```
    ServiceLoader<RouterManagementOutputPort> loaderOutpu
      tRouter =
    ServiceLoader.load(RouterManagementOutputPort.class);
    RouterManagementOutputPort = loaderOutputRouter.find
      First().get();
    ```

    The call on `loaderOutputRouter.findFirst().get()` retrieves a `RouterManagementH2Adapter` object, which is the only available implementation for the `RouterManagementOutputPort` interface.

    With the `RouterManagementInputPort` and `RouterManagementH2Adapter` objects loaded from `ServiceLoader`, we have the required objects to create an input adapter. But first, we need to set up the output port for the use case.

3. This is how we can set a `RouterManagementOutputPort` object in `RouterManagementUseCase`:

    ```
    routerManagementUseCase.setOutputPort(routerManagemen
      tOutputPort);
    ```

    By calling `routerManagementUseCase.setOutputPort(routerManagement-OutputPort)`, we are setting `RouterManagementOutputPort` in `RouterManagementUseCase`.

4. Now, we can create a new `RouterManagementGenericAdapter` adapter by passing `RouterManagementUseCase`, which we have just created, to its constructor:

    ```
    this.routerManagementGenericAdapter =
    new RouterManagementGenericAdapter(routerManagemen
      tUseCase);
    ```

Now, let's move on and learn how to initialize `SwitchManagementGenericAdapter`.

Initializing SwitchManagementGenericAdapter

Still inside the `loadPortsAndUseCases` method, we need to use `ServiceLoader` to find an available implementation for `SwitchManagementUseCase`. We'll perform the following steps for the same reason:

1. In the following code, we are retrieving a `SwitchManagementUseCase` implementation:

    ```
    ServiceLoader<SwitchManagementUseCase> loaderUseCas
      eSwitch = ServiceLoader.load(SwitchManagementUse
    ```

```
          Case.class);
SwitchManagementUseCase switchManagementUseCase =
  loaderUseCaseSwitch.findFirst().get();
```

By calling `ServiceLoader.load(SwitchManagementUseCase.class)`, we are retrieving a `ServiceLoader` object containing all the available implementations for `SwitchManagementUseCase`. In our case, the only available implementation is the `SwitchManagementInputPort` input port. To load such an implementation, we must call `loaderUseCaseSwitch.findFirst().get()`.

We also need an implementation for the `SwitchManagementOutputPort` output port.

2. The following code shows how we can get a `SwitchManagementOutputPort` implementation:

```
ServiceLoader<SwitchManagementOutputPort> loaderOut
  putSwitch = ServiceLoader.load(SwitchManagementOut
    putPort.class);
SwitchManagementOutputPort = loaderOutputSwitch.find
  First().get();
```

Output adapters implement output ports. So, to get an output port implementation, we should call `ServiceLoader.load(SwitchManagementOutputPort.class)` to load the `SwitchManagementH2Adapter` implementation and then call `loaderOutputSwitch.findFirst().get()` to retrieve that implementation object.

3. Now, we can use the output port object to set it in the use case:

```
switchManagementUseCase.setOutputPort(switchManagemen
  tOutputPort);
```

4. Finally, we can initiate the input adapter:

```
this.switchManagementGenericAdapter =
new SwitchManagementGenericAdapter(
routerManagementUseCase, switchManagementUseCase);
```

To instantiate `SwitchManagementGenericAdapter`, we need to pass references for both the `RouterManagementUseCase` and `SwitchManagementUseCase` use cases.

Now, let's move on and learn how to initialize `NetworkManagementGenericAdapter`.

Initializing NetworkManagementGenericAdapter

For `NetworkManagementGenericAdapter`, we only need to load an implementation for `NetworkManagementUseCase`. Follow these steps to do so:

1. The following code shows how we should use `ServiceLoader` to get a `NetworkManagementUseCase` object:

    ```
    ServiceLoader<NetworkManagementUseCase> load
      erUseCaseNetwork = ServiceLoader.load(NetworkManage
        mentUseCase.class);
    NetworkManagementUseCase networkManagementUseCase =
      loaderUseCaseNetwork.findFirst().get()
    ```

2. Then, we must reuse `RouterManagementOutputPort`, which we loaded previously, to set `NetworkManagementUseCase`:

    ```
    networkManagementUseCase.setOutputPort(routerManage
      mentOutputPort);
    ```

3. Finally, we can initiate `NetworkManagementGenericAdapter`:

    ```
    this.networkManagementGenericAdapter = new NetworkMan
      agementGenericAdapter(switchManagementUseCase, net
        workManagementUseCase);
    ```

    To initiate a new `NetworkManagementGenericAdapter` adapter, we must pass references for the `SwitchManagementUseCase` and `NetworkManagementUseCase` use cases.

This section taught us how to retrieve interface implementations using `ServiceLoader` in conjunction with JPMS service providers. With this technique, we can structure code that only relies on abstractions rather than implementations.

Summary

In this chapter, we started by looking into the motivations and benefits behind the JPMS. We discovered that one of the problems the JPMS solves is that of JAR hell, where it's difficult to control the dependencies that an application should expose and use. The JPMS addresses this problem by closing access to every public type in a module, requiring the developer to explicitly state which packages containing public types should be visible to other modules. Also, the developer should state the modules that a given module depends on in the `module` descriptor.

Next, we discussed the DIP and recognized the use cases, input ports, input adapters, and output adapters as components that we can apply to the DIP. Then, we used JPMS features such as consumers, services, and providers to refactor the topology and inventory system to enable dependency inversion in conjunction with hexagonal architecture components.

By employing the DIP, we created a more supple design, an important characteristic when it comes to building change-tolerant systems. We learned that the JPMS is a Java technology that we can use to implement DIP. Such technology also enables us to provide robust encapsulation by isolating related code into modules. This capability is paramount if we wish to establish and enforce boundaries between the Domain, Application, and Framework hexagons.

In the next chapter, we'll start our journey into the cloud-native world by learning about the Quarkus Framework and how to use it to prepare and optimize a hexagonal system to run in a cloud-native environment.

Questions

Answer the following questions to test your knowledge of this chapter:

1. Which JAR dependency problem does the JPMS aim to solve?
2. Which JPMS directive should we use to enable access to a package containing public types?
3. To declare a dependency on a module, which JPMS directive should we use?
4. When applying dependency inversion on the hexagonal architecture, which components can be regarded as high-level, abstraction, and low-level?

Answers

Here are the answers to this chapter's questions:

1. The JAR hell problem.
2. The exports directive.
3. The requires directive.
4. Input adapters, use cases, and input ports, respectively.

Further reading

- *The Dependency Inversion Principle*, by Robert C. Martin, C++ Report, 1996.

Part 3: Becoming Cloud-Native

In this part, you will integrate the Quarkus framework into a hexagonal application, making it truly modern cloud-native software that's ready to be deployed in cloud environments.

We'll learn how to add Quarkus to our existing topology and inventory system. Then, we'll explore some of the exciting Quarkus features, such as CDI beans, RESTEasy Reactive, and Hibernate Reactive. After combining Quarkus and hexagonal architecture, we'll learn how to dockerize and create Kubernetes objects to deploy our hexagonal application to a Kubernetes cluster.

This part has the following chapters:

- *Chapter 10, Adding Quarkus to a Modularized Hexagonal Application*
- *Chapter 11, Leveraging CDI Beans to Manage Ports and Use Cases*
- *Chapter 12, Using RESTEasy Reactive to Implement Input Adapters*
- *Chapter 13, Persisting Data with Output Adapters and Hibernate Reactive*
- *Chapter 14, Setting Up Dockerfile and Kubernetes Objects for Cloud Deployment*

10

Adding Quarkus to a Modularized Hexagonal Application

This chapter will expand our horizons by exploring the concepts and technologies to turn our hexagonal application into a cloud-native one. To support us in our journey to the cloud, we have Quarkus as the key technology, which is a prominent Java cloud-native framework. To understand Quarkus and learn how to leverage its features to enhance a hexagonal system, we need to revisit some fundamental knowledge related to the inner workings of the **Java Virtual Machine** (**JVM**). By understanding the main JVM characteristics and how they work, we can better understand the problems Quarkus aims to solve.

In this chapter, we'll also conduct a brief tour of Quarkus's main features to get an idea of what we can do with such a fine piece of software. Once we're acquainted with Quarkus, we'll take our first step in transforming our hexagonal system into a cloud-native one. To accomplish that, we'll create a brand-new Java module and configure Quarkus dependencies.

These are the topics that we'll cover in this chapter:

- Revisiting the JVM
- Introducing Quarkus
- Adding Quarkus to a modularized hexagonal application

By the end of this chapter, you'll know how to configure Quarkus to work with a hexagonal application. That's the first step in preparing a system to receive all the cloud-native features that Quarkus has to offer.

Technical requirements

To compile and run the code examples presented in this chapter, you need the latest **Java Standard Edition (SE) Development Kit** and **Maven 3.8** installed on your computer. They are all available for Linux, Mac, and Windows operating systems. You can find the code files for this chapter on GitHub at https://github.com/PacktPublishing/-Designing-Hexagonal-Architecture-with-Java---Second-Edition/tree/main/Chapter10.

Revisiting the JVM

The **Virtual Machine** (**VM**) concept wasn't something new when Java arrived back in 1995. Before that time, many other languages used VMs, although they weren't so popular among developers. Java architects decided to use VMs because they wanted a mechanism to create platform independence to improve developer productivity.

Before elaborating on the VM concept, let's first check what we can run inside a VM for Java. In languages such as C or C++, we compile source code into native code tailored for a specific operating system and CPU architecture. When programming in Java, we compile the source code into bytecode. The JVM understands the instructions contained in bytecode.

The VM idea comes from the concept of running programs in an intermediate or virtual environment sitting atop a real machine. In such an arrangement, the program does not need to communicate directly with the underlying operating system – the program deals only with a VM. The VM then converts bytecode instructions into native-code ones.

We can express one of the JVM's advantages with a well-known Java motto – *write once, run anywhere*. Back in the day, and I think even now, it was very appealing to use a language that allowed you to develop software that, without recompilation, could run on different operating systems and CPU architectures. For other languages such as C++, you'd need to adjust your code for every targeted operating system and CPU architecture, prompting more effort to make your program compatible with different platforms.

In today's world of cloud computing, we have services such as Docker and Kubernetes that make software units more portable than ever. To achieve portability in Java, we have the prerogative to execute the same compiled bytecode into different JVMs running on different operating systems and CPU architectures. Portability is possible because every JVM implementation must comply with the JVM specification, no matter where or how it's implemented.

Conversely, we can use container virtualization to achieve portability by packing the compiled software with its runtime environment and dependencies into a container image. A container engine running on different operating systems and CPU architectures can create containers based on container images.

The JVM's appeal in making portable software at the expense of converting bytecode into native code is no longer attractive when you have faster and cheaper alternatives. Today, you can pack your application – without the need for a JVM and also recompilation – into a Docker image and distribute it across different operating systems and CPU architectures. However, we should not forget how robust and time-tested a piece of software such as the JVM is. We'll return to our discussion on Docker and Kubernetes soon, but for now, let's examine some more interesting JVM characteristics.

Another important JVM aspect is related to memory management. With Java, a developer doesn't need to worry about how the program deals with memory release and allocation. Such responsibility is transferred to the JVM, so the developer can focus more on their program's functional details than on the technical ones. Ask any C++ developer how much fun it is to debug memory leaks on large systems.

The feature responsible for managing memory inside the JVM is called a **garbage collector**. Its purpose is to automatically check when an object is no longer used or referenced so that the program can free the unused memory. A JVM can use algorithms that trace object references and mark for releasing those that no longer reference any object. Different garbage collector algorithms exist, such as the **Concurrent Mark and Sweep** (**CMS**) and the **Garbage First Garbage Collector** (**G1 GC**). Since the JDK7 Update 4, the G1 GC has superseded the CMS due to its emphasis on first identifying and releasing the mostly empty Java object heap regions, making more memory available, and doing it faster than the CMS approach.

Garbage collectors are not required to exist in every JVM implementation, but as long as memory resources remain a constraint in computation, we'll often see JVM implementations with garbage collectors.

JVM is also in charge of the whole life cycle of an application. It all starts with the loading of a Java class file into the VM. When we compile a Java source file, the compiler generates a Java class file containing bytecode. Bytecode is a format recognizable by the JVM. A VM's primary goal is to load and process this bytecode through algorithms and data structures that implement and respect a JVM specification.

The following diagram illustrates what it takes to execute a Java program:

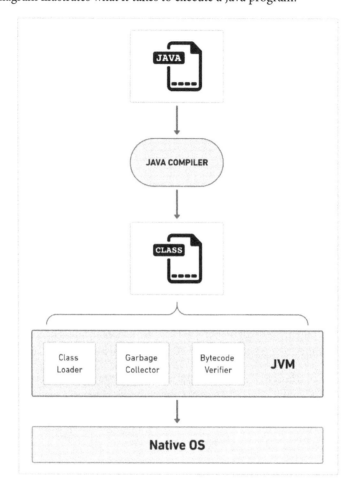

Figure 10.1 – Java compilation and class loading on JVM

It all starts with the Java source code file that is compiled into a Java class file (bytecode) by the Java compiler. This bytecode is read by the JVM and translated into instructions that are understood by the **native OS**.

This bytecode thing has been an object of relentless work for people trying to find faster ways to deal with it.

As time went on, the JVM received good improvements and enhanced techniques that considerably improved the bytecode loading performance. Among these techniques, we can quote **Just-in-Time (JIT)** and **Ahead-of-Time (AOT)** compilations. Let's examine both of them.

Speeding up runtime performance with JIT compilation

JIT compilers arose from the idea that certain program instructions can be optimized for better performance while a program is running. So, to accomplish such optimization, the JIT compiler seeks program instructions with the potential to be optimized. In general, these instructions are the ones most executed by the program.

Because these instructions are executed so often, they consume a significant amount of computer time and resources. Remember that these instructions are in the bytecode format. A traditional compiler would compile all the bytecode into native code before running the program. With a JIT compiler, things are different, as shown in the following diagram:

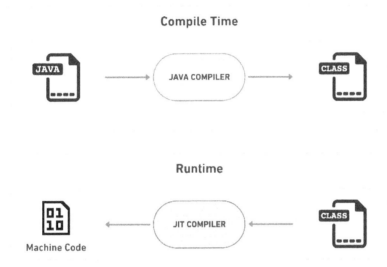

Figure 10.2 – How JIT works

A JIT compiler selects, by using its dynamic optimization algorithms, some parts of the bytecode. Then, it compiles and applies optimizations to these bytecode parts. The result is optimized native code that is tweaked to provide better performance for the system. The term *JIT* is used because the optimizations are made right before the code is executed.

However, there is no such thing as a free lunch when using JIT compilers. One of the most well-known drawbacks of JIT compilers is the increased startup time of an application because of the initial optimizations a JIT compiler does before running the program. In order to overcome this startup problem, there is another technique called AOT compilation. Various cloud-native frameworks, including Quarkus, have used this technique. Let's see how AOT compilation works.

Improving startup time with AOT compilation

AOT is so appealing on the Java scene because traditional Java systems – mainly those based on enterprise application servers such as **JBoss** and **WebLogic** – take too much time to initiate. In addition to slower startup times, we have to consider the amount of computer power those application servers consume. These characteristics are a deal-breaker for anyone who wants to migrate Java workloads to the cloud, where instances and Kubernetes Pods are brought up and down frantically. So, by employing AOT in Java, we give up the cross-platform capability provided by the JVM and its bytecode for a better performance provided by AOT and its native code. The cross-platform problem is mitigated to some extent with the usage of container technologies such as Docker and Kubernetes.

Here, we have a representation showing how straightforward the AOT compilation process is to transform Java bytecode into **machine code**:

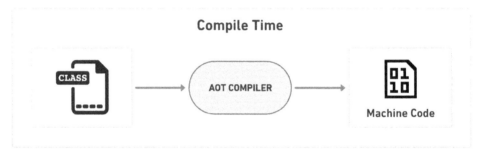

Figure 10.3 – How AOT works

Not everything is an advantage with AOT in Java. An AOT compiler spends more time generating a native binary than a Java compiler needs to create bytecode classes. So, AOT compilation can have a considerable impact on **Continuos Integration** (**CI**) pipelines. Also, the developer needs to do some additional work to get things working properly to use reflection. **GraalVM** is the AOT compiler used to provide a native binary for Java and other JVM-based languages.

With Quarkus, we have the prerogative to create applications using either JIT or AOT compilation methods. It's up to us to decide which technique suits our needs better.

In this section, we gained some background knowledge about the inner workings of the JVM and how it tries to improve bytecode loading with JIT and AOT compilation. Such knowledge is important to understand how Quarkus works under the hood and achieves considerable performance improvements.

Now that we are acquainted with some JVM fundamentals and essential compilation techniques, let's dive in and learn more about Quarkus' main features.

Introducing Quarkus

If you develop enterprise Java applications, you have already worked with Spring Boot. Time-tested and widely used in the industry, Spring Boot is a robust piece of software with a vibrant community. Its libraries increase developed productivity by providing out-of-the-box solutions for security, persistence, APIs, and many more things that a typical enterprise application requires. You may wonder why this book does not discuss Spring Boot but Quarkus. There are two reasons. First, more material is available covering Spring Boot than Quarkus, which is understandable, as Spring Boot has been around longer and has a bigger community. The second reason is that Quarkus was built with cloud-native development at its core, while Spring Boot has been adapted to it. And since this book focuses on cloud-native development with hexagonal architecture, Quarkus was chosen because it is a cloud-first framework.

Focused on performance, Quarkus comes with built-in support for native executables based on GraalVM, making it possible to achieve swift startup times.

To attract developers, it offers valuable things such as live development, a feature that enhances productivity by avoiding the need to restart an application whenever something changes in your code.

Targeting cloud-native environments, Quarkus comes equipped with the proper tooling, allowing you to deal with constraints and leverage the benefits that come when developing software to run on container-based environments, such as Kubernetes.

Borrowing good ideas from enterprise development, Quarkus is built on top of well-established standards such as the **Contexts and Dependency Injection** (**CDI**) framework, the **Jakarta Persistence API** (**JPA**) specification with Hibernate ORM implementation, and the **Jakarta RESTful Web Services** (**JAX-RS**) specification implemented by RESTEasy. For those immersed in the Java **Enterprise Edition** (**EE**) world, this means the learning curve to master Quarkus is shallow because much of their already acquired enterprise development knowledge can be reused to develop Quarkus applications.

Created by Red Hat, Quarkus sets itself apart from its competitors by being a software development framework designed from scratch to deal with cloud technologies. Contrary to other more aged frameworks that bring boilerplate code and features from an older era, Quarkus presents itself as a fresh and modern piece of software.

Built upon other well-established open source projects, Quarkus is the cloud-native framework we'll use to prepare our hexagonal system for the cloud. Before that, though, we'll explore some of the main features this framework provides. Let's get started by looking first at how to create REST endpoints with Quarkus.

Creating REST endpoints with JAX-RS

It's very straightforward to create REST endpoints using Quarkus. In order to do so, the framework relies on a JAX-RS implementation called RESTEasy. This implementation is available in the following Maven dependency:

```
<dependency>
    <groupId>io.quarkus</groupId>
    <artifactId>quarkus-resteasy</artifactId>
</dependency>
```

Look at the following example, which shows how to use RESTEasy to create REST services:

```
package dev.davivieira.bootstrap.samples;

import javax.ws.rs.GET;
import javax.ws.rs.Path;
import javax.ws.rs.Produces;
import javax.ws.rs.core.MediaType;

@Path("/app")
public class RestExample {

    @GET
    @Path("/simple-rest")
    @Produces(MediaType.TEXT_PLAIN)
    public String simpleRest() {
        return "This REST endpoint is provided by Quarkus";
    }
}
```

We set the endpoint address with the `@Path` annotation. With `@GET`, we set the HTTP method supported by that endpoint. With `@Produces`, we define the return type for the request.

In this same `RestExample` class, we can inject dependencies to be used together with the REST endpoints. Let's see how to accomplish this.

Employing dependency injection with Quarkus DI

Quarkus has its own dependency injection mechanism based on **Quarkus ArC**, which, in turn, comes from the CDI specification, which has its roots back in **Java EE 6**. With CDI, we no longer need to control the creation and life cycle of dependency objects we provide to a system. Without a dependency injection framework, you have to create objects this way:

```
BeanExample beanExample = new BeanExample();
```

When using CDI, you just have to annotate the `class` attribute with the `@Inject` annotation, like this:

```
@Inject
BeanExample beanExample
```

For the `@Inject` annotation to work, we first need to declare the dependency as a managed bean. Take a look at the example here:

```
package dev.davivieira.bootstrap.samples;

import javax.enterprise.context.ApplicationScoped;
import javax.validation.Valid;

@ApplicationScoped
public class BeanExample {
    public String simpleBean() {
        return "This is a simple bean";
    }
}
```

The `@ApplicationScoped` annotation states that this bean will be available as long as the application is not terminated. Also, this bean is accessible from different requests and calls across the entire system. Let's update our `RestExample` to inject this bean, as follows:

```
package dev.davivieira.bootstrap.samples;

import javax.inject.Inject;
import javax.ws.rs.GET;
import javax.ws.rs.Path;
import javax.ws.rs.Produces;
import javax.ws.rs.core.MediaType;

@Path("/app")
public class RestExample {

    @Inject
    BeanExample beanExample;

    /** Code omitted **/

    @GET
    @Path("/simple-bean")
    @Produces(MediaType.TEXT_PLAIN)
    public String simpleBean() {
        return beanExample.simpleBean();
```

```
        }
    }
```

Right at the top, we inject the `BeanExample` dependency with the `@Inject` annotation. Then, we call the `simpleBean` method from the injected `BeanExample` dependency.

Next, let's see how to validate objects that are created when the system receives an HTTP request.

Validating objects

We learned how to create REST endpoints and also how to inject dependencies in the application. *But how about object validation? How can we ensure that the data provided by a given request is valid?* Quarkus can help us in that matter. The Quarkus validation mechanism is available in the following Maven dependency:

```
<dependency>
    <groupId>io.quarkus</groupId>
    <artifactId>quarkus-hibernate-validator</artifactId>
</dependency>
```

The Quarkus validation mechanism is based on **Hibernate Validator**.

To see how it works, let's first create a sample object containing the fields we expect in a request, as follows:

```
package dev.davivieira.bootstrap.samples;

import javax.validation.constraints.Min;
import javax.validation.constraints.NotBlank;

public class SampleObject {
    @NotBlank(message = "The field cannot be empty")
    public String field;

    @Min(message = "The minimum value is 10", value = 10)
    public int value;
}
```

With the `@NotBlank` annotation, we state that the `field` variable should never be empty. Then, by using the `@Min` annotation, we ensure that the `value` variable should always contain a number equal to or higher than `10`. Let's return to the `RestExample` class and create a new REST endpoint to validate the request, as follows:

```
@POST
@Path("/request-validation")
```

```
@Produces(MediaType.APPLICATION_JSON)
@Consumes(MediaType.APPLICATION_JSON)
public Result validation(@Valid SampleObject sampleObject) {
    try {
        return new Result("The request data is valid!");
    } catch (ConstraintViolationException e) {
        return new Result(e.getConstraintViolations());
    }
}
```

When `ConstraintViolationException` is caught, the system returns an `HTTP 400 Bad Request` failure response.

Note the `@Valid` annotation just before `SampleObject`. By using that annotation, we trigger a validation check whenever a request hits the `/app/request-validation` endpoint. Check out the following results:

```
$ curl -H "Content-Type: application/json"  -d '{"field": "", "value":
10}' localhost:8080/app/request-validation | jq
{
  "exception": null,
  "propertyViolations": [],
  "classViolations": [],
  "parameterViolations": [
    {
      "constraintType": "PARAMETER",
      "path": "validation.arg0.field",
      "message": "The field cannot be empty",
      "value": ""
    }
  ],
  "returnValueViolations": []
}
```

In the previous POST request, the field is empty, which results in a failure response with an `HTTP 400 Bad Request` code.

In the next request, we set `value` to a number less than 10, as follows:

```
$ curl -s -H "Content-Type: application/json"  -d '{"field": "test",
"value": 9}' localhost:8080/app/request-validation | jq
{
  "exception": null,
  "propertyViolations": [],
  "classViolations": [],
  "parameterViolations": [
```

```
    {
      "constraintType": "PARAMETER",
      "path": "validation.arg0.value",
      "message": "The minimum value is 10",
      "value": "9"
    }
  ],
  "returnValueViolations": []
}
```

Again, the constraint was violated, and the result showed that the validation had failed. The failure was caused because we sent the number 9, and the minimum value accepted is 10.

Here is a proper request with valid data:

```
$ curl -s -H "Content-Type: application/json"  -d '{"field": "test",
"value": 10}' localhost:8080/app/request-validation | jq
{
  "message": "The request data is valid!",
  "success": true
}
```

The field parameter is not null, nor is value less than 10. So, the request returns a valid response.

Configuring a data source and using Hibernate ORM

Quarkus allows you to connect to a data source in two ways. The first and traditional way is based on a JDBC connection. To connect using this method, you need the agroal library and the JDBC driver of the specific database type you want to connect. The second – and reactive – way allows you to treat the database connection like a stream of data. For that mode, you need Vert.x reactive drivers.

In the following steps, we'll set up a data source connection using the traditional JDBC method:

1. To get started, we need the following dependencies:

    ```
    <dependency>
      <groupId>io.quarkus</groupId>
      <artifactId>quarkus-agroal</artifactId>
    </dependency>
    <dependency>
      <groupId>io.quarkus</groupId>
      <artifactId>quarkus-jdbc-h2</artifactId>
    </dependency>
    <dependency>
      <groupId>io.quarkus</groupId>
    ```

```
<artifactId>quarkus-hibernate-orm</artifactId>
</dependency>
```

`quarkus-hibernate-orm` refers to the Hibernate ORM implementation of JPA. It is this dependency that provides the capability to map Java objects to database entities.

2. Next, we need to configure the data source settings in the `application.properties` file, as follows:

```
quarkus.datasource.db-kind=h2
quarkus.datasource.jdbc.url=jdbc:h2:mem:de
    fault;DB_CLOSE_DELAY=-1
quarkus.hibernate-orm.dialect=org.hibernate.dia
    lect.H2Dialect
quarkus.hibernate-orm.database.generation=drop-and-
    create
```

`quarkus.datasource.db-kind` is optional, but we use that to emphasize that the application uses an H2 in-memory database. We use `quarkus.datasource.jdbc.url` to inform the connection string. The `quarkus.hibernate-orm.dialect` option sets the dialect used for the data source communication, and `quarkus.hibernate-orm.database.generation=drop-and-create` forces the creation of a database structure at startup.

If there is an `import.sql` file in `classpath`, this `drop-and-create` option enables the use of that file to load data into the database. Something very interesting about this `drop-and-create` option is that every change on application entities or in the `import.sql` file is picked automatically and applied to the database without restarting the system. For this to work, a system needs to run in live development mode.

Let's create a `SampleEntity` class to persist in the database, as follows:

```
@Entity
@NamedQuery(name = "SampleEntity.findAll",
        query = "SELECT f FROM SampleEntity f ORDER BY
          f.field",
        hints = @QueryHint(name =
          "org.hibernate.cacheable",
        value = "true") )
public class SampleEntity {

    @Id
    @GeneratedValue(strategy = GenerationType.AUTO)
    private Long id;

    @Getter
    @Setter
```

```
    private String field;

    @Getter
    @Setter
    private int value;
}
```

The `SampleEntity` class corresponds to the `SampleObject` class we created earlier. The requirement to use the `SampleEntity` class as a database entity is to annotate it with the `@Entity` annotation. Following that annotation, we have `@NamedQuery`, which we'll use later to retrieve all entities from the database. To automatically generate ID values, we will use `GenerationType.AUTO`. The `field` and `value` variables from `SampleEntity` are mapped to the same variables that exist in the `SampleObject` class.

Let's now create a new bean called `PersistenceExample` to assist us in creating and retrieving database entities. Here's how to do this:

```
package dev.davivieira.bootstrap.samples;

import javax.enterprise.context.ApplicationScoped;
import javax.inject.Inject;
import javax.persistence.EntityManager;
import javax.transaction.Transactional;
import java.util.List;

@ApplicationScoped
public class PersistenceExample {

    @Inject
    EntityManager em;
    /** Code omitted **/
}
```

To interact with the database, the first thing we have to do is to inject `EntityManager`. Quarkus will take care of retrieving an `EntityManager` object with all the database connection settings we provided in the `application.properties` file. Continuing the `PersistenceExample` implementation, let's create a method to persist entities, as follows:

```
@Transactional
public String createEntity(SampleObject sampleObject) {
    SampleEntity sampleEntity = new SampleEntity();
    sampleEntity.setField(sampleObject.field);
    sampleEntity.setValue(sampleObject.value);
    em.persist(sampleEntity);
```

```
        return "Entity with field "+sampleObject.field+"
          created!";
}
```

The `createEntity` method persists an entity in the database.

The `@Transactional` annotation above the method declaration will make the `EntityManager` object flush the transaction once the database operation is committed. This is illustrated in the following code snippet:

```
@Transactional
public List<SampleEntity> getAllEntities(){
    return em.createNamedQuery(
    "SampleEntity.findAll", SampleEntity.class)
            .getResultList();
}
```

The `getAllEntities` method retrieves all entities from the database.

Now, let's return to `RestExample` to create REST endpoints to trigger the creation and retrieval of database entities. We will start by injecting `PersistenceExample` so that we can use this bean to begin operations on the database. The code is illustrated in the following snippet:

```
@Inject
PersistenceExample persistenceExample;
```

Then, we create a `/create-entity` endpoint, as follows:

```
@POST
@Path("/create-entity")
@Produces(MediaType.TEXT_PLAIN)
@Consumes(MediaType.APPLICATION_JSON)
public String persistData(@Valid SampleObject sampleObject) {
    return persistenceExample.createEntity(sampleObject);
}
```

We pass `SampleObject` as the parameter. This object represents the body of the POST request.

Finally, we create a `/get-all-entities` endpoint to retrieve all entities from the database, as follows:

```
@GET
@Path("/get-all-entities")
public List<SampleEntity> retrieveAllEntities() {
    return persistenceExample.getAllEntities();
}
```

The `retrieveAllEntities` method calls on `getAllEntities` from the `PersistenceExample` bean. The result is a list of `SampleEntity` objects.

Let's see what we get when we hit `/create-entity` to create a new entity. You can see the output here:

```
$ curl -s -H "Content-Type: application/json"  -d '{"field": "item-a",
"value": 10}' localhost:8080/app/create-entity
Entity with field item-a created!
$ curl -s -H "Content-Type: application/json"  -d '{"field": "item-b",
"value": 20}' localhost:8080/app/create-entity
Entity with field item-b created!
```

To see the entities we've created, we send a request to `/get-all-entities`, as follows:

```
$ curl -s localhost:8080/app/get-all-entities | jq
[
  {
    "field": "item-a",
    "value": 10
  },
  {
    "field": "item-b",
    "value": 20
  }
]
```

As expected, we received all the entities we persisted previously in the database in a JSON format.

Quarkus is a vast and continuously growing framework that's absorbing more and more capabilities. The features we have seen cover some of the basic things required to develop modern applications.

We'll be able to use RESTEasy when reimplementing input adapters to support REST on our hexagonal application. Quarkus DI will enable us to better manage the life cycle of objects from the Framework and Application hexagons. The Quarkus validation mechanisms will contribute to validating the data entering the hexagonal system. The data source configuration and Hibernate ORM will support the restructuring of output adapters.

In this section, we learned how to tweak the `application.properties` file to configure a database connection on Quarkus, and we briefly explored Hibernate's ORM capabilities that help map Java classes to database entities. We'll explore this subject further in *Chapter 13, Persisting Data with Output Adapters and Hibernate Reactive*.

Let's now see how to integrate Quarkus into the hexagonal system.

Adding Quarkus to a modularized hexagonal application

To recap, we structured the topology and inventory system in three modularized hexagons: **Domain**, **Application**, and **Framework**. A question that may arise is, *which module should be responsible for starting the Quarkus engine?* Well, to avoid blurring the responsibilities of each module in the topology and inventory system, we'll create a dedicated module whose sole purpose is to aggregate the other hexagonal system modules and bootstrap the Quarkus engine. We will name this new module **Bootstrap**, as illustrated in the following diagram:

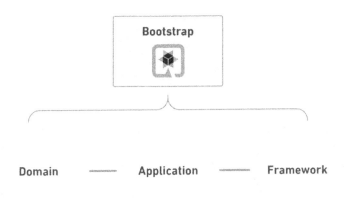

Figure 10.4 – The Bootstrap aggregator module

The `bootstrap` module is an aggregator module that provides, from one side, the dependencies required to initialize Quarkus and, from the other side, the `hexagonal` module dependencies for use in conjunction with Quarkus.

Let's create this new `bootstrap` module in the topology and inventory system, as follows:

1. In the Maven root project of the topology and inventory system, you can execute the following Maven command to create this `bootstrap` module:

```
mvn archetype:generate \
-DarchetypeGroupId=de.rieckpil.archetypes  \
-DarchetypeArtifactId=testing-toolkit \
-DarchetypeVersion=1.0.0 \
-DgroupId=dev.davivieira \
-DartifactId=bootstrap \
-Dversion=1.0-SNAPSHOT \
-Dpackage=dev.davivieira.topologyinventory.bootstrap \
-DinteractiveMode=false
```

This Maven command creates a basic directory structure for the `bootstrap` module. We set `artifactId` to `bootstrap` and `groupId` to `dev.davivieira`, as this module is part of the same Maven project that holds the modules for other topology and inventory system hexagons. The final high-level structure should be similar to the one shown here:

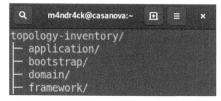

Figure 10.5 – The topology and inventory high-level directory structure

2. Next, we need to set up Quarkus dependencies in the project's root `pom.xml` file, as follows:

```
<dependencyManagement>
  <dependencies>
    <dependency>
      <groupId>io.quarkus</groupId>
      <artifactId>quarkus-universe-bom</artifactId>
      <version>${quarkus.platform.version}</version>
      <type>pom</type>
      <scope>import</scope>
    </dependency>
</dependencyManagement>
```

The `quarkus-universe-bom` dependency makes all the Quarkus extensions available.

Because we're working with a multi-module application, we need to configure Quarkus to discover CDI beans in different modules.

3. So, we need to configure `jandex-maven-plugin` in the Maven project's root `pom.xml` file, as follows:

```
<plugin>
  <groupId>org.jboss.jandex</groupId>
  <artifactId>jandex-maven-plugin</artifactId>
  <version>${jandex.version}</version>
  <executions>
    <execution>
      <id>make-index</id>
      <goals>
        <goal>jandex</goal>
      </goals>
    </execution>
  </executions>
</plugin>
```

Without the preceding plugin, we'd have a problem setting up and using CDI beans on both the Framework and Application hexagons.

4. Now comes the most crucial part – the configuration of `quarkus-maven-plugin`. To make the `bootstrap` module the one that will start the Quarkus engine, we need to configure `quarkus-maven-plugin` in that module properly.

    Here is how we should configure `quarkus-maven-plugin` on `bootstrap/pom.xml`:

    ```
    <build>
      <plugins>
        <plugin>
          <groupId>io.quarkus</groupId>
          <artifactId>quarkus-maven-plugin</artifactId>
          <version>${quarkus-plugin.version}</version>
          <extensions>true</extensions>
          <executions>
            <execution>
              <goals>
                <goal>build</goal>
                <goal>generate-code</goal>
                <goal>generate-code-tests</goal>
              </goals>
            </execution>
          </executions>
        </plugin>
      </plugins>
    </build>
    ```

    The important part here is the line containing `<goal>build</goal>`. By setting this build goal for the `bootstrap` module, we make this module responsible for starting the Quarkus engine.

5. Next, we need to add the Maven dependencies from the topology and inventory system's hexagons. We do that in the `bootstrap/pom.xml` file, as follows:

    ```
    <dependency>
      <groupId>dev.davivieira</groupId>
      <artifactId>domain</artifactId>
    </dependency>
    <dependency>
      <groupId>dev.davivieira</groupId>
      <artifactId>application</artifactId>
    </dependency>
    <dependency>
      <groupId>dev.davivieira</groupId>
    ```

```
    <artifactId>framework</artifactId>
</dependency>
```

6. And finally, we create a `module-info.java` Java module descriptor with the `requires` directives for Quarkus and the topology and inventory hexagon modules, as follows:

```
module dev.davivieira.bootstrap {
    requires quarkus.core;
    requires domain;
    requires application;
    requires framework;
}
```

To aggregate the three hexagon modules into one deployment unit, we'll configure Quarkus to generate an uber `.jar` file. This kind of JAR groups up all dependencies required to run an application in one single JAR. To accomplish that, we need to set the following configuration in the project's root `pom.xml` file:

```
<quarkus.package.type>uber-jar</quarkus.package.type>
```

Then, we're ready to compile the application by running the following Maven command:

mvn clean package

This Maven command will compile the entire application and create an uber `.jar` file that we can use to start the application by executing the following command:

java -jar bootstrap/target/bootstrap-1.0-SNAPSHOT-runner.jar

Note that the artifact we use is generated from the `bootstrap` module, which aggregates all the other modules. The following screenshot shows us what a running Quarkus application should look like:

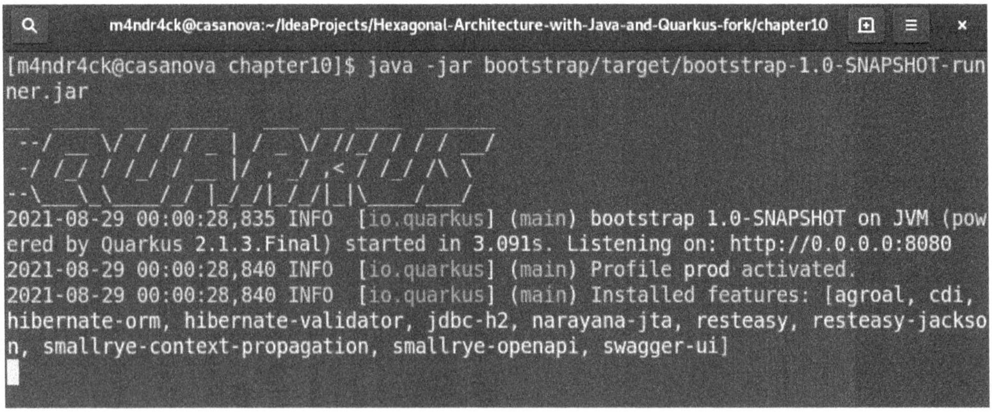

Figure 10.6 – A running Quarkus application

The application seen in the preceding screenshot is running in the `prod` profile. In that profile, some features are deactivated for security purposes. We can also see the installed features running in the application. These features are activated when we add Quarkus extension dependencies on `pom.xml`.

The `bootstrap` module acts as a bridge, allowing us to connect the external development framework to the hexagon modules that comprise the hexagonal system. For the topology and inventory application, we used Quarkus, but we could also use other development frameworks. We cannot say that we are totally decoupling the system logic from the development framework; after all, there will be some system logic that benefits from framework features. However, the approach presented in this chapter shows that part of that system can be developed first and the development framework introduced later.

Summary

In this chapter, we revisited the fundamentals of JVM, assessing some of its features related to JIT compilation and AOT compilation. We learned that JIT improves runtime performance, whereas AOT helps boost application startup time, which proves to be an essential feature for frameworks targeting cloud environments, as in this case with Quarkus.

After getting acquainted with some JVM concepts, we moved on to learn about Quarkus and some important features it offers. Finally, we integrated Quarkus into our already-developed hexagonal system topology and inventory. In order to accomplish such an integration, we created a new `bootstrap` module to act as a bridge between the hexagonal system modules and the development framework. We now know what it takes to integrate Quarkus into a modularized hexagonal application.

In the next chapter, we dive deeper into the integration between Quarkus and hexagonal architecture. We will learn how to refactor use cases and ports from the Application hexagon to leverage Quarkus DI features.

Questions

1. What is the advantage of using the JIT compilation?

2. Which benefit do we get by using the AOT compilation?

3. Quarkus is a development framework specially designed for which kind of environment?

4. What is the role of the `bootstrap` module in hexagonal architecture?

Answers

1. JIT improves the runtime performance of an application.

2. AOT boosts the startup time of an application.

3. Quarkus was designed to develop applications for cloud environments.

4. Its role is to integrate the Quarkus framework with the hexagonal system.

11

Leveraging CDI Beans to Manage Ports and Use Cases

Quarkus provides its own dependency injection solution called **Quarkus DI**. It stems from the **Contexts and Dependency Injection (CDI)** for **Java 2.0** specification. We employ CDI to delegate the responsibility of providing object instances to an external dependency and managing their life cycle across an application. Several dependency injection solutions on the market take such responsibility. Quarkus DI is one of them.

The value of using a dependency injection mechanism is that we no longer need to worry about how and when to provide an object instance. A dependency injection solution enables us to automatically create and provide objects as dependencies in classes that depend on those objects, generally using annotation attributes.

In the context of hexagonal architecture, the Framework and Application hexagons are good candidates to leverage the benefits a CDI solution can provide. Instead of using constructors that inject dependencies using concrete classes, we can use the CDI discovery mechanisms to automatically look up interface implementations and provide them to the application.

In this chapter, we'll learn how to enhance the provisioning of ports and use cases by turning them into beans. We'll explore bean scopes and their life cycles and understand how and when to use the available bean scopes. Once we know about the CDI fundamentals, we'll learn how to apply them to a hexagonal system.

The following topics will be covered in this chapter:

- Learning about Quarkus DI
- Transforming ports, use cases, and adapters into CDI beans
- Testing use cases with Quarkus and Cucumber

By the end of this chapter, you'll know how to integrate Quarkus DI into a hexagonal application by transforming use cases and ports into managed beans that can be injected across the hexagonal system. You'll also know how to test use cases by using Quarkus in conjunction with Cucumber.

Technical requirements

To compile and run the code examples presented in this chapter, you will need the latest **Java SE Development Kit** and **Maven 3.8** installed on your computer. They are available for Linux, Mac, and Windows operating systems.

You can find the code files for this chapter on GitHub at `https://github.com/ PacktPublishing/-Designing-Hexagonal-Architecture-with-Java---Second- Edition/tree/main/Chapter11`.

Learning about Quarkus DI

Quarkus DI is the dependency injection solution provided by the Quarkus framework. This solution, also called **ArC**, is based on the CDI for the **Java 2.0 specification**. Quarkus DI does not completely implement such a specification. Instead, it provides some customized and changed implementations that are more inclined toward the Quarkus project's goals. However, these changes are more visible when you go deeper into what the Quarkus DI provides. For those working only with the basics and most recurrent features described in the CDI for Java 2.0 specification, the Quarkus DI experience is similar to other CDI implementations.

The advantage we get by using Quarkus DI or any dependency injection solution is that we can focus more on the business aspects of the software we're developing, rather than on the plumbing activities related to the provisioning and life cycle control of the objects that the application needs to provide its features. To enable such an advantage, Quarkus DI deals with so-called beans.

Working with beans

Beans are special kinds of objects we can use to inject dependencies or that act as dependencies themselves to be injected into other beans. This injection activity takes place in a container-managed environment. This environment is nothing more than the runtime environment in which the application runs.

Beans have a context that influences when and how their instance objects are created. The following are the main contexts that are supported by Quarkus DI:

- `ApplicationScoped`: A bean marked with such a context is available to the entire application. Only one bean instance is created and shared across all system areas that inject this bean. Another important aspect is that `ApplicationScoped` beans are lazily loaded. This means that the bean instance is created only when a bean's method is called for the first time. Take a look at this example:

```
@ApplicationScoped
class MyBean {

    public String name = "Test Bean";

    public String getName(){
        return name;
    }
}

class Consumer {

    @Inject
    MyBean myBean;

    public String getName() {
        return myBean.getName();
    }
}
```

The `MyBean` class is available not only to the `Consumer` class but also to other classes that inject the bean. The bean instance will be created only once when `myBean.getName()` is called for the first time.

- `Singleton`: Similar to `ApplicationScoped` beans, for `Singleton` beans, only one bean object is created and shared across the system. The only difference, though, is that `Singleton` beans are eagerly loaded. This means that once the system is started, the `Singleton` bean instance is started as well. Here is the code that exemplifies this:

```
@Singleton
class EagerBean { ... }

class Consumer {

    @Inject
    EagerBean eagerBean;
}
```

The `EagerBean` object will be created during the system's initialization.

- RequestScoped: We usually mark a bean as `RequestScope` when we want to make that bean available only for as long as the request associated with that bean lives. The following is an example of how we can use `RequestScope`:

```
@RequestScoped
class RequestData {

    public String getResponse(){
        return "string response";
    }
}

@Path("/")
class Consumer {

    @Inject
    RequestData requestData;

    @GET
    @Path("/request")
    public String loadRequest(){
        return requestData.getResponse();
    }
}
```

Every time a request arrives at `/request`, a new `RequestData` bean object will be created and destroyed once the request has finished.

- Dependent: Beans marked as `Dependent` have their scope restricted to places where they are used. So, `Dependent` beans are not shared across other beans in the system. Also, their life cycle is the same as the one defined in the bean injecting them. For example, if you inject a `Dependent`-annotated bean into a `RequestScoped` bean, the former bean uses the latter's scope:

```
@Dependent
class DependentBean { ... }

@ApplicationScoped
class ConsumerApplication {

    @Inject
    DependentBean dependentBean;
}
```

```
@RequestScoped
class ConsumerRequest {

    @Inject
    DependentBean dependentBean;
}
```

The DependentBean class will become ApplicationScoped when injected into ConsumerApplication and RequestScoped into ConsumerRequest.

- SessionScoped: We use this scope to share the bean context between all the requests of the same HTTP session. We need the quarkus-undertow extension to enable SessionScoped on Quarkus:

```
@SessionScoped
class SessionBean implements Serializable {
    public String getSessionData(){
        return "sessionData";
    }
}

@Path("/")
class Consumer {

    @Inject
    SessionBean sessionBean;

    @GET
    @Path("/sessionData")
    public String test(){
        return sessionBean.getSessionData();
    }
}
```

In the preceding example, a SessionBean instance will be created after the first request is sent to /sessionData. This same instance will be available for other requests coming from the same session.

To summarize, Quarkus offers the following bean scopes: ApplicationScoped, RequestScoped, Singleton, Dependent, and SessionScoped. For stateless applications, most of the time, you may only need ApplicationScoped and RequestScoped. By understanding how these scopes work, we can select them according to our system needs.

Now that we know about the advantages of Quarkus DI and the basics of how it works, let's learn how to employ dependency injection techniques with the ports and use cases from the hexagonal architecture.

Transforming ports, use cases, and adapters into CDI beans

When designing the Application hexagon for the topology and inventory system, we defined the use cases as interfaces and input ports as their implementations. We also defined output ports as interfaces and output adapters as their implementations in the Framework hexagon. In this section, we'll refactor components from both the Application and Framework hexagons to enable the usage of dependency injection with Quarkus DI.

The first step to working with Quarkus DI is to add the following Maven dependency to the project's root `pom.xml`:

```
<dependency>
  <groupId>io.quarkus</groupId>
  <artifactId>quarkus-resteasy</artifactId>
</dependency>
```

In addition to the RESTEasy libraries, this `quarkus-resteasy` library also provides the required libraries to work with Quarkus DI.

Let's start our refactoring efforts with the classes and interfaces related to router management.

Implementing CDI for router management objects

When developing the topology and inventory system, we defined a set of ports, use cases, and adapters to manage router-related operations. We'll walk through the required changes to enable dependency injection in such operations:

1. We start by transforming the `RouterManagementH2Adapter` output adapter into a managed bean:

    ```
    import jakarta.enterprise.context.ApplicationScoped;

    @ApplicationScoped
    public class RouterManagementH2Adapter implements
      RouterManagementOutputPort {
        @PersistenceContext
        private EntityManager em;
      /** Code omitted **/
          private void setUpH2Database() {
          EntityManagerFactory entityManagerFactory =
          Persistence.createEntityManagerFactory(
            "inventory");
          EntityManager em =
    ```

```
        entityManagerFactory.createEntityManager();
        this.em = em;
    }
}
```

We turn this class into a managed bean by putting the @ApplicationScoped annotation on top of the RouterManagementH2Adapter class. Note the EntityManager attribute – we can use dependency injection on that attribute as well. We'll do that in *Chapter 13*, *Persisting Data with Output Adapters and Hibernate Reactive*, but we won't touch on it for now.

2. Before changing the RouterManagementUseCase interface and its implementation, RouterManagementInputPort, let's analyze some aspects of the current implementation:

```
public interface RouterManagementUseCase {

    void setOutputPort(
    RouterManagementOutputPort
      routerManagementOutputPort);
    /** Code omitted **/
}
```

We defined the setOutputPort method to receive and set an instance type of RouterManagementOutputPort, which is fulfilled by a RouterManagementH2Adapter output adapter. As we'll no longer need to explicitly provide this output adapter object (because Quarkus DI will inject it), we can remove the setOutputPort method from the RouterManagementUseCase interface.

The following code demonstrates how RouterManagementInputPort is implemented without Quarkus DI:

```
@NoArgsConstructor
public class RouterManagementInputPort implements
  RouterManagementUseCase {

    private RouterManagementOutputPort
    routerManagementOutputPort;

    @Override
    public void setOutputPort(
    RouterManagementOutputPort
      routerManagementOutputPort) {
        this.routerManagementOutputPort =
        routerManagementOutputPort;
    }
    /** Code omitted **/
}
```

To provide an object of the `RouterManagementOutputPort` type, we need to use the previously mentioned `setOutputPort` method. After implementing Quarkus DI, this will no longer be necessary, as we'll see in the next step.

3. This is what `RouterManagementOutputPort` should look like after implementing Quarkus DI:

    ```
    import jakarta.enterprise.context.ApplicationScoped;
    import jakarta.inject.Inject;

    @ApplicationScoped
    public class RouterManagementInputPort implements
      RouterManagementUseCase {

        @Inject
        RouterManagementOutputPort
          routerManagementOutputPort;
        /** Code omitted **/
    }
    ```

    First, we add `ApplicationScoped` on top of `RouterManagementInputPort` to enable it to be injected into other system parts. Then, by using the `@Inject` annotation, we inject `RouterManagementOutputPort`. We don't need to refer to the output adapter's implementation. Quarkus DI will find a proper implementation for this output port interface, which happens to be the `RouterManagementH2Adapter` output adapter that we turned into a managed bean earlier.

4. Finally, we must update the `RouterManagementGenericAdapter` input adapter:

    ```
    @ApplicationScoped
    public class RouterManagementGenericAdapter {

        @Inject
        private RouterManagementUseCase
          routerManagementUseCase;
        /** Code omitted **/
    }
    ```

    Instead of initializing `RouterManagementUseCase` using a constructor, we must provide the dependency through the `@Inject` annotation. At runtime, Quarkus DI will create and assign a `RouterManagementInputPort` object to that use case reference.

That's it for the changes we must make to the classes and interfaces related to router management. Now, let's learn what we need to change regarding the classes and interfaces for switch management.

Implementing CDI for switch management objects

In this section, we'll follow a similar path to the one we followed when we refactored the ports, use cases, and adapters related to router management:

1. We start by transforming the `SwitchManagementH2Adapter` output adapter into a managed bean:

    ```
    import jakarta.enterprise.context.ApplicationScoped;

    @ApplicationScoped
    public class SwitchManagementH2Adapter implements
      SwitchManagementOutputPort {

        @PersistenceContext
        private EntityManager em;
        /** Code omitted **/
    }
    ```

    The `SwitchManagementH2Adapter` adapter also makes use of `EntityManager`. We won't modify how the `EntityManager` object is provided, but in *Chapter 13*, *Persisting Data with Output Adapters and Hibernate Reactive*, we will change it to use dependency injection.

2. We changed the definition of the `SwitchManagementUseCase` interface in *Chapter 9*, *Applying Dependency Inversion with Java Modules*, and defined the `setOutputPort` method:

    ```
    public interface SwitchManagementUseCase {

        void setOutputPort(
        SwitchManagementOutputPort
          switchManagementOutputPort)
    /** Code omitted **/
    }
    ```

    As Quarkus DI will provide a proper `SwitchManagementOutputPort` instance, we'll no longer need this `setOutputPort` method, so we can remove it.

3. The following code shows how `SwitchManagementInputPort` is implemented without dependency injection:

    ```
    @NoArgsConstructor
    public class SwitchManagementInputPort implements
      SwitchManagementUseCase {

        private SwitchManagementOutputPort
        switchManagementOutputPort;

        @Override
    ```

```
public void setOutputPort(
SwitchManagementOutputPort
  switchManagementOutputPort) {
    this.switchManagementOutputPort =
    switchManagementOutputPort;
}
/** Code omitted **/
}
```

We call the `setOutputPort` method to initialize a `SwitchManagementOutputPort` object. When using dependency injection techniques, there is no need to explicitly instantiate or initialize objects.

4. The following is what `SwitchManagementInputPort` should look like after implementing dependency injection:

```
import jakarta.enterprise.context.ApplicationScoped;
import jakarta.inject.Inject;

@ApplicationScoped
public class SwitchManagementInputPort implements
  SwitchManagementUseCase {

    @Inject
    private SwitchManagementOutputPort
    switchManagementOutputPort;
    /** Code omitted **/
}
```

We use the `@ApplicationScoped` annotation to convert `SwitchManagementInputPort` into a managed bean and the `@Inject` annotation to make Quarkus DI discover a managed bean object that implements the `SwitchManagementOutputPort` interface, which happens to be the `SwitchManagementH2Adapter` output adapter.

5. We still need to adjust the `SwitchManagementGenericAdapter` input adapter:

```
public class SwitchManagementGenericAdapter {

    @Inject
    private SwitchManagementUseCase
      switchManagementUseCase;
    @Inject
    private RouterManagementUseCase
      routerManagementUseCase;
    /** Code omitted **/
}
```

Here, we are injecting dependencies for both the SwitchManagementUseCase and RouterManagementUseCase objects. Before using annotations, these dependencies were provided in this way:

```
public SwitchManagementGenericAdapter (
RouterManagementUseCase routerManagementUseCase,
  SwitchManagementUseCase switchManagementUseCase){
    this.routerManagementUseCase =
      routerManagementUseCase;
    this.switchManagementUseCase =
      switchManagementUseCase;
}
```

The improvement we get is that we no longer need to rely on the constructor to initialize the SwitchManagementGenericAdapter dependencies. Quarkus DI will automatically provide the required instances for us.

The next section is about the operations related to network management. Let's learn how we should change them.

Implementing CDI for network management classes and interfaces

We have fewer things to change for the network part because we did not create a specific output port and adapter for the network-related operations. So, the implementation changes will only take place on the use cases, input ports, and input adapters:

1. Let's start by looking at the NetworkManagementUseCase use case interface:

   ```
   public interface NetworkManagementUseCase {

       void setOutputPort(
       RouterManagementOutputPort
         routerNetworkOutputPort);
       /** Code omitted **/
   }
   ```

   As we did in the other use cases, we also defined the setOutputPort method to allow the initialization of RouterManagementOutputPort. After implementing Quarkus DI, this method will no longer be needed.

2. This is how NetworkManagementInputPort is implemented without Quarkus DI:

   ```
   import jakarta.enterprise.context.ApplicationScoped;
   import jakarta.inject.Inject;
   public class NetworkManagementInputPort implements
   ```

```
NetworkManagementUseCase {

  private RouterManagementOutputPort
  routerManagementOutputPort;

  @Override
  public void setOutputPort(
  RouterManagementOutputPort
    routerManagementOutputPort) {
      this.routerManagementOutputPort =
    routerManagementOutputPort;
  }
  /** Code omitted **/
}
```

The `NetworkManagementInputPort` input port only relies on `RouterManagementOutputPort`, which, without dependency injection, is initialized by the `setOutputPort` method.

3. This is what `NetworkManagementInputPort` looks like after implementing Quarkus DI:

```
@ApplicationScoped
public class NetworkManagementInputPort implements
  NetworkManagementUseCase {

    @Inject
    private RouterManagementOutputPort
    routerManagementOutputPort;
    /** Code omitted **/
}
```

As you can see, the `setOutputPort` method has been removed. Quarkus DI is now providing an implementation for `RouterManagementOutputPort` through the `@Inject` annotation. The `@ApplicationScoped` annotation converts `NetworkManagementInputPort` into a managed bean.

4. Finally, we have to change the `NetworkManagementGenericAdapter` input adapter:

```
import jakarta.enterprise.context.ApplicationScoped;
import jakarta.inject.Inject;

@ApplicationScoped
public class NetworkManagementGenericAdapter {

    @Inject
    private SwitchManagementUseCase
```

```
      switchManagementUseCase;
    @Inject
    private NetworkManagementUseCase
      networkManagementUseCase;
  /** Code omitted **/
}
```

The `NetworkManagementGenericAdapter` input adapter relies on the `SwitchManagementUseCase` and `NetworkManagementUseCase` use cases to trigger network-related operations on the system. As we did in the previous implementations, here, we are using `@Inject` to provide the dependencies at runtime.

The following code shows how these dependencies were provided before Quarkus DI:

```
public NetworkManagementGenericAdapter(
SwitchManagementUseCase switchManagementUseCase, Net
  workManagementUseCase networkManagementUseCase) {
    this.switchManagementUseCase =
      switchManagementUseCase;
    this.networkManagementUseCase =
      networkManagementUseCase;
}
```

After implementing the injection mechanism, we can safely remove this `NetworkManagementGenericAdapter` constructor.

We have finished making all the necessary changes to convert the input ports, use cases, and adapters into components that can be used for dependency injection. These changes showed us how to integrate the Quarkus CDI mechanisms into our hexagonal application.

Now, let's learn how to adapt the hexagonal system to mock and use managed beans during tests.

Testing use cases with Quarkus and Cucumber

While implementing the Application hexagon in *Chapter 7, Building the Application Hexagon*, we used Cucumber to aid us in shaping and testing our use cases. By leveraging the behavior-driven design techniques provided by Cucumber, we could express use cases in a declarative way. Now, we need to integrate Cucumber so that it works with Quarkus:

1. The first step is to add the Quarkus testing dependencies to the `pom.xml` file from the Application hexagon:

```
<dependency>
  <groupId>io.quarkiverse.cucumber</groupId>
  <artifactId>quarkus-cucumber</artifactId>
  <version>1.0    .0</version>
  <scope>test</scope>
```

```
    </dependency>
    <dependency>
      <groupId>io.quarkus</groupId>
      <artifactId>quarkus-junit5</artifactId>
      <scope>test</scope>
    </dependency>
```

The quarkus-cucumber dependency provides the integration we need to run tests with Quarkus. We also need the quarkus-junit5 dependency, which enables us to use the @QuarkusTest annotation.

2. Next, we must add the necessary Cucumber dependencies:

```
    <dependency>
      <groupId>io.cucumber</groupId>
      <artifactId>cucumber-java</artifactId>
      <version>${cucumber.version}</version>
      <scope>test</scope>
    </dependency>
    <dependency>
      <groupId>io.cucumber</groupId>
      <artifactId>cucumber-junit</artifactId>
      <version>${cucumber.version}</version>
      <scope>test</scope>
    </dependency>
    <dependency>
      <groupId>io.cucumber</groupId>
      <artifactId>cucumber-picocontainer</artifactId>
      <version>${cucumber.version}</version>
      <scope>test</scope>
    </dependency>
```

With the cucumber-java, cucumber-junit, and cucumber-picocontainer dependencies, we can enable the Cucumber engine on the system.

Let's see how Cucumber is configured without Quarkus:

```
package dev.davivieira.topologyinventory.application;

import io.cucumber.junit.Cucumber;
import io.cucumber.junit.CucumberOptions;
import org.junit.runner.RunWith;

@RunWith(Cucumber.class)
@CucumberOptions(
        plugin = {"pretty", "html:target/cucumber-result"}
```

```
)
public class ApplicationTest {


}
```

The `@RunWith(Cucumber.class)` annotation is used to activate the Cucumber engine. When using Quarkus, this is how `ApplicationTest` should be implemented:

```
package dev.davivieira.topologyinventory.application;

import io.quarkiverse.cucumber.CucumberQuarkusTest;
import io.quarkus.test.junit.QuarkusTest;

@QuarkusTest
public class ApplicationTest extends CucumberQuarkusTest {


}
```

The `@QuarkusTest` annotations activate the Quarkus testing engine. By extending the `CucumberQuarkusTest` class, we also enable the Cucumber testing engine.

There are no tests on the `ApplicationTest` class because this is just a bootstrap class. Remember that Cucumber tests were implemented in separate classes. Before changing these classes, we need to mock the managed beans that are required to provide instances for `RouterManagementOutputPort` and `SwitchManagementOutputPort`.

Let's create a mocked bean object for `RouterManagementOutputPort`:

```
package dev.davivieira.topologyinventory.application.mocks;
import dev.davivieira.topologyinventory.applica
    tion.ports.output.RouterManagementOutputPort;
import dev.davivieira.topologyinventory.domain.en
    tity.Router;
import dev.davivieira.topologyinventory.domain.vo.Id;
import io.quarkus.test.Mock;

@Mock
public class RouterManagementOutputPortMock implements
    RouterManagementOutputPort {
      @Override
      public Router retrieveRouter(Id id) {
          return null;
      }

      @Override
```

```
    public Router removeRouter(Id id) {
        return null;
    }
    @Override
    public Router persistRouter(Router router) {
        return null;
    }
}
```

This is a dummy mocked bean that we created to prevent Quarkus from throwing `Unsatis-fiedResolutionException`. By using the `@Mock` annotation, Quarkus will instantiate the `RouterManagementOutputPortMock` class and serve it as a bean to be injected during the tests.

In the same way, we will mock `SwitchManagementOutputPort`:

```
package dev.davivieira.topologyinventory.application.mocks;

import dev.davivieira.topologyinventory.applica
  tion.ports.output.SwitchManagementOutputPort;
import dev.davivieira.topologyinventory.domain.en
  tity.Switch;
import dev.davivieira.topologyinventory.domain.vo.Id;
import io.quarkus.test.Mock;

@Mock
public class SwitchManagementOutputPortMock implements
  SwitchManagementOutputPort {
    @Override
    public Switch retrieveSwitch(Id id) {
        return null;
    }
}
```

For `SwitchManagementOutputPort`, we created `SwitchManagementOutputPortMock` to provide a dummy managed bean so that Quarkus can use it for injection during the tests. Without mocks, we'd need real instances from the `RouterManagementH2Adapter` and `SwitchManagementH2Adapter` output adapters.

Although we don't refer directly to output interfaces and output port adapters during tests, Quarkus still tries to perform bean discovery on them. That's why we need to provide the mocks.

Now, we can refactor the tests to use the dependency injection provided by Quarkus DI. Let's learn how to do that on the `RouterAdd` test:

```
public class RouterAdd extends ApplicationTestData {

    @Inject
    RouterManagementUseCase routerManagementUseCase;
    /** Code omitted **/
}
```

Before using Quarkus DI, this is how we got the implementation for `RouterManagementUseCase`:

```
this.routerManagementUseCase = new RouterManagementInput
    Port();
```

The preceding code can be removed once the `@Inject` annotation has been implemented.

We can follow the same approach of adding the `@Inject` annotation and removing the constructor call to instantiate input port objects when refactoring other test classes.

The output you'll get after running Quarkus tests integrated with Cucumber will be similar to the following:

```
[INFO] -------------------------------------------------------
[INFO]  T E S T S
[INFO] -------------------------------------------------------
[INFO] Running dev.davivieira.topologyinventory.application.
ApplicationTest
2021-09-08 22:44:15,596 INFO  [io.quarkus] (main) Quarkus 2.2.1.Final
on JVM started in 1.976s. Listening on: http://localhost:8081
2021-09-08 22:44:15,618 INFO  [io.quarkus] (main) Profile test
activated.
2021-09-08 22:44:15,618 INFO  [io.quarkus] (main) Installed features:
[cdi, cucumber, smallrye-context-propagation]


@RouterCreate
Scenario: Creating a new core router
#dev/davivieira/topologyinventory/application/routers/RouterCreate.
feature:4
.   Given I provide all required data to create a core router
#dev.davivieira.topologyinventory.application.RouterCreate.create_
core_router()
.   Then A new core router is created
#dev.davivieira.topologyinventory.application.RouterCreate.a_new_core_
router_is_created()
```

Note that in the installed feature's output entry, Quarkus mentions `CDI` and `Cucumber` as extensions that are being used.

In this section, we learned how to configure Quarkus to work together with Cucumber properly. This configuration was required to configure Quarkus mocks and refactor test classes to inject input port objects instead of creating them with constructor calls.

Summary

In this chapter, we had the opportunity to learn how Quarkus provides dependency injection through Quarkus DI. We started by reviewing some of the concepts defined by the CDI for **Java 2.0** specification, the specification that Quarkus DI is derived from. Then, we proceeded to implement these concepts in our hexagonal application. We defined the managed beans and injected them while refactoring use cases, ports, and adapters. Finally, we learned how to integrate Quarkus with Cucumber to get the best of both worlds while testing our hexagonal application.

By implementing Quarkus dependency injection mechanisms into a hexagonal system, we are also turning it into a more robust and modern system.

In the next chapter, we'll turn our attention to adapters. Quarkus provides powerful capabilities for creating reactive REST endpoints and we'll learn how to integrate them with hexagonal system adapters.

Questions

1. Quarkus DI is based on which Java specification?

2. What is the difference between the `ApplicationScoped` and `Singleton` scopes?

3. What is the annotation we should use to provide dependencies through Quarkus DI instead of using calling constructors?

4. To enable Quarkus testing capabilities, which annotation should we use?

Answers

1. It's based on the CDI for **Java 2.0** specification.

2. When using `ApplicationScope`, the objects are lazily loaded. With `Singleton`, the objects are eagerly loaded.

3. The `@Inject` annotation.

4. The `@QuarkusTest` annotation.

12

Using RESTEasy Reactive to Implement Input Adapters

An **input adapter** is like a front door that exposes all the features provided by a hexagonal system. Whenever a user or other application wants to communicate with a hexagonal system, they reach one of the available input adapters. With such adapters, we can provide different ways to access the same functionality within the hexagonal system. If a client does not support HTTP communication, we can implement an adapter using a different protocol. The significant advantage here is that removing or adding new adapters does not influence the domain logic.

Due to the hexagonal architecture's decoupling and well-encapsulating nature, we can change technologies without any or major changes occurring in the system domain logic.

In this chapter, we'll continue our journey in exploring the exciting features of Quarkus. One feature that fits quite well with implementing input adapters is the **RESTEasy Reactive JAX-RS implementation**, which is a part of the Quarkus framework. RESTEasy Reactive proposes an asynchronous and event-driven way to expose HTTP endpoints. So, we'll learn how to integrate such Reactive capabilities with input adapters from a hexagonal system.

We'll cover the following topics in this chapter:

- Exploring the approaches to handling server requests
- Implementing input adapters with RESTEasy Reactive
- Adding OpenAPI and Swagger UI
- Testing Reactive input adapters

By the end of this chapter, you'll know how to implement and test input adapters with reactive behavior. You'll also know how to publish the API for these input adapters using OpenAPI and Swagger UI.

Technical requirements

To compile and run the code examples presented in this chapter, you need the latest **Java SE Development Kit** and **Maven 3.8** installed on your computer. They are available for the Linux, Mac, and Windows operating systems.

You can find the code files for this chapter on GitHub at `https://github.com/ PacktPublishing/-Designing-Hexagonal-Architecture-with-Java---Second- Edition/tree/main/Chapter12`.

Exploring the approaches to handling server's requests

In client-server communication, we have a process flow where a client sends a request, the server receives it, and it starts to do some work. Once the server finishes its work, it replies to the client with a result. From the client's perspective, this flow does not change. It's always about sending a request and receiving a response. What can change, though, is how the server can internally handle how a request is processed.

There are two approaches to handling the server's request processing: **reactive** and **imperative**. So, let's see how a server can handle requests imperatively.

Imperative

In a traditional web application running on **Tomcat**, every request that's received by the server triggers the creation of a worker thread on something called a **thread pool**. In Tomcat, a thread pool is a mechanism that controls the life cycle and availability of worker threads that serve application requests. So, when you make a server request, Tomcat pulls a dedicated thread from the thread pool to serve your request. This worker thread relies on blocking I/O to access databases and other systems. The following diagram illustrates how the imperative approach works:

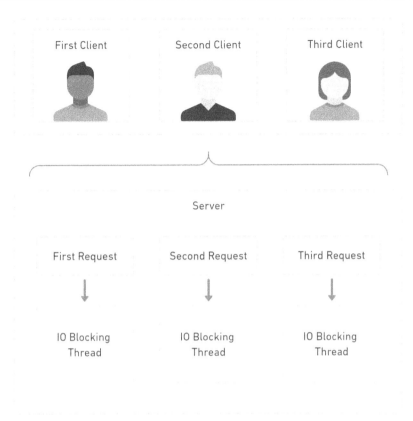

Figure 12.1 – The imperative approach

As shown in the preceding diagram, **Server** needs to create a new I/O blocking worker thread for each request.

Once a worker thread has been created and allocated to serve a request, it is blocked until the request is fulfilled. The server has a limited number of threads. If you have lots of long-running requests and continue to send such requests before the server can finish them, the server will run out of threads, which will lead to system failures.

Thread creation and management is also expensive. The server expends valuable resources in creating and switching between threads to serve client requests.

So, the bottom line of the imperative approach is that a worker thread is blocked to serve one – and only one – request at a time. To serve more requests concurrently, you need to provide more worker threads. Also, the imperative approach influences how the code is written. Imperative code is somewhat more straightforward to understand because things are treated sequentially.

Now, let's see how the reactive approach contrasts with the imperative one.

Reactive

As you may imagine, the idea behind the reactive approach is that you don't need to block a thread to fulfill a request. Instead, the system can use the same thread to process different requests simultaneously. In the imperative approach, we have worker threads that handle only one request at a time, while in the reactive approach, we have I/O non-blocking threads that handle multiple requests concurrently. Here, we can see how the reactive approach works:

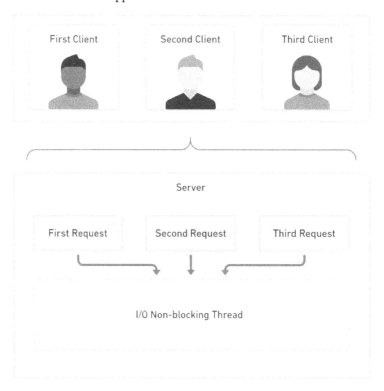

Figure 12.2 – The reactive approach

As shown in the preceding diagram, a single non-blocking thread can handle multiple requests.

In the reactive approach, we have a sense of continuation. Instead of the sequential nature of the imperative approach, with Reactive, we can see that things have continuity. By continuation, we mean that whenever a Reactive-ready server receives a request, such a request is dispatched as an I/O operation with an attached continuation. This continuation works like a callback that is triggered and continues to execute the request once the server returns with a response. If this request needs to fetch a database or any remote system, the server won't block the I/O thread while waiting for a response. Instead, the I/O thread will trigger an I/O operation with an attached continuation and will release the I/O thread to accept other requests.

The following diagram illustrates how I/O threads trigger I/O operations:

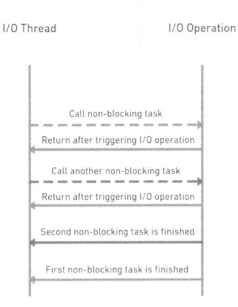

Figure 12.3 – I/O thread flow

As we can see, an I/O thread calls a non-blocking task that triggers an I/O operation and returns immediately. This happens because the I/O thread does not need to wait for the first I/O operation to finish to call a second one. While the first I/O operation is still executing, the same I/O thread calls for another non-blocking task. Once the I/O operation has concluded, the I/O thread resumes execution by finishing the non-blocking tasks.

By avoiding wasting any time and resources that exist in the imperative approach, the reactive approach makes makes optimized use of threads as they don't while waiting for an I/O operation to be finished.

Next, we'll learn how to implement reactive input adapters using the RESTEasy Reactive JAX-RS implementation provided by Quarkus.

Implementing input adapters with RESTEasy Reactive

RESTEasy Reactive is a JAX-RS implementation that supports both imperative and reactive HTTP endpoints. Such an implementation integrates with **Vert.x**, which is a toolkit that we can use to build distributed Reactive systems. RESTEasy Reactive and Vert.x work together in Quarkus to provide Reactive capabilities.

To understand what a Reactive endpoint looks like, we will integrate RESTEasy Reactive with the input adapters of the topology and inventory system.

Let's start by configuring the required Maven dependencies:

```
<dependencies>
  <dependency>
    <groupId>io.quarkus</groupId>
    <artifactId>quarkus-resteasy-reactive</artifactId>
  </dependency>
  <dependency>
    <groupId>io.quarkus</groupId>
    <artifactId>quarkus-resteasy-reactive-
      jackson</artifactId>
  </dependency>
</dependencies>
```

With `quarkus-resteasy-reactive`, we bring the Reactive libraries, including Reactive RESTEasy and the `Mutiny` library, which we'll use to create code in a reactive fashion. We will use `quarkus-resteasy-reactive-jackson` for deserialization tasks involving the Reactive responses.

Once we have the dependencies configured, we can start implementing the Reactive input adapter for router management in the topology and inventory system.

Implementing the Reactive input adapter for router management

We'll work on top of the existing input adapters that we created in *Chapter 8*, *Building the Framework Hexagon*. We'll change those input adapters to enable JAX-RS and Reactive capabilities. We'll execute the following steps to do so:

1. Let's start by defining the top-level path for requests related to router management on the `RouterManagementAdapter` class:

    ```
    @ApplicationScoped
    @Path("/router")
    public class RouterManagementAdapter {

        @Inject
        RouterManagementUseCase routerManagementUseCase;
        /** Code omitted **/
    }
    ```

    We use the `@Path` annotation to map a URL path to a resource in the system. We can use this annotation on top of a class or a method.

    The only field of this class is `RouterManagementUseCase`, which is injected using the `@Inject` annotation. By utilizing this use case reference, we gain access to system features related to router management.

2. Next, let's define a Reactive endpoint to retrieve a router:

```
@GET
@Path("/{id}")
public Uni<Response> retrieveRouter(Id id) {
    return Uni.createFrom()
            .item(
                routerManagementUseCase.
                retrieveRouter(id))
            .onItem()
            .transform(
             router -> router != null ?
             Response.ok(f) :
             Response.ok(null))
            .onItem()
            .transform(Response.Response
                Builder::build);
```

The @GET annotation says that only HTTP GET requests are allowed. The @Path("/{id}") annotation from the method level is concatenated with the @Path("/router") annotation from the class level. So, to reach this retrieveRouter method, we have to send a request to /router/{id}.

Also, note the @PathParam("id") annotation, which we use to capture a parameter from the URL.

What makes this endpoint a Reactive one is its Uni<Response> response type. Uni is one of the two types provided by the Mutiny library. In addition to Uni, there is also the Multi type.

We use the Uni and Multi types to represent what kind of data we're dealing with. For example, if your response returns just one item, you should use Uni. Otherwise, if your response is like a stream of data, such as those that come from a messaging server, then Multi may be more suited for your purpose.

By calling Uni.createFrom().item(routerManagementUseCase.retrieveRouter(id)), we're creating a pipeline that executes routerManagementUseCase.retrieveRouter(id). The result is captured on transform(f -> f != null ? Response.ok(f) : Response.ok(null)). If the request is successful, we get Response.ok(f); otherwise, we get Response.ok(null). Finally, we call transform(Response.ResponseBuilder::build) to transform the result into a Uni<Response> object.

Response.ResponseBuilder::build is a method reference that could be written as the following lambda expression: (Response.ResponseBuilder responseBuilder) -> responseBuilder.build(). responseBuilder represents the object parameter we receive, followed by the build method call to create a new Response object. We favor the method reference approach because we write less code to accomplish the same thing.

The remaining endpoints we are about to implement all follow a similar approach to the one described previously.

3. After implementing an endpoint to retrieve a router, we can implement an endpoint to remove a router from the system:

```
@DELETE
@Path("/{id}")
public Uni<Response> removeRouter(@PathParam("id") Id
  id) {
    return Uni.createFrom()
              .item(
               routerManagementUseCase.removeRouter(id))
              .onItem()
              .transform(
               router -> router != null ?
               Response.ok(router) :
               Response.ok(null))
              .onItem()
              .transform(Response.Response
                 Builder::build);
}
```

The @DELETE annotation corresponds to the HTTP DELETE method. Again, we are defining a Path parameter on the @Path("/{id}") annotation. The method body has a Uni pipeline that executes routerManagementUseCase.removeRouter(id) and returns Uni<Response>.

4. Let's implement the endpoint to create a new router:

```
@POST
@Path("/")
public Uni<Response> createRouter(CreateRouter cre
  ateRouter) {
    /** Code omitted **/
    return Uni.createFrom()
              .item(
                 routerManagementUseCase.
                 persistRouter(router))
              .onItem()
              .transform(
               router -> router != null ?
               Response.ok(f) :
               Response.ok(null))
              .onItem()
              .transform(Response.Response
```

```
                    Builder::build);
    }
```

We use the @POST annotation because we're creating a new resource. The @Path("/") annotation at the method level, when concatenated with the @Path("/router") annotation at the class level, generates the /router/ path. We have the Reactive code in the method body to handle the request and return Uni<Response>.

5. Next, we will implement the endpoint so that a router can be added to a core router:

```
@POST
@Path("/add")
public Uni<Response> addRouterToCoreRouter(AddRouter
    addRouter) {
    /** Code omitted **/
    return Uni.createFrom()
            .item(routerManagementUseCase.
                    addRouterToCoreRouter(router,
                        coreRouter))
            .onItem()
            .transform(
            router -> router != null ?
            Response.ok(router) :
            Response.ok(null))
            .onItem()
            .transform(Response.Response
                Builder::build);
    }
```

Again, we use the @POST annotation here. The @Path("/add") annotation at the method level, when concatenated with @Path("/router") at the class level, generates the /router/ add path. The Reactive code creates a pipeline to execute routerManagementUseCase. addRouterToCoreRouter(router, coreRouter) and return Uni<Response>.

6. Finally, we must implement the endpoint to remove a router from a core router:

```
@DELETE
@Path("/{routerId}/from/{coreRouterId}")
public Uni<Response> removeRouterFromCoreRouter(
    /** Code omitted **/
    return Uni.createFrom()
            .item(routerManagementUseCase.
                    removeRouterFromCoreRouter(
                    router, coreRouter))
            .onItem()
            .transform(
```

```
                    router -> router != null ?
                        Response.ok(f) :
                        Response.ok(null))
                .onItem()
                .transform(Response.Response
                    Builder::build);
    }
```

Here, we use the @DELETE annotation to handle HTTP DELETE requests. In the @Path annotation, we have two path parameters – routerId and coreRouterId. We use these two parameters to obtain the Router and CoreRouter objects when we call routerManagementUseCase. removeRouterFromCoreRouter(router, coreRouter) inside the pipeline provided by Uni.

As we can see, when using Quarkus, it does not take too much to shift from an imperative to a Reactive way of implementing REST endpoints. Much of the work is done behind the scenes by the framework and its libraries.

Now, let's move on and implement Reactive input adapters for switch management.

Implementing the Reactive input adapter for switch management

Following a similar approach to the one we followed in the previous section, we can implement the Reactive input adapters for switch management by executing the following steps:

1. We will start by enabling JAX-RS on the SwitchManagementAdapter class:

    ```
    @ApplicationScoped
    @Path("/switch")
    public class SwitchManagementAdapter {

        @Inject
        SwitchManagementUseCase switchManagementUseCase;
        @Inject
        RouterManagementUseCase routerManagementUseCase;
        /** Code omitted **/
    }
    ```

    This class is annotated with @Path("/switch"), so all the switch management-related requests will be directed to it. Following this, we inject both SwitchManagementUseCase and RouterManagementUseCase to execute operations on the Application hexagon.

2. To enable switch retrieval in the topology and inventory system, we need to implement the Reactive behavior on the `retrieveSwitch` method:

```
@GET
@Path("/{id}")
public Uni<Response> retrieveSwitch(@PathParam("id")
  Id switchId) {
    return Uni.createFrom()
            .item(
             switchManagementUseCase.
             retrieveSwitch(switchId))
            .onItem()
            .transform(
             aSwitch -> aSwitch != null ?
             Response.ok(aSwitch)  :
             Response.ok(null))
            .onItem()
            .transform(Response.Response
               Builder::build);
}
```

By adding the `@GET` and `@Path` annotations, we activate JAX-RS on the `retrieveSwitch` method. We place `switchManagementUseCase.retrieveSwitch(switchId)` so that it's executed inside a `Mutiny` pipeline that returns `Uni<Response>`.

The call on `item` returns immediately. It triggers the operation that's executed by the `retrieveSwitch` method and allows the thread to continue serving other requests. The result is obtained when we call `onItem`, which represents the continuation of the operation that's triggered when we call `item`.

3. Next, we must add Reactive behavior to the `createAndAddSwitchToEdgeRouter` method:

```
@POST
@Path("/create/{edgeRouterId}")
public Uni<Response> createAndAddSwitchToEdgeRouter(
            CreateSwitch createSwitch,
            @PathParam("edgeRouterId") Id
               edgeRouterId){
    /** Code omitted **/
    return Uni.createFrom()
            .item((EdgeRouter)
              routerManagementUseCase.
              persistRouter(router))
            .onItem()
            .transform(
             router -> router != null ?
```

```
                    Response.ok(f)  :
                    Response.ok(null))
                    .onItem()
                    .transform(Response.Response
                       Builder::build);
        }
```

The preceding method handles the HTTP POST requests to create a switch object and add it to an edge router. We call the routerManagementUseCase.persistRouter(router) method here, which is wrapped inside a Mutiny pipeline, to return Uni<Response>.

4. Finally, we must define the Reactive endpoint to remove a switch from an edge router:

```
@DELETE
@Path("/{switchId}/from/{edgeRouterId}")
public Uni<Response> removeSwitchFromEdgeRouter(
        @PathParam("switchId") Id switchId,
        @PathParam("edgeRouterId") Id
          edgeRouterId) {
    /** Code omitted **/
    return Uni.createFrom()
             .item(
               (EdgeRouter)routerManagementUseCase.
               persistRouter(router))
             .onItem()
             .transform(
               router -> router != null ?
               Response.ok(f)  :
               Response.ok(null))
             .onItem()
             .transform(Response.Response
                Builder::build);
    }
```

As we did with our previous removal operation, where we removed a router from a core router, we use the @DELETE annotation to make the removeSwitchFromEdgeRouter method only accept the HTTP DELETE requests. We pass the Path parameters, switchId and edgeRouterId, to obtain the switch and edge router objects required for the operation.

After defining the Reactive endpoints for retrieveSwitch, createAndAddSwitchToEdgeRouter, and removeSwitchFromEdgeRouter, we can start implementing the Reactive input adapter for network management.

Implementing the Reactive input adapter for network management

As you may imagine, the `network` Reactive input adapter follows the same standard that's used by the router and switch Reactive adapters. In the following steps, we will enable Reactive behavior for endpoints related to network management:

1. Let's start by enabling JAX-RS on the `NetworkManagementAdapter` input adapter:

    ```
    @ApplicationScoped
    @Path("/network")
    public class NetworkManagementAdapter {

        @Inject
        SwitchManagementUseCase switchManagementUseCase;
        @Inject
        NetworkManagementUseCase networkManagementUseCase;
        /** Code omitted **/
    }
    ```

    At this point, you may be familiar with the `@Path` annotation at the class level. We inject the `SwitchManagementUseCase` and `NetworkManagementUseCase` uses cases to assist in the operations that are executed by this input adapter.

2. Next, we must define a Reactive endpoint so that networks can be added to a switch:

    ```
    @POST
    @Path("/add/{switchId}")
    public Uni<Response> addNetworkToSwitch(AddNetwork
      addNetwork, @PathParam("switchId") Id switchId) {
        /** Code omitted **/
        return Uni.createFrom()
                .item(
                  networkManagementUseCase.
                  addNetworkToSwitch(
                  network, networkSwitch))
                .onItem()
                .transform(
                  f -> f != null ?
                  Response.ok(f) :
                  Response.ok(null))
                .onItem()
                .transform(Response.Response
                  Builder::build);
    }
    ```

The idea we apply here is the same one we applied to the previous implementations. Inside the `addNetworkToSwitch` method, we add some Reactive code that will use a `Mutiny` pipeline to call `networkManagementUseCase.addNetworkToSwitch( network, networkSwitch)` and return `Uni<Response>`.

3. Finally, we must define the Reactive endpoint to remove a network from a switch:

```
@DELETE
@Path("/{networkName}/from/{switchId}")
public Uni<Response> removeNetworkFromSwitch(@Path
  Param("networkName") String networkName, @Path
    Param("switchId") Id           switchId) {
    /** Code omitted **/
    return Uni.createFrom()
            .item(
             networkManagementUseCase.
             removeNetworkFromSwitch(
             networkName, networkSwitch))
            .onItem()
            .transform(
              f -> f != null ?
              Response.ok(f) :
              Response.ok(null))
            .onItem()
            .transform(Response.Response
              Builder::build);
}
```

Here, we use the `@DELETE` annotation and two path parameters, `networkName` and `switchId`, to remove a network from a switch. Inside the `Mutiny` pipeline, we call `networkManagementUseCase.removeNetworkFromSwitch(networkName, networkSwitch)`. The pipeline result is `Uni<Response>`.

With that, we have finished implementing the Reactive input adapter for network management. Now, the `RouterManagementAdapter`, `SwitchManagementAdapter`, and `NetworkManagementAdapter` input adapters are ready to serve HTTP requests in a Reactive way.

These three input adapters and their endpoints form the hexagonal system API.

In this section, we not only learned how to create ordinary REST endpoints, but we also went the extra mile by using RESTEasy Reactive to enable Reactive behavior on the input adapter's endpoints. That's a fundamental step to tap into the advantages that a Reactive approach can provide. With the Reactive approach, we no longer need to depend on I/O blocking threads, which may consume more computing resources than I/O non-blocking threads. I/O blocking threads need to wait for I/O operations to finish. I/O non-blocking threads are more efficient because the same thread can handle several I/O operations at the same time.

The next section will cover how to use OpenAPI and Swagger UI to publish the system API.

Adding OpenAPI and Swagger UI

Understanding and interacting with third-party systems is sometimes a non-trivial undertaking. In the best scenario, we may have the system documentation, an organized code base, and a set of APIs that, together, help us understand what the system does. In the worst scenario, we have none of these things. This challenging situation requires courage, patience, and persistence to venture into trying to understand a tangled code base with intricate complexities.

OpenAPI represents an honorable effort to increase our capacity to express and understand what a system does. Originally based on the Swagger specification, the OpenAPI specification standardizes how APIs are documented and described so that anyone can grasp the capabilities offered by a system without much effort.

We spent the previous section implementing the Reactive input adapters that form the API of our hexagonal system. To make this system more understandable to other people and systems, we'll use OpenAPI to describe the functionalities provided by the input adapters and their endpoints. Also, we'll enable **Swagger UI**, a web application that presents a clear and organized view of the system's APIs.

Quarkus comes with built-in support for the **OpenAPI v3** specification. To enable it, we need the following Maven dependency:

```
<dependencies>
  <dependency>
      <groupId>io.quarkus</groupId>
      <artifactId>quarkus-smallrye-openapi</artifactId>
  </dependency>
</dependencies>
```

The `quarkus-smallrye-openapi` dependency provides the libraries that contain the OpenAPI annotations we can use to describe the Reactive endpoint methods on the input adapter classes. This dependency lets us configure Swagger UI, too.

Remember that we configured four Java modules: `domain`, `application`, `framework`, and `bootstrap`. To activate and configure Swagger UI, we need to create the `resource/application.properties` file inside the `bootstrap` module. Here is how we can configure this file:

```
quarkus.swagger-ui.always-include=true

quarkus.swagger-ui.urls-primary-name=Topology & Inventory
quarkus.swagger-ui.theme=material
quarkus.swagger-ui.title=Topology & Inventory - Network
  Management System
quarkus.swagger-ui.footer=&#169; 2021 | Davi Vieira
quarkus.swagger-ui.display-operation-id=true
```

```
mp.openapi.extensions.smallrye.info.title=Topology & Inven
  tory API
mp.openapi.extensions.smallrye.info.version=1.0
mp.openapi.extensions.smallrye.info.description=Manage net
  works assets
```

We set `quarkus.swagger-ui.always-include` to `true` to ensure that Swagger UI will also be available when the application is started using the `prod` (production) profile – one of the built-in Quarkus profiles. With `quarkus.swagger-ui.theme`, we can configure the interface theme. We will use the remaining properties to provide a high-level description of the API.

Let's learn how to use the OpenAPI annotations to expose and describe the hexagonal system's endpoints. Look at the following example from the `RouterManagementAdapter` class:

```
@ApplicationScoped
@Path("/router")
@Tag(name = "Router Operations", description = "Router man
  agement operations")
public class RouterManagementAdapter {

    @GET
    @Path("/retrieve/{id}")
    @Operation(operationId = "retrieveRouter",
    description = "Retrieve a router from the network
      inventory")
    public Uni<Response> retrieveRouter(@PathParam("id")
      Id id) {
     /** Code omitted **/
}
```

The `@Tag` annotation, which is used at the class level, lets us define the metadata information that's applied for all the endpoints defined in the `RouterManagementAdapter` class. This means that the method endpoints, such as the `retrieveRouter` method in the `RouterManagementAdapter` class, will inherit that class-level `@Tag` annotation.

We use the `@Operation` annotation to provide details of an operation. In the preceding code, we're describing the operation that's performed at the `/retrieve/{id}` path. We have the `operationId` parameter here, which is used to uniquely identify the endpoint, and the `description` parameter, which is used to provide a meaningful operation description.

To make Quarkus and Swagger UI display a fancy UI of our hexagonal system's API, we just need to add these OpenAPI annotations to the classes and methods (properly configured with JAX-RS) that we want to expose on Swagger UI.

You can compile and run the application using the code from this book's GitHub repository. Make sure that you execute the following commands in the `chapter12` directory:

```
$ mvn clean package
$ java -jar bootstrap/target/bootstrap-1.0-SNAPSHOT-runner.jar
```

This will open the following URL on your browser:

```
http://localhost:8080/q/swagger-ui/
```

Also, you'll see something similar to the following screenshot:

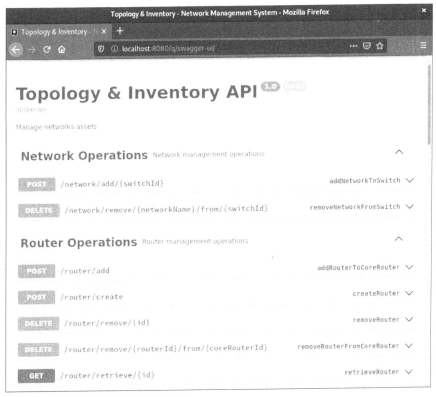

Figure 12.4 – Swagger UI from topology and inventory system

In the preceding screenshot, the operations are grouped into **Network Operations**, **Router Operations**, and **Switch Operations**. These groups come from the `@Tag` annotation we inserted for each of the input adapter classes. Each endpoint inherited its respective `@Tag` metadata information.

So far, we have our hexagonal system properly configured with Reactive endpoints that are well documented with OpenAPI and Swagger UI. Now, let's learn how to test these endpoints to ensure they are working as expected.

Testing Reactive input adapters

Our testing efforts started on the Domain hexagon by unit testing the core system components. Then, we moved on to the Application hexagon, where we could test the use cases using **behavior-driven design** techniques. Now that we have implemented Reactive REST endpoints on the Framework hexagon, we need to find a way to test them.

Fortunately, Quarkus comes well equipped when it comes to endpoint testing. To get started, we need the following dependency:

```
<dependencies>
  <dependency>
    <groupId>io.rest-assured</groupId>
    <artifactId>rest-assured</artifactId>
    <scope>test</scope>
  </dependency>
</dependencies>
```

The `rest-assured` dependency allows us to test HTTP endpoints. It provides an intuitive library that's very useful for making requests and extracting responses from HTTP calls.

To see how it works, let's implement a test for the `/router/retrieve/{routerId}` endpoint:

```
@Test
@Order(1)
public void retrieveRouter() throws IOException {
    var expectedRouterId =
      "b832ef4f-f894-4194-8feb-a99c2cd4be0c";
    var routerStr = given()
            .contentType("application/json")
            .pathParam("routerId", expectedRouterId)
            .when()
            .get("/router/retrieve/{routerId}")
            .then()
            .statusCode(200)
            .extract()
            .asString();
    var actualRouterId =
    getRouterDeserialized(routerStr).getId().getUuid()
      .toString();
    assertEquals(expectedRouterId, actualRouterId);
}
```

To create a request, we can use the static `io.restassured.RestAssured.given` method. We can specify the content type, parameters, HTTP method, and body of a request with the `given` method. After sending the request, we can check its status with `statusCode`. To obtain the response, we call `extract`. In the following example, we're getting the response in the form of a string. This is because the return type of the Reactive endpoint is `Uni<Response>`. So, the result is a JSON string.

We need to deserialize the JSON string into a `Router` object before running assertions. The deserialization work is accomplished by the `getRouterDeserialized` method:

```
public static Router getRouterDeserialized(String jsonStr)
  throws IOException {
    var mapper = new ObjectMapper();
    var module = new SimpleModule();
    module.addDeserializer(Router.class, new
      RouterDeserializer());
    mapper.registerModule(module);
    var router = mapper.readValue(jsonStr, Router.class);
    return router;
}
```

This method receives a JSON string as a parameter. This JSON string is passed to an `ObjectMapper` mapper when we call `mapper.readValue(jsonStr, Router.class)`. In addition to providing a mapper, we also need to extend and implement the `deserialize` method from the `com.fasterxml.jackson.databind.deser.std.StdDeserializer` class. In the preceding example, this implementation is provided by `RouterDeserializer`. This deserializer will transform the JSON string into a `Router` object, as shown in the following code:

```
public class RouterDeserializer extends StdDeserial
  izer<Router> {

    /** Code omitted **/

    @Override
    public Router deserialize(JsonParser jsonParser,
    DeserializationContext ctxt)
            throws IOException {
        JsonNode node =
        jsonParser.getCodec().readTree(jsonParser);
        var id = node.get("id").get("uuid").asText();
        var vendor = node.get("vendor").asText();
        var model = node.get("model").asText();
        var ip = node.get("ip").get("ipAddress").asText();
        var location = node.get("location");
        var routerType = RouterType.valueOf(
```

```
            node.get("routerType").asText());
        var routersNode = node.get("routers");
        var switchesNode = node.get("switches");
        /** Code omitted **/
    }
```

The `deserialize` method intends to map every relevant JSON attribute to a domain type. We perform this mapping by retrieving the values we want from a `JsonNode` object. After mapping the values that we want, we can create a `router` object, as shown in the following code:

```
var router = RouterFactory.getRouter(
        Id.withId(id),
        Vendor.valueOf(vendor),
        Model.valueOf(model),
        IP.fromAddress(ip),
        getLocation(location),
        routerType);
```

Once all the values have been retrieved, we call `RouterFactory.getRouter` to produce a `Router` object. Because a router may have child routers and switches, we call `fetchChildRouters` and `fetchChildSwitches` so that they also have `StdDeserializer` implementations:

```
fetchChildRouters(routerType, routersNode, router);
fetchChildSwitches(routerType, switchesNode, router);
```

We call the `fetchChildRouters` and `fetchChildSwitches` methods because a router may have child routers and switches that need to be deserialized. These methods will perform the required deserialization.

After deserializing the JSON string response, we can run the assertion on a `Router` object:

```
var actualRouterId = getRouterDeserialized(router
  Str).getId().getUuid().toString();
assertEquals(expectedRouterId, actualRouterId);
```

To test the `/router/retrieve/{routerId}` endpoint, we are checking whether the ID of the router that's been retrieved by the Reactive endpoint is equal to the one we passed in the request.

You can run this and other tests that are available in this book's GitHub repository by executing the following command inside the `Chapter12` directory:

```
$ mvn test
```

The output of the preceding code will be similar to the following:

```
[INFO] ------------------------------------------------------
[INFO]  T E S T S
[INFO] ------------------------------------------------------
[INFO] Running dev.davivieira.topologyinventory.framework.adapters.
input.rest.NetworkManagementAdapterTest
2021-09-29 00:47:36,825 INFO  [io.quarkus] (main) Quarkus 2.2.1.Final
on JVM started in 2.550s. Listening on: http://localhost:8081
2021-09-29 00:47:36,827 INFO  [io.quarkus] (main) Profile test
activated.
2021-09-29 00:47:36,827 INFO  [io.quarkus] (main) Installed features:
[cdi, resteasy-reactive, resteasy-reactive-jackson, smallrye-context-
propagation, smallrye-openapi, swagger-ui]
[EL Info]: 2021-09-29 00:47:38.812--ServerSession(751658062)-
-EclipseLink, version: Eclipse Persistence Services -
3.0.1.v202104070723
[INFO] Tests run: 2, Failures: 0, Errors: 0, Skipped: 0, Time elapsed:
5.418 s - in dev.davivieira.topologyinventory.framework.adapters.
input.rest.NetworkManagementAdapterTest
[INFO] Running dev.davivieira.topologyinventory.framework.adapters.
input.rest.RouterManagementAdapterTest
[INFO] Tests run: 5, Failures: 0, Errors: 0, Skipped: 0, Time elapsed:
0.226 s - in dev.davivieira.topologyinventory.framework.adapters.
input.rest.RouterManagementAdapterTest
[INFO] Running dev.davivieira.topologyinventory.framework.adapters.
input.rest.SwitchManagementAdapterTest
[INFO] Tests run: 3, Failures: 0, Errors: 0, Skipped: 0, Time elapsed:
0.085 s - in dev.davivieira.topologyinventory.framework.adapters.
input.rest.SwitchManagementAdapterTest
2021-09-29 00:47:39,675 INFO  [io.quarkus] (main) Quarkus stopped in
0.032s
```

The preceding output describes the execution of the Reactive endpoint tests for the RouterManagementAdapter, SwitchManagementAdapter, and NetworkManagementAdapter input adapters.

One benefit of executing these endpoint tests is that we are not only testing the endpoint functionality on the Framework hexagon but also performing comprehensive tests that check the behavior of all the hexagons of the system.

Summary

In this chapter, we had the opportunity to dive into more Quarkus features, especially RESTEasy Reactive. We started by reviewing what imperative and reactive mean in the context of client-server communication.

Then, we learned that Quarkus provides RESTEasy Reactive as its JAX-RS implementation, enabling us to implement Reactive endpoints on input adapters. After that, we exposed the hexagonal system's API using OpenAPI and Swagger UI. To ensure we implemented the Reactive endpoints correctly, we wrote the endpoint tests using the `rest-assured` library.

In the next chapter, we'll continue exploring the Reactive capabilities offered by Quarkus and emphasize the data persistence aspects with Hibernate Reactive.

Questions

1. What is the difference between imperative and reactive requests?

2. What is the name of the JAX-RS implementation provided by Quarkus?

3. What is the purpose of OpenAPI?

4. Which library should we use in Quarkus to test HTTP endpoints?

Answers

1. Imperative can only handle one request at a time using an I/O blocking worker thread. Reactive can handle multiple requests using I/O non-blocking threads.

2. RESTEasy Reactive.

3. It's used to standardize the way APIs are described and documented.

4. We should use the `rest-assured` library.

Persisting Data with Output Adapters and Hibernate Reactive

In the previous chapter, we learned about some of the advantages that can be brought to a system by using Quarkus reactive capabilities. Our first step on the reactive road was to implement Reactive input adapters using **RESTEasy Reactive**. Although the input adapters' endpoints are being served reactively, we still have the output adapters working in a synchronous and blocking fashion.

To turn the hexagonal system into a more Reactive one, in this chapter, we'll first learn how to configure **Object Relational Mapping (ORM)** on system entities by using Hibernate Reactive and `Panache`. Once the system entities are properly configured, we'll learn how to use these entities to connect to a MySQL database reactively.

The following are the topics we'll cover in this chapter:

- Introducing Hibernate Reactive and `Panache`

- Enabling reactive behavior on output adapters

- Testing reactive output adapters

As we have already implemented reactive input adapters in the previous chapter, our goal here is to extend the reactive behavior in a hexagonal system by implementing reactive output adapters. This implementation takes place at the Framework hexagon, which is the architecture element where we concentrate on adapters.

By the end of this chapter, you'll have learned how to integrate Quarkus with a hexagonal system to access databases reactively. By understanding the required configuration steps and fundamental implementation details, you'll be able to implement reactive output adapters. This knowledge will help you tackle situations where non-blocking I/O requests offer more advantages than I/O-blocking ones.

Technical requirements

To compile and run the code examples presented in this chapter, you need the latest **Java SE Development Kit** and **Maven 3.8** installed on your computer. They are all available for Linux, Mac, and Windows operating systems.

Also, you'll need **Docker** installed on your machine.

You can find the code files for this chapter on GitHub at `https://github.com/ PacktPublishing/-Designing-Hexagonal-Architecture-with-Java---Second- Edition/tree/main/Chapter13`.

Introducing Hibernate Reactive and Panache

The available technologies and techniques to handle database operations in Java have evolved a lot in the last few years. Based on the **Java Persistence API (JPA)** specification, we've been presented with different ORM implementations such as Spring Data JPA, EclipseLink, and, of course, Hibernate. These technologies make our lives easier by abstracting away much of the plumber work required to deal with databases.

Quarkus is integrated with Hibernate ORM and its reactive counterpart, Hibernate Reactive. Also, Quarkus comes with a library called `Panache`, which simplifies our interaction with databases.

Next, we'll take a brief look at Hibernate Reactive and Panache's main features.

Hibernate Reactive features

It's rare, if not impossible, to find a silver-bullet solution that solves all problems related to database access. When we talk about the reactive and imperative approaches to database handling, it's fundamental to understand the advantages and disadvantages of both approaches.

What's so appealing about the imperative approach to database access is the simplicity with which you develop your code. There are fewer things to adjust and think about when you need to read or persist things using an imperative approach. However, this approach may cause setbacks when its blocking nature starts to impact the use cases of your system. To avoid such setbacks, we have the reactive approach, enabling us to deal with databases in a non-blocking fashion, but not without additional complexities in our development and the new problems and challenges that arise when reactively handling databases.

The original Hibernate implementation was conceived to solve the problems that developers had to deal with when mapping Java objects to database entities. The original implementation relies on I/O blocking synchronous communication to interact with databases. It's been, and still is, the most conventional way to access databases in Java. On the other hand, Hibernate Reactive arose from the urge for reactive programming movements and the need for asynchronous communication to database access. Instead of I/O blocking, Hibernate Reactive relies upon I/O non-blocking communication to interact with databases.

The entity mapping properties remain the same in a reactive implementation. However, what changes is how we open a database's Reactive connection and how we should structure the software code to handle database entities reactively.

When using Quarkus, there is no need to provide a reactive persistence configuration based on the `persistence.xml` file because Quarkus already configures it for us. Still, we will briefly explore it to have an idea of how Hibernate Reactive alone works.

To set up Hibernate Reactive, you can follow the standard approach to configuring the META-INF/ `persistence.xml` file, as shown in the following example:

```
<persistence-unit name="mysql">

    <provider>
        org.hibernate.reactive.provider
        .ReactivePersistenceProvider
    </provider>

    <class>dev.davivieria.SomeObject</class>

    <properties>
    <property name=»javax.persistence.jdbc.url»
        value=»jdbc:mysql://localhost/hreact"/>
    </properties>

</persistence-unit>
```

Note that we're using `ReactivePersistenceProvider` to open a reactive connection to the database. Once the `persistence.xml` file is properly configured, we can start using Hibernate Reactive in our code:

```
import static javax.persistence.Persistence.createEnti
  tyManagerFactory;
SessionFactory factory = createEntityManagerFactory (
persistenceUnitName ( args ) ).unwrap(SessionFac
  tory.class);

/** Code omitted **/
public static String persistenceUnitName(String[] args) {
    return args.length > 0 ?
    args[0] : "postgresql-example";
}
```

We start by importing the static `javax.persistence.Persistence.createEntityMan-agerFactory` method provided by Hibernate Reactive. This static method facilitates the creation of `SessionFactory` objects.

In order to create a `SessionFactory` object, the system uses the properties defined by the `persistence.xml` file. With `SessionFactory`, we can start reactive communication with the database:

```
SomeObject someObject = new SomeObject();
factory.withTransaction(
    (
org.hibernate.reactive.mutiny.Mutiny.
  Transaction session,
org.hibernate.reactive.mutiny.Mutiny.Transaction tx) ->
    session.persistAll(someObject)).subscribe();
```

To persist data, first, we need to create a transaction by calling the `withTransaction` method. Inside a transaction, we call the `persistAll` method from `SessionFactory` to persist an object. We call the `subscribe` method to trigger the persistence operation in a non-blocking way.

By establishing a layer between the application and the database, Hibernate provides all the basic things we need to handle databases in Java.

Now, let's see how `Panache` can make things even simpler.

Panache features

`Panache` sits on top of Hibernate and enhances it even more by providing a simple interface for handling the database entities. `Panache` was primarily developed to work with the Quarkus framework, and it is a library aimed to abstract much of the boilerplate code required to handle the database entities. With `Panache`, you can easily apply database patterns such as **Active Record** and **Repository**. Let's briefly see how to do that.

Applying the Active Record pattern

In the **Active Record** pattern, we use the class that represents the database entity to make changes in the database. To enable this behavior, we need to extend `PanacheEntity`. Look at the following example:

```
@Entity
@Table(name="locations")
public class Location extends PanacheEntity {

    @Id @GeneratedValue
    private Integer id;
```

```
    @NotNull @Size(max=100)
    public String country;

    @NotNull @Size(max=100)
    public String state;

    @NotNull @Size(max=100)
    public String city;
}
```

The preceding `Location` class is a regular Hibernate-based entity that extends `PanacheEntity`. Besides extending `PanacheEntity`, there is nothing new in this `Location` class. We have annotations such as `@NotNull` and `@Size` that we use to validate the data.

The following are some of the things we can do with an Active Record entity:

- To list entities, we can call the `listAll` method. This method is available on `Location` because we're extending the `PanacheEntity` class:

    ```
    List<Location> locations = Location.listAll();
    ```

- To delete all the `Location` entities, we can call the `deleteAll` method:

    ```
    Location.deleteAll();
    ```

- To find a specific `Location` entity by its ID, we can use the `findByIdOptional` method:

    ```
    Optional<Location> optional = Location.findByIdOp
      tional(locationId);
    ```

- To persist a `Location` entity, we have to call the `persist` method on the `Location` instance we intend to persist:

    ```
    Location location = new Location();
    location.country = "Brazil";
    location.state = "Sao Paulo";
    location.city = "Santo Andre";
    location.persist();
    ```

Every time we execute one of the preceding described operations, they are immediately committed to the database.

Now, let's see how to use `Panache` to apply the Repository pattern.

Applying the Repository pattern

Instead of using an entity class to perform actions on the database, we use a separate class that is usually dedicated to providing database operations in the Repository pattern. This kind of class works like a repository interface for the database.

To apply the Repository pattern, we should use regular Hibernate entities:

```
@Entity
@Table(name="locations")
public class Location {
/** Code omitted **/
}
```

Note that at this time, we're not extending the `PanacheEntity` class. In the Repository pattern, we don't call the database operations directly through the entity class. Instead, we call them through the repository class. Here is an example of how we can implement a repository class:

```
@ApplicationScoped
public class LocationRepository implements PanacheReposi
  tory<Location> {

    public Location findByCity(String city){
        return find ("city", city).firstResult();
    }

    public Location findByState(String state){
        return find("state", state).firstResult();
    }

    public void deleteSomeCountry(){
        delete ("country", "SomeCountry");
    }
  }
```

By implementing `PanacheRepository` on the `LocationRepository` class, we're enabling all the standard operations such as `findById`, `delete`, `persist`, and so on that are present in the `PanacheEntity` class. Also, we can define our own custom queries, as we did in the preceding example, by using the `find` and `delete` methods provided by the `PanacheEntity` class.

Note that we annotated the repository class as an `@ApplicationScoped` bean. This means we can inject and use it in other classes:

```
@Inject
LocationRepository locationRepository;
```

```
public Location findLocationByCity(City city){
    return locationRepository.findByCity(city);
}
```

Here, we have the most common operations available on the repository class:

- To list all the Location entities, we need to call the listAll method from LocationRepository:

  ```
  List<Location> locations = locationReposi
    tory.listAll();
  ```

- By calling deleteAll on LocationRepository, we remove all the Location entities:

  ```
  locationRepository.deleteAll();
  ```

- To find a Location entity by its ID, we call the findByIdOptional method on LocationRepository:

  ```
  Optional<Location> optional = locationReposi
    tory.findByIdOptional(locationId);
  ```

- To persist a Location entity, we need to pass a Location instance to the persist method from LocationRepository:

  ```
  Location location = new Location();
  location.country = "Brazil";
  location.state = "Sao Paulo";
  location.city = "Santo Andre";
  locationRepository.persist(location);
  ```

In the preceding examples, we are executing all database operations using the repository class. The methods we call here are the same as those present in the entity class from the Active Record approach. The only difference here is the usage of the repository class.

By learning how to use Panache to apply the Active Record and Repository patterns, we increase our capacity to provide good approaches to handling database entities. There is no better or worse pattern. The project's circumstances will ultimately dictate which pattern is more suitable.

Panache is a library made especially for Quarkus. So, the best way to connect Hibernate Reactive objects such as SessionFactory and Transaction to Panache is by delegating the database configuration to Quarkus, which will automatically provide these objects to you.

Now that we're acquainted with Hibernate Reactive and Panache, let's see how we can implement output adapters in a hexagonal system.

Enabling reactive behavior on output adapters

One of the most important benefits of using hexagonal architecture is the improved flexibility to change technologies without significant refactoring. The hexagonal system is designed so that its domain logic and business rules are oblivious to the technologies utilized to execute them.

There is no free lunch – when we decide to use the hexagonal architecture, we have to pay the price for the benefits that this architecture can provide. (By price, I mean a considerable increase in the effort and complexity required to structure the system code by following the hexagonal principles.)

If you're concerned about code reuse, you may find some practices awkward to decouple code from specific technologies. For example, consider a scenario in which we have a domain entity class and a database entity class. We may argue, *why not have just one class that serves both purposes?* Well, in the end, it's all a matter of priorities. If the coupling of the domain and technology-specific classes is not an issue for you, go ahead. In this case, you will not have the burden of maintaining a domain model plus all the infrastructure code that supports it. However, the same code would serve different purposes, thus violating the **Single Responsibility Principle** (**SRP**). Otherwise, if you see a risk in using the same code for serving different purposes, then the output adapters can help.

In *Chapter 2, Wrapping Business Rules Inside the Domain Hexagon*, we introduced an output adapter that integrated the application with the filesystem. In *Chapter 4, Creating Adapters to Interact with the Outside World*, we created a more elaborated output adapter to communicate with an H2 in-memory database. Now that we have the Quarkus toolkit at our disposal, we can create reactive output adapters.

Configuring reactive data sources

To continue the reactive effort that we started in the previous chapter by implementing reactive input adapters, we'll create and connect reactive output adapters to these reactive input adapters by executing the following steps:

1. Let's get started by configuring the required dependencies in the `pom.xml` file of the Framework hexagon:

    ```
    <dependencies>
      <dependency>
        <groupId>io.quarkus</groupId>
        artifactId>quarkus-reactive-mysql-client
          </artifactId>
      </dependency>
      <dependency>
        <groupId>io.quarkus</groupId>
       <artifactId>quarkus-hibernate-reactive-panache</ar
          tifactId>
      </dependency>
    </dependencies>
    ```

The `quarkus-reactive-mysql-client` dependency contains the libraries we need to open a reactive connection with MySQL databases and the `quarkus-hibernate-reactive-panache` dependency contains Hibernate Reactive and `Panache`. It's important to note that this library is especially suited for reactive activities. For non-reactive activities, Quarkus offers a different library.

2. Now, we need to configure the database connection on the `application.properties` file from the Bootstrap hexagon. Let's start with the data source properties:

```
quarkus.datasource.db-kind = mysql
quarkus.datasource.reactive = true
quarkus.datasource.reactive.url = mysql://lo
  calhost:3306/inventory
quarkus.datasource.username = root
quarkus.datasource.password = password
```

The `quarkus.datasource.db-kind` property is not mandatory because Quarkus can infer the database kind by looking into the specific database client that is loaded from Maven dependencies. With `quarkus.datasource.reactive` set to `true`, we're enforcing reactive connections. We need to specify the reactive database connection URL on `quarkus.datasource.reactive.url`.

3. Finally, we have to define the Hibernate configuration:

```
quarkus.hibernate-orm.sql-load-script=inventory.sql
quarkus.hibernate-orm.database.generation = drop-and-
  create
quarkus.hibernate-orm.log.sql = true
```

After Quarkus has created the database and its tables, you can load a `.sql` file to execute more instructions on the database. By default, it searches for and loads a file called `import.sql`. We can change this behavior by using the `quarkus.hibernate-orm.sql-load-script` property.

Be aware of not using `quarkus.hibernate-orm.database.generation = drop-and-create` in production. Otherwise, it will drop all your database tables. If you don't set any value, the default one, `none`, is used. The default behavior doesn't make any changes to the database.

And, finally, we enable `quarkus.hibernate-orm.log.sql` to see which SQL queries Hibernate is executing behind the hood. I recommend you enable the `log` feature only for development purposes. When running the application in production, don't forget to disable this option.

Let's now see how to configure application entities to work with a MySQL database.

Configuring entities

The topology and inventory system requires four database tables to store its data: routers, switches, networks, and location. Each one of these tables will be mapped to a Hibernate entity class properly configured to work with a MySQL data source.

We'll apply the Repository pattern, so we won't have the entities to perform database operations. Instead, we'll create separate repository classes to trigger actions on the database, but before creating repository classes, let's start by implementing Hibernate entities for the topology and inventory system. We'll configure these entities to work with MySQL databases.

The Router entity

For this entity and the others that will be implemented subsequently, we should create classes in the `dev.davivieira.topologyinventory.framework.adapters.output.mysql.data` package of the Framework hexagon.

Here is what the `Router` entity class should look like:

```
@Entity(name = "RouterData")
@Table(name = "routers")
@EqualsAndHashCode(exclude = "routers")
public class RouterData implements Serializable {

    @Id
    @Column(name="router_id", columnDefinition =
      «BINARY(16)")
    private UUID routerId;

    @Column(name="router_parent_core_id",
    columnDefinition = "BINARY(16)")
    private UUID routerParentCoreId;
  /** Code omitted **/
}
```

For the `routerId` and `routerParentCoreId` fields, we must set `columnDefinition`, the `@Column` annotation parameter, to `BINARY(16)`. It's a requirement to make UUID attributes work on MySQL databases.

Then, we create the relationship mapping between routers and other tables:

```
{
    /**Code omitted**/
    @ManyToOne(cascade = CascadeType.ALL)
    @JoinColumn(name="location_id")
    private LocationData routerLocation;
```

```
@OneToMany(cascade = {CascadeType.MERGE},
fetch = FetchType.EAGER)
@JoinColumn(name="router_id")
private List<SwitchData> switches;

@OneToMany(cascade = CascadeType.ALL, fetch =
  FetchType.EAGER)
@JoinColumn(name="router_parent_core_id")
private Set<RouterData> routers;
/**Code omitted**/
}
```

Here, we define a many-to-one relation between routers and location. After that, we have two one-to-many relationships with switches and routers, respectively. The `fetch = FetchType.EAGER` property is used to avoid any mapping errors that may occur during the reactive connections.

Let's move on to the configuration of the `Switch` entity class.

The Switch entity

The following code shows us how we should implement the `Switch` entity class:

```
@Entity
@Table(name = "switches")
public class SwitchData {

    @ManyToOne
    private RouterData router;

    @Id
    @Column(name="switch_id", columnDefinition =
      «BINARY(16)")
    private UUID switchId;

    @Column(name="router_id", columnDefinition =
      «BINARY(16)")
    private UUID routerId;

    @OneToMany(cascade = CascadeType.ALL, fetch =
      FetchType.EAGER)
    @JoinColumn(name="switch_id")
    private Set<NetworkData> networks;

    @ManyToOne
```

```
@JoinColumn(name="location_id")
private LocationData switchLocation;

/**Code omitted**/
}
```

We have omitted other column attributes to focus only on the IDs and relationships. We start by defining a many-to-one relationship between switches and a router. The primary key is the `switchId` field, which happens to be a `UUID` attribute. We have another `UUID` attribute for mapping the `routerId` field.

Also, there is a one-to-many relationship between a switch and networks, and a many-to-one relationship between switches and a location.

Now, let's configure the `Network` entity class.

The Network entity

Although we do not consider networks to be entities in the domain model, they have a separate table in the database. So, at the Framework hexagon level, we treat them as database entities, but when they reach the Domain hexagon, we treat them as value objects. This example shows that the hexagon system dictates how the data will be treated at the Domain hexagon level. By doing so, the hexagonal system shields the domain model from technical details.

We implement the `Network` entity class as follows:

```
@Entity
@Table(name = "networks")
public class NetworkData {

    @ManyToOne
    @JoinColumn(name="switch_id")
    private SwitchData switchData;

    @Id
    @GeneratedValue(strategy = GenerationType.IDENTITY)
    @Column(name="network_id")
    private int id;

    /**Code omitted**/
}
```

This is a straightforward entity class with a many-to-one relationship between networks and a switch. For networks, we rely on the database to generate network IDs. Also, networks are not considered entities in the domain model. Instead, we treat networks as value objects that are controlled by an aggregate. For aggregates, we need to handle the `UUID`, but for value objects, we do not. That's why we don't handle UUIDs for network database entities.

We still need to implement one last entity for location. Let's do that.

The Location entity

In networks, location is not considered an entity at the Domain hexagon level, but because we have a separate table for location, we need to treat it as a database entity at the Framework hexagon level.

The following code is used to implement the `Location` entity class:

```
Entity
@Table(name = "location")
public class LocationData {

    @Id
    @Column(name="location_id")
    @GeneratedValue(strategy = GenerationType.IDENTITY)
    private int locationId;

    @Column(name="address")
    private String address;

    @Column(name="city")
    private String city;

    /**Code omitted**/
}
```

We again rely on the database's built-in ID generation mechanism to handle IDs for location data. After that, we have attributes such as `address` and `city` that are part of a location.

Now that we have all the required entities adequately configured, we can move ahead and use `Panache` to create reactive repository classes, which we'll use to trigger database operations with the entities we've configured.

Implementing reactive repository classes

By implementing the `PanacheRepositoryBase` interface, you create a reactive repository class. We'll need one repository class for router operations and another for switch operations.

It's paramount to define only one repository for the aggregate root. In our case, the `Router` entity is the aggregate root for router management operations, and `Switch` is the aggregate root for switch management operations. The purpose of an aggregate is to ensure consistency across all objects that are controlled by such an aggregate. The entry point for any aggregate is always the aggregate root. To ensure aggregate consistency in a database transaction, we define only one repository class, which is dedicated to controlling the database operations based on the aggregate root.

The classes we're about to implement are located in the dev.davivieira.topologyinventory. framework.adapters.output.mysql.repository package:

- The following code implements the RouterManagementRepository class:

```
@ApplicationScoped
public class RouterManagementRepository implements Pa
  nacheRepositoryBase<RouterData, UUID> {


}
```

Note that we're passing RouterData as the entity we're working on and UUID as the attribute type mapped to be used by the ID. If we don't need any custom queries, we can leave this class empty because Panache already provides lots of standard database operations.

Note that we're also annotating that class with @ApplicationScoped, so we can inject that component in other places, such as the output adapter, which we'll implement soon.

- The following code implements the SwitchManagementRepository class:

```
@ApplicationScoped
public class SwitchManagementRepository implements Pa
  nacheRepositoryBase<SwitchData, UUID> {


}
```

Here, we're following the same approach we did for the RouterManagementRepository class.

With the reactive repository classes properly implemented, we're ready to create reactive output adapters. Let's do that!

Implementing reactive output adapters

Just to recap, we need to provide an adapter implementation for the RouterManagementOutputPort output port interface:

```
public interface RouterManagementOutputPort {
    Router retrieveRouter(Id id);

    boolean removeRouter(Id id);

    Router persistRouter(Router router);
}
```

When implementing the MySQL output adapter, we'll provide a reactive implementation for each one of the preceding method declarations.

We also need to implement the `SwitchManagementOutputPort` output adapter interface:

```
public interface SwitchManagementOutputPort {
    Switch retrieveSwitch(Id id);
}
```

It's simpler, as there's just one method for which we need to provide a reactive implementation.

Let's start by implementing the reactive output adapter for router management.

Reactive router management of the MySQL output adapter

In order to enable the hexagonal system to communicate with a MySQL database, we need to create a new output adapter to allow such integration (because we're using Quarkus, such an output adapter implementation is fairly simple). We'll use the following steps to do so:

1. We start by injecting the `RouterManagementRepository` repository class:

    ```
    @ApplicationScoped
    public class RouterManagementMySQLAdapter implements
      RouterManagementOutputPort {

        @Inject
        RouterManagementRepository
          routerManagementRepository;
        /** Code omitted **/
    }
    ```

    We'll use the `RouterManagementRepository` repository to make database operations.

2. Then, we implement the `retrieveRouter` method:

    ```
    @Override
    public Router retrieveRouter(Id id) {
        var routerData =
        routerManagementRepository.findById(id.getUuid())
          .subscribe()
          .asCompletionStage()
          .join();
        return RouterMapper.routerDataToDomain(router
          Data);
    }
    ```

    When we call `routerManagementRepository.findById(id.getUuid())`, the system starts an I/O non-blocking operation. This `subscribe` call tries to resolve the item produced by the `findById` operation. Then, we call `asCompletionStage` to receive the item. Finally, we call `join`, which returns the result value when the operation is complete.

3. Now, we need to implement the `removeRouter` method:

```
@Override
public Router removeRouter(Id id) {
 return routerManagementRepository
       .deleteById(
       id.getUuid())
       .subscribe().asCompletionStage().join();
}
```

Here, we call the `routerManagementRepository.deleteById(id.getUuid())` Panache operation to remove a router from the database. After that, we call `subscribe`, `asCompletionStage`, and `join` to execute the operations reactively.

4. Finally, we implement the `persistRouter` method:

```
@Override
public Router persistRouter(Router router) {
    var routerData =
    RouterH2Mapper.routerDomainToData(router);
    Panache.withTransaction(
    ()->routerManagementRepository.persist
    (routerData));
    return router;
}
```

The construct is different here. To ensure that the transaction will not be lost between the client and server during the request, we wrap the persistence operation inside `Panache.withTransaction`. This is a requirement for operations where we need to persist data.

Let's now implement the reactive output adapter for switch management.

Reactive switch management of the MySQL output adapter

The approach used here is the same one utilized when we implemented the reactive output adapter for router management. We'll execute the following steps to implement the reactive output adapter:

1. Let's start by injecting the `SwitchManagementRepository` repository class:

```
@ApplicationScoped
public class SwitchManagementMySQLAdapter implements
  SwitchManagementOutputPort {

   @Inject
   SwitchManagementRepository
     switchManagementRepository;
```

```
        /** Code omitted **/
    }
```

As we already saw, the injection of a repository class is required so we can use it to trigger database operations.

2. After that, we implement the `retrieveSwitch` method:

    ```
    @Override
    public Switch retrieveSwitch(Id id) {
        var switchData =
        switchManagementRepository.findById(id.getUuid())
            .subscribe()
            .asCompletionStage()
            .join();
        return RouterMapper.switchDataToDo
          main(switchData);
    }
    ```

    We use this method to retrieve a `Switch` object reactively. There are no persistence methods because all the write operations should always occur through a router management output adapter.

By implementing reactive output adapters in the hexagonal system, we can tap into the advantages of reactive programming techniques. With hexagonal architecture, it's not a big deal to have both reactive and imperative output adapters serving different needs in the same system.

The Quarkus reactive features for databases are paramount for anyone venturing into developing reactive systems. We can provide a reactive alternative to how our application deals with databases by understanding how to use these features. That does not mean that the reactive approach is always a better choice than the traditional imperative one; it's up to you and your project's needs to decide which approach is more suitable.

Now that we've implemented the `RouterManagementMySQLAdapter` and `SwitchManagementMySQLAdapter` output adapters, let's test them.

Testing the reactive output adapters

We need to implement unit tests to ensure the methods from the output adapters are working as expected. Here is an example of how we can create unit tests for `RouterManagementMySQLAdapter`:

```
@QuarkusTest
public class RouterManagementMySQLAdapterTest {

    @InjectMock
    RouterManagementMySQLAdapter
    routerManagementMySQLAdapter;
```

```
@Test
public void testRetrieveRouter() {
    Router router = getRouter();
    Mockito.when(
    routerManagementMySQLAdapter.
    retrieveRouter(router.getId())).thenReturn(router);
    Router retrievedRouter =
    routerManagementMySQLAdapter.
    retrieveRouter(router.getId());
    Assertions.assertSame(router, retrievedRouter);
}
/** Code omitted **/
}
```

It's possible to use the @InjectMock annotation to mock the RouterManagementMySQLAdapter output adapter. When executing the testRetrieveRouter test method, we can mock a call to routerManagementMySQLAdapter.retrieveRouter(router.getId) by using Mockito. when. The thenReturn method returns the object that our mock test should return. In this case, it is a Router object. With Assertions.assertSame(router, retrievedRouter), we can assert the result for the execution of retrieveRouter(router.getId).

We won't need to implement new test classes to execute integration tests for Reactive output adapters. We can rely on the same tests used in the previous chapter to test the reactive input adapters. These tests call the input adapters, which, in turn, call the output adapters by using the use case operations.

However, what changes is that we'll need a MySQL database to test the reactive output adapters.

Quarkus provides Docker-based containers that we can use for development purposes or testing. In order to enable such a database container, there is no need to provide a detailed data source connection configuration in the application.properties file. Here is how we should configure that file for testing purposes:

```
quarkus.datasource.db-kind=mysql
quarkus.datasource.reactive=true
quarkus.hibernate-orm.database.generation=drop-and-create
quarkus.hibernate-orm.sql-load-script=inventory.sql
quarkus.vertx.max-event-loop-execute-time=100
```

Note that we're not specifying a database connection URL. By doing that, Quarkus understands that it needs to provide a database. The previously described application.properties file should be placed in the tests/resource/ directory. Inside this directory, we should also place the inventory.sql file, which loads data into the database. This .sql file is available in this chapter's GitHub repository.

You can override entries in `application.properties` to use environment variables. This may be useful for configurations such as `quarkus.hibernate-orm.database.generation` where you can set the property value based on the application's environment variables. For example, for local or development purposes, you can use `${DB_GENERATION}`, an environment variable that resolves to `drop-and-create`. In production, this environment variable can resolve to `none`.

After properly setting up the `application.properties` and `inventory.sql` files, we can test the application by running the following command in the project's root directory:

```
$ mvn test
```

The following output shows the MySQL Docker container being brought up to be used during tests:

```
2021-10-10 01:33:40,242 INFO   [  .0.24]] (build-10) Creating container
for image: mysql:8.0.24
2021-10-10 01:33:40,876 INFO   [  .0.24]]
(build-10) Starting container with ID:
67e788aab66f2f2c6bd91c0be1a164117294ac29cc574941ad41ff5760de918c
2021-10-10 01:33:41,513 INFO   [  .0.24]] (build-
10) Container mysql:8.0.24 is starting:
67e788aab66f2f2c6bd91c0be1a164117294ac29cc574941ad41ff5760de918c
2021-10-10 01:33:41,520 INFO   [  .0.24]] (build-10) Waiting
for database connection to become available at jdbc:mysql://
localhost:49264/default using query 'SELECT 1'
2021-10-10 01:34:01,078 INFO   [  .0.24]] (build-10) Container is
started (JDBC URL: jdbc:mysql://localhost:49264/default)
2021-10-10 01:34:01,079 INFO   [  .0.24]] (build-10) Container
mysql:8.0.24 started in PT20.883579S
2021-10-10 01:34:01,079 INFO   [io.qua.dev.mys.dep.
MySQLDevServicesProcessor] (build-10) Dev Services for MySQL started.
```

Quarkus creates a database called `default`, where the tables are created. The `inventory.sql` file is run against this `default` database.

After the database is ready, Quarkus starts testing the system, resulting in a result similar to the following one:

```
[INFO] Tests run: 2, Failures: 0, Errors: 0, Skipped: 0, Time elapsed:
32.672 s - in dev.davivieira.topologyinventory.framework.adapters.
input.rest.NetworkManagementAdapterTest
[INFO] Running dev.davivieira.topologyinventory.framework.adapters.
input.rest.RouterManagementAdapterTest
[INFO] Tests run: 5, Failures: 0, Errors: 0, Skipped: 0, Time elapsed:
0.232 s - in dev.davivieira.topologyinventory.framework.adapters.
input.rest.RouterManagementAdapterTest
[INFO] Running dev.davivieira.topologyinventory.framework.adapters.
input.rest.SwitchManagementAdapterTest
[INFO] Tests run: 3, Failures: 0, Errors: 0, Skipped: 0, Time elapsed:
0.088 s - in dev.davivieira.topologyinventory.framework.adapters.
```

```
input.rest.SwitchManagementAdapterTest
[INFO] Running dev.davivieira.topologyinventory.framework.adapters.
input.rest.outputAdapters.RouterManagementMySQLAdapterTest
[INFO] Tests run: 3, Failures: 0, Errors: 0, Skipped: 0, Time elapsed:
0.116 s - in dev.davivieira.topologyinventory.framework.adapters.
input.rest.outputAdapters.RouterManagementMySQLAdapterTest
[INFO] Running dev.davivieira.topologyinventory.framework.adapters.
input.rest.outputAdapters.SwitchManagementMySQLAdapterTest
[INFO] Tests run: 1, Failures: 0, Errors: 0, Skipped: 0, Time elapsed:
0.013 s - in dev.davivieira.topologyinventory.framework.adapters.
input.rest.outputAdapters.SwitchManagementMySQLAdapterTest
```

In order to test the output adapters, we need to call the input adapters. If we can test the input adapters successfully, that means we're also testing the output adapters successfully.

Summary

Hibernate Reactive and `Panache` make our lives much easier when we need to handle databases reactively using Quarkus. We learned that Hibernate Reactive is built on top of the traditional Hibernate implementation but with the addition of reactive features.

While looking into `Panache`, we learned that it can help us implement the Active Record and Repository patterns to implement database operations. For the hands-on part, we implemented database entities, repositories, and reactive output adapters, which we used together to interact with the MySQL database. Finally, we configured the hexagonal system tests to use the MySQL Docker container that Quarkus provides.

In the next chapter, we'll learn about some techniques for packaging the hexagonal system in a Docker image. We'll also learn how to run the hexagonal system in a Kubernetes cluster. This knowledge will enable us to make our hexagonal application ready to be deployed in cloud-based environments.

Questions

1. Which Java specification does Hibernate Reactive implement?
2. What is the difference between the Active Record and Repository patterns?
3. Which interface should we implement to apply the Repository pattern?
4. Why should we run write operations inside the `withTransaction` method?

Answers

1. Hibernate Reactive implements the **JPA** specification.

2. The Active Record pattern allows us to use the entity class to perform operations on the database, whereas we have a dedicated class in the Repository pattern to perform such operations.

3. We should implement the `PanacheRepositoryBase` interface.

4. To ensure the database transaction won't be lost during the reactive operation.

14

Setting Up Dockerfile and Kubernetes Objects for Cloud Deployment

We spent the previous chapters exploring some of the amazing features that Quarkus provides to help us create cloud-native applications. Going even further, we also learned how to integrate Quarkus into a hexagonal system.

Now, we need to prepare the hexagonal system so that it can be deployed in cloud environments. Docker and Kubernetes are the leading technologies that dominate the cloud scene nowadays. If your application is prepared to run on these technologies, you're safe to make it run on most cloud providers.

So, in this chapter, we'll learn how to wrap the hexagonal system in a Docker image and run it on a Kubernetes cluster. For Docker images, we'll explore two techniques for creating such images: one that relies on an executable `.jar` and another that uses a native executable. We'll also learn how to deploy the hexagonal system in a local **minikube**-based Kubernetes cluster.

The following topics will be covered in this chapter:

- Preparing the Docker image
- Creating Kubernetes objects
- Deploying on minikube

By the end of this chapter, you'll know how to make the hexagonal system run in a cloud-native environment based on Docker and Kubernetes. Nowadays, most modern applications run on the cloud. By turning the hexagonal system into a cloud-native one, you'll be able to tap into the advantages that exist when you're on the cloud.

Technical requirements

To compile and run the code examples presented in this chapter, you will need the latest **Java SE Development Kit** and **Maven 3.8** installed on your computer. They are available for the Linux, macOS, and Windows operating systems.

You'll also need **Docker** and **minikube** installed on your machine.

You can find the code files for this chapter on GitHub at `https://github.com/ PacktPublishing/-Designing-Hexagonal-Architecture-with-Java---Second- Edition/tree/main/Chapter14`.

Preparing the Docker image

Container-based virtualization technology is not something new. Long before Docker, there were technologies such as OpenVZ, which applied the same fundamental concepts that are applied by Docker as well. Even today, we have alternatives such as **Linux Containers (LXC)**, which provides a robust container-based solution. What sets Docker apart is how easy and intuitive it makes handling containerized applications. Docker takes portability to another level, simplifying and making containers a viable technology for larger audiences.

In the past, other container platforms were not as straightforward to use as Docker is today. Containers were a topic more related to system administrators than to software developers. Today, the scenario is different because of the simple yet powerful container-based solution we have with Docker. Because of its simplicity, Docker rapidly became popular among developers, who started to incorporate it into their projects.

As I mentioned previously, Docker's strength is in its simplicity to use and learn. Take, for example, how Docker abstracts the complexity required to wrap an application inside a container. You just need to define a Dockerfile describing how the application should be configured and executed inside the container. You can do this by using a simple set of instructions. So, Docker shields the user from low-level complexities that existed in previous container technologies.

One of the things that makes Quarkus so special is that it's a container-first framework. It's designed to build container-based applications. So, Quarkus is an excellent choice if you're targeting container-based environments.

With Quarkus, we can generate Docker images using `.jar` artifacts or native executable artifacts. We'll explore both of these approaches next.

Creating a Docker image with an uber .jar artifact

Our approach here is to wrap the uber `.jar` artifact in the Docker image so that the container can start and run the application by executing that `.jar` file. To build a Docker image, we need to create a Dockerfile with instructions to build such an image.

The following code shows how to create a Dockerfile for the topology and inventory system that uses the uber `.jar` file:

```
FROM eclipse-temurin:17.0.8_7-jdk-alpine
ENV APP_FILE_RUNNER bootstrap-1.0-SNAPSHOT-runner.jar
ENV APP_HOME /usr/apps
EXPOSE 8080
COPY bootstrap/target/$APP_FILE_RUNNER $APP_HOME/
WORKDIR $APP_HOME
ENTRYPOINT ["sh", "-c"]
CMD ["exec java -jar $APP_FILE_RUNNER"]
```

This Dockerfile should be placed in the project's root directory.

The first line is the base **JDK 17** image that we'll build our image from. Then, we define the APP_FILE_ RUNNER and APP_HOME environment variables to define the artifact's name and path, respectively. Because Quarkus is configured to run on port 8080, we have to use the EXPOSE property to expose this port externally. The COPY command will copy the artifact generated by Maven. WORKDIR defines the path that the commands will be executed from within the container. With ENTRYPOINT and CMD, we can define how the container will execute the application's uber `.jar` file.

Follow these steps to generate the Docker image and start the container:

1. First, we need to compile and generate an uber `.jar` file:

    ```
    $ mvn clean package
    ```

2. Then, we can generate the Docker image:

    ```
    $ docker build . -t topology-inventory
    Sending build context to Docker daemon  38.68MB
    Step 1/8 : FROM eclipse-temurin:17.0.8_7-jdk-alpine
     ---> 9b2a4d2e14f6
    Step 2/8 : ENV APP_FILE_RUNNER bootstrap-1.0-SNAPSHOT-runner.jar
     ---> Using cache
     ---> 753b39c99e78
    Step 3/8 : ENV APP_HOME /usr/apps
     ---> Using cache
     ---> 652c7ce2bd47
    Step 4/8 : EXPOSE 8080
     ---> Using cache
     ---> 37c6928bcae4
    Step 5/8 : COPY bootstrap/target/$APP_FILE_RUNNER $APP_HOME/
     ---> Using cache
     ---> 389c28dc9fa7
    Step 6/8 : WORKDIR $APP_HOME
    ```

```
 ---> Using cache
 ---> 4ac09c0fe8cc
Step 7/8 : ENTRYPOINT ["sh", "-c"]
 ---> Using cache
 ---> 737bbcf2402b
Step 8/8 : CMD ["exec java -jar $APP_FILE_RUNNER"]
 ---> Using cache
 ---> 3b17c3fa0662
Successfully built 3b17c3fa0662
Successfully tagged topology-inventory:latest
```

The preceding output describes all the steps that need to be executed to generate the Docker image. Here, we can see that Docker Engine starts building our image on top of the `eclipse-temurin:17.0.8_7-jdk-alpine` image. Then, it proceeds by defining the environment variables and handling the application artifact by preparing it to be executed every time a new container from that image is created.

3. Now, we can start the container with the following command:

    ```
    $ docker run -p 5555:8080 topology-inventory
    ```

    With the `-p` parameter, we're mapping the `5555` host port to the `8080` container port. So, we'll need to use the `5555` port to access the system.

4. To confirm that the application is running on the Docker container, we can access the Swagger UI URL at `http://localhost:5555/q/swagger-ui`.

Now, let's learn how to generate a Docker image using the native executable.

Creating a Docker image with a native executable

In *Chapter 10, Adding Quarkus to a Modularized Hexagonal Application*, we learned that Quarkus uses **Ahead-Of-Time** (**AOT**) compilation techniques to optimize the bytecode and generate native code that offers improved performance, mainly during application startup.

This native executable is a product of the AOT compilation that's performed by Quarkus. Contrary to the uber `.jar` file, which can be distributed to run on different operating systems and CPU architectures, the native executable file is platform-dependent. But we can overcome this limitation by wrapping the native executable into a Docker image that can be distributed to different operating systems and CPU architectures.

There are different approaches to generating a native executable. Some of them require us to install a **GraalVM** distribution and other software. However, to keep things simple, we'll follow an uncomplicated and convenient approach where Quarkus generates the native executable for us inside a Docker container that contains GraalVM.

Follow these steps to generate a Docker image with a native executable:

1. In the pom.xml file from the project's root directory, we need to include the following code before the </project> tag:

    ```
    <profiles>
      <profile>
        <id>native</id>
        <properties>
          <quarkus.package.type>native
            </quarkus.package.type>
        </properties>
      </profile>
    </profiles>
    ```

    The preceding configuration creates a profile that sets the quarkus.package.type property to native, causing Quarkus to build a native executable artifact.

2. Then, we must create the ReflectionConfiguration class on the bootstrap hexagon:

    ```
    @RegisterForReflection(targets = {
            CoreRouter.class,
            EdgeRouter.class,
            Switch.class,
            Id.class,
            IP.class,
            Location.class,
            Model.class,
            Network.class,
            Protocol.class,
            RouterType.class,
            SwitchType.class,
            Vendor.class,
    })
    public class ReflectionConfiguration {}
    ```

    One of the limitations of the native executable is that it offers partial support for reflection. **Reflection** is a technique that allows us to inspect or modify the runtime attributes of Java components, such as classes and methods. When we're running an application inside a JVM, the system can detect the classes/methods/fields that are indirectly connected. The same is not true when we're running a native executable. The reason for that is only classes that are directly connected are visible for reflection.

To overcome this limitation, we need to register all the classes for reflection that are not directly connected. There are two ways to do that: we can put such classes in a `.json` configuration file, or we can create a class annotated with the `@RegisterForReflection` annotation containing the classes we want to register for reflection. In the preceding code, we are using the latter approach, which relies on the annotated class.

3. To generate a native executable, we have to run the following command:

    ```
    $ mvn clean package -Pnative -Dquarkus.native.container-
    build=true -Dnative-image.xmx=6g
    ```

    The compilation process of a native executable is a very expensive one in terms of memory consumption. So, we need to increase memory limits to avoid out-of-memory errors. If `6g` is not enough for you, feel free to increase it to prevent errors.

4. Next, we must create a file called `Dockerfile-native` that contains instructions for building a Docker image with the native executable:

    ```
    FROM registry.access.redhat.com/ubi8/ubi-minimal
    ENV APP_FILE_RUNNER bootstrap-1.0-SNAPSHOT-runner
    ENV APP_HOME /work
    EXPOSE 8080
    COPY bootstrap/target/$APP_FILE_RUNNER $APP_HOME/
    WORKDIR $APP_HOME
    RUN echo $APP_FILE_RUNNER
    CMD ["./bootstrap-1.0-SNAPSHOT-runner", "-
       Dquarkus.http.host=0.0.0.0"]
    ```

    Instead of the JDK 17 base image, we're using the `ubi-minimal` image from the official **Red Hat** registry. This image is suitable for running native executables.

5. Then, we must generate the Docker image with the following command:

    ```
    $ docker build . -t topology-inventory-native -f Dockerfile-
    native
    ```

    You should run the preceding command from the project's root directory.

    We use `-t topology-inventory-native:latest` and `-f Dockerfile-native` to create a different Docker image based on the native executable rather than the uber `.jar` file. The output of this `docker build` command will be similar to the one we generated when we created the Docker image for the uber `.jar` file. The only difference will be the entries related to the native executable artifact.

6. Tag and upload your image to your personal Docker registry:

    ```
    $ docker tag topology-inventory-native:latest s4intlaurent/
    topology-inventory-native:latest
    $ docker push s4intlaurent/topology-inventory-native:latest
    ```

```
The push refers to repository [docker.io/s4intlaurent/topolo-
gy-inventory-native]
f3216c6ba268: Pushed
0b911edbb97f: Layer already exists
54e42005468d: Layer already exists
latest: digest: sha256:4037e5d9c2cef01bda9c4bb5722bccbe0d-
003336534c28f8245076223ce77273 size: 949
```

We'll use the system's native image when deploying the application on a minikube cluster.

7. Now, we can start the container:

```
docker run -p 5555:8080 topology-inventory-native:latest
```

Note that the application is bootstrapping much faster!

8. To confirm that the application is running on the Docker container, we can access the Swagger UI URL at `http://localhost:5555/q/swagger-ui`.

With that, we have configured the Docker images for both the uber `.jar` and native executable artifacts. These Docker images can be deployed on a Kubernetes cluster. However, to do that, we need to create the required Kubernetes objects to allow the deployment. So, in the next section, we'll learn how to create Kubernetes objects for the containerized hexagonal system.

Creating Kubernetes objects

Docker Engine does not provide any fault-tolerance or high availability mechanism. It only offers container-based virtualization technology. So, if you plan on running a critical-mission application using Docker, you may either need to work out your solution to ensure the containers are reliable while running or delegate this responsibility to a container orchestrator.

Container orchestrators arose as a response to the increased use of containers in the IT industry. Among these orchestrators, we can quote Docker Swarm, Rancher, and the one that dominates the industry: **Kubernetes**.

Initially conceived at Google as a closed source software called Borg, it was open-sourced with the name Kubernetes. It's a powerful technology that can run on your computer for development purposes or control a fleet of hundreds, even thousands, of server nodes, providing Pods for the running applications.

You may be wondering, *what is a Pod?* We'll find out soon.

It's not our intent here to dive deep into Kubernetes' internals, but we'll review some basic concepts to ensure we're on the same page.

Reviewing Kubernetes' main objects

As we saw earlier, Kubernetes is a container orchestrator that helps us manage containers. To accomplish this, most – if not all – Kubernetes configuration can be done through `.yaml` files. In Kubernetes, we have the notion of the current state and the desired state. When the former meets the latter, we're fine. Otherwise, we have problems.

The backbone of this currently desired state approach is the Kubernetes configuration mechanism based on YAML files. With these files, we can express the desired state of things inside the cluster. Kubernetes will do its magic to ensure that the current state always matches the desired state. But, you may be wondering, *the state of what?* The answer is the state of Kubernetes objects. Let's look at some of them:

- **Pod**: A Pod is a Kubernetes object that controls the life cycle of containers in a Kubernetes cluster. It's possible to attach more than one container to the same Pod, although this is not a common practice.

- **Deployment**: If a Pod controls the life cycle of containers, we can state that a `Deployment` object controls the life cycle of Pods. With a Deployment, you can specify how many Pods you want to provide for your application. Kubernetes will take care of finding the available resources in the cluster to bring up these Pods. If, for some reason, one of the Pods goes down, Kubernetes will try to bring a brand-new Pod to ensure the desired state is being met.

- **Service**: When we deploy Pods on the Kubernetes cluster, they are not immediately available internally for other Pods or externally for clients outside the cluster. To make a deployed Pod available in the network, we need to create a `Service` object attached to that Pod. This `Service` object acts as a DNS entry point that provides basic load balancing access to the Pods. For example, if you have an application running on three Pods, the `Service` object will handle application requests for one of the three Pods sitting behind the `Service` object. More sophisticated load balancing features can be achieved by using service mesh technologies such as **Istio**.

- **ConfigMap**: If you need to provide environment variables or mount a configuration file inside a Pod, `ConfigMap` is the object that can help you with that.

- **Secret**: This works similarly to `ConfigMap` but can be used to store sensitive information such as credentials or private keys. The data in a `Secret` object should be encoded with `base64`.

Now that we're more acquainted with some of the most important Kubernetes objects, let's see how we can use them to prepare our hexagonal system to be deployed on a Kubernetes cluster.

Configuring Kubernetes objects for the hexagonal system

Before creating the Kubernetes objects, first, let's configure Quarkus to enable YAML configuration and also a health check mechanism. We'll need both of these when we're deploying the application on Kubernetes:

```
<dependencies>
  <dependency>
```

```
      <groupId>io.quarkus</groupId>
      <artifactId>quarkus-config-yaml</artifactId>
    </dependency>
    <dependency>
      <groupId>io.quarkus</groupId>
      <artifactId>quarkus-smallrye-health</artifactId>
    </dependency>
  </dependencies>
```

With `quarkus-config-yaml`, we can use the `application.yaml` file for most of the Quarkus configurations. And to enable health checks endpoints, we can use `quarkus-smallrye-health`.

Before creating the Kubernetes objects, let's configure the `application.yaml` file on the `bootstrap` hexagon:

```
quarkus:
  datasource:
    username: ${QUARKUS_DATASOURCE_USERNAME:root}
    password: ${QUARKUS_DATASOURCE_PASSWORD:password}
    reactive:
      url: ${QUARKUS_DATASOURCE_REACTIVE_URL:
        mysql://localhost:3306/inventory}
```

This `.yaml` file allows us to use most, but not all, of the configurations available on Quarkus. So, it's normal to use both `application.yaml` and `application.properties`. We're using the YAML configuration because we can employ a technique called **variable interpolation**. Take, for example, the following configuration entry:

```
${QUARKUS_DATASOURCE_USERNAME:root}
```

When the application starts, it will try to resolve an environment variable named `QUARKUS_DATASOURCE_USERNAME`. If the application can't resolve the variable name, it will fall back to the default value of `root`. This technique is very useful for defining default configurations for local development where environment variables may not be set.

You may have noticed the presence of the `QUARKUS_DATASOURCE_USERNAME`, `QUARKUS_DATASOURCE_PASSWORD`, and `QUARKUS_DATASOURCE_REACTIVE_URL` environment variables. Kubernetes will provide these environment variables with the `Secret` and `ConfigMap` objects. So, let's learn how to configure these and the other Kubernetes objects that are required to deploy the topology and inventory system (the files we will describe here are put inside a directory called `k8s` in the project's root directory):

1. We will start by configuring the `configmap.yaml` file:

    ```
    apiVersion: v1
    kind: ConfigMap
    ```

```
metadata:
  name: topology-inventory
data:
  QUARKUS_DATASOURCE_REACTIVE_URL:
    «mysql://topology-inventory-mysql:3306/inventory»
```

This ConfigMap provides a QUARKUS_DATASOURCE_REACTIVE_URL environment variable with the reactive database URL that the application needs to connect to the MySQL database.

2. Then, we must configure the secret.yaml file:

```
apiVersion: v1
kind: Secret
metadata:
  name: topology-inventory
type: Opaque
data:
  QUARKUS_DATASOURCE_USERNAME: cm9vdAo=
  QUARKUS_DATASOUCE_PASSWORD: cGFzc3dvcmQK
```

In the preceding Secret, we define the QUARKUS_DATASOURCE_USERNAME and QUARKUS_DATASOUCE_PASSWORD environment variables as the credentials to connect to the system's MySQL database.

3. To generate base64, you can execute the following command on Unix-based systems:

```
$ echo root | base64 && echo password | base64
cm9vdAo=
cGFzc3dvcmQK
```

We use the root and password values as the credentials to authenticate on the MySQL database.

4. Let's configure the deployment.yaml file:

```
apiVersion: apps/v1
kind: Deployment
metadata:
  name: topology-inventory
  labels:
    app: topology-inventory
spec:
  replicas: 1
  selector:
    matchLabels:
      app: topology-inventory
  template:
    metadata:
```

```
    labels:
        app: topology-inventory
/** Code omitted **/
```

Here, we describe some of the metadata entries from the `deployment.yaml` file:

- The `metadata.labels.app` field: A Kubernetes `Service` object can apply load balancing by using the `labels` property to identify the Pods that are part of the same `Deployment`. We'll see how the `Service` object references that label shortly.

- The `replicas` field: This defines that this `Deployment` will provide just one Pod.

5. Still in the `deployment.yaml` file, we can start defining the entries for the container configuration:

```
spec:
  initContainers:
    - name: topology-inventory-mysql-init
      image: busybox
      command: [ <sh>, <-c>, <until nc -zv
        topology-inventory-mysql.default.svc.clus
          ter.local 3306; do echo waiting
        for topology-inventory-mysql.de
          fault.svc.cluster.local; sleep 5;
        done;> ]
  containers:
    - name: topology-inventory
      image: s4intlaurent/topology-
        inventory:latest
      envFrom:
      - configMapRef:
          name: topology-inventory
      livenessProbe:
        httpGet:
          path: /q/health/ready
          port: 8080
        initialDelaySeconds: 30
        timeoutSeconds: 5
        periodSeconds: 3
      ports:
  - containerPort: 8080
```

Let's look at the entries that are used for the container configuration:

- The `initContainers` field: This is used when we need to execute some tasks or wait for something before the main container starts. Here, we're using an `init` container to wait for a MySQL database to be available. The `.yaml` file that loads the database is available in this book's GitHub repository for this chapter.

- The `Containers` field: This is where we set the configuration for the container that the Pod runs.

- The `image` field: This is where we inform the image location of our application. It can be a public or private registry.

- The `configMapRef` field: This is used to inject `ConfigMap` data into the container.

- The `livenessProbe` field: Kubernetes can send probe packets to check whether the application is alive. This is where we'll use the health check mechanism we configured earlier.

- The `containerPort` field: This is where we'll inform the port about the exposed Docker container.

6. Finally, we will configure the `service.yaml` file:

```
apiVersion: v1
kind: Service
metadata:
  name: topology-inventory
  labels:
    app: topology-inventory
spec:
  type: NodePort
  ports:
    - port: 8080
      targetPort: 8080
      nodePort: 30080
      protocol: TCP
  selector:
    app: topology-inventory
```

Kubernetes provides three different Service types: `ClusterIP` for internal communication, and `NodePort` and `LoadBalance` for external communication. We're using `NodePort` to access the application from outside the Kubernetes cluster. Let's take a look at the most important fields:

- The `port` field: This field declares the Service port that is available internally for other Pods in the Kubernetes cluster

- The `targetPort` field: This field specifies the port that the container is exposing

- The `nodePort` field: This field specifies the external port, which allows external clients to access the application

It's not a trivial undertaking to prepare an application to be deployed on a Kubernetes cluster. In this section, we learned about the main objects of Kubernetes. Understanding these objects is essential because they are the building blocks for any application running on a Kubernetes cluster.

With all the required Kubernetes objects adequately configured, we can deploy the hexagonal system in a Kubernetes cluster.

Deploying on minikube

minikube is a Kubernetes cluster that was made for development purposes. It allows us to create and destroy clusters with ease. Because of its simplicity, we'll use minikube to deploy our hexagonal system by following these steps (I recommend following the instructions at `https://minikube.sigs.k8s.io/docs/start/` to install minikube on your machine):

1. Once you have installed minikube, you can start your cluster by issuing the following command:

    ```
    $ minikube start
    :) minikube v1.4.0 on Fedora 30
       Creating virtualbox VM (CPUs=2, Memory=2000MB, Disk=20000MB)
    ...
       Preparing Kubernetes v1.16.0 on Docker 18.09.9 ...
       Pulling images ...
       Launching Kubernetes ...
       Waiting for: apiserver proxy etcd scheduler controller dns
       Done! kubectl is now configured to use "minikube"
    ```

    The default cluster configuration consumes 2 CPUs, 2 GB of RAM, and 20 GB of disk space.

2. To confirm that your cluster is alive, run the following command:

    ```
    $ kubectl get nodes
    NAME        STATUS    ROLES    AGE    VERSION
    minikube    Ready     master   5m     v1.16.0
    ```

    Nice! Now, we can deploy the topology and inventory system to our local Kubernetes cluster.

3. The Deployment process is fairly simple. All we have to do is apply the Kubernetes YAML files we created in the previous section:

    ```
    $ kubectl apply -f k8s/
    configmap/topology-inventory created
    deployment.apps/topology-inventory-mysql created
    service/topology-inventory-mysql created
    deployment.apps/topology-inventory created
    secret/topology-inventory created
    service/topology-inventory created
    ```

4. Then, we can run the following command to see whether the topology and inventory system is up and running:

```
$ kubectl get pods
NAME                                      READY    STATUS    RES
TARTS     AGE
topology-invento-
ry-76f4986846-zq5t8          1/1      Running   0            73s
topology-inventory-mysql-dc9dbf-
c4b-7sct6     1/1      Running    0            73s
```

5. To access the application, we need to use the minikube cluster IP. You can use the following code to retrieve that IP on a Unix-based operating system:

```
$ minikube ssh "ip addr show eth0" | grep "inet\b" | awk '{print
$2}' | cut -d/ -f1
192.168.49.2
```

6. With that IP, we can query the health check endpoint to see whether the topology and inventory system is alive:

```
$ curl -s http://192.168.49.2:30080/q/health/ready | jq
{
  "status": "UP",
  "checks": [
    {
      "name": "Reactive MySQL connections health
        check",
      "status": "UP",
      "data": {
        "<default>": "UP"
      }
    }
  ]
}
```

This shows that both the application and its database connection are healthy.

You can also access the Swagger UI URL at `http://192.168.49.2:30080/q/swagger-ui`, as shown in the following screenshot:

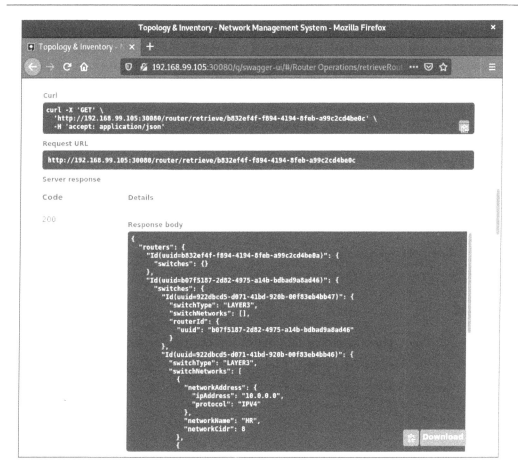

Figure 14.1 – Swagger UI from topology and inventory running on minikube

Note that we are using port `30080` to access the Swagger UI URL on minikube. `30080` is the Kubernetes node port that we configured to enable external access to the application.

With that, we have completed the fundamental steps to turn the hexagonal system into a cloud-native one. Our application is ready to be deployed on a local minikube cluster and any cloud provider that offers Kubernetes clusters.

Summary

We started this chapter by learning about the building blocks that we can use to create a Docker image for the hexagonal system. Then, we created two Docker image types. The first one was based on the uber `.jar` file, which is used to package and run the application, while the second one was based on native executables, where we could leverage the features Quarkus provides to create a native executable artifact.

Then, we created the Kubernetes objects that were required to deploy the hexagonal system in a Kubernetes cluster. Finally, we deployed the hexagonal system in a local minikube cluster. More than a hexagonal system, we now have a cloud-native hexagonal system ready to tap into the advantages provided by cloud environments.

In the next chapter, we will learn how hexagonal architecture relates to layered architecture, an architectural style used by many applications. Understanding the differences between these two architectures helps us assess which architecture may be better to employ when starting or refactoring a software project.

Questions

1. What is the advantage of the native executable over the uber `.jar` artifact?

2. Which Kubernetes object can we use to store environment variables and mount configuration files?

3. What Service type is used to make a Kubernetes Pod externally available?

Answers

1. The startup time is much faster than the traditional uber `.jar` artifact.

2. We can use the `ConfigMap` object.

3. The `NodePort` Service type.

Part 4: Hexagonal Architecture and Beyond

You will learn in this part what distinguishes hexagonal architecture from the widely used layered architecture. We will highlight the differences between both and allow you to make a more informed decision regarding which architecture to use when starting your next software project.

We will then explore how SOLID principles can be combined with hexagonal architecture ideas to build better, change-tolerant applications.

Finally, to finish the book, we'll discuss some good design practices you can follow to create robust hexagonal systems.

This part has the following chapters:

- *Chapter 15, Comparing Hexagonal Architecture with Layered Architecture*
- *Chapter 16, Using SOLID Principles with Hexagonal Architecture*
- *Chapter 17, Good Design Practices for Your Hexagonal Application*

15

Comparing Hexagonal Architecture with Layered Architecture

Hexagonal architecture is just one of several software architecture approaches. Among these approaches, one that stands out is the so-called layered architecture, which has been widely used in enterprise software development for years. Its vast adoption is because it's reasonably simple to apply the layered architecture principles and also because this is one of the patterns that may naturally emerge when there is no conscious decision made regarding which architectural approach to use for new projects.

Understanding layered architecture and being aware of its differences when comparing it to hexagonal architecture is good to help us make more informed decisions regarding which software architecture approach to use when starting or refactoring a software project. That's why in this chapter, we will begin by reviewing layered architecture ideas. Then, based on those ideas, we will implement a simple application to learn how to apply the layered architecture concepts. We will then proceed by refactoring that simple application using hexagonal architecture ideas so we can better grasp the contrasts between the two architectures. Finally, we will finish by assessing the advantages and disadvantages of hexagonal and layered architectures.

The following topics will be covered in this chapter:

- Reviewing the layered architecture
- Creating an application using the layered architecture
- Rewriting a layered architecture application into a hexagonal one
- Assessing the benefits and disadvantages of hexagonal and layered architectures

By the end of this chapter, you will understand the difference between layered and hexagonal architecture, enabling you to make better, informed decisions on your next software project.

Technical requirements

To compile and run the code examples presented in this chapter, you will need the latest **Java SE Development Kit** and **Maven 3.8** installed on your computer. They are available for the Linux, Mac, and Windows operating systems.

You can find the code files for this chapter on GitHub at `https://github.com/ PacktPublishing/-Designing-Hexagonal-Architecture-with-Java---Second-Edition/tree/main/Chapter15`.

Reviewing the layered architecture

Layered architecture, in my view, may emerge when a group of developers in charge of a project do not stop to think about which kind of architecture is more suitable for the software they want to develop. I have observed this scenario in projects where without conscious team planning, the code structure would evolve to some level of separation of concerns where the presentation/API code would be somewhat isolated from the business and infrastructure code. You would not see core business logic in the classes responsible for providing a REST endpoint, for example. You may notice, in such projects, packages named `model`, `repository`, `service`, and `controller` as hints to a system based on the layered architecture ideas. They are hints because each of those packages usually represents an intent to allocate a specific software responsibility. The code present in the `model` package is used to represent database entities. The `repository` package contains classes showing which kind of database operations the system can do based on the model entities. `service` is a package where some business logic is executed over the data retrieved from the database using classes from the `repository` package. Finally, the `controller` package contains classes exposing API endpoints to allow triggering one of the supported application behaviors.

As a form of layered architecture, we can see the code structure based on the `model`, `repository`, `service`, and `controller` packages. Each package represents a layer with its responsibility that depends directly on the code from the package/layer that comes next or is below it. The controller depends on the service, which depends on the repository, which depends on the model. It's not uncommon to see slight variations of this pattern where more layers are introduced, even though the general idea of downward dependency is always there. There may even be situations where a layer bypasses the next layer and relies on the classes from another layer. We can see how a backend application based on layered architecture is usually structured in the following figure:

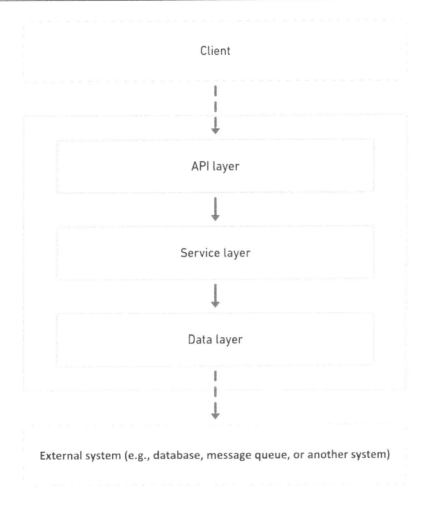

Figure 15.1 – Layered architecture example

Instead of a presentation layer, which would make sense if we were developing a web application, we have the API layer containing classes with REST endpoint logic. These classes are responsible for receiving the client request and triggering some application behavior in the service layer. This layer usually contains business logic that depends on external data. To handle external data, we have the data layer containing classes responsible for getting, persisting, and mapping external data. I don't use the term persistence here to avoid implying the data source will be a database. The data can come from anywhere, including a database.

I have seen this pattern being employed in a few software development projects in large enterprises and start-ups. Curiously, if you ask developers involved in the project which architecture they used, they would probably say no specific architecture was applied, even though their code suggests the software was developed based on the layered architecture.

Because layered architecture has existed for many years, it has kind of become a standard architecture for enterprise software projects. The idea of segregating responsibilities based on high-level system components seems to accommodate a good deal of the necessities we see in enterprise software, usually because this kind of software follows, most of the time, the same pattern of receiving input, getting data from somewhere, performing data processing, and then persisting or sending that data to another system. Given that many enterprise applications are developed following this pattern, what significantly changes between those applications is the data-processing part containing the business rules specific to a given application. The other parts may also change but not so considerably because how APIs are exposed and how data is retrieved/persisted may be standardized across different applications of the same organization, especially when the same team maintains those applications.

Although layered architecture helps to provide some level of decoupling, it does not entirely avoid situations where changes in one layer may also require changes in another. When you have the business/service layer depending on the persistence layer, changes on the latter can impact the former. Next, I will share an experience using the layered architecture.

I recall a situation where the team I was working with decided to change the database technology in the middle of the project. During the implementation, it turned out that an ORM feature available for the previous database technology was unavailable to the new database. The problem was that the system had some business rules that relied directly on that missing feature from the new database. Ultimately, we had to adjust our approach by significantly changing how those business rules would be processed. This application, in particular, evolved without a team discussion on what architectural principles should have been followed. Eventually, the project evolved into something with layered architecture characteristics.

To better understand the layered architecture, let's develop an application based on this architecture idea.

Creating an application using the layered architecture

In the previous section, we saw how a backend application based on layered architecture can be structured. Our example has three layers: API, service, and data. Following this structure, we will develop a simple user application that allows user registration and login. We will implement the data layer, then proceed to the service layer, and then the API layer. The application will be based on Quarkus, so we can rely on the framework to provide REST endpoints and connect to a database.

Implementing the data layer

The data layer is responsible for allowing getting, persisting, and mapping external data. We rely on a database for the user application to store user information:

1. So, let's start by preparing Quarkus to enable us to use an H2 in-memory database:

```
quarkus.datasource.db-kind=h2
quarkus.datasource.jdbc.url=jdbc:h2:mem:default;DB_CLO
```

```
  SE_DELAY=-1.;NON_KEYWORDS=user
quarkus.hibernate-orm.database.generation=drop-and-
  create
```

The `quarkus.datasource.db-kind` property tells Quarkus to use the H2 driver. `quarkus.datasource.jdbc.url` configures an in-memory database that will live while the application is running. Finally, we set `quarkus.hibernate-orm.database. generation` to allow the automatic creation of the database on the application startup.

2. In the `dev.davivieira.layered.data.entity` package, we create the `User` ORM entity class:

```
package dev.davivieira.layered.data.entity;

import jakarta.persistence.Entity;
import jakarta.persistence.GeneratedValue;
import jakarta.persistence.GenerationType;
import jakarta.persistence.Id;
import lombok.*;

@Entity
@Getter
@Setter
@RequiredArgsConstructor
@NoArgsConstructor
public class User {

    @Id
    @GeneratedValue(strategy =
    GenerationType.IDENTITY)
    private Long id;
    @NonNull
    private String email;
    @NonNull
    private String password;
}
```

`User` is an ORM entity because the Jakarta `@Entity` annotation is placed on top of the class. The `id` attribute is annotated with `@GeneratedValue`, so the underlying database generates the `id` value. We finished the implementation with the `email` and `password` attributes required for new user registration and login.

3. In the `dev.davivieira.layered.data.repository` package, we create the
    `UserRepository` class:

    ```
    package dev.davivieira.layered.data.repository;

    import dev.davivieira.layered.data.entity.User;
    import io.quarkus.hibernate.orm.
      panache.PanacheRepository;
    import jakarta.enterprise.context.ApplicationScoped;

    import java.util.Optional;

    @ApplicationScoped
    public class UserRepository implements PanacheReposi
      tory<User> {

        public Optional<User> findByEmail(String email) {
            return find("email",
            email).firstResultOptional();
        }
    }
    ```

    By implementing `PanacheRepository`, we get predefined standard database operations
    to allow fetching, saving, and deleting data. In addition to those predefined operations, we
    create `findByEmail` to search `User` entities using the email address. If no data is found, it
    returns an empty `Optional`.

The `User` entity and repository comprise the data layer, allowing us to persist and retrieve user data
from a database. Let's now implement the service layer.

Implementing the service layer

We need a place to put the logic to check whether the email address already exists when registering a new
user or validating the user credentials during the login. The service layer is where we place that logic:

1. In the `dev.davivieira.layered.service` package, we start the implementation of
    the `UserService` class:

    ```
    @ApplicationScoped
    public class UserService {

        @Inject
        UserRepository userRepository;
        /** Code omitted **/
    }
    ```

We inject `UserRepository` to enable the service class to handle external data through the data layer.

2. We won't map client requests directly to an ORM entity when receiving them. Instead, we map those requests to a `UserDto` class:

```
public record UserDto (String email, String password)
    {}
```

The `record` class will automatically generate the class constructor, getters, and setters for the email and password fields.

3. Continuing with the `UserService` class, we implement the `createAccount` and `isEmailAlreadyUsed` methods:

```
@Transactional
public String createAccount(UserDto userDto) throws
  Exception {
     isEmailAlreadyUsed(userDto.email());

     var user = new User(userDto.email(),
     userDto.password());
     userRepository.persist(user);

     return "User successfully created";
}

private void isEmailAlreadyUsed(String email) throws
  Exception {

     if(userRepository.findByEmail(email).isPresent()){
         throw new Exception("Email address already
                             exist");
     }
}
```

The `createAccount` method receives the `UserDto` parameter. We get the email from this parameter and pass it to the `isEmailAlreadyUsed` method, which uses `findByEmail` from `UserRepository` to check whether the email already exists.

4. To finish the `UserService` implementation, we create the `login` and `isThePasswordValid` methods:

```
public String login(UserDto userDto) {
     var optionalUser =
     userRepository.findByEmail(userDto.email());
     if (optionalUser.isPresent()) {
```

```
            var user = optionalUser.get();
            var isThePasswordValid =
            isThePasswordValid(user, userDto);
            if (isThePasswordValid) {
                return "Authenticated with success";
            } else {
                return "Invalid credentials";
            }
        } else {
            return "Invalid credentials";
        }
    }

    private boolean isThePasswordValid(User user, UserDto
        userDto) {
        return
        user.getPassword().equals(userDto.password());
    }
```

In the `login` method, we get the email from `UserDto` and use it to check whether the user account exists for that email. If not, we return the invalid credentials message. Otherwise, we check whether the password from `UserDto` matches the password from the `User` entity retrieved from the database using `UserRepository`.

Creating a user account and validating the user credentials for login are the responsibilities of the service layer. It accomplishes that by relying on the data layer to get user data from the database. Now we need to expose an API to allow clients to send requests to our application.

Implementing the API layer

The last layer, the API layer, is where we implement REST endpoints for user creation and user login requests:

1. In the `dev.davivieira.layered.api` package, we start the implementation of the `UserEndpoint` class:

    ```
    @Path("/user")
    public class UserEndpoint {

        @Inject
        UserService userService;
        /** Code omitted **/
    }
    ```

    We inject `UserService` to access the `createAccount` and `login` methods from the service layer.

2. We first define the register endpoint:

```
@POST
@Produces(MediaType.TEXT_PLAIN)
@Consumes(MediaType.APPLICATION_JSON)
@Path("/register")
public String register(UserDto userDto) throws Excep
  tion {
    return userService.createAccount(userDto);
}
```

That is a straightforward REST endpoint implementation, receiving a JSON payload mapped to UserDto and returning plain text. UserDto is passed directly to the createAccount method from the UserService class on the service layer.

3. Finally, we define the login endpoint:

```
@POST
@Produces(MediaType.TEXT_PLAIN)
@Consumes(MediaType.APPLICATION_JSON)
@Path("/login")
public String login(UserDto userDto) {
    return userService.login(userDto);
}
```

As we did in the previous register endpoint, here we are simply exposing the REST endpoint and passing the DTO directly to the service layer.

The API layer is responsible only for exposing the REST endpoints and nothing more. We avoid putting any business logic on this layer to ensure we separate the concerns among this and the other layers.

Let's see now how we can test this layered application.

Testing the layered application

We will test the service layer by focusing only on the logic that checks whether the email already exists and the credentials are valid. The following is what one of the tests would look like:

```
@QuarkusTest
public class UserServiceTest {

    @Inject
    UserService userService;

    @Test
    public void
```

```
givenTheUserEmailAlreadyExistsAnExceptionIsThrown()
throws Exception {
    var userDto = new UserDto("test@davivieira.dev",
    "password");
    userService.createAccount(userDto);
    Assertions.assertThrows(
            Exception.class,
            ()-> userService.createAccount(userDto)
    );
}
/** Code omitted **/
}
```

The preceding test checks whether an exception is thrown when the email address already exists. Note that for this test to work, the service layer depends on the data layer, which requires a database to persist data. So, the core system logic, present in the service layer, depends directly on the data layer that is composed of the ORM entity and repository classes. How we handle external data dictates what we can do in the service layer.

Suppose we want to avoid creating this dependency, where the core system's logic depends on and sits so close to data-handling code. In that case, hexagonal architecture can help us with a different arrangement where the core system's logic does not depend on anything and provides the flexibility to evolve that core logic without any concerns regarding how external data is handled. Let's see how that can be done by refactoring our layered architecture application into a hexagonal one.

Refactoring a layered architecture application into a hexagonal one

By now, we have an idea of how to implement a layered architecture application. Let's refactor this application we have just developed into a hexagonal one. This exercise will highlight the significant differences between the two architectures.

Implementing the Domain hexagon

The Domain hexagon contains data and behaviors with core system logic. In the following steps, we'll see how to refactor some data and behaviors from the layered application using the hexagonal approach:

1. While using the layered architecture, we started developing the system by implementing the data layer. We'll refactor it into a Domain hexagon containing only a `User` domain entity class:

    ```
    @Getter
    @Setter
    @RequiredArgsConstructor
    ```

```
@NoArgsConstructor
public class User {
    private Long id;
    @NonNull
    private String email;
    @NonNull
    private String password;

    public User(Long id, String email, String
    password) {
        this.id = id;
        this.email = email;
        this.password = password;
    }
    /** Code omitted **/
}
```

The major difference is that this entity is not an ORM used to map database entities. This entity is a POJO that contains not only data but also behaviors. Let's implement these behaviors.

2. In the User entity class, we implement the isEmailAlreadyUsed method:

```
public void isEmailAlreadyUsed(Optional<User> op
  tionalUser) throws Exception {
    if(optionalUser.isPresent()) {
        throw new Exception(
        "Email address already exist");
    }
}
```

isEmailAlreadyUsed receives an Optional<User> parameter. If the value is present, then we throw an exception.

3. To finish the User entity class implementation, we create the login and isPasswordValid methods:

```
public String login(Optional<User> optionalUser) {
    if (optionalUser.isPresent()) {
        var user = optionalUser.get();
        var isThePasswordValid =
        isThePasswordValid(user);
        if (isThePasswordValid) {
            return "Authenticated with success";
        } else {
            return "Invalid credentials";
        }
```

```
        } else {
            return "Invalid credentials";
        }
    }

    private boolean isThePasswordValid(User user) {
        return user.getPassword().equals(this.password);
    }
```

The logic is similar to the methods we implemented in the layered application, but instead of using a `UserDto` class, we operate directly on the `User` domain entity class.

Following a DDD approach, we pushed logic from the Service Layer into the Domain hexagon in the hexagonal application. Methods containing core system logic that used to be on the service layer are now part of the `User` domain entity class in the Domain hexagon.

The significant difference here is that the Domain hexagon does not depend on anything. In contrast, in the layered architecture approach, the Service layer containing the core system logic depends on the data layer.

Implementing the Application hexagon

We implemented the `User` domain entity class on the Domain hexagon containing core logic to handle user registration and login. We need to define how, in an agnostic way, the behaviors will be triggered and how external data will be retrieved. By agnostic, I mean expressing the need for external data without going into the technology details to provide such data. We employ use cases and input and output ports in the Application hexagon:

1. Let's start by defining the `UserAccessUserCase` interface:

    ```
    public interface UserAccessUseCase {
        String createAccount(User user) throws Exception;
        String login(User user);
    }
    ```

    Creating an account and being able to log in are the two use cases supported by our application.

2. To allow handling external data, we define the `UserAccessOutputPort` interface:

    ```
    public interface UserAccessOutputPort {
        Optional<User> findByEmail(String email);
        void persist(User user);
    }
    ```

This interface is just a POJO containing the `findByEmail` and `persist` method definitions. In the layered architecture approach, we had these methods as part of the repository class in the data layer. In the repository class, it was implied that the data would come from a database. In the hexagonal approach, we express, through the output port interface, that the data can come from anywhere.

3. We finish by implementing the `UserAccessInputPort` class:

```java
@ApplicationScoped
public class UserAccessInputPort implements UserAcces
  sUseCase {

@Inject
UserAccessOutputPort userAccessOutputPort;

@Override
public String createAccount(User user) throws
Exception {
        user.isEmailAlreadyUsed
            (userAccessOutputPort.findByEmail
              (user.getEmail()));
    userAccessOutputPort.persist(user);
    return "User successfully created";
}

@Override
public String login(User user) {
    return
    user.login(
    userAccessOutputPort
    .findByEmail(user.getEmail()));
  }
}
```

`UserAccessInputPort` implements the `UserAccessUseCase` interface. Note we are injecting `UserAccessOutputPort`. It's through this output port that the input port will handle external data. The `createAccount` method checks whether the email already exists by relying on the logic provided by the `isEmailAlreadyUsed` method from the `User` domain entity class. The `login` method also relies on the Domain hexagon by calling the `login` method present in the `User` domain entity class.

The Application hexagon allowed us to express how the system should handle external data in conjunction with the core system's logic from the Domain hexagon. Contrary to what we did in the layered architecture approach, the core system logic and external data handling have been defined without specifying whether the data is coming from a database or somewhere else.

This approach of expressing, through output ports, what data the system needs without exposing how the system will get that data is a significant difference between layered and hexagonal architecture.

Implementing the Framework hexagon

The Application hexagon orchestrates external data with core system logic from the Domain hexagon. Still, we need to provide a way to get that external data. In the layered architecture approach, the data layer allowed us to get data from a database, and the API layer exposed REST endpoints. In the Framework hexagon, we use input adapters to provide the REST endpoints and output adapters to get data from a database. Let's implement it:

1. We start with the `UserAccessInputAdapter` class:

    ```
    @Path("/user")
    public class UserAccessInputAdapter {

        @Inject
        UserAccessUseCase userAccessUseCase;
        /** Code omitted **/
    }
    ```

    We inject `UserAccessUseCase` to access the operations available in the Application hexagon.

2. In the `UserAccessInputAdapter` class, we implement the `register` method:

    ```
    @POST
    @Produces(MediaType.TEXT_PLAIN)
    @Consumes(MediaType.APPLICATION_JSON)
    @Path("/register")
    public String register(UserDto userDto) throws Excep
      tion {
        return userAccessUseCase.createAccount(new
        User(userDto.email(), userDto.password()));
    }
    ```

    We map `UserDto` directly to the `User` domain entity class. Then, we pass it to the `createAccount` method from `UserAccessUseCase`.

3. To finish the `UserAccessInputAdapter` implementation, we create the `login` method:

    ```
    @POST
    @Produces(MediaType.TEXT_PLAIN)
    @Consumes(MediaType.APPLICATION_JSON)
    @Path("/login")
    public String login(UserDto userDto) {
        return userAccessUseCase.login(new
        User(userDto.email(), userDto.password()));
    }
    ```

As we did in the register method, we map `UserDto` to the `User` domain entity class and then pass it to the `login` method.

We still need to implement the output adapter. Let's do that.

4. `UserAccessOutputAdapter` implements `UserAccessOutputPort`:

```
@ApplicationScoped
public class UserAccessOutputAdapter implements
  UserAccessOutputPort {

    @Inject
    UserRepository userRepository;
    /** Code omitted **/
}
```

By injecting `UserRepository`, we are effectively turning this output adapter into one that deals with databases.

5. We need to implement the `findByEmail` method:

```
@Override
public Optional<User> findByEmail(String email) {
    return UserMapper
            .userDataToDomain(
            userRepository.findByEmail(email));
}
```

We use `UserRepository` when implementing `findByEmail` from the `UserAccessOutputPort` interface. `UserMapper` is a helper class to map the ORM entity class called `UserData` into the `User` domain entity class.

6. Finally, we implement the `persist` method:

```
@Transactional
@Override
public void persist(User user) {
    var userData = UserMapper.userDomainToData(user);
    userRepository.persist(userData);
}
```

We again use the `UserMapper` helper class to map the `User` domain entity class into the `UserData` ORM entity class. That is required because we cannot persist the domain entity. So, we pass the `UserData` ORM entity class to the `persist` method from `UserRepository`.

Introducing the Framework hexagon allows clients to access the system's API provided by input adapters and connect the hexagonal application to an external data source, a database in our case. The input adapter from the Framework hexagon does not differ much when compared to the REST endpoints provided by the API layer. Both approaches expose similar methods, rely on DTO classes to map client requests, and send them downstream to either the service layer or the Application hexagon.

What significantly changes is how external data is handled. In the hexagonal approach, the output adapter implements an output port, which provides flexibility with the output port abstraction. A new output adapter can be implemented without disrupting the core system's logic. On the other hand, there is no such abstraction in the layered architecture approach. The service layer relies directly on the repository classes from the data layer.

Let's see now how we can test the hexagonal application.

Testing the hexagonal application

Because the core system's logic is part of the Domain hexagon, we can create unit tests to validate the User domain entity behaviors. The following is what one of those unit tests would look like:

```
@QuarkusTest
public class UserServiceTest {

@Test
public void givenTheUserEmailAlreadyExistsAnException
    IsThrown() {
      var user = new User("test@davivieira.dev", "password");
      var optionalUser = Optional.of(user);
      Assertions.assertThrows(
              Exception.class,
              ()-> user.isEmailAlreadyUsed(optionalUser)
      );
}
/** Code omitted **/
}
```

In the layered approach, we had to inject a service class and provide a database to test whether the email was already being used. In the hexagonal approach, we are testing the logic directly from the User domain entity class. Moving the core system logic from the service layer, in the layered architecture, to the Domain hexagon in the hexagonal architecture provided the flexibility to run more constrained tests without dependencies on external resources.

Based on our implementation of the same application using layered and hexagonal architecture, let's assess the pros and cons of each architecture.

Assessing the benefits and disadvantages of hexagonal and layered architectures

The structure of a layered application is more straightforward than a hexagonal one. In the layered approach, we have the service layer depending directly on the data layer. This dependence implies that the core system logic relies on the ORM entity and repository classes from the data layer. Contrary to the hexagonal approach, there is no abstraction regarding external data access, and the core system logic is embedded with code that handles external data. Is this good or bad? As with most things in software development, it depends on your context.

The experience I shared at the beginning of the chapter, where my team had to change the database technology in the middle of the project, is an example where employing the hexagonal approach would have been beneficial. If you expect considerable requirement changes in your project, then the hexagonal approach may be a good idea to make it easier for your application to accommodate those changes. Otherwise, the layered architecture is a good choice, given it's fast to bootstrap a new application with such architecture.

The layered architecture provides a simple and fast approach to developing new applications. Most backend developers are acquainted with having an API layer to expose endpoints, a service layer containing core system logic, and the data layer usually providing database access. So, it's a small undertaking to onboard new team members to maintain applications based on this architecture. The trade-off is that this architecture offers less flexibility when infrastructure components need to change.

On the other hand, the hexagonal architecture allows us to decouple the core system logic code from the infrastructure/external data-handling code. Still, this decoupling does not come for free. Hexagonal architecture slightly increases the code complexity due to additional components, such as the ports, use cases, and adapters we use to ensure the decoupling. The major benefit is a change-tolerant application shielded from the unpredictability of unexpected system requirements. Onboarding new team members may represent an additional effort because hexagonal architecture is less widely used than its layered counterpart. Hence, people need more time to grasp the hexagonal approach ideas to start contributing to the project.

Summary

This chapter explored layered architecture and its differences from hexagonal architecture. We started by reviewing the purpose of layered architecture to provide some level of separation of concerns through logical layers containing code with specific responsibilities. After reviewing the idea of the layered approach, we dirtied our hands by implementing a simple user access application from scratch containing the API, service, and data layers. To highlight the differences between the layered and hexagonal architectures, we refactored the user access application to use the hexagonal approach. By doing so, we saw that the layered architecture does not entirely protect the application from major changes, such as those that touch on infrastructure components such as external data access handling. Finally, we assessed the advantages and disadvantages of the layered and hexagonal architectures, concluding that the layered one is a good choice when no significant project requirement changes are expected, and the hexagonal architecture is recommended when one needs a more change-tolerable application capable to accommodate considerable system changes, especially at the infrastructure level. In the next chapter, we will explore how SOLID principles can be used with hexagonal architecture.

Questions

1. Why would you choose layered architecture over hexagonal architecture in a new project?

2. Although layered architecture provides some level of separation of concerns, it does not completely decouple core system logic from infrastructure code. Why?

3. In which scenario does using hexagonal architecture instead of layered architecture make sense?

Answers

1. It provides a simple and fast way to bootstrap new applications.

2. Because the core system logic depends directly on the infrastructure code, usually when there is a service layer depending on a data layer.

3. When project requirements are expected to change, using hexagonal architecture allows the creation of change-tolerable applications capable of accommodating those requirements.

16

Using SOLID Principles with Hexagonal Architecture

The idea of having a set of principles to help us develop better software amuses me. Over the years, programmers have faced many problems; some happened so often that patterns to solve such issues emerged, giving rise to the so-called **design patterns**. These patterns have been employed to solve specific software development problems. Complementing design patterns that act more on recurrent and specific coding problems, ideas have emerged on tackling maintainability problems in software projects. A remarkable and influential set of those ideas has been synthesized into what is known as **SOLID principles**.

This chapter will explore SOLID principles and how we can tap into them while using hexagonal architecture. We will start by reviewing each principle, and then we will proceed to see how they can be applied in the context of a hexagonal system. Finally, we will discuss how design patterns, such as builder and abstract factory, can be used with hexagonal architecture.

The following topics will be covered in this chapter:

- Understanding SOLID principles
- Applying SOLID on a hexagonal architecture system
- Exploring other design patterns

After completing this chapter, you will be able to employ SOLID principles in conjunction with hexagonal architecture techniques. Also, you will know how to use design patterns, such as chain of responsibility, decorator, builder, and singleton, while developing a hexagonal system.

Technical requirements

To compile and run the code examples presented in this chapter, you will need the latest **Java SE Development Kit** and **Maven 3.8** installed on your computer. They are available for the Linux, MacOS, and Windows operating systems.

You can find the code files for this chapter on GitHub at `https://github.com/PacktPublishing/-Designing-Hexagonal-Architecture-with-Java---Second-Edition/tree/main/Chapter16`.

Understanding SOLID principles

Since the advent of programming, developers have discussed ideas and captured principles to help develop better software. These principles arose as a response to help handle highly complex code. After suffering multiple times from the same recurrent problems, developers started recognizing those problems' patterns and devised techniques to prevent such issues. A notable example is the **Gang of Four (GoF)** book on design patterns, which caused a tremendous impact in the object-oriented world and continues to influence generations of developers to this day. Another remarkable and influential example is the ideas formulated by Robert Martin that led to SOLID principles.

SOLID stands for the following principles:

- **Single Responsibility Principle (SRP)**
- **Open Closed Principle (OCP)**
- **Liskov Substitution Principle (LSP)**
- **Interface Segregation Principle (ISP)**
- **Dependency Inversion Principle (DIP)**

These principles aim to help developers create robust and easy-to-change software through code, based on a set of rules defined by those principles. I believe that using these principles does not fully guarantee that software is free of maintainability problems. However, such principles can significantly improve overall code quality. In essence, it's all about employing techniques that allow the introduction of changes to a code base in a sustainable way. I mean, the software will grow, but its complexity will be kept under control.

SOLID principles work in a similar way to hexagonal architecture because both aim to provide techniques to develop more maintainable, change-tolerant software. Therefore, it makes sense to explore how those principles can be applied in the context of a hexagonal application. Let's start our exploration by reviewing each one of the SOLID principles.

Single Responsibility Principle (SRP)

It's not hard for me to remember a situation where I would witness or be the author of a code change that caused side effects, discovered only after an application was deployed to a staging or, even worse, production environment. A stakeholder would report problems in the application that started to occur right after the change that caused the side effect was deployed. So, although the change solved the problem for one stakeholder, it created a problem for another. Why? Because the change responsible for the problem has violated the SRP. The violation occurred because the same system logic served two different stakeholders. The change solved the problem for one stakeholder but created a side effect that caused trouble for the other.

An SRP violation can also occur when we define abstractions too early. Suppose we define an abstract class with certain data and behaviors we believe will be common to all future implementations of that abstract class. Then, later on, we discover, through an unfortunate incident report, that some data or behavior from that abstract class causes unexpected outcomes in a recent implementation provided by another developer, who assumed the behaviors and data provided by that abstraction would work in the implementation that causes the trouble.

The SRP ensures a method or function is changed based on requests from only one type of stakeholder or actor, usually a department or a line of business in an organization. It is important to ensure the logic from department A, for example, does not mess up the logic from department B, which can be accomplished by arranging the code in a way that the logic to serve different stakeholders is adequately separated.

Open-Closed Principle (OCP)

The idea behind this principle lies in increasing what software can do without changing the existing things in it. In order to do this, a software component or module should be open for extension but closed for modification. I can recall an experience where I was implementing a reporting feature. Instead of having one class to deal with all kinds of reports, I created a base abstract class with basic attributes common to reports. Every time a new type of report had to be implemented, a new concrete class would be created by implementing the base abstract class. Additional attributes and functions would be appended to the basic attributes of the base abstract class.

We use the OCP to avoid those situations where we want to add a new feature, and to do so, we also need to change some piece of logic already supporting an existing feature. By doing that, we violate the OCP. Instead, we need to arrange code so that we can add new features without modifying the code already serving existing features.

Liskov Substitution Principle (LSP)

Based on the reporting example I gave in the OCP description, let's suppose we have a `Report` class containing the `print` method declaration. According to a given problem domain, the `print` method is a behavior supported by any report. In addition to the `Report` class, imagine we have the `WorkdayReport` and `WeekendReport` classes extending it. The LSP prescribes that if we pass objects of type `WorkdayReport` or `WeekendReport` to a method expecting a `Report` type, that method will be able to trigger the behaviors inherent to all kinds of reports – in this case, the `print` method. The bottom line is that the `Report` type should be designed so that its declared methods, when overridden for sub-types, should be coherent with the subtype's purpose.

Interface Segregation Principle (ISP)

The ISP is helpful whenever we want to provide clients with an interface containing only the method declarations they need. This principle is usually employed when we have a single interface with many method declarations, and a given client only implements some methods and provides dummy implementations for those they don't need. By employing the ISP, we break that single interface with multiple interfaces tailored for specific client needs.

Dependency Inversion Principle (DIP)

Stable and unstable software components have distinct concepts. *Stable* means those components that don't change too often, while *unstable* is the opposite. Having a client component depending directly on an unstable component may be risky because changes in unstable code can trigger changes in the client. Most of the time, the unstable component is a concrete class with implementation details that don't need to be exposed to its clients.

To avoid exposing such implementation details and protect the client from dependency changes, DIP prescribes that clients should always depend on abstractions rather than concretions. The unstable component – a concrete class with implementation details – should derive from an abstraction by implementing an interface, for example. Then, the client should rely on a stable component, an interface implemented by the unstable component (a concrete class). We call an interface a stable component because it acts as a contract, and contracts are less susceptible to change.

Let's see in the next section how we can apply SOLID principles to an application developed using hexagonal architecture.

Applying SOLID on a hexagonal architecture system

To see how each SOLID principle is applied, we will go back to the topology and inventory system we have developed throughout the book. Let's start by seeing how the SRP can be applied in the topology and inventory system.

Applying the SRP

Just to recap, the topology and inventory system manages network resources such as routers and switches. Such a system is suited for telecommunication or **Internet Service Provider** (ISP) companies that want to keep an inventory of the network resources they use to serve their customers.

In the topology and inventory system, we have core and edge routers. Core routers handle high-load network traffic from one or more edge routers. Edge routers are used to handle traffic from end users. Edge routers connect to network switches.

Consider a scenario where core and edge routers change locations. For example, a core router that is now localized in France needs, for some reason, to be re-provisioned in Italy, and an edge router that is in Frankfurt needs to be re-provisioned in Berlin. Consider also that network changes across countries are handled by actor A, and network changes across cities are handled by actor B.

Let's change the topology and inventory application to fulfill the described requirement. The changes described as follows are made in the Domain hexagon:

1. Create the `AllowedCountrySpec` specification class:

```
public final class AllowedCountrySpec extends Ab
    stractSpecification<Location> {

    private List<String> allowedCountries =
    List.of(
    "Germany", "France", "Italy", "United States");

    @Override
    public boolean isSatisfiedBy(Location location) {
        return allowedCountries
                .stream()
                .anyMatch(
                allowedCountry -> allowedCountry
                .equals(location.country()));
    }
    /** Code omitted **/
}
```

This specification limits which countries can be chosen through the `allowedCountries` attribute. That's not how you should represent it in a real application, but it is enough to illustrate the SRP idea.

2. Now, create the `AllowedCitySpec` specification class:

```
public final class AllowedCitySpec extends Ab
    stractSpecification<Location> {

    private List<String> allowedCities =
    List.of(
    "Berlin", "Paris", "Rome", "New York");

    @Override
    public oolean isSatisfiedBy(Location location) {
        return allowedCities
                .stream()
                .anyMatch(
                allowedCountry -> allowedCountry
                .equals(location.city()));
```

```
    }
    /** Code omitted **/
}
```

Following the same idea from the previous specification, here we limit which cities are allowed through the `allowedCities` attribute.

3. Declare the `changeLocation` method in the `Router` abstract class:

    ```
    public abstract sealed class Router extends Equipment
      permits CoreRouter, EdgeRouter {
      /** Code omitted **/
      public abstract void changeLocation(
      Location location);
      /** Code omitted **/
    }
    ```

    Note that `Router` is an abstract sealed class, allowing only the `CoreRouter` and `EdgeRouter` classes to implement it.

4. Provide an implementation for `CoreRouter`:

    ```
    @Override
    public void changeLocation(Location location) {
        var allowedCountrySpec = new AllowedCountrySpec();
        allowedCountrySpec.check(location);
        this.location = location;
    }
    ```

    We use the `AllowedCountrySpec` to check whether the new router `Location` is allowed. If a non-allowed country is provided, an exception is thrown. Otherwise, the new location is assigned to the `location` variable from the `Router` object.

5. Provide an implementation for `EdgeRouter`:

    ```
    @Override
    public void changeLocation(Location location) {
        var allowedCountrySpec = new AllowedCountrySpec();
        var allowedCitySpec = new AllowedCitySpec();
        allowedCountrySpec.check(location);
        allowedCitySpec.check(location);
        this.location = location;
    }
    ```

    The `EdgeRouter` implementation is slightly different. In addition to `AllowedCountrySpec`, we also have `AllowedCitySpec`. A new `Location` will be assigned to the `Router` object only after fulfilling these two specifications.

Let's review what we have done here. We started by creating the `AllowedCountrySpec` and `AllowedCitySpec` specifications; then, we declared the `changeLocation` method on the `Router` abstract class. As both `CoreRouter` and `EdgeRouter` implement this class, we had to override the `changeLocation` method to serve the needs of actor A and actor B. Actor A is responsible for handling location changes across countries – in this case, `CoreRouter`. Actor B is in charge of handling location changes across cities, which is the responsibility of `EdgeRouter`.

Suppose that instead of declaring `changeLocation` as abstract, we provided a concrete implementation shared by both the `CoreRouter` and `EdgeRouter` classes. That would violate the SRP because the `changeLocation` logic would serve different actors.

Applying the OCP

We have not stated it yet, but the arrangement between the `Router`, `CoreRouter`, and `EdgeRouter` classes represents an application of the OCP. Observe the following Unified Modeling Language (UML) diagram:

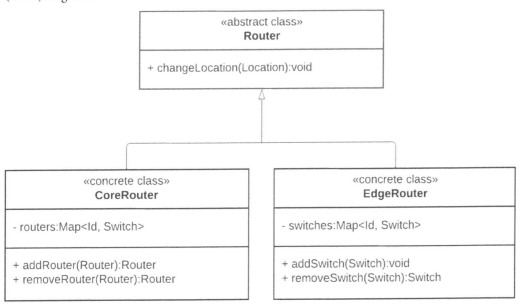

Figure 16.1 – Applying the OCP

The OCP ensures that a module or component is closed for change but open for extension. Instead of providing a class design where one single class would contain the logic to handle both core and edge routers, we leverage the inheritance capability from Java to extend the possibilities of the `Router` abstract class, without changing its attributes and behaviors. Such extensions are possible through the `CoreRouter` and `EdgeRouter` concrete class implementations.

Applying the LSP

To demonstrate the application of the LSP, we need to make more changes in the topology and inventory system. While applying the SRP and OCP, we changed the Domain hexagon. Now, we will make changes in the Application hexagon:

1. Declare the `changeLocation` method in the `RouterManagementUseCase` interface:

    ```
    public interface RouterManagementUseCase {
        /** Code omitted **/
        Router changeLocation(
        Router router, Location location);
        /** Code omitted **/
    }
    ```

    Changing a router's location is a new use case that we add to the topology and inventory system, so we add the `changeLocation` method declaration to express that use case.

2. Implement the `changeLocation` method in `RouterManagementInputPort`:

    ```
    public class RouterManagementInputPort implements
      RouterManagementUseCase {
        /** Code omitted **/
        @Override
        public Router changeLocation(Router router,
        Location location) {
            router.changeLocation(location);
            return persistRouter(router);
        }
        /** Code omitted **/
    }
    ```

    The `changeLocation` method from `RouterManagementInputPort` calls `changeLocation` from `Router` by passing a `Location` object. `changeLocation` from `Router` has a logic that checks whether the provided `Location` is allowed. If everything is fine, we call `persitRouter` to persist `Router` with its new `Location`.

    The LSP application can be observed when we implement the `changeLocation` method in `RouterManagementInputPort`. Note that `changeLocation` expects a `Router` type:

    ```
    public Router changeLocation(Router router,
      Location location) {
        router.changeLocation(location);
        return persistRouter(router);
    }
    ```

It means we can pass here either a `CoreRouter` or an `EdgeRouter` object because both extend `Router`, and both provide an implementation of `changeLocation`, a behavior inherent to all routers.

Applying the ISP

While applying the LSP, we created `RouterManagementUseCase` and `RouterManagementInputPort` in the Application hexagon. Let's finish our implementation by providing an input adapter in the Framework hexagon to connect the input adapter to the input port:

1. Implement the `changeLocation` method in the `RouterManagementAdapter` class:

```
@Transactional
@POST
@Path("/changeLocation/{routerId}")
@Operation(operationId = "changeLocation", description
  = "Change a router location")
public Uni<Response> changeLocation(@PathParam
  ("routerId") String routerId, LocationChange loca
    tionChange) {
    Router router = routerManagementUseCase
        .retrieveRouter(Id.withId(routerId));
    Location location =
        locationChange.mapToDomain();
        return Uni.createFrom()
        .item(routerManagementUseCase.changeLocation(ro
        uter, location))
        .onItem()
        .transform(f -> f != null ? Response.ok(f) :
              Response.ok(null))
            .onItem()
            .transform(
               Response.ResponseBuilder::build);
}
```

With the `POST` and `PATH` annotations, we turn this method into a `REST` endpoint to receive requests sent to the `/router/changeLocation/{routerId}` URI. The router part of the URI comes from the top-level definition of the `PATH` annotation of the `RouterManagementAdapter` class.

This input adapter gets `Router` using the `retrieveRouter` method from `RouterManagementUseCase`. Then, it converts the `LocationRequest` object into a `Location` domain object. Finally, it passes `Router` and `Location` to the `changeLocation` method from `RouterManagementUseCase`.

To confirm that our implementation works, let's implement a test to check the entire flow.

2. Implement the following test in the `RouterManagementAdapterTest` class:

```
@Test
public void changeLocation() throws IOException {
    var routerId =
        "b832ef4f-f894-4194-8feb-a99c2cd4be0c";
    var expectedCountry = "Germany";
    var location = createLocation("Germany",
        "Berlin");
    var updatedRouterStr = given()
            .contentType("application/json")
            .pathParam("routerId", routerId)
            .body(location)
            .when()
            .post("/router/changeLocation/{routerId}")
            .then()
            .statusCode(200)
            .extract()
            .asString();
    var changedCountry =
    getRouterDeserialized(
    updatedRouterStr).getLocation().country();

    assertEquals(expectedCountry, changedCountry);
}
```

This test changes the location of the Router, which is a core router located in the United States. After sending a POST request containing a `Location` object with `Germany` as the country and `Berlin` as the city, we run an assertion to ensure that the returned `Router` object has the changed location – Germany instead of the United States.

The ISP can be observed in making use-case operations available to the input adapter. We have the `RouterManagementInputPort` class implementing the `RouterManagementUseCase` interface. The ISP is employed because all method declarations from the `RouterManagementUseCase` interface are relevant and implemented by `RouterManagementInputPort`.

Applying the DIP

We discussed dependency inversion in *Chapter 9, Applying Dependency Inversion with Java Modules*, where we used the **Java Platform Module System (JPMS)** to apply dependency inversion. To recap, let's review the following diagram:

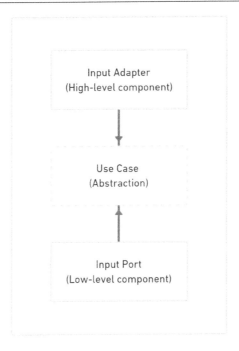

Figure 16.2 – Reviewing dependency inversion

The DIP states that clients should always depend on abstractions rather than concretions. That is precisely what we are doing by making RouterManagementAdapter depend on the RouterManagementUseCase interface, rather than the RouterManagementInputPort concrete class:

```
public class RouterManagementAdapter {
    @Inject
    RouterManagementUseCase routerManagementUseCase;
    /** Code omitted **/
}
```

In *Chapter 9*, *Applying Dependency Inversion with Java Modules*, the RouterManagementUseCase interface implementation – a RouterManagementInputPort object – is provided by the JPMS. In the current implementation, we use Quarkus with the @Inject annotation to provide RouterManagementInputPort.

Exploring other design patterns

In previous chapters, we applied some design patterns while developing the topology and inventory system. These patterns helped us arrange code to support application needs better. So, in this section, we will review the design patterns we applied while implementing hexagonal architecture.

Singleton

Before introducing Quarkus to our topology and inventory system, we had to provide our own mechanism to create a single database connection object. When handling database-based connections, it's common to have just one instance that connects to a database and shares that connection with other objects.

Singleton is the pattern we used to create a single database connection instance, as shown in the following example:

```
public class RouterNetworkH2Adapter implements RouterNet
  workOutputPort {

    private static RouterNetworkH2Adapter instance;

    @PersistenceContext
    private EntityManager em;

    private RouterNetworkH2Adapter(){
        setUpH2Database();
    }

    private void setUpH2Database() {
        EntityManagerFactory entityManagerFactory =
        Persistence.createEntityManagerFactory
          ("inventory");
        EntityManager em =
        entityManagerFactory.createEntityManager();
        this.em = em;
    }

    public static RouterNetworkH2Adapter getInstance() {
        if (instance == null) {
            instance = new RouterNetworkH2Adapter();
        }
        return instance;
    }
}
```

To ensure only an object is created, we create a private constructor to prevent clients from creating additional instances. The object creation is handled by the `getInstance` method, which checks whether the instance attribute is `null`. If it is `null`, then it creates a new `RouterNetworkH2Adapter` and assigns it to the `instance` variable. The private constructor then creates a database connection using `EntityManagerFactory`.

When executing `getInstance` for a second time, instead of creating a new `RouterNetworkH2Adapter`, we return the existing instance created previously.

Builder

Builder is a design pattern that helps us expressively create complex objects. It's intended for scenarios with constructors with many parameters and different ways to make the same object. We have used that design pattern to create `CoreRouter` and `EdgeRouter` objects.

Consider the following example, where we create an instance of `CoreRouter` using its constructor:

```
var router = new CoreRouter(
                id,
                parentRouterId,
                vendor,
                model,
                ip,
                location,
                routerType,
                routers);
```

One of the drawbacks of using the constructor directly is that we need to know how to pass the parameters in the correct order. In the previous example, we must pass first `id`, then `parentRouterId`, and so on.

Now, let's see the object creation using builder:

```
var router = CoreRouter.builder()
                .id(id == null ? Id.withoutId() : id)
                .vendor(vendor)
                .model(model)
                .ip(ip)
                .location(location)
                .routerType(routerType)
                .build();
```

Other than skipping some parameters such as `parentRouterId`, we pass the parameters in any order through builder methods such as `vendor` or `model`. Once we are done, we call the `build` method to return the `CoreRouter` instance.

Throughout the book, we have not provided a custom builder implementation. Instead, we relied on the helpful Lombok libraries to create builders by simply adding the `Builder` annotation to the class's constructor:

```
@Builder
public CoreRouter(Id id, Id parentRouterId, Vendor vendor,
  Model model, IP ip, Location location, RouterType router
    Type, Map<Id, Router> routers) {
/** Code omitted **/
}
```

Lombok is probably enough for you if you don't have special requirements for how your objects should be created. Otherwise, you can implement your own builder mechanism. That is usually done when you want to define mandatory or optional parameters and other rules for object creation.

Abstract factory

We discussed in the previous section how applying the LSP enables us to pass a `CoreRouter` or `EdgeRouter` object to a method expecting a `Router` type, and then we can use that object without any issues. The abstract factory pattern comes into play whenever we need to create `CoreRouter` or `EdgeRouter` objects. We did so when we implemented the `RouterFactory` class:

```
public class RouterFactory {

    public static Router getRouter(Id id,
                                   Vendor vendor,
                                   Model model,
                                   IP ip,
                                   Location location,
                                   RouterType routerType){

        switch (routerType) {
            case CORE -> {
                return CoreRouter.builder().
                    Id(id == null ? Id.withoutId() : id).
                    Vendor(vendor).
                    Model(model).
                    Ip(ip).
                    Location(location).
                    routerType(routerType).
                    Build();
            }
            case EDGE -> {
                return EdgeRouter.builder().
```

```
                    Id(id==null ? Id.withoutId():id).
                    Vendor(vendor).
                    Model(model).
                    Ip(ip).
                    Location(location).
                    routerType(routerType).
                    Build();
        }
        default -> throw new
        UnsupportedOperationException(
        "No valid router type informed");
    }
  }
}
```

The `RouterFactory` class contains only the `getRouter` method, which receives some parameters required to create code and edge routers and returns an object of type `Router`. Note that we pass a `RouterType` parameter used in the `switch` statement to identify which kind of router needs to be created, either `CoreRouter` or `EdgeRouter`. Regardless of the specific router subtype, we always return it as the `Router` supertype for use, for example, in scenarios where the LSP can be applied.

Summary

This chapter allowed us to explore how SOLID principles can be employed together with hexagonal architecture. We also reviewed our design patterns while implementing the topology and inventory system. We started by briefly discussing SOLID principles.

After getting a basic understanding of the principles, we moved on to see how they can be applied in the context of a hexagonal application. We then implemented the change router location feature to the topology and inventory system. Finally, we reviewed how design patterns such as builder, singleton, and abstract factory are employed while designing the hexagonal system.

The next and final chapter will explore further design practices to help us build better software.

Questions

1. What does OCP stand for, and what is its purpose?
2. What is the goal of the DIP?
3. Which design pattern can support the LSP?

Answers

1. It stands for the **Open-Closed Principle**. Its purpose is to ensure a software component or module is closed for modification but open for extension.

2. The DIP prescribes that clients should always depend on abstractions rather than concretions. By doing that, we protect clients from changes in the concretions that may require changes in the client code.

3. The abstract factory pattern provides objects based on their supertype, which can be used in LSP, where supertypes are replaced with subtypes while retaining the object's behavior consistency.

17
Good Design Practices for Your Hexagonal Application

While exploring the hexagonal architecture in this book, we learned about some of the principles and techniques that characterize a hexagonal application. By visualizing a system with clearly defined boundaries, we established three hexagons: Domain, Application, and Framework.

Using these hexagons as a guide, we explored how to separate the business code from the technology code. This separation allowed us to explore ways of creating change-tolerant systems. But we did not stop there. Going the extra mile, we learned how the Quarkus framework could be used to turn a hexagonal application into a cloud-native application.

We have reached the end of this book equipped with the fundamental ideas needed to create hexagonal systems. In this chapter, we will explore some helpful design practices we can apply when creating robust hexagonal applications.

In this chapter, we'll cover the following main topics:

- Using **Domain-Driven Design** (**DDD**) to shape the Domain hexagon
- The need for creating ports and use cases
- Dealing with multiple adapter categories
- Conclusion – the hexagonal journey

By the end of this chapter, you'll be aware of the design practices that can make your hexagonal architecture project more robust. These practices will also help you to decide when and how to employ the hexagonal architecture principles.

Technical requirements

To compile and run the code examples presented in this chapter, you need the latest **Java SE Development Kit** and **Maven 3.8** installed on your computer. They are both available for the **Linux**, **Mac**, and **Windows** operating systems.

You can find the code files for this chapter on GitHub:

```
https://github.com/PacktPublishing/-Designing-Hexagonal-Architecture-
with-Java---Second-Edition/tree/main/Chapter17
```

Using Domain-Driven Design to shape the Domain hexagon

When employing the hexagonal architecture to design a system's code structure, we cannot stress enough how important it is to first implement the Domain hexagon. It's the Domain hexagon that sets the tone for the development of the entire application.

As long as you keep the code in the Domain hexagon that purely expresses the problem domain—the code that does not merge business concerns with technology ones—you are on the right path to ensuring the encapsulation level that favors a more change-tolerant design. The technique you'll use to develop the Domain hexagon should not be your main concern at this stage—instead, your aim should be to create a Domain hexagon that is focused on the system's purpose, rather than the technology you might use to implement it. So, you can develop the Domain hexagon using your own set of principles, or you can borrow ideas from others who have addressed a similar problem previously.

The advantage of using DDD is that it means you don't need to reinvent the wheel. Most—if not all—of the concepts and principles that you need to model your problem domain are well established in the rich body of knowledge present in DDD techniques. However, this does not mean you must follow all DDD principles to the letter. The recommended approach is to adopt and adapt the things you find helpful for your project.

Next, we'll explore some of the approaches you can follow when using DDD to design the Domain hexagon.

Understanding the business we are in

A good application design reflects a good understanding of the business it is intended to serve. The design journey does not start in the code but by seeking business knowledge. I'm not telling you to become a business expert in the field you intend to build software for. However, I think it's important to understand the fundamentals because if you don't, mistakes made at the start of the design phase can cause irreversible damage that will extend through the software project.

In the best scenario, the project can survive these early mistakes, but not without paying the high cost of tangled and hard-to-maintain software. In the worst scenario, the result is unusable software, and starting a new project from scratch is the best thing to do.

Understanding the business fundamentals is the first thing we should do. The business details are important too, and we should pay close attention to them if we want to make top-notch software. But mistakes relating to details aren't as serious as mistakes relating to fundamentals. The former is generally easier and cheaper to fix than the latter.

Let's revisit the topology and inventory system for a moment. We have a business rule stating that only edge routers from the same country can be connected to each other. We use the edge routers to handle regional traffic because they have less traffic capacity than core routers. The core routers can be located in different countries because they have more traffic capacity.

The whole domain model has been built based on these business premises. We compromise the entire system development if we fail to understand and translate these business premises into a cohesive domain model. Everything we build on top of such a model will be based on weak or wrong assumptions. That's why we need to spend whatever time is necessary to grasp the business fundamentals.

Now, let's see some of the techniques we can use to build business knowledge.

Business Model Canvas

An excellent exercise to understand how the business works can be done with the Business Model Canvas technique. A **Business Model Canvas** is a tool for creating business models. It provides instruments to analyze and understand the main elements of a business. By providing a structured and simplified way to identify a business's main aspects, the Business Model Canvas can be the starting point to draw the big picture you and your team need to understand the business fundamentals.

The tool's main benefit is its focus on the key elements that are crucial for the profitability of a business. Another helpful aspect is how it represents customers and partners in the overall business landscape. This helps us to understand how well the business model is fulfilling the expectations of both customers and partners.

A disadvantage is that it does not provide a deep and comprehensive view of how a business should operate to produce good results. Also, it does not touch on the business strategy. Much of its emphasis is on end results instead of long-term goals.

There is a variation of—and an alternative to—the Business Model Canvas called the **Lean Canvas**, which is more directed toward start-ups. The main difference with this approach is that it focuses on the high uncertainty level that start-ups face when they try to develop new ideas and products.

Here is an illustration of the Business Model Canvas:

Figure 17.1 – The Business Model Canvas

As we can see in the preceding figure, the Business Model Canvas lets us structure each business aspect in distinct parts. This separation helps us to visualize the main elements comprising the business. Here are the elements of the Business Model Canvas:

- The **Key Partners** element represents our key partners and suppliers and contains information about the key resources or activities that are involved in that relationship

- In **Key Activities**, we state the value propositions required for the key activities

- For **Key Resources**, we need to identify the value propositions required to enable the key resources

- In **Value Propositions**, we describe the elements of value we intend to deliver to the customer

- The **Customer Relationships** element is about the expectations of each customer segment in establishing and maintaining a relationship with us

- In **Channels**, we identify the communication channels through which our customer segments will reach us

- The **Customer Segments** element represents the groups of people we want to deliver value to

- The **Cost Structure** element describes the highest costs involved in enabling the business model

- The **Revenue Streams** element shows the value our customers are really willing to pay for

In addition to the Business Model Canvas, we also have the Event Storming technique as an alternative, which is geared more toward DDD projects. Let's examine it now.

Event storming

If you do not find the Business Model Canvas a suitable approach, another technique called **event storming** can help you understand your business needs. Created by Alberto Brandolini, event storming uses colored sticky notes to map business elements into domain events, commands, actors, and aggregates. Each one of these sticky note elements has its own color, as shown in the following flowchart:

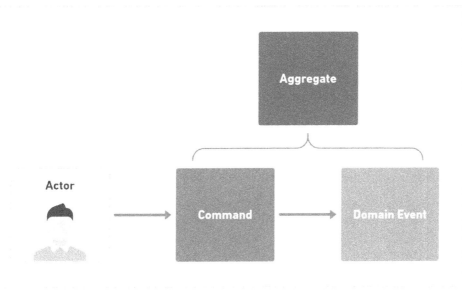

Figure 17.2 – The Event Storming technique

As we can see in the preceding diagram, the sticky notes from event storming use the same terminology we encounter when dealing with DDD. That's because event storming was created especially for those who use DDD and need to understand the business requirements for their project.

The event storming sessions should be conducted by developers, domain experts, and a facilitator who coordinates the session to ensure the mapping efforts go in the right direction.

The starting point of an event storming session is usually a challenging business process to model. In these sessions, it's common to discuss how actors and their actions influence the business processes. Another central point is how external systems support and interact with the business processes. Risks and pain points are also essential subjects to map to identify business-critical areas. To learn more about event storming, check out its website at https://www.eventstorming.com.

Once we understand how the business works, we need to translate that knowledge into a domain model. In the next section, we'll see how collaboration can help us to increase our knowledge about the business.

Promoting collaboration to increase knowledge

The domain model is the outcome of people trying to understand the business and translating that understanding into code. In order to get the most out of this process, collaboration plays a vital role where the degree of complexity is high and things are hard to accomplish. To overcome this complexity, we need to establish a collaborative atmosphere where everyone involved in the project can contribute with relevant information that helps to build the big picture. The collaborative approach helps to ensure that everyone is on the same page regarding the problem domain, leading to a domain model that better reflects the business concerns.

Aside from using the code itself to capture and convey the problem domain knowledge, written documentation is another useful tool for collaboration. I'm not talking about writing long and comprehensive documentation – I mean the opposite. Let me explain.

Concise documentation that is focused on explaining the building blocks of a system can help people who aren't acquainted with the code to make their first steps into understanding the system and, consequently, the problem domain. Sometimes, an introduction to the system's main elements quickly leads to a comprehensive understanding of the problem domain.

What I'm saying may seem obvious, but very often, I've stumbled upon a complex code base with poor or no documentation at all. When the problem domain is complex, it's natural for the code to be complex too. Without documentation to explain the basic system, what's already complicated becomes even harder to grasp.

I recommend allocating some time at the end of the project to write the system documentation. New joiners, in particular, will benefit from a friendly document providing an overview of the system's big picture.

Now that we know how important it is to have a solid foundation based on an understanding of the business requirements and have discussed the value of collaboration in increasing our knowledge of the problem domain, let's explore some of the DDD techniques to adopt when building the Domain hexagon.

Applying DDD techniques to build the Domain hexagon

In this section, we'll explore some design practices to help us establish clear boundaries in the hexagonal system. Complementing what we saw in *Chapter 2, Wrapping Business Rules inside Domain Hexagon*, we'll see the importance of creating subdomains, searching for a ubiquitous language, and defining bounded contexts to distinguish the different aspects of the problem domain.

Subdomains

The purpose of a **subdomain** is to group the elements that support the core domain but cannot be considered elements that express the core domain. These supporting elements are essential for the activities conducted by the core domain. Without the supporting elements, the core domain cannot work. There are also generic subdomains whose purpose is to provide additional capabilities to both core domains and supporting subdomains. A generic subdomain works as a standalone component that doesn't depend on things provided by other domains.

We can say that we have primary activities in the core domain. And in the subdomain, we have secondary activities that enable the primary ones. If we blend primary and secondary activities, we'll end up with a domain model with mixed concerns. It may not be a big deal for smaller systems, but in larger ones, it can add a considerable complexity that can undermine the productivity of anyone trying to understand the system. That's why it's a good approach to break a domain into subdomains. We'll always have a core domain concentrating on the most important part of the code.

Let's use a banking system as an example to explore the subdomain idea further. In such a system, it's possible to identify the following domains:

- As a core domain, we have **Transactions** that allow users to receive and send money

- As supporting subdomains, we may have **Loans** and **Insurances** that add more capabilities to the system but rely on the **Transactions** core domain to enable such capabilities

- Finally, we have **Authentication** as a generic subdomain, serving both the core domain and supporting subdomains that require every transaction to be authenticated

The following diagram shows how subdomains relate to the core domain:

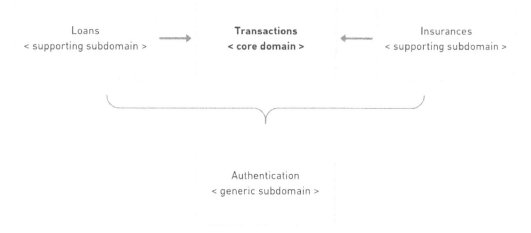

Figure 17.3 – Banking system subdomains

The **Transactions** core domain contains the system's building block elements. These elements are also present in the **Loans** and **Insurances** subdomains, but for different purposes. The generic **Authentication** subdomain knows nothing about the other domains. It only provides an authentication mechanism that is shared across the core domain and supporting subdomains.

Ubiquitous language

One of DDD's touchstones is its emphasis on how we use language to describe a domain model. This emphasis aims to avoid the pitfall of ambiguities in our general communication seeping into the system code we want to create.

As human beings, we have much more capacity than computers to handle ambiguities in language because we can add context to our words. Computers, on the other hand, don't have this ability unless we provide it for them. In order to decrease the ambiguity level of a system, a ubiquitous language seeks precise terminology to describe the things that comprise the domain model.

Defining precise terminology, however, is not enough to ensure that we'll always convey the right meaning in the domain model, as similar words may have a different meaning depending on the context in which they are used. That's why there's another technique in DDD called bounded context that we can use to deal with differences in meaning within a domain model.

Bounded context

The **bounded context** idea is a response to the fact that words have a different meaning depending on the context in which they are used. When we bring this idea to DDD, we may find that a domain model element can have a different meaning or behave differently depending on the context where it's applied. If we do not actively take action to explicitly define a context to clarify the meaning of such a domain model element, we are contributing to the ambiguity within the system.

For example, take the topology and inventory system. Suppose that other than inventory capabilities, we want to allow the system to get a real-time status and basic information from routers and other network equipment. This new feature could result in two contexts: one for inventory and the other for status.

From the inventory perspective, a router means a static record in a database. On the other hand, from the status perspective, a router is a *living* thing that issues real-time data. By expressing this distinction in the form of a bounded context, we ensure that our understanding of one context does not blur with another. More than that, by structuring the code within the clear boundaries that a bounded context can provide, we're creating a system that can evolve and receive changes in a more organized way. Also, we are enforcing the Single Responsibility Principle at the level of modules. This means a module should change only for a single reason and not multiple reasons.

The DDD techniques discussed in this session don't offer much value if we don't first grasp our business needs. That's why we started by exploring some of the techniques we can use to enhance our understanding of the business model. Once we know about the business we're in, we can safely employ the DDD techniques (such as subdomains and bounded contexts) to establish boundaries between different system components and remove ambiguities within the domain model.

So, let's see how we can implement bounded contexts and subdomains in a hexagonal system.

Implementing bounded contexts and subdomains in a hexagonal system

Our approach to implementing a bounded context relies on the creation of a subdomain. Here, we discuss both bounded contexts and subdomains.

Bounded contexts can exist with or without a subdomain. We've already seen that the topology and inventory system can check the status of network equipment. Suppose we determine that the status element is an integral and critical characteristic of the problem domain. In that case, we can make the status element part of the core domain instead of putting it into a supporting subdomain. But we'd still need to deal with the ambiguity of having domain elements serving different purposes. To solve this problem, we'd have to establish two bounded contexts within the core domain: one bounded context for inventory and another for status.

If we decide that the status element is not a part of the core domain, we can model it as a subdomain, as we'll see next.

When developing the topology and inventory system, we placed a single domain model inside the Domain hexagon. This domain model meets the business requirements related to the inventory management of network assets. Consider the scenario where the topology and inventory system can access network equipment to check its status. To avoid mixing concerns between inventory management and status information, we'll break the **Domain Hexagon** into two domain models. The first one is a **Core Domain** serving inventory management needs. The second domain model is a **Subdomain** for status information needs. The following diagram shows the representation of the new **Domain Hexagon**:

Domain Hexagon

Figure 15.4 – The Domain Hexagon

Inside the **Domain Hexagon**, we now have the **Inventory Core Domain** and the **Status Subdomain**. In the following steps, we'll configure the Domain hexagon module to reflect the new structure:

1. In the project's root `pom.xml` file, we add the new Maven `modules` element, which represents the core domain and subdomains:

    ```
    <modules>
      <module>domain</module>
      <module>domain/inventory-core-domain</module>
      <module>domain/status-sub-domain</module>
      <module>application</module>
      <module>framework</module>
      <module>bootstrap</module>
    </modules>
    ```

    Note, we added the `domain/inventory-core-domain` and `domain/status-sub-domain` Maven modules in the `pom.xml` file.

    Before proceeding, please ensure to move all the files from `domain/src/main/java` to `domain/inventory-core-domain/src/main/java`. The `domain` Maven module will be used as a parent project to aggregate both the core domain and subdomain projects.

2. Next, we'll configure the `pom.xml` file from the `domain` Maven module:

    ```
    <?xml version="1.0" encoding="UTF-8"?>
      <!-- Code omitted -->
      <artifactId>domain</artifactId>

      <dependencies>
        <dependency>
          <groupId>dev.davivieira</groupId>
          <artifactId>inventory-core-domain</artifactId>
        </dependency>
        <dependency>
          <groupId>dev.davivieira</groupId>
          <artifactId>status-sub-domain</artifactId>
        </dependency>
      </dependencies>

    </project>
    ```

    The `domain` Maven module depends on `inventory-core-domain` and `status-sub-domain`. We kept the `domain` module but broke it into two parts. With this approach, there will be no need to change anything in the Application and Framework hexagons.

3. We also need to reconfigure the `module-info.java` module descriptor:

```
module domain {
    requires transitive inventory_core_domain;
    requires transitive status_sub_domain;
}
```

The `transitive` keyword is necessary to ensure the exports from `inventory_core_domain` and `status_sub_domain` are visible for other modules depending on the `domain` module.

4. Next, we configure the `pom.xml` file for the `inventory-core-domain` Maven module:

```xml
<?xml version="1.0" encoding="UTF-8"?>
  <!-- Code omitted -->
  <parent>
    <groupId>dev.davivieira</groupId>
    <artifactId>topology-inventory</artifactId>
    <version>1.0-SNAPSHOT</version>
  </parent>

  <artifactId>inventory-core-domain</artifactId>

</project>
```

The preceding example is a straightforward `pom.xml` file containing only the `artifactId` and the `parent` coordinates. In addition to `pom.xml`, we need to provide a `module-info.java` file, as shown here:

```
module inventory_core_domain {
    exports
      dev.davivieira.topologyinventory.domain.entity;
    exports
      dev.davivieira.topologyinventory.domain.service;
    exports
      dev.davivieira.topologyinventory.domain
      .specification;
    exports
      dev.davivieira.topologyinventory.domain.vo;
    exports
      dev.davivieira.topologyinventory.domain.entity
      .factory;
    requires static lombok;
}
```

This Java module provides better encapsulation for the inventory core domain. Note that we're also exporting the `entity`, `service`, `specification`, and `vo` packages. They are all part of the core domain.

5. Next, we configure the pom.xml file of the status-sub-domain Maven module:

```xml
<?xml version="1.0" encoding="UTF-8"?>

  <!-- Code omitted -->
  <artifactId>status-sub-domain</artifactId>

  <dependencies>
    <dependency>
      <groupId>dev.davivieira</groupId>
      <artifactId>inventory-core-domain</artifactId>
      <version>1.0-SNAPSHOT</version>
    </dependency>
  </dependencies>
</project>
```

We declare a dependency on the inventory-core-domain Maven module because we use the same entities present in the core domain to provide status information capabilities in the status-sub-domain subdomain Maven module. The difference, though, is that the same entity, in the same way as Router, can have a different meaning (and also a data model) when we are in the status information context.

6. To finish, we need to configure the module-info.java file for status_sub_domain:

```java
module status_sub_domain {
    exports dev.davivieira.topologyinventory.status;
    requires inventory_core_domain;
}
```

We're exporting only one package and declaring that this module depends on inventory_core_domain.

Now that we have the Maven and Java modules properly configured to help us enforce the boundaries between the core domain and subdomain, let's explore the use of a bounded context.

Let's consider that the topology and inventory system can now check the status of a router. To isolate this behavior and establish a context for such activities, we will create a class called RouterInfo in the subdomain:

```java
package dev.davivieira.topologyinventory.status;

import dev.davivieira.topologyinventory.domain.entity.factory.
RouterFactory;
import dev.davivieira.topologyinventory.domain.vo.IP;
import dev.davivieira.topologyinventory.domain.vo.Id;
import dev.davivieira.topologyinventory.domain.vo.Model;
import dev.davivieira.topologyinventory.domain.vo.RouterType;
```

```
import dev.davivieira.topologyinventory.domain.vo.Vendor;

public class RouterInfo {

    public String getRouterStatus () {
        var router = RouterFactory.getRouter(
                Id.withoutId(),
                Vendor.CISCO,
                Model.XYZ0004,
                IP.fromAddress("55.0.0.1"),
                null,
                RouterType.CORE);
        return "Router with "+router.getIp()+" is alive!";
    }
}
```

In the RouterInfo class, we have a dummy method called getRouterStatus, which is just to illustrate that the Router entity can assume a different behavior and data model in the context of status information. It's very simple to make this subdomain feature available for the Application and Framework hexagon.

Let's do that to see how the subdomain fits into the overall hexagonal system by executing the following steps:

1. We start by adding a new method definition in RouterManagementUseCase:

    ```
    public interface RouterManagementUseCase {

        /** Code omitted **/

        String getRouterStatus();
    }
    ```

    The getRouterStatus method integrates with the subdomain to retrieve the router status.

2. Next, we implement getRouterStatus in RouterManagementInputPort:

    ```
    @Override
    public String getRouterStatus() {
        var routerInfo = new RouterInfo();
        return routerInfo.getRouterStatus();
    }
    ```

    Here, we are getting an instance of the RouterInfo object from the subdomain and calling the getRouterStatus method.

3.　Finally, we implement the endpoint in `RouterManagementAdapter`:

```
@Transactional
@GET
@Path("/get-router-status")
@Operation(operationId = "getRouterStatus", description = "Get
router status")
@Produces(MediaType.TEXT_PLAIN)
public Uni<Response> getRouterStatus() {
    return Uni.createFrom()
                .item(routerManagementUseCase
                .getRouterStatus())
                .onItem()
                .transform(
                  router -> router != null ?
                  Response.ok(router) :
                  Response.ok(null))
                .onItem()
                .transform(Response.ResponseBuilder::build);
}
```

Here, we are using the RESTEasy Reactive to implement the `/get-router-status` endpoint that will get the router status information from the subdomain:

```
$ curl -X GET http://localhost:8080/router/get-router-status
```

Running the preceding `curl` command gives us the following output:

```
Router with IP(ipAddress=55.0.0.1, protocol=IPV4) is alive!
```

This implementation of DDD elements such as subdomains and bounded contexts helps us understand how we can integrate these elements with the hexagonal architecture. Using Maven and Java modules, we can emphasize the boundaries between the core domain and subdomain even more.

Now, let's shift our attention to the Application hexagon, which is the realm of ports and use cases.

The need for creating ports and use cases

After putting some effort into modeling the problem domain in the Domain hexagon, the next step is to move on to the Application hexagon and define how the system enables the behaviors that fulfills the business-related operations that come from the Domain hexagon. Actors—who could be both users and other systems—drive these behaviors. They dictate the system's capabilities.

The moment when we start implementing the Application hexagon is crucial because we begin to think in aspects that are not directly related to the domain model. Instead, these aspects may be related to integrations for communicating with other systems. But we shouldn't go so far as to decide which technologies to use. We don't take decisions related to technology when implementing the Application hexagon. Rather, technology concerns are a subject that we go deep into in the Framework hexagon.

We employ use cases to define what a system can do to meet actors' needs. Without considering specific technical details, we can state that a good moment to create a use case is when we need to express an actor's intent on the system. The actor's intent plays a fundamental role in shaping the system's behaviors. By employing use cases, we can describe such behaviors. Input ports come next by defining how the system will actually accomplish the actor's goals. Input ports can be implemented right away or be implemented later. However, they must be implemented before you decide to move on to the Framework hexagon. If you choose to implement the Framework hexagon before implementing input ports, there will be no way to make the Framework hexagon communicate with the Application hexagon. In other words, use cases and ports are the bridge between both hexagons.

There is not much to be concerned about when it comes to output ports because they are interfaces implemented by output adapters in the Framework hexagon. Output adapters, in their turn, can pose some problems if we have multiple categories of them. Next, we'll assess some of the consequences of having multiple adapter categories.

Dealing with multiple adapter categories

In the context of the hexagonal architecture, adapters help us to increase the hexagonal system's compatibility with different protocols and technology. In the Framework hexagon, we finally decide how the system will expose its features through input adapters and how it will communicate with external systems through output adapters.

In a similar way to what happens in the Application and Domain hexagons, the Framework hexagon is encapsulated in its own Java module. This module approach helps us enforce the boundaries between each system hexagon. From the Framework hexagon's perspective, it's good to group all input and output adapters within the same module. Although modularization can help us set boundaries, it is not enough to prevent the maintainability challenges we may face when dealing with multiple adapter categories.

What I mean by adapter category is a classification to group adapters that enable the integration with a specific technology. For example, in the topology and inventory system, we have the `RouterManagementAdapter` and `SwitchManagementAdapter` input adapters. These adapters expose HTTP RESTful endpoints. So, these input adapters comprise the adapter category that provides HTTP support for the hexagonal system. If we want to enable integration with another technology, for example, gRPC, we need to create a new set of adapters in an adapter category that supports exposing gRPC endpoints.

When dealing with input adapters, we don't face a significant maintainability burden by having multiple adapter categories providing support to different technologies in the hexagonal system. However, some issues may arise if we have multiple adapter categories for output adapters.

With output adapters, we can integrate the hexagonal application with external systems. But it's important to pay attention where we need to provide translation mechanisms for every new integration. These translations help us to map data coming in and going out through output adapters. If adapter categories for output adapters grow too large, it can potentially create a maintainability problem. In that scenario, we would need to keep multiple translation mechanisms for every adapter category.

Consider the following scenario. Imagine a system that started out with all of its data being served by a database. As the main system evolved, the developers migrated its parts into smaller subsystems to prevent the main system from becoming too big. But during this migration process, certain use cases could not be fully migrated to the new subsystems, resulting in a situation where the main system still needed to fetch data from both the database and the subsystems in order to fulfill some of its business rules. In this circumstance, the main system requires two output adapters: one for the database and another for the subsystem. Allowing two output adapters to serve the same purpose due to an unfinished migration can potentially increase the maintenance cost. One of the main problems of this approach is the need to translate the domain model data, which comes from the database and the subsystem.

So, for input adapters, we have a low risk when employing multiple adapter categories. However, the same cannot be said about output adapters. The recommendation here is to be aware of the trade-off in having to maintain several translation mechanisms for multiple output adapters.

Conclusion – the hexagonal journey

One of the fascinating things about software development is that we can employ many methods to achieve the same result. This freedom adds to the fun of software development and fosters creativity. Creativity is the main force behind clever solutions for complex problems. That's why we should always leave space for creativity in any software project. But when combined with tight schedules and resources, freedom and creativity should be managed to produce valuable software without adding unnecessary complexity.

I see the hexagonal architecture as an approach that can help us manage these different requirements. It provides a clear set of principles to organize system code within flexible yet consistent boundaries. The hexagonal approach offers a model to direct our creative efforts in an organized and – to a certain extent – standardized way.

The hexagonal architecture is not for everyone, nor is it suitable for every project. However, people seeking ways to standardize their software development practices will find the hexagonal architecture to be a useful blueprint to scaffold their next software project. Nevertheless, it's important to understand the considerable complexity involved in structuring a system using hexagonal principles. If the project is for a medium or large, long-term, and highly mutable system, I believe the hexagonal architecture is an excellent choice to ensure the system's maintainability in the long run. On the other hand, if we're talking about small applications responsible for, let's say, one or two things, then using the hexagonal architecture would be like using a gun to kill an ant. So, you need to carefully assess the scenario to check if the hexagonal architecture will bring more solutions than problems to your project.

The hexagonal architecture is not a silver bullet that will magically solve your technical debt and maintainability issues. These problems have more to do with your attitude to keep things simple than with the software architecture you choose to structure your application. But the hexagonal architecture can help you tackle those issues if you're already committed to an attitude to keep things simple and easy to understand no matter how complex the problem domain you're dealing with is. I encourage you to keep a simple attitude and explore and extend the hexagonal architecture ideas. For me, it's been an unending learning and rewarding experience to design hexagonal systems. I wish the same to you.

Let me finish this book by sincerely thanking you for accompanying me on this hexagonal journey.

Summary

We started this chapter by exploring some ideas relating to DDD, and we discussed the importance of understanding our business needs before jumping straight to development. We also learned about the Business Model Canvas and event storming.

While on the topic of DDD, we learned how subdomains and bounded contexts are essential to help establish clear boundaries within the Domain hexagon. After that, we discussed use cases and ports. We learned that it's essential to implement input ports before starting to build the Framework hexagon.

Next, we learned about the maintainability consequences of having multiple adapter categories, mainly when dealing with output adapters that require translation mechanisms. Finally, we ended the book by reflecting on our hexagonal journey and the importance of keeping software development simple.

When using Quarkus, especially the native image feature, we need to consider the large amount of memory and time required to build a native executable. If your CI environment is constrained, you may face problems caused by insufficient computational resources. Also, bear in mind that compilation time considerably increases when compiling native images. If your priority is faster compilation rather than a more rapid system startup, you may have to reconsider using native images. I always recommend checking the Quarkus documentation and the Quarkus community through the official mailing list and other channels. This can help you learn more about Quarkus and stay updated on common issues and how to solve them. If the community help is not enough, you can seek Quarkus' official support provided by Red Hat.

The hexagonal architecture provides us with the principles to develop robust and change-tolerant systems. Quarkus is a cutting-edge technology that we can use to apply hexagonal principles to create modern, cloud-native applications. By combining hexagonal architecture with Quarkus, we can produce fantastic software. I encourage you to experiment and further explore the possibilities of such a fascinating combination. The hexagonal journey of this book ends here, but you guys can start a new one by applying, tweaking, and evolving the ideas I have presented to you.

Questions

1. What techniques can we use to understand our business needs?

2. Why should we employ subdomains and bounded contexts?

3. Why is it important to define use cases and create input ports before implementing the Framework hexagon?

4. What are the consequences of having multiple adapter categories for output adapters?

Answers

1. The Business Model Canvas and event storming.

2. Subdomains and bounded contexts help us establish clear boundaries to prevent mixing the meaning and concerns of the entities in a domain model.

3. Because use cases and input ports are the bridge between the Framework and Application hexagons.

4. It can lead to several translation mechanisms that may be hard to maintain if we have too many of them.

Index

www.packtpub.com

Subscribe to our online digital library for full access to over 7,000 books and videos, as well as industry leading tools to help you plan your personal development and advance your career. For more information, please visit our website.

Why subscribe?

- Spend less time learning and more time coding with practical eBooks and Videos from over 4,000 industry professionals

- Improve your learning with Skill Plans built especially for you

- Get a free eBook or video every month

- Fully searchable for easy access to vital information

- Copy and paste, print, and bookmark content

Did you know that Packt offers eBook versions of every book published, with PDF and ePub files available? You can upgrade to the eBook version at packtpub.com and as a print book customer, you are entitled to a discount on the eBook copy. Get in touch with us at customercare@packtpub.com for more details.

At www.packtpub.com, you can also read a collection of free technical articles, sign up for a range of free newsletters, and receive exclusive discounts and offers on Packt books and eBooks.

Other Books You May Enjoy

If you enjoyed this book, you may be interested in these other books by Packt:

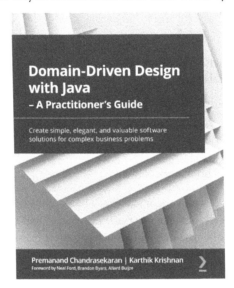

Domain-Driven Design with Java - A Practitioner's Guide

Premanand Chandrasekaran, Karthik Krishnan

ISBN: 978-1-80056-073-4

- Discover how to develop a shared understanding of the problem domain
- Establish a clear demarcation between core and peripheral systems
- Identify how to evolve and decompose complex systems into well-factored components
- Apply elaboration techniques like domain storytelling and event storming
- Implement EDA, CQRS, event sourcing, and much more
- Design an ecosystem of cohesive, loosely coupled, and distributed microservices
- Test-drive the implementation of an event-driven system in Java
- Grasp how non-functional requirements influence bounded context decompositions

Get Your Hands Dirty on Clean Architecture - Second Edition

Tom Hombergs

ISBN: 978-1-80512-837-3

- Identify potential shortcomings of using a layered architecture
- Apply varied methods to enforce architectural boundaries
- Discover how potential shortcuts can affect the software architecture
- Produce arguments for using different styles of architecture
- Structure your code according to the architecture
- Run various tests to check each element of the architecture

Design Patterns and Best Practices in Java

Kamalmeet Singh, Adrian Ianculescu, Lucian-Paul Torje

ISBN: 978-1-78646-359-3

- Understand the OOP and FP paradigms
- Explore the traditional Java design patterns
- Get to know the new functional features of Java
- See how design patterns are changed and affected by the new features
- Discover what reactive programming is and why is it the natural augmentation of FP
- Work with reactive design patterns and find the best ways to solve common problems using them
- See the latest trends in architecture and the shift from MVC to serverless applications
- Use best practices when working with the new features

Packt is searching for authors like you

If you're interested in becoming an author for Packt, please visit `authors.packtpub.com` and apply today. We have worked with thousands of developers and tech professionals, just like you, to help them share their insight with the global tech community. You can make a general application, apply for a specific hot topic that we are recruiting an author for, or submit your own idea.

Share Your Thoughts

Now you've finished *Designing Hexagonal Architecture with Java, Second Edition*, we'd love to hear your thoughts! Scan the QR code below to go straight to the Amazon review page for this book and share your feedback or leave a review on the site that you purchased it from.

`https://packt.link/r/1837635110`

Your review is important to us and the tech community and will help us make sure we're delivering excellent quality content.

Download a free PDF copy of this book

Thanks for purchasing this book!

Do you like to read on the go but are unable to carry your print books everywhere?

Is your eBook purchase not compatible with the device of your choice?

Don't worry, now with every Packt book you get a DRM-free PDF version of that book at no cost.

Read anywhere, any place, on any device. Search, copy, and paste code from your favorite technical books directly into your application.

The perks don't stop there, you can get exclusive access to discounts, newsletters, and great free content in your inbox daily

Follow these simple steps to get the benefits:

1. Scan the QR code or visit the link below

https://packt.link/free-ebook/9781837635115

2. Submit your proof of purchase

3. That's it! We'll send your free PDF and other benefits to your email directly

www.ingramcontent.com/pod-product-compliance
Lightning Source LLC
Chambersburg PA
CBHW060647060326
40690CB00020B/4551